Culture and Adultery

NEW CULTURAL STUDIES

Series Editors
Joan DeJean
Carroll Smith-Rosenberg
Peter Stallybrass
Gary A. Tomlinson

A complete list of books in the series
is available from the publisher.

Culture and Adultery

The Novel, the Newspaper, and the Law, 1857–1914

Barbara Leckie

PENN
University of Pennsylvania Press
Philadelphia

Copyright © 1999 University of Pennsylvania Press
All rights reserved
Printed in the United States of America on acid-free paper

10 9 8 7 6 5 4 3 2 1

Published by
University of Pennsylvania Press
Philadelphia, Pennsylvania 19104-4011

Library of Congress Cataloging-in-Publication Data
Leckie, Barbara.
  Culture and adultery : the novel, the newspaper, and the law, 1857–1914 / Barbara Leckie.
    p. cm.
  Includes bibliographical references and index.
  ISBN 0-8122-3498-7 (alk. paper)
  1. English fiction — 19th century — History and criticism.
2. Adultery in literature.   3. English fiction — 20th century — History and criticism.   4. Adultery — Great Britain — Public opinion — History.   5. Legal stories, English — History and criticism.
6. American fiction — History and criticism.   7. Journalism — History — 19th century.   8. Journalism — History — 20th century.
9. Sensationalism in literature.   10. Law and literature.   I. Title.
PR878.A37L43 1999
823'.809353 — dc21   99-17837
                                                                              CIP

For my parents

Contents

Introduction: Censorship and Adultery ... 1

1. The Democracy of Print: The Mid-Victorian Censorship Debates ... 16
2. Columns of Scandal: The Divorce Court Journalism Debates ... 62
3. An Undercurrent of the Body: The Sensation Novel Debates ... 112
4. A National Habit of Repression: Henry James's Negotiation of Adultery in *The Golden Bowl* ... 154
5. A Good Read: Ford Madox Ford's *A Call* and *The Good Soldier* ... 202

Conclusion: The Narrative of a Waking Body ... 244

Notes ... 257

Works Cited ... 273

Acknowledgments ... 289

Index ... 291

Introduction
Censorship and Adultery

Adultery may seem an unlikely, and perhaps unwise, place from which to begin a study of censorship and culture. Adultery, after all, is the most bourgeois of transgressions. On a continuum of shock-effect it would not occupy a position close to either the high or low extremes that Peter Stallybrass and Allon White argue are so fruitful in interrogations of transgression. But this is a study of middle-class culture and, as I will argue, adultery was never remote from middle-class concerns in Victorian England. For critics of the European novel, adultery, of course, is a pivotal subject; as Tony Tanner notes in *Adultery in the Novel*, many of those novels "canonized as 'great'" take adultery as their central theme (11). In studies of the Victorian and transitional modernist novel in England, however, the topic of adultery is virtually absent from the critical discourse.[1] Franco Moretti's sweeping claim to this effect—"Every great narrative tradition has dealt with the theme of adultery, in France and in Germany, in America and in Russia. In England, nothing—absolutely nothing" (*Way* 188)—is only one example of what is a widely accepted position in literary scholarship.

And yet between 1857 and 1914 adultery was, in fact, everywhere in English print culture:[2] it was discussed in parliamentary debates; it was a front-page "Divorce Court" story in most of the daily newspapers at least twice a week for over fifty years; it was a topic of heated discussion in literary and cultural interest reviews; it was represented in popular novels, and it was a central feature of novels that were eventually "canonized as 'great.'" I define my project, then, in the context of two sets of questions. First, how did adultery become "visible" in this public sphere between 1857 (when divorce shifted from canon law to civil law under the new Matrimonial Causes Act) and 1914? Conversely, why has the discursive history of adultery been overlooked, or rendered "invisible," in the English critical tradition? Is there a relationship between Victorian efforts to censor or regulate representations of adultery—as examples of transgressive sexuality impinging on public morality in a broader political context — and the subsequent critical silence on such representations? How do categories for perception, at different historical moments, condition what is seen and not seen? Second, what can be gained by making adultery a focus of critical study? What political and cultural interests does the interplay between censorship and discursive proliferation serve? Is there a connection between the representation of adultery in England and the development of the novel? The first set of questions addresses the cultural matrices through which certain issues and ideas become visible; the second set analyzes the implications of this tension between visibility and invisibility in relation to the representation of adultery, the cultural work of such representation, and the development of the English novel.

This double context borrows from, and extends, the readings of taboo and transgression advanced by Sigmund Freud, Michel Foucault, and Pierre Bourdieu. Freud's powerful elaboration of the psychoanalytic categories of perception, for example, fundamentally altered the way in which the middle-class humanist subject could be seen and interpreted. In particular, his analysis of dream censorship and censorship effects such as displacement and condensation provides a vocabulary through which broader forms of social and political censorship can be understood.[3] Freud, moreover, was the first theorist to chart the complicated interplay among taboo, contagion, and sexuality for which one finds a strikingly resonant parallel in mid-nineteenth-century novel debates. And Freud's faith in the constructive capacity of discursive exchange and the power of words radically to reshape experience suggests a new angle from which to interpret literary regulation and censorship in the Victorian period. But while psychoanalysis defined a new system of thought which continues to exercise an immense persuasive appeal today, within the boundaries of Freud's system the faultlines have been interpreted as remarkably rigid and reductive.[4] Repression, for example, implies for many critics an event, idea, or experience that is repressed and that can ultimately be located in the complicated nexus of a family Oedipal drama; this conception of repression, then, assumes the recovery and elucidation of the thing repressed for a patient's psychic benefit. In this context, sexuality is also essentialized as the fraught, and usually sublimated, origin of psychological and social problems.

More recently, critics have taken issue with both simple versions of repression and recovery and an essentialized sexual nature at the core of human dilemmas.[5] Foucault has perhaps been most influential in this enterprise. His critique of the fact of sexual repression in the Victorian period —

people were talking about sex everywhere, he argues — goes hand in hand with his critique of the positive effects assumed to stem from the lifting of repression. If "Western man has been drawn for three centuries to the task of telling everything concerning his sex" (*History* 23), then there is nothing new or liberating or transgressive about such discourse. And yet a common misconception prevails that a "censorship of sex" was in place and that talking about sex was, therefore, an act of contestation. Foucault's comments on the tension between the theoretical invisibility of sexuality and its visibility in practice correspond closely to what I have witnessed in Victorian interpretations of adultery: a discursive explosion of representations of adultery exists alongside claims that adultery and the representation of adultery were nonexistent and that any attempt at representation was, therefore, rare and dangerously transgressive. Foucault challenges what he calls Freud's "repressive hypothesis" and the assumed censorship of sex to which it was related by denying that subversive or transformative effects necessarily follow from talking about sex. Instead, he suggests that if sex is so frequently discussed, then it is more likely in the service of dominant powers than at odds with them. Censorship, in other words, can be productive and lead to a proliferation of discourses that support dominant class interests.

Foucault's second challenge to Freud is to insist that sex has a history, as his title *The History of Sexuality* avows. As such, it cannot be essentialized as the universal answer to all therapeutic problems. To historicize sexuality is to attend to the particular institutions through which it becomes visible and meaningful. This claim also holds for an analysis of adultery; adultery, like sexuality, has a history and in my discussions of its representation in legal debates, the newspaper, and the novel I hope to complicate the simple definitions of adultery used by most literary critics. While most critics of the novel assume adultery's subversive status, when one turns to the actual history of adultery, its representation in particular periods, in particular contexts, by particular social actors, a very different picture emerges. In sum, where Freud sees a censorship that needs to be overcome, Foucault sees an absence of successful censorship; and where Freud sees an essentialized sexuality, Foucault sees a historicized sexuality.

But the nexus of censorship and sexuality, of course, is not this straightforward. Foucault readily acknowledges, for example, a distinction between "vocabulary" and "discourses and their domains" (*History* 17–18). He grants an "expurgation" at the level of "the authorized vocabulary" in which there was the codification of "a whole rhetoric of allusion and metaphor," the screening of some words, and a general "policing of statements" (17–18) while at the level of discourses and their domains, by contrast, there was a "discursive explosion" and an "institutional incitement to speak about" sex (17–18). Most important, however, the incitement to speak about sex was also productive of its own institutional censorships or exclusions. Particular people were encouraged to talk about sex in particular ways which, in turn, encouraged particular versions of sexuality and discouraged others. It is here that the work of Bourdieu is useful. As several contemporary critics have pointed out, having a label for one's sexuality cuts two ways: on the one hand, without a label it is difficult to affirm one's identity and petition one's rights; on the other hand, with a label it is easy to have one's identity condemned and one's rights denied.[6] What Bourdieu contributes to this discussion is a sensitive account of the class vectors involved in identity articulations (a doctor's question about one's sexual orientation is different from a friend's, and so on) and the stakes involved in protecting one's position to authorize identity or any other social category.[7]

Bourdieu's work, moreover, first alerted me to the currency of categories of perception, like those I have described in Freud and Foucault to different ends, in an analysis of censorship and literature. The debates related to the transitional modernist novel in England dramatize a symbolic struggle—a struggle over the symbols through which the social world is defined—in two ways. First, the prohibition against the representation of adultery generated extensive debate and conflict; and second, the classification and imposition of disciplinary boundaries were, in the period under question, radically unstable and themselves open to a very different sort of adulteration. When Bourdieu writes that "[m]any 'intellectual debates' are less unrealistic than they seem if one is aware of the degree to which one can modify social reality by modifying the agents' representation of it" (*Language* 128), he offers a crucial insight into Victorian novel debates that can appear trivial and inconsequential in hindsight. He further argues that the "capacity to see (*voir*) is a function of the knowledge (*savoir*), or concepts, that is, the words, that are available to name visible things, and which are, as it were, programmes for perception" (*Distinction* 2). For a study of transgression, this combination of the stakes granted to intellectual debates coupled with the power accrued to programs of perception is absolutely crucial. The debater who ultimately ends up defining social reality simultaneously dictates the programs of perception through which such a social reality is perceived. And it is the program or category of perception that defines what counts as transgressive in a particular social space. Bourdieu takes the transformative capacity of language that Freud attributes to the psychoanalytic setting, and extends it to social and political fields. Unlike Freud, however, Bourdieu relates the transformative effects of one's words to the social power and class position of the speaker, and he notes the powerful role of language in social reproduction as well as in social change.

If Freud makes strikingly visible the place of sexuality in one's personal world through new psychoanalytic categories of perception, Foucault interrogates the ideological work of this visibility in a broader range of contexts and historical periods, and Bourdieu, while also attentive to the ideological work of symbolic power, offers a sophisticated account of how new categories of perception compete for acceptance in diverse, competitive, and overlapping social fields. And if Freud links sexuality to censorship in the individual's psychic structure, Foucault offers a more subtle account of censorship that derives from the ways in which speakers talk about sex as well as from the ways in which they are silent, and Bourdieu sharpens Foucault's institutional analysis in stricter and more rigorous sociological terms. Censorship sometimes follows not only from an explicit law, but also, and most important, from a network of institutional formations. It is not only prohibitive but also *productive*, as both Foucault (in his contrast between law and discipline) and Bourdieu (in his contrast between rules and strategy) argue. In this context, to gain an understanding of the place of adultery in the novel only in terms of transgression, as many critics have endeavored to do, requires considerable revision.

This book, it should be stressed, is a work of literary criticism. I am interested in the role that the novel and the institution of the novel play in shaping what counts as taboo and in negotiating a social and political field in which certain subjects, like adultery, are targeted as transgressive and, therefore, outside the boundary of permissible literary representation. I want to bring novels, novel theory, and a concrete analysis of a specific "transgressive" practice—adultery—into dialogue with psychoanalysis, historiography, and reflexive sociology to rethink a theory of transgression. I further argue that understanding adultery and transgression, sexuality and censorship, between 1857 and 1914 is best accomplished by a consideration of the three intertwined representational fields: the novel, the newspaper, and the law. One premise of this book is that the specific contours of transgression develop very slowly and unevenly and while certain transgressions are, of course, repeatedly named (the taboo against the representation of adultery in the nineteenth-century English novel, for example) the specificity of that transgression developed and continues to develop even as its naming seems to bring about an act of definitive closure. Another premise of this book is that censorship, explicitly enforced or only implicitly made clear, contributes to the production of literary categories. In particular, as will be illustrated, it is related to the articulation of a separate aesthetic sphere from which social and political interests—the public morality threatened by representations of adultery—are evacuated. This move may grant an apparent freedom to the novelist haunted by the specter of censorship, but the cost for this freedom, as Terry Eagleton and others have noted, is higher than cultural critics should be willing to pay.

The title of this book—*Culture and Adultery*—and the title of this Introduction—"Censorship and Adultery"—imply a connection between culture and censorship that I want to approach carefully. Several recent critics have used the idea of censorship to describe culture: for example, Cheryl Herr blatantly claims that "culture is censorship" (11) and Stephen Greenblatt is only slightly less contentious in his formulation of "culture as a system of constraints" ("Culture" 227). Herr and Greenblatt, like Foucault and Bourdieu, however, read the censorious and constraining aspects of culture as themselves productive. My title also echoes Matthew Arnold's *Culture and Anarchy*, although his treatment of culture is apparently remote from any equation between culture and censorship. For Arnold, culture is productive rather than prohibitive in the way that it shapes individual judgment and sensibility and better prepares one to make informed social and political decisions about the world that one inhabits. But the fact that Arnold contrasts culture with anarchy also stresses the way in which culture, for Arnold, is perceived to constrain unruly forces and experiences. Culture, then, ensures a safeguard against anarchy in a manner that is roughly parallel to Mary Douglas's distinction between order and disorder to clarify the social place of "dirt," taboo, and pollution. Douglas argues that "ideas about separating, purifying, demarcating, and punishing transgressions have as their main function to impose system on an inherently untidy experience" (4). In this context, culture is a system of constraints that works to contain and dispel disorder: "The analysis of ritual symbolism," Douglas writes, "cannot begin until we recognize ritual as an attempt to create and maintain a particular culture, a particular set of assumptions by which experience is controlled" (128). While culture is not exactly "ritual symbolism" for Arnold (although the religious connotations are not ill placed), Douglas's terms nevertheless apply to Arnold's understanding of cultural work.

To emphasize the positive performative character of culture Arnold downplays what his definition of culture excludes (all forms of popular culture, working-class culture, political culture, and unauthorized subject matter); his blueprint for culture, therefore, reflects the play between constraint and production that one finds ranging from ritual symbolism to the work of contemporary culture critics. When culture as productive is coupled with culture as prohibitive, a better understanding of the complexity of both the cultural work and the specific place of sexuality in that work is gained. It is in this doubly inflected and mobile sense, moreover, that I will be using the term censorship.[8] Censorship can be understood in a specifically legal context that captures what was perceived to be a very real political threat stemming from the circulation of particular representations in the public sphere (here the debates related to the 1857 Obscene Publications Act, the 1868 *Regina* v. *Hicklin* case, and the 1889 Indecent Advertisements Act are crucial). But it can also be understood in terms of the authorities and institutions (from the individual reviewer to the circulating libraries) through which the limits of acceptable discourse were communicated, informally but powerfully, in specific cultural contexts. I will rely on both of these understandings of censorship and the forces of prohibition and cultural production to which they are related.[9] The ability to define what counts as literature carries immense social and political weight, as Arnold knew in the 1860s and the antagonists to cultural diversity in the university know today; because the category of literature is constantly open to debate and dissent, however, it is also constantly subject to change and revision. While "Arnoldian culture" now serves as a catch-phrase for the established literary canon, even Arnold's sense of what should be included in the category of culture has been altered and contested by subsequent critics who nevertheless support his general idea of literary greatness and the positive benefits that it generates.

One example will illustrate my point: the novel of adultery. In 1867 when Arnold was writing the essays that would later become *Culture and Anarchy,* the novel as a genre was not included in the category of aesthetic culture as Arnold defined it. Very few critics contested this position. In 1884 Walter Besant's essay "The Art of Fiction" and Henry James's response to it in an essay bearing the same title illustrate that almost twenty years later the novel's status as art (or culture in Arnold's sense) was still by no means established. The tone of both Besant's and James's essays indicates that they expected disagreement and dissent, that they were expressing views that took issue with public opinion. A similar attempt was made to exclude the representation of adultery from the broader category of anthropological culture. The novel *of adultery,* therefore, was even further beyond the scope of Arnoldian culture in its explicit invocation of the sexualized body in a literary if not aesthetic genre. In an 1868 critique of the English sensation novels that freely included adultery among their topics, Francis Paget writes that these novels "aid in sensualizing the character of a whole people." Further, Paget, like many other cultural commentators of the period, is worried about the threat that these novels pose to social and political stability: if this novelistic practice is not stopped, Paget warns, something like the French "reign of terror" will most certainly follow (302–3). The novels I consider in this book, then, are often situated in the context of a double prohibition — against the novel form and against adultery as subject matter — and their response to this regulatory context shapes their development and changes the way that such regulation is itself interpreted.

Paget's remarks imply, moreover, that to write on censorship is also to write on reading. Censorship only makes sense in the context of imagined effects of reading and, at the very least, the impulse to censor acknowledges the capacity of words to shape, and possibly transform, social reality. Paget further specifies these reading effects in two ways that are persistent in the nineteenth-century debates on literary regulation: he connects reading and the sensual body; and he connects reading, (the sensual body), and political revolution. I put "the sensual body" in parentheses here because this step in the critic's logic will often be either occluded or assumed (as it is in Paget) in the arguments that support censorship. One outcome of the democratization of reading in the mid-Victorian period is that the new reading public became a subject of regulation precisely in terms of somatic or hysterical reading effects. In England the young female reader, in particular, worked as a constraint delimiting possibilities for novelistic representation; such readers, it was argued, were particularly vulnerable to the hysterical effects and dangerous addictions to fiction (or fiction addictions as I will refer to them hereafter) that unsupervised reading generated. As Hunter, Saunders, and Williamson note, for pornography to exist "a public which might be corrupted by obscene publications had to exist" (88). Naming the young female readers as vulnerable simultaneously created this category of vulnerable readers for whom reading restrictions were then deemed necessary.

In the discussion that follows I turn to the parliamentary debates related to divorce and obscene publications, the newspaper transcriptions of divorce trials and the debates related to the publication of these trials, the sensation novel debates of the 1860s and the sensation novels themselves (with a focus on Caroline Norton's *Lost and Saved* and Mary Elizabeth

Braddon's *The Doctor's Wife*), Henry James's *The Golden Bowl*, Ford Madox Ford's *A Call* and *The Good Soldier*, as well as other novels and cultural documents.[10] Arnold and many of his contemporaries, as noted above, drew a circle around culture that would have excluded all of these works. Something happened between 1857 and 1914, however, to reconfigure the Arnoldian circle such that about half the works treated here are considered canonical; part of my aim is to trace this reconfiguration. These works, nonetheless, are never "canonized as great" in the context of their representation of adultery and, because I argue that their literary stature is related to their representation of adultery, I will also address this exclusion. Many critics will still be surprised to find sensation novels, newspapers, and divorce trials considered alongside James and Ford, to find central Victorian texts considered alongside modernist works. This surprise is a reminder of the constraints and boundaries that we always impose to define what counts as legitimate scholarship or to demarcate a legitimate area of inquiry.

I am arguing that culture defined both in the narrow Arnoldian aesthetic sense of high literary culture and in the broader anthropological sense—what Raymond Williams calls a "whole way of life" and E. P. Thompson calls "a whole way of struggle"—involves prohibition as well as production. Between 1857 and 1914 adultery was both very visible in the public sphere (especially in the contexts of the newspaper, the novel, and the law) and subject to implicit forms of censorship and regulation. Novelists negotiated this territory carefully. In the process, narrative innovations associated with modernist literary techniques were developed; and the novel as a genre intimately connected to the social world was redefined in terms of its necessary distance, indeed powerlessness, in the face of worldly concerns and interests. In both cases—the developments internal to the novel form and the redefinition of the category of the novel itself—adultery's resonance as subversive or transgressive subject matter was reconfigured in terms of the law and legitimate forms of symbolic expression. One encounters fantasies of adulterous desire replaced by fantasies of spectacular surveillance as the novels in the English tradition, again and again, choose to approach adultery not from the perspective of a character involved in adultery, but rather from the perspective of the betrayed party. At the same time, the very phantasmatic construction of adulterous scenes in the novel form takes issue with a bourgeois ideology committed to the absence of adultery, reworks traditional approaches to epistemology, and opens a space for imagining other discursive and sexual possibilities in the cultural field.

To elaborate the shift from the Victorian realist novel to the transitional modernist novel it is helpful to look in more detail at how the category or institution of literature itself changes. Peter Burger is attentive to the category of "art as institution" and "the social function of literary works" (*Theory* lii). Burger's work dovetails in important ways with Bourdieu's sociology of culture discussed above. Burger points out, for example, that the "commonly held view that one need only look closely to grasp the peculiarity of poetic texts . . . does not take into account that this 'looking' already rests on certain assumptions (such as the assumption that there is a difference between poetic and nonpoetic texts) and ideas, however vague they may be" (*Theory* lv). What is interesting is that in the shift to modernist culture, the relationship between literature and social action, which is arguably the driving force behind both Arnold's *Culture and Anarchy* (the subtitle of which is "An Essay in Political and Social Criticism") and the very different negative spins on the burgeoning novel genre expressed by other critics, is reconfigured. When Paget, for example, suggests a possible link between sensation novels and some social or political disturbance analogous to the French Revolution's Reign of Terror he assumes a dynamic relationship between the novel and society that is overturned in modernism's commitment to aesthetic autonomy.

Increasingly, art is distanced from questions related to social stability or social change and instead participates in what Burger calls "the neutralization of critique" (*Theory* 13). But what prompts this shift? As Edward Said notes: "If it is true that, according to an art-for-art's sake theory, the world of culture and aesthetic production subsists on its own, away from the encroachments of the State and authority, then we must still be prepared to show [how] that independence was gained and, more important, how it is maintained" ("American" 169). What, Said later asks, are the "reasons for this confinement" of "the isolation of literature and literary studies away from the world?" (173). Burger describes art's separation from the social sphere as follows: "the autonomy status of art within bourgeois society is by no means undisputed but is the precarious product of overall social development. That status can always be called into question by society (more precisely, society's rulers) when it seems useful to harness art once more. Not only the extreme example of the fascist politics of art that liquidates the autonomy status, but the large number of legal proceedings against artists for offenses against morality, testify to that fact" (*Theory* 24–25). I want to reverse Burger's connection here between the possibility of literature being harnessed to the social field and literary censorship to recover a sense of the historical development that marks the shift to modernism and aesthetic autonomy precisely in the context of censorship.[11] Arnold's general views on culture, Paget's opposition to the sensation novel in the 1860s, and the widespread implicit censorship of adultery in the English novel all assume a connection between literary representations and the social field that is rejected by modernism. When this connection was perceived to threaten the nation's aesthetic development, either in the implicit forms of censorship already developed by Arnold in his appeals to the State, the powerful regulating force of the circulating libraries, the numerous reviews condemning the representation of selected subjects, or in the explicit censorship of French novels and English translations of French novels in England, then a critical shift developed, again slowly and unevenly, to separate art from the social sphere.

Richard Stang begins his influential study *The Theory of the Novel in England* by taking issue with those critics who have not fully credited the existence of English novel theory before the advent of Henry James's criticism. He questions the fact that critics again and again return to the 1880s as the genesis of English novel criticism and speculates that the "chief reason for the wholesale dismissal of this large literature [mid-Victorian criticism of fiction] is that most of it is buried away in the files of Victorian periodicals" (xi). This explanation, however, begs the question of why it has remained buried away, and why, for that matter, it continues to be buried away even after Stang's impressive research. I suspect that the answer is closer to what Stang himself describes as this criticism's persistent interest in literature's role in social and political questions. Like Stang, I think that there is marvelous work in this period, but I relate its critical neglect more to the history of censorship than to an act of forgetting. Peter Keating provocatively suggests that "the complex battles over literary censorship" and the "repeated attempts to impose moral controls on fiction [in late-nineteenth-century England] were symptomatic of much deeper struggles taking place throughout Europe and America on the questions of what form modern mass democracy should take and whether literature was to have a significant place in whatever kind of democratic society eventually emerged" (283–84).[12] This book looks more closely at the role of literature in modern mass democracy and traces the process, intimately related to diverse forms of censorship, by which literature's participation in democratic society was increasingly constructed as irrelevant.

In his introduction to *Aesthetics and Ideology,* George Levine argues both for literature's potential to be socially and politically disruptive and for the articulation of a separate aesthetic sphere to protect these destabilizing interests. Levine's goals are admirable and timely but in accepting the aesthetic's necessary distance from the social and political world about which it speaks, Levine short-circuits the very contestatory potential of the art that he promotes. Levine refers to "the destabilizing power of the affective" (12), the "visceral moments of aesthetic pleasure" (15), and "the goose bumps of intense personal encounters with literature and art" (17). But he creates an aesthetic domain that is remote from both goose bumps and politics as a strategic response to the possibility of censorship.[13] Levine describes how important it is to resist "the pure logic that leads to arguments against academic freedom and against the First Amendment" and he gives the example of Said's description of an "intellectual free space that might be associated with the realm of the aesthetic" (15, 14). He cites from Said's *Culture and Imperialism* as follows: "I have availed myself of the utopian space still provided by the university, which I believe must remain a place where such vital issues are investigated, discussed, reflected on. For it to become a site where social and political issues are actually either imposed or resolved would be to remove the university's function and turn it into an adjunct to whatever political party is in power" (14).

But if literature is political, as Levine claims, and those visceral moments of aesthetic pleasure are important defining aspects of the literary experience, then how does one both circumvent censorship — in whatever form it may take (as opposition to academic freedom or the First Amendment, or as an injunction not to represent certain subjects like adultery) — and maintain the active and vital connection with the political and the somatic so important to what we call literature? It should not be forgotten, after all, that the articulation of a separate aesthetic sphere is a political move (as Levine notes) that may be entirely consonant with dominant political interests (as Levine does not note, but as my own study demonstrates).

It is necessary, in other words, to consider the implications of the avowed separation of literature from politics, ethics, and worldly concerns. In the Preface to their edited collection *Formations of Fantasy*, Burgin, Donald, and Kaplan describe a film in which a political prisoner is condemned for "harbouring thoughts likely to disrupt public order" (1). Literature, following Levine and others, is often about the literary expression of exactly such thoughts. As Burgin, Donald, and Kaplan note, the liberal tradition maintains a distinction between the mind and the deed — or in John Stuart Mill's terms, the word and the deed — that protects both the political prisoner and the novelist (or novel) from undue persecution. In this move, however, the political power of thoughts and words is often forgotten. This book documents a period in which such power was very much alive, in which hysterical outcries against obscene publications were regularly recorded in the House of Commons reports, the newspapers, and cultural journals, and in which the power of words, even the words found in a work of fiction, were assumed to have the capacity to transform social and political relations. At the same time, it should be remembered that forms of contestation and opposition can participate in the very heuristic structures that they are seeking to refute or undercut; as D. A. Miller notes, "the novel's critical relation to society, much advertised in the [Victorian] novel and its literary criticism, masks the extent to which modern social organization has made even 'scandal' a systematic function of its routine self-maintenance" (*Novel* xii). In nineteenth-century debates about literary regulation it is usually the social and political conservatives (represented also by various vice groups) who oppose the free circulation of "obscene" publications and the liberals who support a relatively unrestricted freedom. But, as Burgin, Donald, and Kaplan argue, one consequence of the democratic left's failure to consider any connection between psychology and the political (and, I would add, between literature and the political) "has been that the mobilizing force of *fantasy* has been effectively ceded to the right" (1). My study of culture and adultery in nineteenth- and early twentieth-century England does not directly ask the implicit question here: how can the mobilizing force of fantasy be recuperated for the democratic left? The indirect route, however, has its advantages; it tells a story of adultery that has not been told before and it also tells a story of the aesthetic — as politically engaged and somatically invested — that needs to be told again.

It is generally accepted that marriage was central to the development of middle-class bourgeois ideology, and yet its central infraction — adultery — remains largely unexplored in the English novel. To understand the representation of adultery in this context requires an understanding of a complex and contradictory set of codes and institutions through which adultery was both condemned and eroticized. Between 1857 and 1914 the representation of adultery was neither invisible in the English novel, as Moretti claims, nor invisible in other cultural formations. Instead it was part of a rapidly growing discursive economy in which representations of adultery were both vigorously prohibited by reviewers and readers and actively promoted in the daily journalistic documentation of divorce trails. On the one hand, an attempted censorship; on the other hand, an extraordinary proliferation of discursive activity. It was in this context, where the only legitimate way to discuss adultery was to translate it as a domestic detective story in the service of the law, that Victorian and transitional modernist novelists developed both a theory of the novel and formal novelistic innovations through which to negotiate censorship and represent adultery in a manner that, to cite Moretti, would make it look like "nothing."

I argue, then, that the cultural history of the representation of adultery is both a history of modernist literary innovations in negotiating censorship and a history of the separation of the body and politics from the aesthetic sphere. In the context of the debates between print regulation and print freedom prompted by both the developing novel genre and the divorce court journalism, novelists developed strategies through which to make adultery visible in the serious novel. First, adultery was translated not as a question of passion, but as a question of epistemology. This shift, as noted above, was effected by putting a focus on the deceived party in an adulterous triangle (as the divorce court also did, by definition); sex, to follow Foucault, becomes a question of truth, and adultery becomes a question of truth, *and* detection and punishment. Second, a series of formal innovations—multiple points of view, unreliable narrations, nonlinear plots, and an absence of closure—related to the representation of adultery as a domestic detective story were developed that also resembled the pattern of divorce court documentation. On the one hand, these strategies are remarkably consistent with Foucault's analysis of discipline. On the other hand, these strategies, make possible a discussion of sexuality that would not otherwise have taken place and that cannot entirely be folded into a Foucauldian disciplinary matrix; there are, as Foucault notes and Bourdieu affirms, points of resistance. Indeed, it is in the powerful force of fantasy— Isabel's fantasies in *The Doctor's Wife*, Maggie's fantasies in *The Golden Bowl*, and Dowell's fantasies in *The Good Soldier*—that one could begin to chart another narrative possibility and find a potent explanation for the articulation of a separate, eviscerated, aesthetic sphere.

After 1857 the representation of adultery moved from a marginal position that worked to affirm mainstream cultural norms to center stage in the daily newspapers and the novel. This shift produced a fascinating cultural dilemma, overlooked by historians of culture and literature, that contributed to the generation of texts like Matthew Arnold's *Culture and Anarchy* and the vast array of cultural works that participate in the struggle to reorient categories of perceptions and lines of classification so as to accommodate the "anomaly" of the publicity of adultery as a norm rather than a disturbance. The *representation* of adultery in the public sphere, moreover, and the regulatory schemes and censorships to which it gave rise, also provide an excellent material example of the intersection of culture and politics at a particularly charged historical moment.

My aim is simultaneously to interrogate the categories of perception through which adultery and the novel become "visible" and "invisible" in the social field and to analyze the place of adultery in the English novel's development. The question is not: does the representation of adultery in the novel carry a transgressive or conservative effect? but rather: how does the category of transgression work in the social field? How is it socially constructed and effective? In whose interests? To what ends? I hope to reanimate the Victorian debates over literary regulation that were always also debates over competing categories of perception in order to demonstrate the stakes at play in these struggles and their very real, but not stable, material effects. At the same time, I hope to shift the category of perception through which the English novel (and culture, more generally) is seen by tracing new lines of relation, as well as by illuminating the necessary exclusions that the establishment of any category involves. This study, then, considers print censorship, flexibly understood, and the enormously rich and complicated terrain of intellectual obsession and ambivalence, thwarted desire and expansive fantasy, forbidden reading and somatic pleasures. It seeks to uncover the obscured tracks of knowledge as sexuality, as reading, as addiction, and as the body, which the exploration of adultery in the Victorian and transitional modernist print culture makes visible.

I

The Democracy of Print
The Mid-Victorian Censorship Debates

> There took root and eventually flourished in nineteenth-century England a revolutionary social concept: that of the democracy of print.
>
> Richard Altick, *The English Common Reader*

In Wilkie Collins's 1888 *The Legacy of Cain* a father tells his daughter a story about her distant cousins. When the daughter asks about her cousin's marriage, however, the father abruptly stops his narrative. "The marriage was dissolved by law," he tells her, "and the wife was the person to blame. I am sure, Helena, you don't wish to hear any more of *this* part of the story." Helena writes in her diary: "I did wish. But I saw that he expected me to say No — so I said it" (101). Helena at once desires to hear the prohibited story and masks her desire in an apparent collusion with her father's authority and censure. No, she says to her father, I don't want to hear that story. Yes, she says inwardly, that is a story that I very much wish to hear. As Helena's simultaneous rebellion and compliance suggest, she manufactures her innocence the better to pursue the averted narrative and complete the story of adultery that her father initiates.

Examples of reading in this novel, moreover, only aggravate the fears that Helena's crafty submission would provoke in cultural authorities concerned, like Helena's father, to curb the circulation of stories of adultery. Helena's sister Eunice, for example, shares her desire for forbidden representations. She overhears two teachers reading an article in the newspaper — both sisters are explicitly prohibited from reading newspapers and novels — and listens with a lively interest. The mayor's wife, they read, is incensed by a "disgusting" photograph of the Venus de' Medici in a shop window. Intrigued, Eunice decides to take a look at the photograph herself. What she learns speaks to fears incited by what Richard Altick resonantly calls the new "democracy of print" (*Common Reader* 1): she becomes aware of herself (she is a little less ignorant, a little less uneducated); and she becomes aware of her body (she has, she thinks, a shapely, appealing, possibly seductive body). Armed with this knowledge she responds boldly to her lover's kisses.

But Eunice's experience is tame by contrast to Helena's. For it is only one short step from Helena's desire to hear the untold story of adultery to the fulfillment of that desire by way of other avenues more within her control. First she tries reading English novels but, like an addict, she soon wants stronger, more potent reading material alive to what she calls "the splendid fascinations of crime" (*Legacy* 174). To this end, she experiments with cheap translations of French novels. And like Eunice, Helena learns from her "secret course of reading" (272). Her reading inspires her to act on desires that she had hitherto only vaguely imagined. She swiftly seduces Eunice's lover, Philip, thereby transforming the untold story of adultery into the lived story of her life. And in a burst of melodramatic excess, Collins carries her wayward reading practices a step further. Stumbling upon an account of a maid, a mistress, and a mysterious poisoning, Helena again mirrors what she reads in her actions. It slowly emerges that Philip, ill and bedridden, is being poisoned by none other than Helena, the "innocent" young female reader.

In these three stories Collins captures with wonderful economy several points salient to the interplay between censorship and adultery in English print culture. First, adultery is invoked in the context of the law both in terms of the father's official reference to divorce law and in his unofficial censorship of references to a woman's adultery. Second, Collins's novel articulates a perceived link between reading and social action. Something material happens when readers read. This link, moreover, invokes the body and the nation in surprisingly predictable and insistent ways. The fact that Eunice reads and becomes aware of her body, for example, reflects an obsession with the body that also arises in the mid-century print censorship debates.[1] Helena's fascination with French novels reflects an obsession with questions of nation and national identity that similarly informs the debates. Third, this link between reading and social action raises another set of questions with which the debates grappled. Were aesthetic works as dangerous to social welfare as non-aesthetic works? And how could one tell the difference between the two? Should art be restricted or circumscribed to prevent the material effects of reading? And perhaps most important, who decides these questions? Finally, these examples focus on female reading practices. While the cultural authorities on whom I focus in the debates discussed below are obsessed with the social function of print culture—an obsession, to be sure, that also preoccupies critics of contemporary culture—it is more precise to say that they care most deeply about the social function of print culture *for particular readers*. In the process they produce the category of the young female reader that plays such a vital role in the history of the English novel and censorship.

Taken together, these three stories—the exchange between father and daughter, Eunice's experience with newspapers, and Helena's experience with novels—illuminate the tension between prohibition and expression that has intrigued me in English print culture as a whole. Adultery, after all, is forbidden but it is not unspoken. For if adultery resonates in this novel by way of what is not said (the father's refusal to tell the story of his cousin's marital breakdown) it also resonates by way of what is said (Helena's seduction of her sister's lover). Running alongside claims that adultery is either unspeakable or nonexistent, then, is the very story of adultery to which these claims allude. At the same time, the discourse on censorship contributes to the articulation of the categories of the young female reader and nation to which I refer above. The father's interdiction, for example, generates the young woman's desire, and the narrator's description of this exchange constructs the daughter as a dissembler, a construction that in turn fuels the need for reading regulations in the first place.

These points all find broader parallels in several legal debates and trials in the mid-Victorian period that contributed to the public visibility of sexuality. The debates over the Matrimonial Causes Act, recurrent throughout the 1850s, discussed adultery and domestic cruelty at length; the Obscene Publications Act debates in 1857 discussed representations of sexuality in print culture; the *Madame Bovary* trial in France, also in 1857, provided a more specific public treatment of the representation of adultery; and the 1857 Madeleine Smith murder trial in England provided yet another angle on the charged intersection of sexuality and the law. The outcome of the first example—the 1857 Matrimonial Causes Act—carries important implications for the proliferation of representations of adultery in English print culture. The latter three examples, by contrast, address the potential censorship of representations of adultery and, in the process, contribute to the central categories of perception through which adultery would be visible in English print culture.

Like *The Legacy of Cain*, these debates vividly demonstrate the tension between prohibition and production, made potent by the ostensible democracy of print, in the public sphere. In the novel debates, in particular, cultural commentators repeatedly refer to the *absence* of public representations of adultery. Such representations, many claim, are not permitted in English print culture. Indeed, enormous critical energy is expended on at once denying the fact that representations of adultery exist, prohibiting such representations, and cataloguing the perilous consequences of allowing such representations to circulate freely. Claims that adultery was not permitted in English print culture seem to support the widely maintained position that the representation of adultery was not relevant to the development of the English novel, and that, as Judith Armstrong puts it, English writers avoided adultery "like the plague" (30). I am suggesting, by contrast, that we should look more closely at a print culture in which the representation of adultery is so incessantly and vigorously denied. Instead of assuming that adultery was not relevant to the English novel, I want to consider how an understanding of adultery was constructed *through* the English discourse on censorship and what bearing this construction had on the English novel. This nexus of contradictory concerns—denial, prohibition, and affirmation—loosely corresponds to what Foucault has called the "logic of censorship": "affirming that such a thing is not permitted, preventing it from being said, denying that it exists" (*History* 84). As Foucault also implies, there is a tight link between the existence of a thing or act and its expression. The Victorian discourse on censorship was motivated, in many ways, by the ardent desire to keep adultery out of language; presumably as long as it was not spoken, it could not exist.

And yet this discourse on censorship contributed to the social production of the very topics—sexuality and adultery—that it worked so vigorously to deny. If debates related to adultery and censorship testified to a certain degree of instability in the social field, they also made adultery visible and discussable in new ways. On the one hand, the absence of adultery in the English public sphere was forcefully wedded to the categories of nation and gender in a manner that amplified the stakes at play in print censorship. On the other hand, the cultural commentators who advocated some form of print regulation did not go unchallenged. As nation and gender increasingly became the categories of perception through which adultery became visible and censorship advisable, a symbolic struggle related to the resonance and critical purchase of these categories also developed. Both the attempt to restrict representations of adultery and the challenge to this attempt, then, contributed to ways in which adultery became meaningful and intelligible.

It would be misleading, in this context, simply to refer to a widespread effort to subdue and restrict transgressive representations, although a considerable amount of passion and zeal was devoted precisely to this task. What interests me more is what the English discourse on censorship produced. Censorship, I have noted, assumes a connection between print culture and political or social action. And yet in mid-nineteenth-century England this connection is not evenly distributed among all readers. Eunice reads and becomes aware of her body; Helena reads and, more gravely, initiates acts of infidelity and attempted murder. Where Altick refers optimistically to the democracy of print, Peter Keating, more skeptically, questions the role of print in democracy. What role will print play, he asks, in modern mass democracy? In the context of censorship, it is only one short step from focusing on the role of print to focusing on the role of the reader for whom the benefits of democracy should be most palpable and pressing. What role will the new readers play, ominously referred to as the millions of readers, in the tentative steps toward democratic culture? By shifting the debate from the repression of certain works targeted as transgressive to the articulation of the categories of gender and nation and the construction of a new category of readers, we can begin to see both how a particularly English perception of adultery developed and how it inventively countered the celebrated democracy of print.

"Printed Poison": The Reader's Body and the Body Politic

While this book traces a distinctive history of English representations of adultery, I want to turn initially to a French cultural event, the 1857 censorship trial of *Madame Bovary*, to illuminate the English discourse on censorship. At first glance, Flaubert's novel could not be more remote from English cultural concerns; as Fitzjames Stephen writes shortly after the trial's resolution, "there is no fear that our [English] novelists will outrage public decency" in a similar manner (40). In English fiction, W. R. Greg similarly writes, it "is forbidden to describe or even to allude to" adultery, and his claim that such "violations of the moral and social law meet with the severest and most unqualified condemnation" is, for the most part, borne out in the criticism ("Lowest" 402). The representation of adultery in England, Greg's comment suggests, was regulated by the critic's condemnation and explicit censorship trials were accordingly unnecessary. Both Stephen's and Greg's comments, however, contribute to a larger cultural discussion concerned to dictate acceptable novelistic subject matter and to address the novel's role in the new public sphere. In this context, the trial of *Madame Bovary* both provided a highly public and dramatic example of everything that the English hoped to avoid and, at the same time, articulated potent issues at the heart of the censorship debate that would powerfully inform the English approach to print censorship.

Early in 1857 Flaubert was charged with posing an "offense to public morals and religion" ("Trial" 345) for the publication of *Madame Bovary*.[2] On 30 January 1857, Flaubert listened to a spirited defense of his novel by the defense attorney, Marie-Antoine-Jules Senard, in response to Ernest Pinard's scathing condemnation of its "poisonous" character on behalf of the prosecution. The indictment of Flaubert's novel was motivated by Pinard's belief that the continuity between reading and transgressive practices posed a threat to social and political stability. At the outset, then, it was the concern with public morals that marked the novel for prosecution. The contamination of the reader's body, it was argued during the trial, contagiously infected the body politic. Flaubert himself communicates the perceived link between the sexual body and the body politic in a vivid metaphor: "[b]rothels," he writes to his lover Louise Colet, "provide condoms as protection against catching the pox from infected vaginas. Let us always have a vast condom within us to protect the health of our soul and the filth into which it is plunged. The pleasure is diminished, it is true, and sometimes the sheath splits" (*Letters* 210). Here he articulates, idiosyncratically to be sure, the prevailing sense that one negotiates social and sexual ills at one's peril; the "filth" was too extreme, the available forms of protection were unreliable. The metaphor is most forcefully, and ironically, demonstrated when Flaubert's own novel comes under the scrutiny of the law: Emma Bovary's sexuality, specifically her adultery, contaminates — in a move that figuratively translates reading as sexual contact — French society.

The threat posed by novel reading, moreover, was thematically treated in Flaubert's novel itself. Emma's discontent with Charles and their marriage derives, in part, from her impassioned reading of novels. Charles's mother vehemently objects to Emma's reading. If the owner of the lending library will not stop giving Emma books then Charles's mother's only recourse, she warns, will be the police: "Would they not have the right to tell the police, if the librarian still persisted in his poisonous trade?" (101). Emma's ingestion of arsenic, in this context, is an extension of her novel-reading habit, a point that lends a cruel irony to the apothecary's response to Emma's poisoned body: "Don't panic! . . . It is simply a question of administering some powerful antidote. What poison was it?" (Flaubert 259). What indeed? It was the question, figuratively speaking, that preoccupied both the prosecution and the defense. Was there any "powerful antidote" to counter the negative effects of reading? More urgently, how could one distinguish between poisonous reading and healthy reading?

The trial debates record a symbolic struggle to determine the words and categories through which the mid-century cultural field would be defined; in particular, the debates address the competing understandings of the social function of print culture. With respect to the *Bovary* trial, these competing understandings unfold in the context of Pinard's and Senard's construction of aesthetic value. To what extent does aesthetic value either neutralize or serve as an antidote to the novel of adultery? Pinard pays attention to the category of literature only to discredit what he calls Flaubert's chosen genre, realism. Otherwise, the question of aesthetic value is not perceived to impinge on the questions that the debates wrestle to resolve. Senard, by contrast, devotes almost half of his discussion to authorial intention and aesthetic value. He situates Flaubert in the context of a respected family, and he situates his novel in the context of respected works. Flaubert had a similar idea before the trial: "I am cramming the margins next to the incriminated passages," he writes his brother, "with embarrassing quotations drawn *from the classics*, to show by means of that simple parallel that for the past three hundred years there hasn't been a line of French literature that couldn't be indicted as undermining morality and religion" (*Letters* 224). At the trial itself, Senard indignantly argues: "you will see his sources and God knows it is strange to have to justify them; you will see him . . . entirely permeated with the writings of Bousset and Massillon" ("Trial" 355). Indeed, the most offensive passages in the novel owe a debt to these writers whom, Senard later points out, no one would think of prosecuting. Senard's bullying tone here is an excellent example of the exercise of cultural competence by way of the privileged modes of interpretation and privileged contexts of association through which aesthetic value itself was articulated.

Pinard, however, is preoccupied with an argument that, for him, overrides, or at least comes into serious conflict with, any appeal to the aesthetic value of the text in question. He urges counsel to take the reader into consideration. Is it possible to protect a text, whatever its aesthetic value, if it corrupts the reader? The situation is even more serious, Pinard argues, when one considers the specific audience for novels like *Madame Bovary*. He puts his point succinctly: "who is it who reads Monsieur Flaubert's novels? Are they read by men engaged in social and political economy? No!

The light pages of *Madame Bovary* fall into hands that are even lighter, into the hands of young girls, sometimes of married women. Well then! When the imagination has been seduced [by *Madame Bovary*], when this seduction will have reached into the heart, when the heart will have spoken to the senses, do you think that a very dispassionate argument will be very effective against this seduction of the senses and the feelings?" ("Trial" 345). Here reading is eroticized; it seduces the senses and disturbs the reader's capacity for rational argument. And this seduction is gendered: it is young women and married women who are most at risk. Pinard, however, is not simply identifying a state of affairs; he is also performatively invoking a class of readers, readers like Emma, Eunice, and Helena, who require regulation. Instead of discussing the category of the young female reader as a descriptive category, then, it is more accurate to approach it as a constructed category, a naming that, following Bourdieu, "brings into existence that which it utters" (*Language* 42).

It is worth considering the implications of this performative. When Pinard pits reason against the body and denigrates the latter accordingly, he makes a distinction between what Bourdieu calls a "taste of reflection" and a "taste of sense." Bourdieu understands this distinction as integral to both the demarcation between high and popular culture and the legitimation of "social differences" that such a distinction enforces (*Distinction* 6–7). The "taste of reflection" describes a category of reading that is educated, detached, and objective; the "taste of sense," by contrast, describes a category of reading that is uneducated, involved, and subjective. The codes through which readers interpret the novel divide these readers into two groups: the educated reader for whom the novel does not pose a threat; and the vulnerable reader, for whom the novel, as Pinard puts it, is "poison" ("Trial" 345). This division has consequences, moreover, for newly visible readers like Eunice, Helena, and Emma who are perceived to be voraciously indulging in newspapers, novels, and other forms of print culture made available by the democracy of print. For if it can be demonstrated that their reading practices conform to the taste of sense and that a trajectory can be charted from the printed page to the readers' sensual body and a level of narrative involvement bespeaking serious social costs (from specific examples of adultery, attempted murder, and suicide to the more general disintegration of a feminine ideal), then the new reading practices will accordingly be discredited and the new readers will be both excluded from positions of cultural authority and limited in their access to print culture.

Indeed, it is no surprise that Collins highlights Eunice's sudden awareness of her body — it is as if her body *materializes* — when he describes her encounter with a prohibited form of print culture. The danger that is repeatedly flagged both in the *Bovary* trial and in the mid-century censorship debates is a form of reading that bypasses reason to lodge itself, sexually and/or hysterically, in the reader's body.[3] The conflation of hysteria and reading, for example, which is so persistent in the literature of the period, is also a conflation of women and reading that pathologizes women's reading practices (Vrettos 26).[4] As Janet Beizer puts it, "reading, women, and hysteria" were "knotted into the texture of the time" (56). Men, reading, and wisdom, on the other hand, formed the knot that tied men's reading practices to a domain impermeable to the diseases and addictions that afflicted reading women.

In the trial of *Madame Bovary* the category of the vulnerable reader was invoked and contested — would the female reader be seduced by the text, as Pinard claimed, or would she learn a lesson from the text, as Senard argued? — as it competed with other categories of perception to determine the outcome of the trial. Ultimately, Flaubert's stature and the seriousness of the novel itself overrode considerations of the reader's potential vulnerability, and on 7 February 1857 Flaubert's novel was officially recognized as literature rather than obscenity.[5] If the French were concerned with the connection between reading and social action, the English were concerned with this relation specifically in the context of French novels. *Madame Bovary* was only an extreme example of a type of novel perceived to be tremendously damaging to the English national fabric.

This trial offers one particularly vivid and fractious example of the intersection of law and culture: it articulates the terms of a debate between moral and aesthetic value that persisted throughout the century, and it isolates the female reader as a figure to be regulated. The vocabulary of the trial, moreover, was informed by somatic metaphors — references to poison, addiction, and disease — that linked the reader's poisoned or addicted body to a similarly ravaged body politic. In England, cultural commentators were confident that the English novel escaped a similar need for legal intervention. It should be noted, however, that the "logic of censorship" dictated a series of conflicting claims — that adultery did not exist in England, that it was not represented, and that it needed to be censored. The absence of such a trial in England does not, of course, indicate that the English were not as wary and watchful with respect to fiction and adultery as the French; it also does not mean that equally pressing concerns with respect to print censorship did not obtain in England.

The periodical literature of mid-century England is full of references to the absence of adultery in the English novel and betrays a massive investment in distinguishing the English novel from the French along these lines. As I noted above, Fitzjames Stephen reassures his readers that Flaubert has not set a trend and that French ideas will not infect English literature. England, he writes, is "safe" from the "contamination" of French subjects (by which he means adultery): "Their [English novelists'] weaknesses forbid such dangerous eccentricity quite as much as their virtues" (40). Robert Buchanan similarly writes: "There is no danger of our writers indulging in indecencies. Whatever our private life may be, our literature is singularly alive to the proprieties" (297). While Stephen's review refers specifically to *Madame Bovary*, other cultural commentators rallied together to decry the representation of adultery in the French novel in general and to applaud the absence of adultery in the English novel. A writer for the *Spectator*, for example, observes:

The state of French fiction has at length become such that it is scarcely possible to give in the English language and within the settled conventions of English writing an accurate account of any of its more characteristic productions. The plot not only abounds in incidents, but essentially depends on relations between men and women which English books never mention, which Englishmen call *en masse* immoral, which none of us, without Continental assistance, would have the patience or the wish to pursue into their natural complexities. An English writer would consider he was advancing into debatable if not forbidden ground, if he treated the events with which Sir Cresswell Cresswell is specially concerned. Divorce and adultery are, perhaps, within the present limits of English art, if treated with rapidity and delicacy, and if admitted to be immoral. Not one in twenty even of our most popular novelists could handle such topics graphically and dramatically, and yet not overstep the prescribed boundaries. Almost every one would hazard some expression or venture on some dangerous scene, which exclude his book from "family" perusal, and thereby deprive it of saleability, and him of his remuneration. We pay our writers to be moral, and they are moral. ("*Griffe*" 1029)

A reviewer in 1866 similarly writes: "[the French] have a whole mass of literature which represents the entire population to be thinking about nothing but how to commit, or not to commit, or to hinder or not to hinder other people in committing adultery. . . . If art suffers from our stricter system, there are higher considerations even than the welfare of art" ("Immoral" 637).[6] These higher considerations were, of course, the moral and political health of the nation — the body politic — in light of which aesthetic pretensions were quickly sacrificed. English novels, Mrs. Oliphant claims in 1867, prefer "a certain sanity, wholesomeness, and cleanliness unknown to other literature of the same class" over "the highest development of art" ("Novels" 257).[7] "That corruption which has so fatally injured the French school has," she continues, "it has been our boast, scrupulously kept away from ours. . . . The English mind is still so far *borne* that we do not discuss the seventh commandment with all that effusion and fulness of detail which is common on the other side of the channel" (257–58; see also Maxwell 1054). And Greg solemnly warns against adopting the subject matter of "diseased and indecorous" French fiction—"so strange, so repellent, . . . so appalling"—in English fiction ("Lowest" 401). Adultery was repeatedly perceived to be not only the subject matter of choice in French fiction, but also linked both to the French revolutionary spirit and what Greg calls French society's "hideous and cancerous corruption" (425).[8]

In the mid-Victorian print censorship debates, then, the prohibition against the representation of adultery was articulated through the prism of the French novel. Adultery was French; faithful marriage was English. As Greg puts it, "it is as rare to find a successful French novel that is not scandalous as an English one that is" ("Lowest" 401). The interpretation of this "fact" was straightforward; France was morally depraved and England was morally pure. But if these comments successfully link the French novel with moral decline and political revolution (affirming Paget's link between reading, the sensual body, and revolution), they do something else as well. For the English novelist, the representation of adultery involved not simply a moral question, but also a national question as a link was forged between sexual representation and national identity. A sense of Englishness, in other words, caught up with the sense of nation, was articulated in the context of the *invisibility* of adultery in England.

On the one hand, the French novel was used as a counterpoint against which to distinguish the morally superior English novel and through which to articulate the English taboo against the representation of adultery. On the other hand, the concerns of the French censorship trial—the competing demands of moral and aesthetic questions, the focus on the female reader—were also powerfully applicable to the English cultural context. What is interesting here is the close relationship critics perceived between the representation of adultery and the possibility of aesthetic innovation. Nevertheless, as the passages above indicate, in England the moral value of fiction was consistently privileged over aesthetic innovation or "the welfare of art" ("Immoral" 637). How could a critic applaud aesthetic innovation, after all, if it prefigured moral decline and political revolution? The moral question became even more compelling when one considered the novel's central reader. As the *Saturday Review* notes, "the largest novel-consuming class of the day" is "young ladies" ("Novels" 439).[9] Similarly, in response to Wilkie Collins's "The Unknown Public," Thomas Wright argues in 1883 that the "bulk of this great body of readers [the new reading public] comes from classes that . . . are several 'cuts' above the domestic class. They belong to the 'young ladies' classes" (281).

While Pinard's prosecution was motivated by the desire to protect the young, sometimes married, female reader, the social construction of a new class of vulnerable readers was even more the hallmark of the English tradition, where the blush on the cheek of the young girl operated as a barometer for what was and was not acceptable in the novel. Georgina Podsnap in Dickens's *Our Mutual Friend* is the most frequently cited example of the blushing young woman. Dickens writes: "A certain institution in Mr. Podsnap's mind which he called 'the young person' may be considered to have been embodied in Miss Podsnap, his daughter. It was an inconvenient and exacting institution, as requiring everything in the universe to be filed down and fitted to it. The question about everything was, would it bring a blush into the cheek of the young person?" (175–76). Similarly, a reviewer for the *Spectator* reflects on the role of the female reader in the context of print censorship. If in France "[b]ooks seem at first to have been written for men only," in England "[t]hey now scarcely seem to be written for men at all" (*"Griffe"* 1030). They "are written," the reviewer continues, "for every part of the species *except* men. . . . We have taken young ladies into the club. Every remarkable work of fiction is certain at present to be read by immature minds of the feebler sex before it has been many days published. On such minds an outspoken literature might easily produce very pernicious effects. A large experience proves that the moral constitution of the female mind loses its tone far more easily than the masculine; it is in the good sense and the bad a more delicate constitution" (*"Griffe"* 1030).

Kate Flint, in *The Woman Reader*, documents how the construction of this reader regulated the literary market and English cultural production: "the awareness of Victorians and Edwardians of that discrete category, 'the woman reader,' and the hypotheses about her special characteristics, as well as her presumed needs and interests, affected the composition, distribution, and marketing of literature. The category was continually drawn upon by reviewers, who could use the figure of 'the woman reader,' or 'the young person' (by implication invariably female), as a touchstone against which to place fiction with undesirably explicit sexual content, or as a marker to suggest a work's sentimentality and presumed appeal" (13). The English, of course, had their reasons for deferring to the young female reader. As Mrs. Oliphant noted, it was preferable to have all novels available to the new reading public than to have certain inappropriate novels cautiously locked away ("Novels" 281). Implicit print censorship would then allow young female readers to participate more fully in the rapidly expanding print culture. But the fact that this censorship was inspired by a democratic impulse — the desire to make all novels available to all readers — should not prevent us from seeing the larger social implications of this approach. Like many paternalistic measures, the obsessive references to the young female reader's need for protection belied less straightforward forms of ideological work and cultural classification.

Like Pinard's reference to the typical reader of *Madame Bovary*, references to the default reader in England highlight the "seduction of the senses" to which these readers are vulnerable. And, as in the *Madame Bovary* trial, the references are informed by a rhetoric that focuses on reading as poison, addiction, and disease. The attention to seduction and the reading body accordingly divides and classifies readers; at the same time, social hierarchies that the democracy of print is perceived to dismantle are reinforced. The same threats and fears, after all, are not relevant to educated readers who have been schooled in the "taste of reason"; and if print is increasingly available to the new reading public, it is not, following the discourse on the vulnerable reader, received in the same way by diverse readers. In this context the metaphor of the blushing cheek is particularly apt insofar as it is the female reader's *body* — her face — that registers a reading effect and warns of possibly greater and more disturbing effects to come. In other words, the metaphor for signaling reading danger is a metaphor that embodies, so to speak, exactly what the danger is imagined to be. Alfred Austin makes this connection concisely — "as their [reader's] minds, so their bodies" (256) — and it arises repeatedly in reviews and criticism from the 1860s. Ironically, however, if female readers needed to be protected to ensure their role as custodians and transmitters of moral values, the very policies mobilized to protect these readers contributed to the eroticization of the female reading body and a conflation of the female reader with the adulterous reader. Much more disturbing than the prostitute, to whom Coventry Patmore's "angel in the house" is typically contrasted, is the reader in the house who, as a middle-class, literate woman should conform to the angelic ideal but, because she reads, perilously slides, like Emma and Helena, into the region of adultery, addiction and forbidden desire.[10]

Indeed, the Victorian discourse on censorship generates a discourse on readers and the new reading public that is central to the representation of adultery in the novel. It situates the novel as a political force in a dynamic, potentially volatile relation to society. Most important, the discourse on censorship insists on understanding the novel as a social practice. If this approach allows some critics to underestimate the aesthetic value of a work in question and to mock increasingly sophisticated appeals to versions of aesthetic autonomy, it does keep alive a sense of the vital interchange between novels and readers that informed contemporary cultural production and reception. This discourse on readers, moreover, contributes to a history of the reader that is too often neglected in social histories and theories of the novel. In the very important and useful efforts to understand how readers actually read and who readers were in Victorian period, the issue of how nineteenth-century commentators described readers, how these readers were constructed to read, and who these readers were constructed to be, is not sufficiently analyzed. By attending to the ways in which readers were constructed to read we can see how the new—and, in the case of the novel, specifically female—reader is shaped through popular and critical discourses concerned less with factual description and more with the regulation of readers. We can see how these constructions of the reader at once played a role in the democracy of print culture and in discourses devoted to the suppression of feminist politics. By isolating a default female reader for whom a novelist was obliged to restrict her or his representations, for example, the discourse on censorship effectively rewrote and reinscribed cultural hierarchies and classifications perceived to be threatened by the new democracy of print. And by defining the default reader in terms of her somatic reading practices and limited reading competence, the discourse on censorship reduced the already radically constricted potential for women's political authority in the public sphere.

I want to stress, however, that the construction of the default reader as female was not the only variation on the discourse of vulnerable reading during this period. The categories of youth and class were similarly deployed to create a group of vulnerable, and potentially dangerous readers who required regulation. Nicola Beisel, for example, isolates youth, class, and ethnicity in her study of obscenity regulation in New York City in the late nineteenth century ("Constructing" 105). These categories—especially the category of youth—also had significant critical purchase in England. Nevertheless, the main category of critical concern for English critics of the novel was the female reader. Because this female reader is so often grouped with other vulnerable readers, the ideological work of this particular category—its participation in the containment, regulation, and definition of women—is too often overlooked.

The perceived ability of the novel of adultery to afflict the vulnerable reader's body and, accordingly, the body politic also has an important bearing on the development of the English novel. The repeated appeals to the prohibition against adultery in the English novel work in two ways. By assuming a link between reading and revolution in the context of adultery, they serve as potent warnings to the English novelist. These indictments of the representation of adultery do not carry a legally authorized or institutional capacity to censor print production, of course, but their force in the mid-century cultural field should not be underestimated. They exert a powerful pressure on the novelist and exemplify one of the extralegal avenues through which censorship was advanced. At the same time, however, the very repetitiveness of these references indicates an instability in the social field. They open a space to question the stringent restrictions imposed upon the English novelist and to speculate on the relationship between moral value and aesthetic innovation. The English response to *Madame Bovary*, and to French fiction in general, grappled with the tension between English moral superiority (and the national pride to which it was related) and an aesthetic superiority reluctantly conceded to the French.

Could aesthetic accomplishment, for example, also be secured for the English novel without relinquishing the English commitment to moral fiction? As the quotations above indicate, many cultural critics were comfortable with the English system of print regulation; but there were nevertheless a substantial number of critics, and an even larger number of novelists, who were uneasy with the delimitation of subject matter in the novel. These critics tended to maintain the terms of the debate—that fiction should be moral and that it was intimately wedded to public interest—but they questioned the means by which this goal was obtained. Did print censorship really produce moral purity? Should authors always tailor their fiction to the requirements of young female readers? Was silence with respect to adultery as potentially immoral as the discussion of adultery? Conversely, were there ways in which the representation of adultery could be rendered moral?

Stephen's review of *Madame Bovary* is a case in point. While Stephen is clearly sympathetic with the unsuccessful prosecution—Flaubert's novel, he writes, is "one of the most revolting productions that ever issued from a novelist's brain" (40)—his review is nevertheless ambivalent about literary prescriptions prohibiting the representation of certain subject matters.[11] Indeed, he pauses at the very places where other critics are most assured and his tentative questions expose how vulnerable the fabric of English novel theory was during this period. When Stephen refers to the "virtues" *and* "weaknesses" of the English novelist's reluctance to approach taboo topics (40), for example, he prepares the way for his equivocation with respect to the English novelist's tacit policy of avoiding such reputedly dangerous topics as adultery. He writes: "There are probably half a dozen scenes in it [*Madame Bovary*] which no English author of reputation would venture to insert in any of his publications; and indeed there is no subject on which we are so apt to plume ourselves as the modern purification of our light literature." At this point he introduces his first pause: "But is this true? And if it is, how far does it prove that we are more moral than our neighbours? It is true in one sense, no doubt, that our light literature is pure enough. That is, it is written upon the principle that it is never to contain anything which a modest man might not, with satisfaction to himself, read aloud to a young lady. But surely it is very questionable whether it is desirable that no novels should be written except those which are fit for young ladies to read. It is not so with any other branch of literature" (40–41). English light literature might be "pure enough" but there is a clear implication in Stephen's language — "is this true?"; "if it is [true]"; "[i]t is true" — that "pure enough" is both not as pure as one might hope and purer than the intelligent reader may want. Like Pinard, Stephen assumes a category of female readers for whom literary subject matter is carefully tailored. But in England, Stephen implies, the situation is more grievous because *no* novels may be written that transgress the moral boundaries as they are implicitly dictated by the lowest common denominator, a readership of young ladies.[12] In France Pinard attempted to prosecute *Madame Bovary* by appealing to what young women and married women could or, in this case, could not understand; in England the novel was restricted in advance by following such guidelines without the advice of a prosecuting attorney.

It does not necessarily follow, Stephen argues, that the "modern purification" of the novel which sets England apart from other nations guarantees moral superiority. England's fiction may be purer than France's, but its morals may be equally debased.[13] Many popular writers, for example, "seem to think that the highest function of the poet is the amusement of children; but we are by no means prepared to say that emasculation produces purity" (41). Stephen's next suggestion endows the relationship between reading and social action with a very different emphasis: "Whether a light literature entirely based on love, and absolutely and systematically silent as to one important side of it, may not have some tendency to stimulate passions to which it is far too proper ever to allude, is a question which is too wide for our limits on the present occasion" (41). Does the novel's silence on sexual questions act as a stimulant? What exactly is the status of the silent story of adultery to which Helena's father alludes, for example? Even to *think* this question was to depart from the accepted theories of social transgression by which the English cultural field was shaped. Like Pinard and Senard, Stephen approaches the novel in terms of the moral lessons that it may teach, a strategy that would have been familiar to his readers. Unlike Senard, however, Stephen only gingerly broaches the tension between aesthetic accomplishments and moral lessons that the topic of adultery typically raised; instead, he chooses to rethink, without in any way resolving, the relationship between self-censorship and purity that most English critics took for granted.

Eleanor Marx's and Henry James's approaches to *Madame Bovary*, by contrast, speculate on the moral lessons to be gained from the explicit representation of sexual transgression. When Eleanor Marx first translated *Madame Bovary* into English in 1884, she included an introduction that mimics several of the moves made by Senard almost thirty years earlier. She situates Flaubert in the context of illustrious precursors and respected contemporaries, she reminds her reader that the trial exonerated the novel, and she engages the relationship between reading and social action. Was *Madame Bovary* "printed poison" or was it essentially "moral and healthy" as she herself believes (xvii)?[14] Henry James echoes Marx's approach in a review that indicates the impact of the trial in shaping one's reading. James frames his discussion of *Madame Bovary* with the scandal that the novel provoked: "It is a book adapted for the reverse of what is called family reading, and yet I remember thinking, the first time I read it, in the heat of my admiration for its power, that it would make the most useful of Sunday-school tracts." Where Stephen speculates on the purity of the English novel, James speculates on the purity of the French novel. In both cases, however, as reviewers they read against the grain of dominant interpretations. It is established that the English novel is pure, but is it really? It is established that the French novel is impure, but is it? James continues: "one is dragged into the very current and tissue of the story; the reader seems to live in it all, more than in any novel I can recall. At the end the intensity of the illusion becomes horrible" (173). What James describes here—a seductive power, a strange intensity—is similar to Emma's equivocal reading stance in Flaubert's text. Reading has the power to grip one's very body and the feeling may be quite "horrible." And this somatic register to reading is precisely what defines the vulnerable female reader's reading practices. The novel may carry an instructive moral as James claims, but as soon as it lodges itself in the reader's body, the moral of the story is eclipsed by the narrative's seductive and dangerous appeal.

These responses to *Madame Bovary* were part of a broader effort to rethink the restrictions imposed on English fiction. As J. Herbert Stack asked in one of the most penetrating and comprehensive contemporary accounts of English novels of adultery: "what are the proper limits to the novelist's license?" While most of the reviewers cited earlier took for granted the taboo against adultery, other reviewers were increasingly questioning the taboo, its social implications, and its role in the novel's development. "What is the proper range" for the novel, Stack continues, "or is there any? Which of the broken commandments may he [the novelist] illustrate? If allowed to take as his hero a murderer or a thief, is he also free to invest the adulterer or adulteress with the interest of romance? In the old Greek drama and in modern French fiction this question has been answered emphatically and elaborately in the affirmative" (731). In English fiction, by contrast, the question is more complicated.

Stack's essay is important because it speculates on what an English version of adultery might look like. English novelists, he insists, cannot copy the French without seriously compromising their art and the credibility of their narration. In this context, he criticizes George Alfred Lawrence's *Anteros* for not being alive to the necessary national distinctions: "He [Lawrence] has drawn a novel of *English* life [and adultery], and simply on account of the national and local tone, the whole story seems absurd, unnatural, and untrue. It may be asked, are there not unfaithful wives in England as in France? There are; but the whole tone of English feeling on the subject is entirely different from what it is in France" (733). In England, for example, there is a greater freedom of choice with respect to marriage partners; the English, therefore, are less likely to be sympathetic with a wayward spouse. And because divorce is a more viable possibility in England, the tragic sense of marital entrapment and despair typical of the French novel of adultery does not obtain. Stack explains the first distinction as follows: "her [the woman's] original freedom of choice appears as a bar to the after-right of revolt; and it is certainly no exaggeration to say that while nineteen out of twenty Frenchmen may follow with interest the unfaithful wife, nineteen out of twenty Englishmen will think with sympathy of the deserted husband the broken-up home. . . . It is inevitable therefore that an English novel of infidelity in married life should awaken in English readers sympathies the very opposite of those aroused by French stories of the same class in French minds" (734). With respect to the second point Stack argues that the divorce court turns France's "illicit poetry" of adultery into England's "legal prose" (735). The very improbability of adultery in England's legal prose, Stack suggests, leads to "the entire exclusion of adultery from English fiction. We do not see much to regret in that" (738–39).

And yet, at the same time, Stack offers a canny description of both the difficulties besetting the novelist who desires to represent adultery and what this representation might involve: "But it may be asked, Why should not the sorrows of the desolate hearth be painted for us in accordance with this English sentiment? It may be that some day a writer will arise to do so; but we can understand the difficulties of the case. The pain is domestic; associated superficially with what is tame and trivial; and yet linked in reality with emotions so deep and so delicate that words fail to reach them" (734). To represent adultery in the English novel, as Stack notes, accordingly requires the most careful and sensitive negotiation of both what makes the English experience of adultery distinctive and of what English cultural authorities will potentially permit. In Chapter 2 I focus on the extensive English treatment of adultery in the daily newspapers: the "legal prose" of these narrative accounts of divorce, I argue, articulated one very visible and dynamic framework through which adultery could be legitimately represented. But the "silent" representations of adultery in English novel criticism—the fact that adultery was both tabooed and denied—also deeply informed the English novel of adultery. The relevance of the category of the female reader to the discourse on censorship, for example, was not lost on the English novelist; indeed, it is striking how many novels of adultery focus, literally or figuratively, on the female reader. But instead of following through on the trajectory that links the reader in the house to the adulteress in the house (as initiated by the criticism and thematized in *Madame Bovary*), English novelists focus, for the most part, on variations of the female reader as the betrayed party in an adulterous triangle. In this context, she becomes a reader of instead of a participant in transgressive behavior; the very text of adultery that the censorship debates deny her is staged within her domestic circle.

Flaubert's novel, in fact, serves as an excellent counterpoint to the English novel of adultery, for everything that this novel is the English novel is not. In *Madame Bovary* the representation of adultery is harshly, painfully clear (there is never any doubt, for example, that Emma Bovary has been an unfaithful wife); the adultery is primarily represented from the point of view of the adulteress and as a result it is Emma's passions and desires, aches and anxieties that are documented; and finally the language of the novel itself, its mobile and reaching engagement with aesthetic questions, is inseparable from what the prosecution calls the "poetry of adultery" ("Trial" 340). In the English novel, by contrast, the representation of adultery is a *question* in the text; it is most frequently represented from the perspective of the betrayed party in an adulterous triangle. As a result, the adultery is communicated through an unreliable lens, by turns dim and sharp, and from surprising angles—the flash of a skirt as it moves across a doorway, a spouse's retreating back, the small hesitation in an otherwise unremarkable greeting, a strangely luminous bowl—to convey an ambiguous and unsteady picture of sexual transgression. Finally, while the English novel of adultery insistently engaged aesthetic questions—questions that were in conflict with the general prohibition against the representation of adultery—it developed these questions not in terms of the "poetry of adultery" but rather in terms of what I will call an epistemology of adultery.

In summary, questions of nation and gender coincide in Victorian discussions of reading, novels, and adultery. Indeed, it would not be an exaggeration to say that the English consider the terms "French novel" and "novel of adultery" to be synonymous. When English reviewers invoke adultery, they do so to name it as taboo for English novelists, to assert a connection between Englishness (in terms of national superiority) and the absence of adultery, or to speculate on its relationship to aesthetic value. In one sense, then, adultery becomes visible in the context of taboo, nation, and aesthetics in a manner that will have an important bearing on the representation of adultery in the English novel. At the same time, however, the representation of adultery prompts a discussion of vulnerable readers. For whom does the representation of adultery pose a threat? And what can be done to offset this threat? The category of the vulnerable reader is then used to stabilize unpredictable and highly somatic reading effects and to reinscribe social classifications and hierarchies.

"Matter Out of Place": The Obscene Publications Act and the *Hicklin* Standard

Four months after the Flaubert trial in France, the prominence of obscene publications came to the attention of the English public and Parliament. In the spring of 1857 Lord Campbell opened the first reading of proposed amendments to the Obscene Publications Act with a potent metaphor. "A sale of poison," he claimed, "more deadly than prussic acid, strychnine, or arsenic—the sale of obscene publications and indecent books—was openly going on" (*Hansard* 145: 102). This poison metaphor, familiar from the Victorian novel debates, is powerful precisely for the ways in which it invokes the reader's body. Obscene publications, after all, are seen as "*more deadly*" than other poisons recognized for their killing properties. And yet problems with the poison metaphor immediately present themselves. Was Lord Campbell, for example, afflicted with the deadly character of obscene publications? Or did he know how to read such publications? In other words, to what extent did reading competence enter into the debate? How was reading competence and the legal construction of a vulnerable reader related to efforts to define obscenity?

These questions have an important bearing on two decisive mid-Victorian obscenity legislation debates: the 1857 Obscene Publications Act debates and the debates related to the 1868 *Regina* v. *Hicklin* trial. Once again, in these debates and the obscenity legislation that followed, the identification of somatic reading practices with certain classes of readers (women, the young, and the working classes) worked to exclude new readers from positions of cultural authority. These readers, for example, were not perceived to share the acumen and reading competence demonstrated by Lord Campbell and others. They were not considered capable of reading and evaluating an obscene publication without undue harm or of being able to distinguish between obscene and non-obscene publications. In this sense, these debates prefigure the modernist construction of an elite readership from which less competent and educated readers are excluded. As the poison metaphor indicates, moreover, the failure to read correctly was related to the reader's body or a form of reading *with* the body particularly apt in the context of obscene publications.

The Obscene Publications Act and the *Hicklin* standard add a legal dimension to the overview of reviewers' approaches to adultery and French fiction. While these cases do not discuss adultery, strictly speaking, they do provide an opportunity to consider the relationship between prohibition and discursive proliferation. Does the prohibition of certain topics result in silence, or even an indictment, of these topics? In a letter to his brother, Flaubert writes: "The police have blundered. . . . (in part thanks to the prosecution) my novel is looked on as a masterpiece" (*Letters* 224). In the cases to be considered here, a discourse on prohibition generates the very obscenity it seeks to subdue. More importantly, however, in its effort to eliminate obscenity the 1857 case also generates a degree of category confusion that will not be dispelled until 1868 with the definitive construction — indeed, legislation — of the vulnerable reader as a legal category.

Both the 1857 trial and the 1868 case stage a relationship between the law and fantasy that has increasingly come under the scrutiny of critics uncomfortable with the liberal framework of repression through which censorship is typically interpreted. The opposition between fantasy and the law that informs the liberal approach has been challenged by critics concerned to address the interimplication of fantasy and the law. Hunter, Saunders, and Williamson argue that in English obscenity cases — in this discussion the *R v. Curll* decision of 1727 — the law did not work simply to repress fantasies: "the law did not supervene in an exemplarily repressive swoop on a field occupied only by the drives and erotic fantasies. Rather, through a single and uncertain common-law court decision, the law entered a field already *dense* with specific forms of social and ethical regulation derived from the religious technology of the flesh and the direction of conscience" (51). It is important, they argue, to attend to the social field in which both law and fantasy are defined. As Judith Butler stresses, the law shapes one's fantasy constructions as fantasy, in turn, shapes the formation of the law ("Force" 111).

In this context, it is instructive to note the comparison between these nineteenth-century debates and current anti-pornography discourse. Where the Victorian debaters posit a causal connection between the young (usually female) reader of novels and forms of sexual depravity, contemporary critic Catharine MacKinnon, for example, posits a causal connection between the male reader or viewer of pornography and forms of sexual depravity. The targeted reader — that is, the reader who requires regulation — has shifted from the female to the male. In the former case, young female readers are threatened by their own reading and viewing; in the latter case women are threatened by men's reading and viewing. MacKinnon does not so much fear that girls or women will become prostitutes after being exposed to pornography as she fears — or, rather, claims that she knows — that boys and men will be prompted to objectify women and that there is a direct relationship between the objectification of women and the abuse, sexual or otherwise, of women.[15] MacKinnon's critique of pornography, then, is not concerned with the vulnerable (female) reader/viewer but rather with the violent (male) reader/viewer. What is most striking, however, is the contrast between the extensive debate and opposition that MacKinnon's argument has excited and the absence of such debate and opposition in the nineteenth century. To be sure, there was a great deal of controversy related to censorship as I outline in this chapter, but there was very little debate on or opposition to the construction of the default reader as a vulnerable reading woman.[16] By contrast, it is not difficult to find numerous critics contesting MacKinnon's translation of the average man in the context of pornography as the violent man.

In "The Discourse on Language" Foucault considers the relationship between production and exclusion that is implicit in the discussion described above. He elaborates on discursive "danger" as follows: "I am supposing that in every society the production of discourse is at once controlled, selected, organized and redistributed according to a certain number of procedures, whose role is to avert its powers and its dangers, to cope with chance events, to evade its ponderous, awesome materiality. In a society such as our own we all know the rules of *exclusion*. The most obvious and familiar of these concerns what is *prohibited*. We know perfectly well that we are not free to say just anything, that we cannot simply speak of anything, when we like or where we like; not just anyone, finally, may speak of just anything" (216). Foucault describes this regulatory production of discourse as self-evident; he is only describing what "we all know," what is "obvious and familiar," what we "know perfectly well." In many ways the debates related to the 1857 Obscene Publications Act were about establishing, institutionalizing, and reinforcing the categories through which culture was understood, about consolidating the "established order of things" ("Discourse" 216). But the intensity of these debates suggests an instability within the dominant categories through which social order was at least minimally maintained. Indeed, M. J. D. Roberts reads the debate as a "moral panic" (612) that reflects a mid-century anxiety about key cultural categories and addresses, specifically "the problem of reconciling the claims of a libertarian ethic of individual responsibility with the claims of an ethic of paternalistic social concern" (611). This libertarian ethic was couched in terms of an aesthetic freedom that closely corresponds to twentieth-century approaches to censorship. But, as Roberts notes, it competed with a paternalistic ethic that framed the discussion quite differently. For Roberts, the focus on youthful, lower- and middle-class (as opposed to working-class) readers suggests "generational tensions building up within the middle-class and lower-middle-class family" (614).

It is Hunter, Saunders, and Williamson, however, who come closest to my reading of the paternalistic ethic to which Roberts quite rightly refers.

"Victorian obscenity law," they write, "emerged not as a monolithic repression of sexual expression but as a sophisticated and discriminating mechanism of regulation" (53). Following Foucault, they want to replace the "story of repression," through which the Obscene Publications Act and other statutes are often understood, with a "history of legal regulation and policing" (73). Their approach, however, obscures two points that are central to my argument: first, the tension between the *competing* discourses of repression and regulation that translate in my reading as the tension between a focus on the text or the author and a focus on the reader; and, second, the specificity of the very regulation to which they point—that is, in the context of the novel the regulation was gendered, it targeted vulnerable *female* readers—under the guise of censorship and public morals. Repression and regulation, in other words, were two competing categories of perception through which to understand and address the relationship between reading and social action in Victorian England. The fact that regulation "won" this particular symbolic struggle had consequences for both the development of the novel and the social construction of women during this period.

Because Hunter, Saunders, and Williamson assume a reading of censorship that corresponds to the framework of regulation, they miss—in fact, deny—an important aspect of the 1857 parliamentary debates related to obscenity. They maintain that in nineteenth-century English law there was an "untroubled distinction between pornography and literature" (92); obscenity, they assert, was self-evident to critical commentators because it was determined according to circumstance rather than as a product in need of an essentialist definition. It is true that the 1857 debates and, more emphatically, the *Hicklin* standard, do *result* in a circumstantial reading of obscenity which they call "variable obscenity." What their perspective overlooks, however, is the *debate*, a debate to which several other commentators have been sensitive (see, for example, Roberts and Manchester). This debate marks a historical moment in which certain "well-known," "obvious" categories—literature and obscenity—are revealed to be unstable. These categories are provisionally stabilized by 1868 with the construction of the vulnerable reader, a construction that is in fact much more surprising and consequential than most censorship histories and histories of the English novel allow.

Campbell's answer to the problem of obscene publications was a proposed bill that would restrict the circulation of obscenity by granting greater freedom to police and magistrates. Magistrates would be authorized to issue search warrants at their discretion and the police would be authorized to investigate suspicious homes, seize whatever pornography they found, and burn it. These suggestions met with a twofold objection related to the definition of obscenity and the contravention of privacy. For the law to operate, it needed to mark out a terrain within which material could be positively identified as pornographic. This task proved more difficult than the supporters for the bill imagined as a series of competing and sometimes overlapping discourses vied for legal credibility. But before turning to this debate I want to return to some of the issues raised by the poison metaphor.

A writer for the London *Times* on 29 June 1857 makes the following observation: "The distinctive industry of Holywell-street [the street in London where obscene publications were most prominently sold] has received a compliment which is wholly undeserved in being classed with the sale of poisons. There is nothing intrinsically wrong in the existence of arsenic or of strychnine. Poison is, as Lord PALMERSTON said of dirt, matter out of its proper place; and there is a risk of interfering with the proper use of drugs which are only incidentally dangerous to life. Bad books, bought and sold only for their badness, may be prohibited without any corresponding inconvenience" (7). In her influential account of pollution and taboo, Mary Douglas also refers to dirt as matter out of place; for example, shoes are not dirty on the back doormat, but the same shoes on the dining room table are dirty (35). The idea that dirt is matter out of place implies two conditions for Douglas: "a set of ordered relations and a contravention of that order. Dirt then, is never a unique, isolated event. Where there is dirt there is system" (35). In fact, it is this sense of a system — an interlocking set of relations between the production and intention evident in the obscene publication, the obscene publication itself, and the reader of the obscene publication — which demands attention. For as the debate unfolds the inaccuracy of the *Times* comment becomes manifestly clear. Bad books were not always bad books; on the contrary, like poison and drugs, bad books were, in some reader's hands, permissible publications, and in others, deadly publications in need of legal suppression.

While Campbell relied on the transparency of his poison metaphor, his opponents questioned exactly what constituted an obscene publication or "bad book." It became increasingly clear that the definition of obscenity was context dependent and that it relied, at least in part, on the reader or spectator. Lord Brougham, for example, asked: "how did he [Campbell] propose to define what was an 'obscene publication'?" Lord Lyndhurst similarly asked: "what is the interpretation which is to be put on the word 'obscene'?" (*Hansard* 146: 330; see also the comments of Wensleydale, Roebuck, and White). These questions clearly indicate that the definition of obscenity was not as self-evident as the authors of *On Pornography* claim; indeed, they prompt a staging of the competing frameworks of intelligibility through which such a definition could be secured. In doing so, they make public and political an instability in categories assumed to be self-evident. They force an articulation of social rules that rely precisely on their non-articulation — they are what "we know perfectly well" — and in doing so the law's own vulnerability is made visible. To be sure, no one anticipated this definitional instability. At one desperate point, for example, Lord Campbell argued that there *must* be an operative definition of obscenity because without one the current law, quite apart from the proposed amendment, would not work.

Lord Brougham was also concerned with the line between obscenity and poetry: "in the works of some of their most eminent poets," he explains, "there were some objectionable passages which, under this measure, might cause them to be considered obscene publications" (*Hansard* 146: 329). To support this point Brougham and others offered several examples of material that would be indicted as obscene under the proposed law; they referred to the paintings of Correggio, sculpture in general, the poems of Rochester, the drama of the Restoration, as well as the works of Wycherley, Congreve, Dryden, Ovid, Shakespeare, and others. Like Lyndhurst, Roebuck again "wanted to know where the line could be drawn" (*Hansard* 147: 1475). Art, he suggested, is even more formative and influential than cruder writings: "in the *Eloisa to Abelard*, one of the most brilliant poems in the English language, there were lines which he would be ashamed to read aloud. They might depend upon it that the passions of youth were not half so much excited by vulgar obscenity as by refined licentiousness. Where were they to stop? They could lay down no rule" (147: 1477). Art posed a danger to dominant cultural definitions precisely because of its internal instability; a work could provoke contemplation in some audiences and masturbation in others. In many ways, this was exactly Campbell's point, and it is a point that was made more forcefully during the Hicklin discussion eleven years later; yet Campbell had reasons for trying to placate the anxieties of his opponents. And, indeed, his comments betray his own confusion with respect to the categories in question. No doubt, he wanted it to be possible both to legislate against obscenity *and* protect art. During the next readings Lord Campbell again tried to reassure his antagonists that art—a category that operated on the basis of implicit criteria—was not at risk. The work in private collections and the dramatists, poets, and novelists to whom his antagonists referred would be exempt from the legislation. Instead the law was designed "to apply exclusively to works written for the single purpose of corrupting the morals of youth" (146: 329). As the debaters were quick to recognize, however, these works—the works in private collections and the works written for youth—were not mutually exclusive. The same volume of poetry enjoyed by a gentleman in his home, for example, might be circulated in cheap editions to a broader and more vulnerable reading public. In some cases, in other words, a copy of Ovid or Dryden or Shakespeare might be a "bad book."

As obscenity is increasingly contested, its teasing, now-you-see-it, now-you-don't connection to the scene of the legal debate itself is stressed. This point is evident in Campbell's approach both to obscene publications and to his legal remedy for such publications. On 9 July 1857 he opens the debate with a commentary, predictably, on French novels. He begins his speech by stating that "for decency's sake, he would not dwell upon" the new obscene publications that had recently come to his attention. But, he continues, he now holds in his hand a copy of Dumas's *The Lady of the Camellias*:

It gave a description of the white camellia and the red camellia, in a manner that trenched upon modesty, and which he could not state. He did not wish to create a category of offences in which this book might be included, although it certainly was of a polluting character. It was only from the force of public opinion and of an improved taste that the circulation of such works could be put a stop to. . . . He was shocked to think that there could be so much circulation for works like the one in his hand—*The Lady of the Camellias*. In this work the lady described her red camellias and her white camellias; but he would not shock their Lordships by going further. He had heard on good authority that the book was sold at all the railway stations. (146: 1152)[17]

Campbell's well-regulated mind is shocked by what he reads, but he pointedly refrains from sharing the content of this reading experience with his listeners. Instead he opens an obscene space of phantasmatic projection. Campbell, moreover, gives no clear sense of why Dumas's novel, given its "polluting character," would not be charged as obscene. The *Law Times*, in this context, may be excused its impression that Lord Campbell wished to name the book as exactly the sort of material the new law would be designed to restrict.

Indeed, on numerous occasions, Campbell himself contributes to the weakening of the very categories he seeks to consolidate. He groups the "literary" works to which his antagonists refer with obscene publications despite his emphatic disavowal of this category collapse throughout the debate. Campbell "thought the particular street to which he had referred, but not named [Holywell Street], would rejoice upon learning that the cause of free trade in obscene publications had been upheld by such distinguished authorities" (146: 337). This comment clearly contradicts Campbell's claim that there was a "broad and marked distinction" between obscenity and literature since the only "obscene publications" defended by Lyndhurst and others were works of "literature." Similarly, an argument between Campbell and Lyndhurst closes with Campbell referring to Lyndhurst's "zeal for these filthy publications" (146: 333). But what filthy publications is Campbell referring to at this point? In his apology several weeks later he says that he had only wanted "to assure" Lord Lyndhurst "that, as he had talked with so much delight of certain works of Correggio and of the prints from them, there was nothing in this Bill which would disturb his enjoyment of them" (146: 1362). Is Correggio, then, a filthy publication? In fact, Correggio may be both a work of art *and* a filthy publication, a point that Campbell is reluctant to admit. Again the London *Times* makes Campbell's point more forcefully than he does himself: "no tribunal would censure a bookseller for supplying his customers with complete editions of the classics, although much may be urged against the morality of PETRONIUS, of NONNUS, of MARTIAL, and even of CATULLUS and OVID. When their works are advertised in low thoroughfares in inflammatory placards, obviously addressed to the young, the ignorant, and the vicious, the law which Lord CAMPBELL wishes to strengthen will become applicable to the case" (29 June 1857, 7). In other words, the classics and other works of "literature" will not always be exempt from legal regulation. Campbell may want to reassure his opponents that literature does not fall within the boundaries of his proposed law, but when that literature is produced in cheap editions or disseminated in "low thoroughfares" then its classification shifts from literature to obscenity under the law. The ostensible "democracy of print," exacerbated by new and cheaper forms of publication and by increased literacy, provokes a perceived erosion of public morals precisely because literature moves into new and unexpected social spaces.

And yet in the 1857 debate the distinction between literature and obscenity could not be stabilized by reference to the consideration of a vulnerable reader as easily as Campbell and the *Times* might wish. Lord Lyndhurst, for example, remarks that his discussion of obscenity inescapably shapes his identity and his reputation: "I am sorry to have detained your lordships with this explanation, but so many misapprehensions and misapplications of what fell from me have gone abroad, that I have felt as though I were upon my trial, and that I was imperatively called upon to justify myself" (146: 1360–61).[18] As obscenity rapidly comes to inform everything that the debate addresses, White comments: "Some people thought that the naked human figure, except to students of art, was objectionable, and he had even heard it whispered that some part of the literary works of Lord Campbell himself—his *Lives of the Lord Chancellors*, and his *Lives of the Lord Chief Justices*—might and would be made the subject of prosecutions, in the event of this Bill becoming law" (*Hansard* 147: 1479). Lord Campbell may feel confident in his ability both to remain unaffected by his exposure to obscene publications—to adopt a "taste of reflection"— and in his ability to distinguish between the obscene and the non-obscene, but this same confidence was not shared by other participants in the debate as they unsuccessfully attempted to formulate a stable and secure definition of what constituted an obscene publication.

Despite these instabilities, the bill passed and Campbell was initially pleased with its effects. But by 1868 it was, as the *Saturday Review* put it, a "dead letter": "Holywell Street literature is not only a phrase, but a very visible and palpable fact of the day. At the present moment the dung-hill is in full heat, seething and steaming with all its old pestilential fume" ("Purity" 646). In this same year, Henry Scott, a metal broker who lived respectably in Wolverton, had a confrontation with the law. Scott was a member of the Protestant Electoral Union and his objectionable pamphlet *The Confessional Unmasked* was very unlike the Holywell street pornography with which the 1857 debates had explicitly taken issue. Indeed, as M. J. D. Roberts notes, it was exactly the sort of publication that Campbell's bill should have exempted from prosecution.

The defense begins with a tactic very similar to that of Campbell's opponents described earlier; they seek to demonstrate that it is impossible to draw a line between obscenity and art because classic works are clearly sometimes obscene. The defense asks, "What can be more obscene than many pictures publicly exhibited, as the Venus in the Dulwich gallery?" to emphasize that in certain circumstances obscenity is condoned. But this proves to be exactly the wrong argument. The prosecution, unlike Campbell, is not prepared to exempt the legislation of works of art in all cases. They respond by saying, "it does not follow that because such a picture is exhibited in a public gallery, that photographs of it might be sold in the streets with impunity" (*Law Reports* 365). And Lord Cockburn expands on this point later in the discussion: "A medical treatise, with illustrations necessary for the information of those whose education or information for the work is intended, may, in a certain sense, be obscene, and yet not the subject of indictment; but it can never be that these prints may be exhibited for any one, boys and girls, to see as they pass. The immunity must depend on the circumstances of publication" (*Law Reports* 367).[19]

Similarly, in 1916 John Sumner, president of the New York Society for the Suppression of Vice, offers a reading of the *Hicklin* standard as follows: "*whereas the circulation of a picture or a book under some circumstances might be illegal, under other circumstances the law would not apply*. For instance, a legitimate work of art exhibited in an art gallery is not disturbed, whereas a copy of the same picture or sculpture, generally circulated and easily accessible to the young and which would create in a youthful mind lewd and sensuous thoughts, is a subject for suppression under the laws referred to" ("Obscene" 95–96). As Cockburn notes, "[t]his work . . . is sold at the corners of streets, and in all directions, and of course it falls into the hands of persons of all classes, young and old, and the minds of those hitherto pure are exposed to the danger of contamination and pollution from the impurity it contains" (*Law Reports* 372). Like Campbell eleven years earlier, Cockburn is concerned with the vulnerable reader; the fact that the work is sold on street-corners and disseminated "in all directions" only underscores the danger of discursive proliferation that the law is designed to contain. And like the *Times*' response to the 1857 debate, this argument similarly suggests that when the classics are distributed in "low thoroughfares" their status as classics is no longer relevant.

Where poison was the operative metaphor in the Obscene Publications Act debate, disease is the metaphor of choice employed in this case. Cockburn notes that "an indictment lies for carrying a child with an infectious disease in the public streets, though there was no intention to do injury to the passersby" (*Law Reports* 368). This analogy, of course, implies that the written work in question might work as an infectious disease, damaging and injuring the bodies of those with whom it comes in contact. Cockburn's metaphor, however, masks what is most powerful about his position. A sick child carried into the street risks infecting everyone with whom she or he comes in contact, regardless of the street, the age, the class, or the gender of the potentially endangered passerby. "Diseased" texts, on the other hand, only risk infecting certain, carefully defined, audiences—those who are not immune, to refer to Cockburn above, those who adopt the "taste of sense." The disease spreads in some directions, but not in others. Unlike the sick child, who is equally sick to each person with whom she or he comes in contact, in this case it is the law that dictates who is most vulnerable and in which direction the disease might spread. While the law appears to protect the public in general from the threat of a sick child it, in fact, legislates — that is, legally creates — a vulnerable public that requires regulation.

The point of both debates, of course, is that bad books are precisely like poisons or *pharmakons*. In some contexts *The Confessional Unmasked*, novels by Dumas, or medical treatises are bad, and in other contexts they are good. The context dictates the pollution behavior and exposes the real focus of social concern as projected readers. This ordering of books has important implications for the maintenance of social boundaries and classifications; as Douglas argues, persuasive ideas related to sexual dangers often perform the work of organizing social hierarchies and symmetries in a manner that is consistent with the dominant social order (3–4). The belief that sexual representations in books were divided into good and bad categories depending on the reader's gender (and other prevalent categories of vulnerability) supported a social hierarchy that devalued certain reading practices; the system that is imposed on disorder, in other words, hierarchizes reading experiences and only secondarily books. Contagion, in this context, threatens categories otherwise discrete as it also underscores the social value of established categories. What the diseased/sick-child metaphor and the poison metaphor indicate is not only an inherent instability in the category of literature (sometimes the sick child is a work of art, so to speak; sometimes the poison is a remedy) but also a shift in the terms of the debate away from the category of literature and toward the regulation of targeted audiences.

This point is best demonstrated in the case's famous definition of obscenity. As noted above, Cockburn, unlike the 1857 debaters, is quick to acknowledge that in several works of English literature there might be subject matter that would warrant an obscene indictment. The following long passage contains Cockburn's famous definition of obscenity in italics, but the context of this definition underscores the problematic distinction between literature and obscenity that I have been discussing:

there are a great many publications of high repute in the literary productions of this country the tendency of which is immodest, and, if you please, immoral, and possibly there might have been subject-matter for indictment in many of the works which have been referred to. But it is not to be said, because there are in many standard and established works objectionable passages, that therefore the law is not as alleged on the part of this prosecution, namely, that obscene works are the subject-matter of indictment; *and I think the test of obscenity is this, whether the tendency of the matter charged as obscenity is to deprave and corrupt those whose minds are open to such immoral influences, and into whose hands a publication of this sort may fall.* Now, with regard to this work [*The Confessional Unmasked*], it is quite certain that it would suggest to the minds of the young of either sex, or even to persons of more advanced years, thoughts of a most impure and libidinous character. The very reason why this work is put forward to expose the practices of the Roman Catholic confessional is the tendency of questions, involving practices and propensities of a certain description, to do mischief to the minds of those to whom such questions are addressed, by suggesting thoughts and desires which otherwise would not have occurred to their minds. (*Law Reports* 371, emphasis mine)

In this awkwardly worded passage, the definition of obscenity is inseparable, both rhetorically and thematically, from the reference to literature. Most commentators only cite the italicized clause here and they miss, therefore, the striking fact that Cockburn builds his definition of obscenity on a reference to literature. Cockburn sharpens Campbell's reference to vulnerable readers above — "the morals of youth," "the youth of this country" — by incorporating the category of literature into his test for obscenity. Following this definition, neither the category of literature nor the author's intention are relevant to the determination of obscenity. Instead obscenity, like literature, generates fantasies; it suggests thoughts and desires that would otherwise remain unarticulated. It is, arguably, this power of suggestion that is most at issue. Even though *The Confessional Unmasked* has a pedagogical and religious intention, it can be indicted for obscenity. Cockburn explains his position on intention as follows: "May you commit an offence against the law in order that thereby you may effect some ulterior object which you have in view, which may be an honest and even a laudable one? My answer is, emphatically no" (*Law Reports* 372). Cockburn next develops his conception of inferred intention; it may be true, he argues, that Scott had no intention to deprave and corrupt his readers but because he must have known the material he distributed was obscene such an intention could be reasonably inferred. Cockburn writes, "I hold that, where a man publishes a work manifestly obscene, he must be taken to have had the intention which is implied from that act" (*Law Reports* 373). Cockburn, then, dismisses the relevance of authorial intention with as much ease as he rejects cultural value; the most decisive factor in determining obscenity is the hands into which a contested work might fall.

The Obscene Publications Act debate and the articulation of the *Hicklin* standard make visible the instability of the categories of obscenity and literature in mid-nineteenth-century England. The result, surprisingly, is neither a definition of literature nor a definition of obscenity, but rather, as noted above, the construction of a vulnerable category of readers. These debates record the struggle between competing discourses to define the boundaries of literary regulation. In 1857 it is difficult to disentangle the different discourses as debaters draw, almost haphazardly, on the arguments best designed to facilitate their competing projects. Thus Lord Campbell is quick to concede that the censorship of literature is undesirable, and debaters on the opposite side are quick to grant that the protection of vulnerable readers is imperative.

By 1868, however, these threads have separated as Cockburn adamantly rejects both cultural value and authorial intention in determining the obscenity of a given work. The cultural value of the "classic" work of literature, for example, is no guarantee that such a work will not be indicted for obscenity; similarly, the stated intentions of an author like Henry Scott are irrelevant to the evaluation of *The Confessional Unmasked* as obscene. Instead obscenity is determined by reference to the category of the vulnerable reader, the reader "into whose hands a publication . . . may fall." It is this reader to whom the somatic metaphors of poison and disease uniquely apply. These debates and the obscenity legislation that follows, then, contribute to the social construction of a new category of readers—readers who adopt a "taste of sense," readers who read with their bodies—and the reinscription of more traditional social boundaries threatened by the democracy of print.

"Not Proven": The Adulteress in the House

"He expected me to say No—so I said it," Helena writes. But her diary, composing a substantial portion of the narration, records the very story of transgressive desire that her father encourages her to disavow. If Helena can call Eunice's diary a "shameless record of passions unknown to young ladies in respectable English life" (150), then her own diary is an even more extreme and condemnatory display of exactly such passions. In many ways, Helena embodies the contradictory and overdetermined characteristics of the new female readers that so excited public controversy. At once transgressive actor and transgressive writer, the narrator also constructs her as a transgressive reader; indeed, to the extent that there is a non-hereditary origin to her moral abandon it is located in her reading practices. In this context, *The Legacy of Cain* taps well-established, if also contested, conventions for both describing and circumscribing female readers. I have been arguing that the construction of such damaging and exaggerated descriptions was a response to women's participation in the new print culture and their sometimes active, sometimes passive claims to positions of cultural authority. It became increasingly clear that it was worth fighting for the authority to "name" the new readers and to articulate their position in a shifting social space defined by the democracy of print. Helena's diary represents her claim to self-expression; the interpretation of her diary, however, represents a challenge to that effort. Like the enthusiastic criminal who leaves a record of her or his crime, Helena provides the material — her diary is "produced in court as evidence against her" (465) — through which she may be indicted. But if this legal resolution effectively usurps Helena's nascent efforts at self-expression, the formal structure of the novel itself defines and delimits the cultural authority of her voice in another way. For both sisters' diaries are framed by another diary written, appropriately enough, by the governor of the prison.

In this section I want to turn to two stories of real women who, like Emma and Helena, contributed to the public visibility of adultery. The Madeleine Smith murder trial in 1857 and the *Robinson* v. *Robinson* divorce trial in 1858 vividly stage the perceived links between adultery, gender, and knowledge that animate the novel debates and the construction of the young female reader. As I noted at the outset, print censorship in the mid-Victorian period obeys a paradoxical logic that at once asserts that a disputed subject does not exist, cannot be expressed, and must be censored. The cases addressed here demonstrate this logic as the female protagonists, Madeleine Smith and Mrs. Robinson respectively, are guilty of sexual crimes that pose a challenge to the evidential and moral claims by which their society was made intelligible. How does one *know* when a spouse has committed adultery? What evidence constitutes indisputable proof? Adultery should not exist and yet two middle-class women seem to have committed adultery. The representation of adultery is not permitted and yet these cases are discussed in great detail in journals and daily newspapers. The attempts to reconcile these contradictions demonstrate the enormous social power invested in making a woman's adultery invisible or nonexistent in the English public sphere.

The first case history has been well documented. In 1857 Madeleine

Smith was accused of murdering her lover. While the literature devoted to the trial emphasized the question of her guilt, I want to stress the case's engagement with the issue of Madeleine's adultery.[20] The details are as follows. In 1855, nineteen-year-old Madeleine Smith caught the attention of Emile L'Angelier as she walked along one of the Glasgow streets where she lived. Everyone agreed that Madeleine was beautiful and vivacious; her friends remarked on her charm and quick intelligence. Emile did not lose any time in arranging, unknown to Madeleine's family, a meeting, and a relationship between the two quickly developed. But Emile was only a shipping clerk and Madeleine's parents, and no doubt Madeleine herself, imagined a different sort of marriage than the secret proposal offered by Emile. Letters from the first year of their correspondence record a series of appeals from Emile and, for the most part, evasions from Madeleine with respect to the question of marriage. These entreaties are made more urgent after Madeleine and Emile have sexual relations although, it should be noted, even before this occurrence they refer to each other as husband and wife, presumably based on their physical intimacy, their loosely proposed marriage plans, and the romantic excitement that their affair generated.

During this period Madeleine, in her letters to Emile, discussed her own body, her sexuality, and her desire in a manner that stunned the trial participants and the British reading public. The judge, looking for regret or repentance in Madeleine's letters says, "is there the slightest appearance of grief or remorse? None whatever. It is the letter of a girl rejoicing in what had passed, and alluding to it, in one passage in particular, in terms which I will not read, for perhaps they were never previously committed to paper as having passed between a man and a woman" (Jesse 14). While Madeleine vigorously denied any regret with respect to her physical intimacy with Emile — "I do not regret that — never did, and never shall," she writes to Emile (Jesse 336) — she most certainly did regret the emotional involvement and tacit responsibilities that such intimacy produced. Nevertheless, Madeleine's letters, as the judge's comment above indicates, disturbed the accepted norm of female behavior. After consummating the relationship with Emile for the first time, she writes: "Beloved, if we did wrong last night it was in the excitement of our love. Yes, beloved, I did truly love you with my soul. I was happy, it was a pleasure to be with you. . . . I did not bleed in the least last night — but I had a good deal of pain during the night" (Jesse 316–17). And later she writes, "I think I would be wishing you to *love* me if I were with you — but I don't suppose you would refuse me" (Jesse 327). And later still she writes: "Our intimacy has not been *criminal*, and I am your wife before God — so it has been no sin — our loving each other. No, darling, fond Emile, I am your wife" (Jesse 329). When Emile and Madeleine decide to refrain from having intercourse again until after they are married, Madeleine writes: "It was a punishment to myself to be deprived of your *loving me*, for it is a pleasure, no one can deny that. It is but human nature. Is not every one that *loves* of the same mind?" (Jesse 336). Yes and no. When Madeleine's letters become an open text for public consumption, they are used to indict Madeleine's style of loving as at once very much at odds with what "every one" does, and yet very much in accord with unspoken desires harboring in the heart of the home.

The story that the letters record becomes trickier to decipher after the autumn of 1856. Several months earlier Madeleine had been introduced to William Minnoch, a friend and colleague of her father's. Emile suspected, rightly, that Minnoch visited the Smith home as Madeleine's suitor and potential fiancé. Madeleine assured Emile that she had no interest in Minnoch, that she loved Emile, that she was his wife and that, in a logic their relationship had created, they would be married soon. But on 28 January 1857 Madeleine became engaged to Minnoch. When Emile learned of the engagement and Madeleine's deception, he threatened to expose their relationship. Madeleine was frightened and implored him as a gentleman to refrain from doing so. On several occasions over the course of her relationship with Emile, Madeleine tried to end the romance and, around the time of her engagement to Minnoch, she made a more emphatic effort in this direction. But after Emile's threats she renewed her commitment to him and intensified the passionate tenor of her letters. One month later Emile was dead. Eight days later Madeleine was arrested.

Was Madeleine guilty of murdering her lover/"husband"? Did she, on three occasions, lace his hot chocolate with arsenic causing him to be ill and, finally, to die, as the prosecution claimed? Or did he, depressed over the loss of Madeleine, commit suicide as the defense argued? The history of Emile's last five weeks (and Madeleine's actions in this period) is revealing. In mid-February, at the time of her first attempt to break off with Emile and his threats to expose her, Madeleine tried to buy arsenic from a local pharmacist and was refused. About five days later Emile became violently ill but he recovered on the following day. Two days later Madeleine successfully bought a small dose of arsenic to "kill rats." On cross-examination she explained that she had not bought the poison to kill rats, as she had told the pharmacist, but rather to improve her complexion. There was a popular belief, circulating around this time, that the ingestion of small doses of arsenic would improve one's complexion and Madeleine's account was, therefore, minimally plausible.[21] A day later Emile again became sick; he vomited green bile and experienced severe internal pains. Again he recovered. A week later, on 18 March, Madeleine bought more arsenic. Five days later, on 23 March, Emile was dead from arsenic poisoning.

In the Madeleine Smith murder trial, poison entered not as a metaphor but as a material fact. This fact, however, underscores the potency of the metaphor. It was only a month earlier that Lord Campbell had acknowledged the danger of the sale of poisons, but he also argued that there was "a sale of poison more deadly" than the sale of "arsenic"—obscene publications. The London *Times*, on the day before the Smith trial began, endorsed Campbell's comment: true, the sale of poisons was bad, but much worse still was the sale of obscene publications. Madeleine's case complicates such hyperbole. After all, she allegedly bought poison and killed her lover; on a scale of dangers posed to society this was stiff competition. Mary Hartman, moreover, argues that Madeleine's "taste for romantic literature and intrigue" (52) shaped her approach to the relationship with Emile, satisfying her desire for excitement and something, anything, to occupy her otherwise idle days. The Manchester *Guardian*, in the context of the Smith case, put it more dramatically: "It is the fashion of our times to set the young free from all restraints. They may read French novels, choose their own acquaintances, and decide a thousand questions for themselves which their grandmothers would not have dreamed of proposing to their daughters at all" (cited in Hartman 281). In this account, the figurative poison that leads to the real poison was not obscene publications but the mainstream, "soft," conduct-book style literature in which Madeleine had been schooled. Girls were told romantic stories without being given the opportunity to fulfill such fantasies in their own lives. Madeleine, through her own attempt to invest her life with drama was forced into a track which she could not have anticipated and from which she desperately recoiled.

But another form of "poison" also emerges: the voluminous transcription of Madeleine's story in daily newspapers and journals. The administration of the law generates the very public story of Madeleine's private life recorded in 151 letters publicized by the trial. It is in this context that Madeleine's sexual relationship with Emile was interrogated and her infidelity made visible. Did she love him? Were her letters reliable? How credible is the voice of a woman who comfortably discusses her own sexuality and sexual pleasure? The prevailing narrative of a young middle-class woman's sexual innocence was powerful enough to rewrite Madeleine's letters as the story of an innocent young woman beguiled by a clever and conniving scoundrel. It would appear that there was enough circumstantial evidence to tell a convincing story of love, deception, and finally murder. But the jury read the evidence differently. The verdict, the result of nine days of exacting testimony that riveted the British reading public: not proven. Madeleine Smith as a free woman was calmly driven home by her brother; the ideological tensions that her case awakened, however, sent ripples through middle-class society.

The most interesting point here is that even in the face of powerful evidence to the contrary the jury preferred to believe in Madeleine's innocence both in terms of the murder and, more surprisingly because it was so well documented, the adultery. The *Saturday Review*, for example, passed quickly over the murder to concentrate on what is called the real "moral anomaly" of the adultery: "Whether MADELEINE SMITH poisoned L'ANGELIER or not, her parallel correspondence with him and with MINNOCH in March is established; and this is the moral anomaly in presence of which the fact of murder is a mere sequence" ("Madeleine" 27). "The problem to solve," the writer continued, "and it is inscrutable, because, as far as we know, absolutely without example—is the co-existence of that burning intensity of mere sexual passion which indisputably led MADELEINE SMITH to discard every restraint, even of common decency, that frailty so generally throws over the acts of sin, with a cool-settled malignity of self-possession, a deliberate hypocrisy in counterfeiting rapturous affection, which, for the credit of human nature, is unparalleled" (26). The writer for the *Saturday Review* promptly, and ingeniously, located the guilt not in Madeleine but in her dead lover. It was Emile (and, no doubt, it helped that he was French) who provoked the "horrible change" in Madeleine; it would be difficult to imagine, the *Saturday Review* argued, "a meaner and more contemptible scoundrel" (26). It was Emile who destroyed the love in Madeleine's heart and inspired her hatred. It was Emile, moreover, who, by provoking such hatred, was wholly responsible for Madeleine's adultery with Minnoch. Indeed, it is much easier to conceive of a woman's hatred for her husband inciting a case of adultery than either her love or her sexual passion: "This is the real characteristic of women. In many cases of adultery, it is not half so much caused by guilty love on the woman's part, as by unquenchable hatred towards the husband" (27).

Following this reviewer, Madeleine turns to Minnoch (and she murders Emile as a mere sequential step) in an expression of her intense hatred; in doing so, she absolves herself of either sexual or moral guilt: "A mere desire to marry a richer suitor, and to stand well with society, would not explain the crime in such a character as we are considering. Hatred whose very intensity almost sanctifies it — and perhaps, when the moral sense is gone, lifts it into a sort of justice — would alone account for the deed, and account also for such easy demeanour at the trial. Hatred as we can conceive hers, if guilty, to have been, does not pale the cheek or check the elastic step" (27). True, she committed a crime and the *Saturday Review* does not even dispute her likely guilt, but her hatred for Emile shifts the crime from guilt into what this reviewer names "conscious innocence" (27). She may have committed adultery, she may have murdered Emile, but she did so unwillingly. The sexual and romantic passion that motivates an adulterous act is rewritten as hatred for one's husband so that in this interpretation the adultery does not look like adultery at all.

This writer ends on a note that will inform almost all representations of adultery in the English public sphere. The *uncertainty* of the case contributes to its power: "It may be that the most solemn lessons of life require an element of mystery and doubt" (26). Indeed, this writer speculates, in social terms "mystery and doubt" may operate in the interests of social justice much more powerfully and incisively than a simple solution — proof of Madeleine's guilt and the requisite hanging — by keeping the discourse alive, by encouraging in the cautious husband a constant doubt and a constant suspicion, by making the home the focus of the keenest and most vigilant of scrutinies. After briefly considering the consequences of the outcome on Madeleine herself the *Saturday Review* article concludes:

But as regards society, we think that the lesson is better and more impressive as it stands. There are thousands who have fallen into the sin of this miserable pair. In all sorts of society, and among the most refined of our social respectabilities, as well as in the experience of the village poor, that particular frailty is — can we venture to deny it? — far from uncommon. How stands the warning? It may have reduced MADELEINE SMITH — the burning, passionate Juliet of decent society, fresh from the school-room, and in the very heart of domestic sanctities — to the murderess of L'ANGELIER. It must have reduced her to that profligate abasement of character which, anyhow, is a world's wonder. It must have produced that degradation which, without a blush, could write the letters to L'ANGELIER and which would have entered MINNOCH's house and home as a bride. It may have brought L'ANGELIER to his doom from the hands of his paramour — it must have brought him to a dog's death, either at his own hands, or at those of somebody whom he had somehow foully wronged. And the simple fact that we have our desperate choice in this alternative of horrors, only shows what may be going on in the inmost core of all that is apparently pure and respectable. (27)

In the "very heart of domestic sanctities," "in the inmost core of all that is apparently pure and respectable," lurks the possibility of evil undetected, sexual passion uncontrolled, criminal plots unchecked. And yet how can one know? The verdict—not proven—spins out a story of "mystery and doubt" that haunts both the halls of the middle-class home and, as I will demonstrate in the chapters that follow, the pages of literature designated for the female reader who, like Madeleine Smith, is innocent and not innocent at once.

The details of the second case I want to discuss are, at first, prosaic enough. Mr. Robinson, a respected civil engineer, married Mrs. Robinson, a widower, in 1844. While friends and family testified that the marriage was apparently happy, by at least the early 1850s Mrs. Robinson was feeling constrained and restless. Around this time the Robinsons became close friends with another couple, Dr. and Mrs. Lane, twenty years their junior. Dr. Lane was a hydrotherapist devoted to his profession and he often helped Mrs. Robinson with her various, vaguely defined, physical complaints. On several occasions the Robinsons looked after the Lanes' four children and, in general, the two couples seemed to enjoy each other's company. Dr. Lane wrote Mrs. Robinson long letters when she was away, walked with her on the grounds of his clinic, and clearly indicated that the two were on amiable terms.

We would know nothing else of these couples if in 1857 Mr. Robinson had not read his wife's diaries. In these pages he was astonished to discover a tantalizing record of her affair with Dr. Lane. "How the evening passed I know not," she writes in a typical passage; "It was full of passionate excitement, long and clinging kisses, and nervous sensations, not unaccompanied with the dread of intrusion. Yet bliss predominated" (*Times*, 13 June 1858: 11). The diary clearly charts the development of the affair, from fond regard to attraction to the "bliss" of adultery. On another occasion, Mrs. Robinson and Dr. Lane go to Moorpart: "We drove off, Alfred [Mrs. Robinson's son] soon taking his place on the box. I never spent so blessed an hour as the one that followed, full of such bliss that I could willingly have died not to wake out of it again" (*Times*, 15 June 1858: 10). Another entry reads as follows: "all at once, just as I was joking my companion [Dr. Lane] on his want of memory, he leaned over me, and exclaimed, 'If you say that again, I will kiss you.' You may believe I made no opposition, for had I not dreamed of him of this full many a time before. What followed I hardly remember—passionate kisses, whispered words, confessions of the past. Oh, God! I never hoped to see this hour or to have any part of my love returned. Yet so it was.

He was nervous, and confused, and eager as myself. At last we raised ourselves and walked on happy, fearful, almost silent" (*Times*, 16 June 1858: 10). On the basis of these and other diary entries, Mr. Robinson immediately petitioned for a separation and then, a year later, a divorce. But Mr. Robinson did not get his divorce. To be granted a divorce it was incumbent upon Mr. Robinson's defense to prove adultery and again the verdict was ambivalent: not proven.

Indeed, despite her age — she was in her early fifties — Mrs. Robinson becomes a case study, like Madeleine Smith above, of the vulnerable "young" woman. Journalists, legal professionals, and doctors alike participate in a mass diagnosis that reads Mrs. Robinson's account of her adultery as an illness, specific to women, that prompts the sufferer to imagine what did not happen. Like novel readers who mistakenly believe that fiction is real, Mrs. Robinson mistakenly believes that her own diary — and it is frequently compared to French writing in the cultural commentaries — is real. The background for this diagnosis is somewhat vague; Mrs. Robinson had a history of "ovarian problems" that, like the link between a woman's womb and hysteria, provoked speculations on her mental stability. Dr. Lane, himself, suggests, without naming it as such, that Mrs. Robinson's ailment is menopause. But the most convincing evidence of Mrs. Robinson's mental condition is the diary itself. The *Saturday Review* does not mince words: "The diary stands self-convicted of insanity" ("Purity" 657). The defense for Lane made a similar argument: "this journal had evidently been written by a woman of so flighty, extravagant, excitable, romantic, and irritable a mind as almost to amount to insanity. He should contend that it had been written under the influence of a disease peculiar to women, which had the effect of producing the most extraordinary delusions upon the mind of the patients, and frequently caused them to accuse themselves of the most horrible crimes" (*Times*, 16 June 1858: 10–11). This special woman's disease was a convenient way to contain the threat posed to British society by a woman's transgressive sexual desire. Like Madeleine's letters, the three thick volumes of Mrs. Robinson's diaries bring a woman's sexuality forcefully into the public sphere; Mrs. Robinson not only unabashedly celebrates her sexual desire but also allows this desire to be directed to a man who is not her husband. Like Madeleine, she expresses neither guilt nor remorse. And like Madeleine, this testimony to her agency as a sexual subject is promptly rewritten in a tamer and, in this case, much more pernicious register by the medical and legal profession that studies her case as one of disease rather than desire.

The alternative to reading Mrs. Robinson's description of adultery as an illness was to read it as a clever strategy by which to escape her husband: "Will the boasted English home gain when it is experimentally ascertained that a wife can get rid of an inconvenient spouse if she is clever enough to keep a faithful diary of all the spots and sores of married life — if she carefully keeps her counsel, and acts consistently with a view to a future suit — if she contrives, by arts not unknown to the feminine mind, to get a husband to overstep the debateable land?" ("Month" 36). This picture of women as artful plotters against their marriage vows is obviously at odds with the more entrenched and, for men, appealing picture of women as angels ministering to husband and home. But this picture of middle-class women also raises the epistemological questions that the divorce court, in a more general sense, staged and restaged. The woman's diary here is not a reflection of an authentic, inner self but rather a *strategy* to be legally deployed. And if a woman's diary is not to be believed, if it does not give a clear and unmediated account of at least the writer's version of her truth, then what can be believed, what is true? This problem of truth extended beyond the evidence of diaries produced at divorce trials; the testimony recounted in the divorce court was itself perceived to be profoundly unreliable: "Much worse is it for public morals when, as must the case in such a suit, it is the interest of one party to exaggerate, embitter, and barb every little detail of temper and infirmity — to magnify the humiliating instances of spite, to envenom the cutting words, to exasperate the provoking tongue, and to cherish and improve instances of the unforgiving temper" ("Month" 36).

Like the Madeleine Smith trial, moreover, this case also raised the question of print censorship as the "gross scandal" shifted from the content of Mrs. Robinson's diaries to the fact of their publication. Again the *Saturday Review* articulates several of the key concerns with the democracy of print in an article entitled "The Purity of the Press." The writer begins by describing newspaper reports of legal cases as unfit or dangerous reading for "decent women" and "the young" and concludes by noting that it is precisely these readers, among others, whom the newspaper reaches in its "hundreds of thousands of readers of all ages and both sexes" who "are invited to gloat over the details of a breach of the seventh commandment, unaccompanied by the slightest hint as to the retribution which it involves" (657). Indeed, a sharp distinction is made between murder trials and divorce trials; in the former, the case works as a deterrent whereas in the latter the case works as a prurient stimulant upon its readers. In the former, transgression is severely punished (crime does not pay) whereas in the latter transgression is frequently left unresolved and hence unpunished. Mrs. Robinson's diaries are described as "perhaps about as filthy compositions as ever proceeded from any human pen" (657), and yet "the whole of these loathsome productions were reprinted at full length in the *Times* and several other daily papers. We cannot imagine what possible justification, or even what excuse, can be made for so gross an outrage on public decency. . . . A man has neither morally nor, as we think, legally any better right to corrupt the public morals by increasing than by originating the circulation of such publications" ("Purity" 657). Here it is clear that divorce, and the representation of adultery to which it was always related, raised questions of censorship and print regulation as much as it did questions of gender equity and social stability.

A shift is then made from the divorce court newspaper reports to light literature. If Emile's cup of cocoa can contain a deadly poison, if Madeleine Smith can conceive the idea of poisoning her lover, then poison may also be found in other places. It is not surprising that this metaphor is once again connected to reading novels, although in this case, with a surprising twist: "clear water may hold in solution the deadliest poison, though it is quite imperceptible either by the smell or by the taste; and we believe that this is emphatically the case with much of the light literature of the day. The principle upon which that literature is written is that it is to contain nothing which a modest man might not read aloud to a modest woman, and accordingly it carefully suppresses all those coarse allusions to the relations between the sexes which we find in Fielding or Defoe; but it indemnifies itself by a sort of luscious sentimentality which appears to us to be infinitely worse" ("Purity" 657). But what does light literature have to do with divorce court reports? If the divorce court columns vividly display a woman's sexuality and the intimate bedroom secrets by which any marriage is constructed and, at times, defeated, light literature, with its default reader and timid approach to what Henry James calls "the great relation between men and women," should exemplify everything that the divorce court report is not. But like Fitzjames Stephen, this writer is by no means confident that censorship — in the shape of the "modest woman" reader — produces safe literature; indeed, the dangers embedded in novels, like the invisible poison in clear water or cocoa, are found everywhere. Mrs. Robinson's journals, for example, testify to the dangers of reading too profusely as Mrs. Robinson reputedly reads light literature and then writes the light pornography of her journals. It is on this note of seeing the "deadliest poison" of sexuality everywhere — in light literature where it is not clearly represented, in Mrs. Robinson's journals where it is coyly represented, and in pornography where it is explicitly represented — that the reviewer closes.

While it would be as difficult to "prove" the slide that this reviewer describes as it was to prove the Smith and Robinson cases, what is clear is that the threat to public decency is also a threat to the boundaries that separate light literature from a middle-class woman's diary from pornography. In many ways, the explicit pornography of Holywell Street with its precisely stated geographical location and its known clientele is less alarming than the shaded pornography of light literature and divorce court reports which is difficult to classify, is not location specific, and appeals to a wide and eclectic readership. Similarly, as I have noted above, the story of adultery challenged the dominant story of domestic stability in a manner that was arguably much more powerful than the story of the prostitute to whom the angel in the house is so often contrasted. The adulteress, after all, is also "in the house" and she can look a lot like the angel as both Madeleine and Mrs. Robinson in their different ways attest. As a marginal character, at once inside and outside of the domestic ideal of Victorian culture, the adulteress cannot be dismissed as totally "other" but neither can she be accommodated within the prevailing gender norms.

The history of these cases is the history of the translation of women's sexuality into anything but female agency: in the case of Madeleine Smith, sexuality becomes the register of Emile's masculine power, and in the case of Mrs. Robinson, it becomes the signal of Mrs. Robinson's insanity. In these readings, women remain innocent while their unreliable character is paradoxically maintained. At the same time, in both cases, adultery is translated into a question of knowledge. The adultery is interrogated, in other words, to determine the truth of the women's crimes, murder and adultery respectively, and, by extension, to determine the truth of the woman or, as the *Saturday Review* puts it, her "moral and psychological character."

The powerful desire not to see adultery — to read arsenic as a symptom of male evil and private confession as a symptom of female insanity — was abetted by the most salient feature of this domestic crime, its resistance to proof. But if adultery becomes a question of epistemology in the divorce court columns as the trials attempt to verify adultery and adjudicate guilt, an epistemology of adultery is also the means by which English novelists evade censorship and disapprobation. The sexual passion that is so disturbing in the divorce court columns (and in the French novels and obscene publications discussed above) is supplanted and in its place is the passion, as real and as relentless, of knowledge. It is remarkable, in fact, that almost all treatments of adultery in the English tradition approach this subject matter primarily from the perspective of the deceived party. The focus on the deceived party, as opposed to the partners in adultery, heightens the instability of knowledge — what counts as evidence? what counts as proof of adultery? how does one know? — as it also informs new narrative developments in the novel. If one imagines *Madame Bovary*, for example, told from the perspective of Charles Bovary rather than Emma, the narrative interest is redirected along very different lines.

While several critics, following Foucault, have linked sexuality to knowledge, adulterous forms of sexuality nuance this distinction; adultery is, at once, explicitly about sexuality *and* about knowledge. By translating adultery as epistemology, English novelists cleverly evade a "censorious world" keen to dictate "better and more correct notions of the relations between men and women" ("Claptrap" 47) and develop narrative innovations that radically transform the genre of the English novel. The epistemological slant promoted by English novels of adultery places an emphasis on doubt, on what one cannot know, and in this way, it is consistent with the way the law itself most effectively operates. As the reviewer above notes, with respect to the Smith case, the verdict of "not proven" is perhaps the best performance of justice.

This chapter documents the complex response in English culture and law to selected representations of adultery and sexuality in the public sphere. It argues that the very discourses designed to subdue or censor representations of adultery contribute to the categories of perception through which adultery was most persistently perceived. By figuring the representation of adultery as a taboo subject, English cultural commentators contributed to the visibility of adultery in specific ways. First, the discourse on taboo linked the absence of adultery in the English social field to positive constructions of national identity (the English, unlike the French, are exempt from moral decay and political revolution) and passive constructions of female identity (represented most consistently by the "angel in the house"). Conversely, the representation of adultery itself was defined in terms of political revolution, moral decay, and national threat, on the one hand, and the eroticization of women's reading practices, on the other. It was relatively easy in this context to slide from a threat posed to the national body to a threat posed to the woman's body and back again. But while the history of censorship typically documents a print culture that is vulnerable to censoring mechanisms, I have been concerned to reorient this perspective to focus less on vulnerable books and authors and more on vulnerable readers. Indeed, the regulation of print culture in Victorian England was inseparable from the construction of a new and vulnerable category of female readers that contributed to the reinscription of social classifications and hierarchies perceived to be threatened by the new democracy of print. The institutionalization of an implicit print censorship, in particular, had a significant impact on the direction of the novel's development in terms of a complex self-censorship that explicitly pivoted on an imagined female reader (as I demonstrate in the following chapters). And if the outcome of the two cases with which I concluded was "not proven," the next chapter demonstrates that the representation of adultery in the public sphere can be more than proven; indeed, the register of this representation charts, in the interstices of the law, the newspaper, and a rapidly accelerated print culture, a new history of censorship and a new history of the novel.

2

Columns of Scandal

The Divorce Court Journalism Debates

> And gradually the secret imperious attraction of the Divorce Court grew clearer to the disgusted and frightened Lawrence than it had ever been before.... Here the moves of the great, universal, splendid, odious game had to be described without reservation.... All the hidden shames were exposed to view, a feast for avid eyes....
>
> The court was filled with a pleasant anticipation.... merely the spectacle of a young virgin compelled to relate, in the presence of public and Press, exactly how she had caught her father in adultery. It was an affair not by any means to be missed.
>
> Arnold Bennett, *Whom God Hath Joined*

No attempt to document the visibility of adultery in nineteenth- and early twentieth-century England would be complete without a consideration of the divorce bill passed as part of the Matrimonial Causes Act in 1857. And yet a detailed analysis of the connections between this divorce bill, the divorce court journalism to which it was related, and literary production is absent in criticism on the English novel. This absence is especially notable when one considers that the legal context of the divorce court provided one of the few Victorian forums in which participants were urged to speak about sex; the publication of these divorce cases in daily newspapers, moreover, made them readily available to diverse readers. The story of adultery, as Bennett notes, was being "listened to by all the world and read without abridgement in evening trains or at morning tables" (83).

In fact, the publication of divorce cases in the daily newspapers served as the dominant discursive framework through which adultery was made visible in the Victorian and transitional modernist periods. Intensely voyeuristic and obsessively detailed, this journalism writes adultery as a domestic detective story; the goal for judge, jury, and reader alike is to read the signs by which adultery betrays itself, to determine the truth of this uniquely domestic crime. How can one *know* that one's spouse has been unfaithful?

What evidence constitutes proof of such suspicions? What stories, what narratives count as evidence? These questions find a compelling parallel, moreover, in novelistic representations of adultery. Indeed, the English novel of adultery is preoccupied with the very epistemological questions that the divorce court poses as most urgent. And the English novel presents these questions in new narrative forms—the story focuses on the betrayed party, it is told from multiple points of view, it disrupts narrative causality, and it tests traditional understandings of closure—that also bear a striking resemblance to the format of the divorce court journalism.

The divorce court journalism provides an excellent framework through which to comprehend better, indeed *see*, the representation of adultery in the English novel. And the divorce court journalism debates provide an excellent account of the impassioned responses to this representation of adultery in the public sphere. Divorce law reform had been a controversial topic during the early 1850s, and in 1857 the prime minister, Palmerston, was anxious to dispel opposition and to see his party's bill ratified. But the bill remained controversial: the Attorney General acknowledged the "great anxiety and even alarm in the country at large" excited by the bill, and his claim that such alarm was "groundless" did little to reassure uneasy members of Parliament (*Hansard* 147: 718). The three central areas of political preoccupation—gender, class, nation—were rehearsed in a series of lengthy and often rancorous parliamentary discussions. These debates serve as a fascinating indication of middle-class attitudes toward divorce in general, and sexuality and adultery in particular, in mid-century England.[1] I am less concerned, however, with the intricacies of divorce reform than with the new journalism to which this reform gave rise. What the mid-century shapers of the Matrimonial Causes Act could not have anticipated was that the newspaper coverage of divorce cases would put adultery vividly in the public sphere in a manner that would make the French novels and obscene publications, discussed in Chapter 1, look mild by comparison.[2]

The new divorce bill shifted matrimonial jurisdiction from canon law to civil law and made it possible for a husband to petition for divorce on the basis of his wife's adultery and for a wife to petition for divorce on the basis of her husband's *aggravated* adultery (adultery plus unwarranted desertion for at least two years, cruelty, rape, sodomy, bigamy, and so on). While the bill maintained a sexual double standard which would not be rectified until 1923, it nevertheless made divorce possible for men *and* women, for the middle classes, and, to a very limited extent, the lower classes. Prior to the bill, divorce had been prohibitively expensive, and while the option of divorcing was theoretically open to women as well as men, only 3 percent of divorces granted were sought by women (Basch 23).³ Pivotal for the history of women, marriage, and adultery, the bill warrants Françoise Basch's claim that it was "the outstanding event of the century" (23) and the *Times*'s editorial comment that it was "one of the greatest social revolutions of our time" (cited in Horstman 97).

The divorce court column in the daily newspapers, usually located on the third or fourth page of the London *Times* and the first page of less "serious" newspapers like the *Pall Mall Gazette* or the *Evening News*, marked the crossing of adultery into the domain of legitimate representation.⁴ Like divorce law reform itself, such a crossing inflamed public opinion. In the context of the Obscene Publications Act, why were such representations permitted? What was the relationship between the euphemism (to which most of the newspapers, more or less, subscribed) and this enormous production of public discourse on divorce and adultery? And, most urgently, what social and political effects would these representations have on English politics and culture? As commentators counted the newspaper columns devoted to these cases (ninety columns in one case), the questions posed (twenty-three hundred questions were directed to one participant alone in an 1890 case), and even the words (one especially contentious case, discussed below, was composed of 180,000 words, just short of the New Testament's 181,258 words), it becomes clear that proud claims attesting to the absence of adultery in the English public sphere figured awkwardly in such a revised print culture.⁵ As William Dean Howells observed: "No one will pretend that there is not vicious love [adultery] beneath the surface of our society; if he did, the fetid explosions of the divorce court would refute him" (71). But, against the evidence, people did persistently pretend. At the same time, the divorce court publications sparked a debate, more populist and more furious than the debate that led to the ratification of the bill in the first place, on censorship and reading that crucially shifted the categories of perception through which adultery was understood in the Victorian and transitional modernist periods.⁶

The extraordinary visibility of adultery in the public sphere, at a time when much less intense and exhaustive representations of adultery in the novel and popular genres were strictly regulated, provoked a challenge to the boundaries by which social order was defined and maintained. In this chapter I will consider this boundary disturbance in the context of the divorce court and representations of the divorce court in the popular imagination. The year 1886 was a watershed in this respect. In addition to the usual bi-weekly divorce dramas, two sensational cases tested already weakened social classifications. These two cases offer an excellent, albeit exaggerated, example of the generic conventions of the divorce court journalism and of the stakes involved in the publications of divorce trials—or, what one Victorian divorce lawyer called "trials of adultery" ("Balance" 122).

In general, the divorce court journalism debates signal a degree of social distress, fraught with contradictions, that demands scrutiny; interestingly for this book, however, they also display a tension between competing categories in the consistently volatile censorship debates. Is the connection between reading and social action more important—that is, more legitimate and more worthy of social consideration—than the category of freedom of speech? In these debates the link between reading and social action (as the central category through which cultural danger is adjudged) is displaced by the category of freedom of speech. In many ways the renewed validity of this category—always resonant, following Mill and others, in English print culture—also opens a space for the articulation of a specifically aesthetic or literary print freedom that I will explore in more detail in the following chapters.

"A Bursting of Wooden Railings": The Divorce Court and the Popular Imagination

In 1861 the Yelverton divorce trial was published in illustrated book form that included a ballad insert and 105 closely printed, tissue-like pages.[7] Like most of these trials, the testimony is at once tantalizing and tedious as witnesses shift back and forth between events pertinent to the marriage, relaying what information they have with amazing patience and care. Like most of these trials, too, the Yelverton case excited the attention of a public that extended well beyond the boundaries of those involved in the trial itself:

This morning for more than an hour before the opening of the court, the space in front of the doors was blocked by a dense crowd, who waited impatiently for the moment which would decide their chance of witnessing the proceedings. . . . The Chief Justice came on the bench at half-past ten o'clock, and an order was then given to open the doors. The scene which then ensued was, for a time, of the most alarming character. The policemen whose duty it was to see that the court should not become overcrowded, were pushed aside by the in-rushing crowd. Several people were dashed down and trampled on. The bursting of wooden railings, and the smashing of glass, increased the apprehension of those who were safely seated inside, that loss of life would be the result of the maddened efforts of thousands of people to crush into a small court, not capable of holding one-twentieth of the number who were struggling to get in. (*Yelverton* 41)[8]

Even allowing for a sensational writing style in this avowedly "full and verbatim report" (9), the description records an intense desire — the "bursting of wooden railings," the "smashing of glass" — to participate in the expansion of discursive boundaries related to sex that the divorce court introduced.[9] "Thousands of people" waited for hours and pressed through the crowd to hear the sex lives of two people discussed in intimate detail. But the divorce court registers more than this material bursting of wooden railings; it also contributes to the bursting of ideological boundaries previously considered secure and the testing of categories of perception previously untried. And if the divorce court publications pushed the limits of visibility, it also provoked an open discussion related to how such visibility might be socially and politically useful.

The bursting of wooden railings, moreover, signaled that the implicit constraints on the accessibility to obscene publications were no longer entirely operative. Despite the Obscene Publications Act and the *Hicklin* standard, these representations were available to all reading members of the population coded as "vulnerable." Where works classified as obscene were often housed in museums with restricted access or written in languages like Latin or French that were only intelligible to the educated classes, the divorce court publications were, as Queen Victoria would note, delivered to every middle-class home that subscribed to a newspaper and written in an easy journalistic prose that was often accessible even to the poorly educated.

It has become popular in recent criticism to expose a sexual undercurrent in Victorian everyday life — in pornography, in prostitution, in the frequentation of brothels (of which *My Secret Life* is a prominent example) — but one does not have to turn to a secret sexual life to demonstrate that sexuality was a central issue in Victorian England. The visibility of the divorce court trials and the vehemence with which they were condemned makes this point undeniably clear. The *Pall Mall Gazette* argues that the divorce court documentation offers a convincing portrait of the period: "the objectionable matter is diluted by an immense quantity of perfectly innocuous and often most highly instructive detail of social life. The Macaulay of the future will find more valuable material for painting his picture of English society at the close of the Victorian era in the reports of the

Dilke and Colin Campbell divorce cases than in any of the publications of recent years, and that altogether irrespective of the question of immorality" (4 Feb. 1887: 1).[10] The notorious volumes of *My Secret Life* to which Foucault also turns to support his claim that the Victorian period witnessed a process of transforming "sex into discourse" finds a compelling parallel, then, in the very public spectacle of divorce trials where sex is equally transformed into discourse both in the courtroom and then, more dramatically, in the divorce court journalism.

While Foucault traces the shift from religious confession to psychoanalytic confession in *The History of Sexuality*, I want to suggest that the divorce court, with its insistent questions and elliptical, by turns hesitant and bold, answers, operated as a legal confession. I am thus not in accord with Foucault's claim that with the discursive explosion relating to sexuality beginning in the late eighteenth century and continuing throughout the nineteenth century marriage became less scrutinized than it had been in previous periods (36–38).[11] Foucault's comments on children's sexuality, for example, are applicable to the treatment of marriage and sexuality in English divorce trials: "Wherever there was the chance they [children's pleasures] might appear, devices of surveillance were installed; traps were laid for compelling admissions; inexhaustible and corrective discourses were imposed; parents and teachers were alerted, and left with the suspicion that all children were guilty, and with the fear of being themselves at fault if their suspicions were not sufficiently strong" (42). Accordingly, Foucault asks: "what does the appearance of all these peripheral sexualities signify? Is the fact that they could appear in broad daylight a sign that the code had become more lax? Or does the fact that they were given so much attention testify to a stricter regime and to its concern to bring them under closer supervision. In terms of repression, things are unclear. There was permissiveness, if one bears in mind that the severity of the codes relating to sexual offenses diminished considerably in the nineteenth century and that law itself often deferred to medicine. But an additional ruse of severity, if one thinks of all the agencies of control and all the mechanisms of surveillance that were put into operation by pedagogy and therapeutics" (40–41). The Matrimonial Causes Act in 1857 is an excellent example of a law that relaxed the regulation relating to divorce and, at the same time, subjected marital sexuality to an exacting surveillance in preparation for the law courts, in the law courts themselves, and in the divorce court journalism. Foucault's comment on such an installation of surveillance and suspicion is telling: "The child's 'vice' was not so much an enemy as a support; it may have been designated as the evil to be eliminated, but the extraordinary effort that went into the task that was bound to fail leads one to suspect that what was demanded of it was to persevere, to proliferate to the limits of the visible and the invisible, rather than to disappear for good" (42). Similarly, following the Matrimonial Causes Act, adultery became, first and foremost, a question of the law. Sexuality is neither beyond the law nor exempt from power relations. The documentation of divorce cases served as a "useful and public discourse" (18) through which the taboo against adultery was kept animated, both in its expression of a sexual double standard and its deployment of public scandal.[12] These proceedings provide a compelling historical intersection between legal and discursive approaches to adultery that coincides with the development of the novel of adultery in England. The divorce court publications, in their exposure of the perpetrators of adultery, made it clear to a population for whom privacy was a personal right, that their sexual crimes were always potentially being watched. As the law retreated, the visibility of the "criminal" and, in these cases, the specifically domestic crime of adultery, became a central mechanism through which the law discreetly operated.

In addition to the copious newspaper accounts of divorce cases that the new court spawned, there was a substantial production of material that registered adultery's visibility in the public sphere by responding directly to the divorce court publications in popular genres. Newspaper trials were sold in bound volumes with pen-and-ink illustrations and portraits of the key players, ballads were written, pamphlets and moral tracts were distributed (even those tracts, like "Divorce" discussed below, that condemned such representations were avidly read by a curious public), a new newspaper, *The Divorce Court Reporter*, was founded in 1857, public and private letters were sent, and short stories and parodies of the more popular cases proliferated (Figures 1, 2). This discursive production, not surprisingly, reflects and contributes to the massive ideological contradictions that the divorce court's institutionalized discourse on adultery generated in "a censorious world" ("Claptrap" 47).

A passage from Sir Arthur Conan Doyle's short story "A Case of Identity" has been made famous by numerous critics for illustrating the remarkable transparency of realist fiction. Sherlock Holmes tells Watson that "life is infinitely stranger than anything which the mind of man could invent. We would not dare to conceive the things which are really mere commonplaces of existence. If we could fly out of that window hand in hand, hover over this great city, gently remove the roofs, and peep in at the queer things

1. "An Old, Old Story With Its Usual End. — As Told So Often In The Divorce Court." *The Days' Doings*, 29 July 1871.

Reading of the Great Divorce Case.
By Albert Chevalier and Fred Cape.

"Have you read this?"
"I've heard about it."

"Then why did she take her aunt with her?"
"Why, don't you see."

"Fancy that now."

"Well I'm——."

"That's good, isn't it?"

"The papers ought not to be allowed to publish such things."

2. "Reading of the Great Divorce Case." *The Idler*, August 1892–January 1893.

which are going on, the plannings, the cross-purposes, the wonderful chain of events, working through generations, and leading to the most *outré* results, it would make all fiction with its conventionalities and foreseen conclusions most stale and unprofitable" (41). What is overlooked by critics, however, is that this comment takes place in the context of a discussion of the divorce court; it was the divorce court, perhaps more than any other nineteenth-century English institution, that generated metaphors of visibility and surveillance at odds with domestic privacy.

A tract on divorce, written by an "Old Bachelor" two years after the new Matrimonial Causes Act, illustrates several of the contradictions in the popular representations of divorce and adultery, contradictions informed by this tension between the ardent exposure of domestic crimes and a deep commitment to domestic privacy. The story that the Old Bachelor tells is of Amy, the innocent wife at home, her husband, a captain in the army, and Captain Howard, a friend of her husband. After "ruining" Amy, Captain Howard conveniently falls off his horse, becomes speechless and disfigured, and dies. Amy's conscience, however, dictates a confession to her husband after which she faints. One recourse for the husband would be the divorce court, but in this tract it is deplored in no uncertain terms. "*He* [Amy's husband] was not the man to drag her—to drag *himself*, his humiliation—through the filthy mire of a court of miscalled justice. He was not the man to feed the public appetite, to gratify prurient curiosity, by the retailing of his inward struggles—his inward wrongs" (64). Here what is most alarming about the new category of perception through which adultery was defined is its *public* visibility. To expose one's inward struggles is not to gain the redress of the law, the Old Bachelor argues, but to feed the public appetite.

In this elision between the law and the public, however, the Old Bachelor identifies, as he also participates in, the new technology of publicity, visibility and surveillance through which the divorce court most effectively works. The law, in other words, works *through* the public exposure of inward struggles. Indeed, the Old Bachelor's tract serves as a perfect example of the effectiveness of the Court: it identifies a large portion of the population as guilty and it encourages a studied practice of both domestic surveillance and self-scrutiny.

Does it [the logic of adultery] not yield a most practical influence upon our morals? Alas! the mass of impurity which is daily shovelled up in our Divorce Court bears witness to its effect. Old Father Thames has got a rival; the accumulated filth that floats on his venerable bosom is not so noxious as the poison that is daily distributed under the sanction our Christian legislature. And to what do we owe this scandal? To ourselves — to our accommodating morals — to the manner in which we educate our women — to the fearful license we grant them, when we allow them to receive, as intimate friends in their homes, men who, if the world's justice were the justice of God, would be expiating in solitary confinement their offenses against the peace and happiness of society. (4)

The plural "ourselves" and "we" is clearly not gender neutral. Rather it is men who have neither regulated women's education nor adequately constrained other men; it is men, accordingly, who are to blame for the scandal of divorce. In this move guilt is effectively dispersed throughout the population: "innocent" men are guilty for the reasons the Old Bachelor states; "guilty" men remain guilty, of course, when they commit adultery; "innocent" women are always potentially guilty because of their inability to withstand seduction; and "guilty" women also remain guilty. This tract further reinforces the dispersal of guilt in its celebration of doubt as a positive value: "Are our doubts always traitors? or the warning whisperings of some unseen protecting agency, merciful to save, to spare. May not the obstacles which we find upon our way be so many blessings to avert years of woe? Who can tell what is good for him?" (12). Like the *Saturday Review*'s endorsement of the efficacy of "mystery and doubt," the Old Bachelor promotes doubt as an "unseen protecting agency." The *Sunday Echo*, in a response to one of the divorce cases discussed below, suggests that the divorce court might, in fact, provide lessons for husbands: "Mr. Finlay made one remark, which ought to be SPECIALLY INTERESTING to married men and even to prospective husbands. Dealing with Lady Colin's repugnance to occupy the same sleeping apartment as her husband, and that the thought of it made her 'ferocious,' counsel said that all who had experience of the Divorce Court know that repugnance to a husband's bed is one of the first signs of the infidelity of a woman" (6). And, despite his aversion to the divorce court, the Old Bachelor concludes on a similar note:

Can men ward off the evils of infidelity? that infidelity which touches many closely, ruins some natures, drives others desperate, and lowers all? Yes — simply. We would all watch a burglar and drive him from our door. . . . Is not a wife man's first, most valuable property. . . . Well! Let him watch her kindly and tenderly. . . . The burglar *is* dangerous; he dreads him: but there is a greater thief than he, and that is the man who will sit and smile, and talk, drinking of the cup, breaking the bread, and eating the salt; speaking soft, courteous words, perchance of gratitude; and *that* man smiles, and smiles, and *yet* is a villain: to his friend's house he has brought a plague —

a leprosy that *even the waters of Shiloah cannot cleanse!* O men! . . . Still if you refuse to be the watchful guardians of your own honour, lose it! (77–79)

Charles Bovary never suspected his wife and he paid the painful price. But this will not be a mistake made by most husbands (and, increasingly, wives) in English fiction. Instead, the watchful spouse, more and more frequently, becomes the canny recorder of her or his partner's wrongdoing.

The exposure of Amy's story and others like it confronted the English public with the anomaly of the middle-class woman who, like the women in Charcot's illuminated theaters of hysteria, openly displayed her sexuality to a curious audience and who, unlike Charcot's patients, talked profusely. Numerous critics attempted to fold the contradictions that such women represented into a neat and convincing package. Others simply told the story again and again as if in the telling a repetitive mastery might be gained. Like Freud's grandson Ernst, who threw and retrieved a spool attached to a string each time his mother left the room in a motion that at once signaled his distress and his control, spools relating stories of a woman's adultery are repeatedly thrown into the public sphere in the years following the new divorce bill.

Augustus Egg's triptych *Past and Present*, exhibited at the Royal Academy in 1858, is an excellent example of just such a story of adultery (Figure 3). T. J. Edelstein is no doubt right to link these paintings with the passage of the Act and the fear, expressed by many, that the new divorce bill was the first step toward the disintegration of morals and the deterioration of the family. Egg's painting, Edelstein argues, "is not simply a narrative of a fallen woman but the realization of a great fear [provoked by the divorce bill]" (210). The three paintings, individually titled *Misfortune*, *Prayer*, and *Despair*, represent respectively a husband's discovery of his wife's affair; the children's dislocation from the happy family to, it is implied, the orphanage; and the wife's catastrophic fall from the parlor to, quite literally, the gutter. The following words accompany the painting: "August the 4th. Have just heard that B —— has been dead more than a fortnight, so his poor children have now lost both parents. I hear *She* was seen on Friday last near the Strand, evidently without a place to lay her head. What a fall hers has been!"

The three paintings capture, with brilliant economy, the central motifs by which adultery was culturally defined in Victorian England, and serve as a point of comparison for representations of adultery in other genres. First, it is the wife who is unfaithful. Nina Auerbach ironically comments in

3. Augustus Leopold Egg, *Past and Present*, 1858. The Trustees of the Tate Gallery.

relation to these paintings that a woman is "a creature whose nature it is to fall . . . and whose identity defines itself only in that fall" (155). One can hardly imagine the roles reversed: the husband lying prostrate on the floor and the wife staring gloomily off into the distance. The woman's fall is reinforced by heavy-handed religious symbolism: a cut apple lies on the floor beside her and a painting of the biblical Fall hangs above her portrait on the back wall. The husband's absence in the following two pictures draws on the often inchoate fear that a woman's adultery threatens the father's status as father. Are his children really his? Where does he fit in the domestic scene if he does not know the answer to this question?

The second motif displayed in the painting is the perspective of the betrayed party. The painting's focus on the discovery and consequences of adultery — always tragic, always instructive — is consistent with the permissible representation of adultery in the novel tradition. I will discuss this

point at greater length below, but it is this focus that has been overlooked when critics read the representation of adultery as resistant to dominant power structures. Third, adultery is associated with reading novels, particularly French novels. A novel by Balzac is clearly visible in the painting and Edelstein suggests that by "placing the volume in the centre of this Victorian drawing room Egg pointedly compares the amorality of Balzac with the theme of his own narrative, that adultery destroys the home and family" (208). Similarly, in the novel itself novel reading is associated with adultery and Emma Bovary is only the most infamous example of the erring wife who gravitates toward adultery via literature. Finally, the house of cards built by the two young daughters in Egg's painting underscores the fragility of the family itself. The painting thus captures both the fear of adultery with respect to the sanctity of the family and the sexual double standard through which adultery was legally, discursively, and pictorially understood. If, as

the Lord Chancellor argued, it was hardly possible for a husband to pardon his wife's adultery, then the painting offered a potent reminder to men and women alike of the consequences adultery posed for the unyielding husband, the penitent wife, and the innocent children.

Another story, "Divorce a Vinculo; or, The Terrors of Sir Cresswell Cresswell," serially published in 1859, also gives a popular account of divorce in which a woman's capacity for sexual deception is equated with her capacity for narrative deception. The story begins by marvelling over Sir Cresswell Cresswell's "incarnate omnipotence" as the judge of the divorce court. His omnipotence resembles Holmes conjecture on complete visibility cited above: "He knows—or can know any time he chooses—what we say, what we do, nay what we think about" (Gamma 185). His power thus extends beyond the husband who watches his wife to the whole of society. "Now the British feminine theory is," the author writes, "that women are angels. This, however, must be a loose way of talking; for, as far as I am aware, it is difficult to bring an angel into Court and institute a comparison" (205). Here the writer makes explicit a tension that will arise repeatedly in the divorce court debates: when the angel in the house becomes a witness in the court her social placement is complicated in a manner that is not easily resolved. Sometimes the woman could be made to conform to the opposite stereotype, as Mrs. Barber does in this story, but not all women could be made to fit this image as was evident both in the courtroom and in the divorce trial journalism.

In "Divorce a Vinculo," however, Mrs. Barber is a parody of the dissembling woman as her lawyer conspires with her to deceive the court: " — this must not be, Gentlemen of the Jury, we have a duty to perform, and must not be diverted from our purpose even by so sorrowful a spectacle as this — Do not fix your eyes on my unfortunate client.' (The Jury all looked at her.) 'Do not attend to her distressing manifestations of grief. She is, I know, doing her utmost to repress them' — (Mrs. Barber here perfectly howled) — 'for she has been well trained and tutored in grief. Turn your thoughts rather to the task of listening to a plain unvarnished tale of the wrongs she has endured, and if I can convince your reason and judgment — for that is all I wish to do — let your verdict to-day free her from the barbarity of her inhuman persecutor" (251). The story also underscores the confusion between the public and the private to which the divorce court gave rise. Mrs. Barber's effrontery, for example, is exacerbated by the manner in which she blurs the boundary between the public legal institution and the celebrated privacy of the home. "As she glanced round the Court — you felt that it was converted into a drawing-room, and Mrs. Barber was the lady of the house. In point of fact, this was no longer Sir C. C.'s celebrated Divorce Court. What we saw was, *Mrs. Barber At Home!*" (271). Where the home was transformed into a modified divorce court by the Old Bachelor, in this story the divorce court is transformed into the home. The breakdown of the boundaries between previously discrete categories, moreover, is again mobilized by a metaphor of contagion as one gentleman worries "that Mrs. Barber's example might be contagious" (341). In fact, it is references to the divorce court itself that are contagious as this "social drama," to borrow Victor Turner's term, is rehearsed again and again in popular versions of English print culture. The divorce court registers in the popular imagination as a place of radical ambivalence; this ambivalence is most marked in the representation of women and the fear that women's sexuality could not be adequately controlled and that women's sexual transgression would not be adequately punished. But the divorce court was also an institution which authorized a certain way of speaking about sexuality—in terms of surveillance and suspicion, evidence and guilt—that demonstrates the law's entanglement in representations of adultery in the Victorian period.

I want to return now to Conan Doyle's story. Holmes invites Watson to consider the strangeness of life, the unexpected twists and unimagined turns, that distinguish lived experience from fiction. Watson, however, refutes Holmes's claim and appeals to the newspaper as a "practical test." In the newspaper, he argues, one finds true stories that are every bit as conventional and predictable as fiction. "Here is the first heading upon which I come," he states. "'A husband's cruelty to his wife.' There is a half column of print, but I know without reading it that it is all perfectly familiar to me. There is, of course, the other woman, the drink, the push, the blow, the bruise, the sympathetic sister or landlady. The crudest of writers could invent nothing more crude" (41). No doubt Watson stumbles first on the divorce column (which includes separation cases) because of its prominent position in the newspaper. The fact that he turns to a divorce case to "unroof" the English home, moreover, is consistent with the continuity between divorce and domestic visibility that I have discussed above. Most important, however, by 1891 when this story was written, there was a well-established discourse on divorce; matrimonial problems are something that the reader can "know without reading," they are "perfectly familiar."

But Holmes, in turn, entreats Watson to confront his complacent assumptions, to be alert to the hidden narrative between the lines, to let himself, in short, be startled and surprised by life. The perfectly familiar, Holmes argues, is, in fact, unfamiliar. Watson imagines "fiction with its conventionalities"; Holmes imagines a life that is infinitely strange and the divorce case supports his argument. "This is the Dundas separation case," he tells Watson, "and, as it happens, I was engaged in clearing up some small points in connection with it. The husband was a teetotaler, there was no other woman, and the conduct complained of was that he had drifted into the habit of winding up every meal by taking out his false teeth and hurling them at his wife, which you will recall is not an action likely to occur to the imagination of the average story-teller" (41). This short anecdote captures the potent complexity of the divorce court: it was both "perfectly familiar" and full of strange surprises. It was perfectly familiar because it was so pervasively in the public spotlight and because its narrative, as Watson intuits, corresponds to narrative patterns adapted from fiction. But it was also perfectly unfamiliar because the field of visibility always makes possible new alignments and new meanings as the terms of the debate are again and again reconfigured. In current criticism not only has the "perfectly familiar" story of the divorce court been lost, but also the unfamiliar story remains untold. While the familiar story is the more easily excavated narrative, I also want to be attentive to the unfamiliar story that the divorce court tells, written between the lines with unknown accents and unpredictable voices, the story that we cannot know without reading.

"Coarse Brutal Adultery": The Dilke and Campbell Cases, 1886

While the documentation of divorce trials in the English newspapers was almost a daily event in the latter half of the nineteenth-century, two particularly sensational cases caught the public eye: the *Crawford* v. *Crawford and Dilke* case in the winter and early summer of 1886 and the *Campbell* v. *Campbell and Others* case in November and December 1886.[13] The trials were so well attended by the public that people were turned away at the courtroom door; and the newspapers, in their desire to increase sales, advertised in-depth coverage of the details for those who were not fortunate enough to attend the courtroom theatrics. Because these trials were well known, and because their documentation was representative, in an exaggerated form, of divorce trials in general—with the exception of the aristocratic stature of the parties involved—I will use them to exemplify the legal regulation of sexuality as it was dramatically translated into a "useful and public discourse."

First, a brief summary of the divorce procedure and an overview of terminology are in order. If a spouse desires a divorce and is willing to undertake the public scandal without which such a measure is impossible, the husband must petition for divorce on the grounds of his wife's adultery with an identified "co-respondent(s)," or the wife must petition for divorce on the grounds of her husband's aggravated adultery (as described earlier). The husband must prove adultery; the wife must prove adultery and an additional charge. The petitioner is the person who requests a divorce; the respondent is her or his spouse; and the co-respondent is the spouse's alleged lover. If the respondent and co-respondent accept the accusation of adultery or aggravated adultery, then the divorce is uncontested and the case is documented in a simple column offering an account of the marriage, "evidence" of adultery (often in the form of a letter to a lover), and the terms of settlement. If the accusation is not accepted, however, the divorce is contested and an investigation into the truth of the accusation is necessary.

In 1886 Sir Charles Dilke was named as a co-respondent in the *Crawford* v. *Crawford and Dilke* divorce case. The accusation shocked British society not only because of Mrs. Crawford's detailed descriptions of the affair but also because of Dilke's position as a prominent politician.[14] The case may be summarized, by Mrs. Crawford's account, as follows. Mrs. Crawford told her husband that she had been "ruined" by Dilke shortly after she and her husband were married. The affair, she claimed, continued for two and a half years until Dilke became "tired" of her. During the affair Dilke allegedly told Mrs. Crawford about several other relationships in which he had been involved and persuaded Mrs. Crawford to participate in a *ménage à trois* with one of Dilke's current lovers, Fanny. "He taught me every French vice," Mrs. Crawford stated (*Times*, 23 July 1886: 4). Dilke denied all the accusations; he had, however, been adulterously involved with a Mrs. Rogerson and a Mrs. Pattison, the latter of whom he married just before the trial.

The case includes all the ingredients of an intriguing detective novel, from the anonymous letter alerting Mr. Crawford to his wife's alleged infidelity, to the inexplicable disappearance of Fanny, and the accusations and counteraccusations presented in court. The letter which Mr. Crawford received reads as follows: "Fool, looking for the cuckoo when he has flown, having defiled your nest. You have been vilely deceived, but you dare not touch the real traitor" (*Times*, 23 July 1886: 4). Mr. Crawford suspects a Captain Forster; the melodrama escalates as Mrs. Crawford discloses the identity of the "real traitor" and the transfixing details of the affair. The *Illustrated Police News* took full sensational advantage of this case with front-page coverage picturing key narrative moments (see Figures 4, 5). While the captions are interesting—"Donald do not believe there is a scrap of truth in that" (as Crawford presumably reads the "real traitor" letter), "She said, 'Yes, it is true,'" "He stooped and kissed me," etc. — the intersection of domestic geography and personality that the pictures record is also worth remarking. Close-ups of the protagonists are included in the context of the exteriors of their homes which will be penetrated as the trial progresses. Thus there is one bedroom scene in the 31 July illustration but the majority of the images depict the facades of homes that are important to the narrative (Figure 4). By 7 August, the viewer has entered the home and this movement of passage is repeatedly signified, in four of the nine images, by a partially opened door (Figure 5). These popular representations, then, serve as

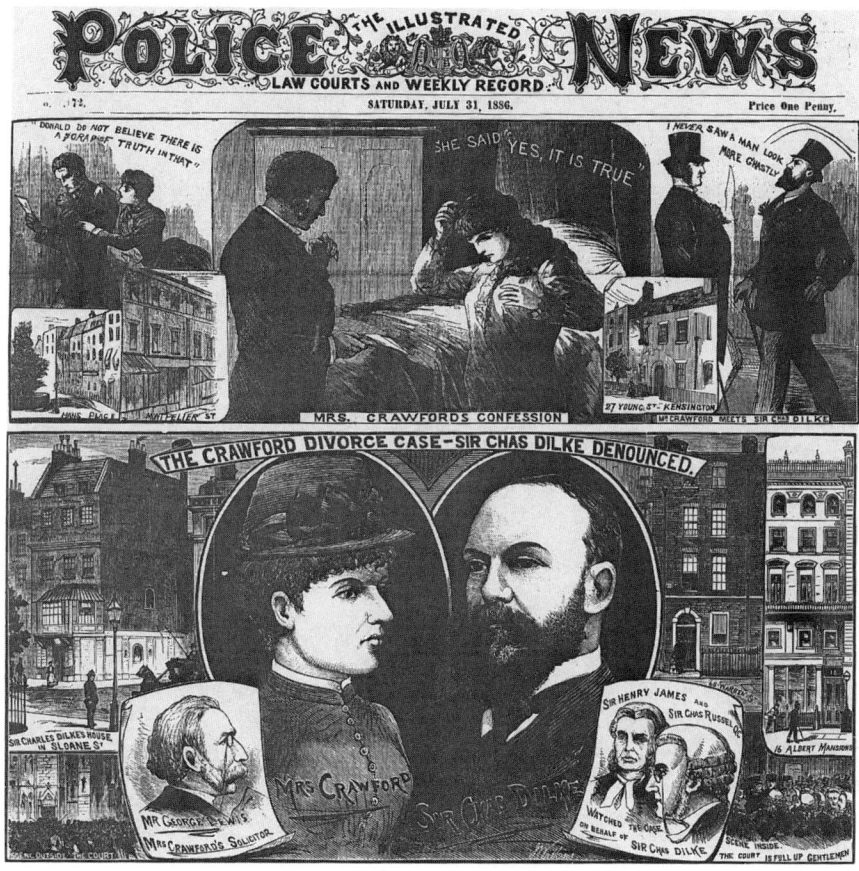

4. "The Crawford Divorce Case—Sir Chas Dilke Denounced." *Illustrated Police News*, 31 July 1886.

a counterpart to the penetration of the private sphere and the encouragement of surveillance that one finds in the written records of the trials.

The case attracted not only the attention of the general public but also of Henry James, who remarked with good humor: "His [Dilke's] long, double liaison with Mrs. Pattison and the other lady [Mrs. Rogerson], of a nature to make it a duty of honour to marry *both* (!!) when they should become free, and the death of each husband at the same time—with the public watching to see *which* he *would* marry—and he meanwhile 'going on' with poor little Mrs. Crawford, who is a kind of infant—the whole thing is a theme for the novelist—or at least for *a* novelist" (*Middle* 169). The "poor

5. "Scenes and Incidents in the Crawford Dilke Case." *Illustrated Police News*, 7 August 1886.

little" Mrs. Crawford's account, however, unlike Mrs. Robinson's and the fictional Mrs. Barber's, carried considerable credibility in the courtroom. In part, Mrs. Crawford's aggrieved demeanor, her apparent aversion to sex, her sense of being cruelly exploited, and her clear expression of regret contributed to the court's willingness to support her testimony. She made it easy, in other words, to shift the desire for sex and, with it, the balance of the blame, to the man.[15] When Mrs. Crawford described the love triangle in which she participated with Dilke and his maid Fanny, the judge responded: "This is a most revolting subject, gentlemen, and one which one would be glad to believe untrue; but the question for you in regard to that is do you think Mrs. Crawford invented the story? . . . Which is the more probable, that a man should do such things or that a woman should invent them?" (*Times*, 5 Aug. 1886: 3). The desire to believe in the woman's credibility clearly informed the judge's approach to this case. But it also led to contradictions. At another point he said of Mrs. Crawford, "I think it is vain to endeavour to put any intelligible construction on the conduct of an hysterical woman who seems to have acted with such grave indiscretion" (*Times*, 5 Aug. 1886: 3). Her testimony is taken as credible and intelligible; her conduct, on the other hand, is incredible and unintelligible. The elision between Mrs. Crawford's accusation and *proof* of her accusation was made in the newspapers, which were quick to condemn Dilke on the basis of what Mrs. Crawford had said, and by the judge who felt justified in calling attention to the "moral evidence" against Dilke, moral evidence which amounted to no more than the accusation itself. In the judge's words, Dilke was accused of committing "ruthless adultery unredeemed by love or affection," "coarse brutal adultery more befitting a beast than a man," of doing what "any man of proper feeling would shrink from doing with a prostitute in a French brothel" (*Times*, 5 Aug. 1886: 4). These comments contradict not only the distinction between hearsay and evidence, but also the assumption of impartial judgment; the judge's comments betray precisely where his feelings lie.

In retrospect, everything about the case points to a conspiracy against Dilke who was rapidly gaining political power in a much divided Parliament. But the interest in the affair extends well beyond fair play. The testimonies of Mr. Crawford's detectives and the tracked Mrs. Crawford exemplify a strategy of surveillance and a proliferation of discourse which leaves very little to the imagination. Mrs. Crawford's description of Dilke's home (the thickness of his carpets, the size of his windows, the floorplan of his bedroom, the position of his bed; Figure 6), as well as her account of Dilke's personal disclosures and his sexual activities, shamelessly violated the nineteenth-century principle of privacy to the wonder and delight of an expectant audience.[16] The wife is not prostrate on the floor as she was in Egg's painting, nor is she celebrating the "bliss" of adultery like Mrs. Robinson; rather, she is defending herself.[17]

The *Campbell* v. *Campbell and Others* trial followed rapidly on the heels of the Dilke case. It was this case to which I referred above in the parallel between the length of divorce court publications and the New Testament. The biblical comparison could not offer a better example of the almost religious fervor with which these cases were followed. The *Pall Mall Gazette*,

6. "Charles Dilke's Bedroom." *Sporting Times*, 24 July 1886.

for example, commented amusingly on the *Observer*'s coverage of the case: "this Sunday morning paper cost fourpence, and contains, as a rule, a very long list of the hours of the church and chapel services which in the various districts of the metropolis invite the thoughts of Londoners heavenward. Last Sunday, however, the usually long list dwindled into the smallest possible proportions, the great mass of the services being crowded out to make room for the details of the filthiest divorce case on record. Presumably the *Observer* thought that its readers would not want to go to church that morning, being occupied in reading the five columns in which it detailed Saturday's evidence" (17 Dec. 1886: 1). These comparisons exemplify, moreover, the rise of sexual discourse which captivated the public. Portraits by Lord and Lady Campbell were sold outside the gates to the divorce court, and many of the newspapers advertised a penny pamphlet on the case entitled "The Colin Campbell Divorce Case." It quickly became clear that this sort of reporting sold newspapers, and the result was a competition between the newspapers to provide the most detailed and explicit account of the trial proceedings. Heath Moon, for example, notes that in relation to the Campbell case the *Evening News* reported "the fullest account possible of the proceedings" and that as a result the newspaper's circulation doubled within a week (252). Again the *Illustrated Police News* vividly depicted the central players in the drama and offered a cartoon caption commentary to highlight the melodramatic moments (Figures 7–9).

Lord Colin petitioned for divorce against his wife on the basis of her alleged adultery with four co-respondents; Lady Colin petitioned, in response, for divorce against her husband on the basis of his alleged adultery with one co-respondent. (His cruelty had already been confirmed in a previous trial.) The newspapers record a battle between a bitterly estranged couple and a cast of almost stock characters: Lady Colin's parents, Mr. and Mrs. Blood; Boyd and Boyd, the two detectives hired by Lord Colin to track his wife; the Duke of Marlborough as one co-respondent, the chief of the fire department as another, and so on. And the questions posed during the trial read like a sordid game of Clue. Did the butler really see the chief of the fire department and Lady Colin in a compromising position when he stealthily squinted through the keyhole? What was Lady Colin doing in her room with the cabman? Did Lord Colin really wish to see the maid with "her hair down"? If he had, in fact, confessed to such a desire, did this mean that he had had sexual relations with her? Did Lady Colin have a miscarriage, an abortion, or was she simply ill? If she had had an abortion, did this mean she had had sexual relations with the doctor? Will the doctors confirm

7. "The Great Campbell Divorce Case." *Illustrated Police News*, 11 December 1886.

that Mary Watson is *virgo intacta*? And what was the nature of Lord Colin's strange illness?

Lord Colin's "complaint of a physical nature" by which he was recurrently troubled throughout his marriage was probably some form of venereal disease resulting from an "indiscretion in his youth" (*Times*, 6 Dec. 1886: 4). As a result, the marriage was not consummated for several months and Lady Colin felt considerable physical aversion toward her husband. Lord Colin, for his part, tried to have his wife arrested in Paris (her activities looked "suspicious," he said) and put in Saint Lazare, a prison well known for its apprehension of prostitutes. The testimony is exacting and tedious and what it avoids in bluntness it makes up for in the sheer accumulation of detail. In the following example Ann Duffy, a nurse for Lord Colin's "illness," is questioned about the period before and after Lady Colin's illness:

Lady Colin took little or no notice of her husband. She came to his room for perhaps five minutes at a time. Mr. Bird was there and he and Lady Colin were much

The Divorce Court Journalism Debates 87

8. "The Great Campbell Divorce Case." *Illustrated Police News*, 18 December 1886.

together. Had seen Mr. Bird in Lady Colin's bedroom more than once, but could fix no dates. In the morning room on one occasion she saw Lady Colin and Mr. Bird at her feet, sitting on a stool. They frequently walked out together. . . . Lady Colin paid no attention to her husband whatever. She seldom, if ever, read to him, and witness nursed him without any help from Lady Colin. Lady Colin used to go out at 11 in the morning, return to lunch, go out afterwards, and would also dine out. She remembered Colonel Butler calling on one occasion. She opened the door to him and conducted him upstairs into the drawing room where Lady Colin was. Subsequently a Lady called and before the door was opened Lady Colin called out "Not at home." Witness thereupon opened the door and told the visitor's footman that Lady Colin was not at home. When Lady Colin appeared on the landing to give the order her hair was disordered and her face was flushed. (*Times*, 4 Dec. 1886: 4)

This passage is followed by a description of a long exchange between the witness and Lord Colin when he returns home and asks about his wife's visitors. The nurse's details and Lord Colin's questions — indeed, the testimony as a whole — combine to provide a blueprint for reading the adulter-

9. "Scenes and Incidents in the Colin Campbell Divorce Case." *Illustrated Police News*, 25 December 1886.

ous body. The jury reached the verdict, after "columns of scandal" had been included in all the daily papers, that neither party was guilty of adultery.

James again was intrigued and dismayed by the case. He wrote to Charles Norton from Milan as follows: "The subject of the moment, as I came away, was the hideous Campbell divorce case, which will besmirch exceedingly the already very damaged prestige of the English upper class. The condition of that body seems to me to be in many ways very much the same rotten and *collapsible* one as that of the French aristocracy before the revolution — minus cleverness and conversation; or perhaps it's more like the heavy, congested and depraved Roman world upon which the barbarians came down" (*Letters*, I: 124).[18] James's use of the word "hideous" in relation to the Campbell case captures the dominant British response to this sociosexual exposé. But while the case could be unanimously condemned as hideous, the response to it — James, after all, was *interested* — was considerably more complicated.

One may dismiss these cases as politically motivated in the first instance and pathetic in the second, but to do so would be to fail to come to terms with the astonishing fact of their presence in the papers at all. Given the sanctity of the home and the value invested in privacy, these cases violate those values which were most esteemed. Adultery is written as a domestic detective story in the service of the law; the divorce court thus defines a version of adultery that is distinguished both from French novels and obscene publications and, is in this context at least minimally legitimate, if also highly sensational, in the English public sphere.

The explicit question which informs the divorce trials — and which appears in the novels to which I will turn — is the following: what constitutes satisfactory proof or evidence of adultery? The difficulty lies in the linguistic character of this proof where one person's language (an aristocrat's, for example) is more reliable than another's (a servant's). The *Daily Telegraph* summarizes the Campbell case as follows: "The weight of accusation was founded on the gossip of the kitchen and the servant's hall. If the reputation of men and women in society were to be taken away because of what can be overheard by eavesdroppers and repeated by the malice of discharged domestics, nobody could be safe for a single instant. Everything that could embitter the case was dragged into the light, and no pity was shown by either side; the result almost being to justify an expression used by one of the counsel engaged, that the Divorce Court would, under certain circumstances, be 'the pest-house of modern society'" (21 Dec. 1886: 4). Even when witnesses were deemed reliable there was nevertheless an assumption of perjury — defined as a "code of honor" — in divorce cases. A letter to the *Pall Mall Gazette* offers a succinct expression of this social code:

If a man has committed adultery with a woman who has a character to lose it is obvious that he has become pledged thereby, as by a solemn oath, to maintain for her sake an inviolable secrecy. If put into the witness-box it is merely a question with him as to which perjury he is to commit. He may violate his pledge to her and expose and ruin her, or he may perjure himself before the judge. . . . until it is recognized, and the fact appreciated, that a co-respondent's evidence is absolutely valueless, trials for divorce, where the petition is contested, are likely to remain a farce. . . . the circumstances of adultery are different from the circumstances of other crimes, inasmuch as the man is the chief criminal and the woman mostly is the victim. Yet upon her, if she is discovered, the whole of the consequences fall. (24 Dec. 1886: 6)

Arnold Bennett also provides an excellent fictional description of this process in *Whom God Hath Joined*. The "eager, spellbound public" listens to a divorce case in which one co-respondent, Dove, fails to perform his role as perjurer convincingly: "With a few clumsy admissions he [Dove] ruined the edifice of innocence which Mrs. Carr and the other co-respondent had so ingeniously erected. The junior Bar, all those acute, clean-shaven, sharp-featured faces, looked at each other with pained and chivalrous contempt of the cad, Dove. Dove had given a woman away. Dove had not lied with sufficient conviction. Dove was unworthy of the name of man, and, if such an outburst had been permissible, the junior Bar would have expressed its disgust by hissing the wretch's performance" (227). This aspect of the divorce court and legal proceedings in general did not escape the attention of novelists concerned with the representation of adultery.

While each divorce case is subject to its own idiosyncrasies, several common features emerge. A rhetoric of scandal, for example, informs both the public's interest and the final legal resolution. Such scandal thrives on suspicion, jealousy, and well-kept secrets, and creates the sense that one's private life is never quite as private as one imagines. Servants, in the events I described earlier, do not hesitate to look through keyholes, intercept letters, and eavesdrop; friends have retained personal letters which are read in court, recorded clandestine meetings which contradict the claims of the accused, and been privy to conversations of a compromising nature. In addition, the marriage is almost always reconstructed as an "affectionate marriage" until one spouse to her or his "great shock" or "surprise" or "astonishment" discovers that her or his partner has been unfaithful. The element of surprise emphasizes the innocence of the betrayed party and elicits the sympathy of the jury; at the same time, it creates the impression that such a shock could befall, and does befall, the most unsuspecting of spouses and the most happy of households.

Divorce trials, moreover, are circular, contradictory, and tediously repetitious accounts of "what happened." Discrepancies in the story have to be accounted for, straightened, and integrated into a coherent and linear narrative form. To discredit a witness's story, for example, the witness must be verified as mentally unbalanced or the testimony must be demonstrated as causally incoherent. Consider Lady Miles's testimony against Lord Colin in the *Campbell* v. *Campbell* case. Lady Miles fixed the date of Lord Colin's affair with Mary Watson by placing a line in her prayer book on 17 July. The court demanded ocular proof and the prayer book was sent from her country home and verified. Lord Colin's lawyer was quick to attack the evidence—a "revolting compound of devotion and depravity"—provided by such a witness. "What could the jury think of Lady Miles with her airs of virtue and her Prayer book?" "What could be the state of mind of this woman who could make a memorandum of such an occurrence in a Prayer book?" he asked (*Times*, 30 Nov. 1886: 18). Second, he illustrated that it could not have happened anyway: the prayer book belonged to Lady Miles's daughter and only came into the possession of Lady Miles after her daughter's death. Her daughter died after the date in question, therefore Lady Miles had not been using the book at the time.

When the crime is a domestic crime buttressed by a legally endorsed gender discrepancy and a powerful ideology relating to marriage and women's sexuality, relating "exactly what happened" is complicated by what arises like a leitmotif in the transcription of these cases: suspicion. Devices of surveillance and suspicion in the divorce trials are evident on a number of levels. First, the spouse is suspicious and watches her or his partner; second, the hired help (servants, maids, drivers) and family friends reveal on the witness stand the comprehensiveness of their own observations, narrating provocative details which the parties involved never imagined that they knew; third, a private detective is often employed in the function of legitimate surveillance, tracking the steps of the suspected spouse (the first private detective in a novel is introduced in Trollope's *He Knew He Was Right*); fourth, all of this information is offered for the evaluation of the jury and judge in their efforts to adjudicate between the competing claims to "what happened"; and finally, the public reads of these domestic and sexually intimate details, transcribed and paraphrased, in the daily newspapers. D. A. Miller, drawing attention to the pervasiveness of power in Balzac's work, suggests that such power gives the impression of a world "not so much totally intelligible as it is totally suspicious" (*Novel* 29–30). The divorce court cases similarly produce a sense of suspiciousness which is not limited only to the world of crime, but also pervades even the smallest domestic details and the domain of the family where they find their locus. In the divorce cases the assumptions according to which a case may be adjudicated quickly evaporate: witnesses are notoriously unreliable and commit perjury without hesitation (the code of honor, as noted above, *assumes* perjury in adultery cases); the judges are biased and use their bias to manipulate the jury; and suspicion itself is enough to create a case on which it is possible to bring someone to trial.

Arriving at truth claims in the divorce cases, moreover, is also a communal activity in a more literal sense. In summarizing the cases, the judge synthesizes the issues and then appeals to the jury's discretion: "the jury should remember . . . ," "here again the jury would ask themselves," "the jury would have to decide," "it would be for the jury to decide," and so on. In a long case there are usually six or seven appeals of this sort that work like a refrain in the text. The counsel for each of the involved parties also participates in such appeals to the jury. Ford's *The Good Soldier* — with the narrator's frequent "I leave it to you" distributed throughout the text — is the best example of this strategy carried into the novel. In the written newspaper report these comments implicitly invite not only the jury's deliberation but also the reader's, and they produce a sense of open-endedness in an otherwise closed context. In other words, while the jury comes to a decision which is a sentence — the end of the case — the reader is constantly aware of the open manner by which this sentence is determined. The English representation of adultery in the novel will take this inherent undecidability, which is an unavoidable function of the trial's form, and make it self-consciously explicit.

"Everybody Reads It": The Divorce Court Journalism Debate

The content of divorce trial journalism — in particular, the representation of marriage, women, and sexuality — belied a bourgeois ideology committed to the integrity of these categories. And the form — the serial format, the multiple points of view, the non-linear narration, the equivocal closure — emphasized the unreliability of Victorian evidential claims and anticipated modernist literary principles. But what Mary Poovey, in another context, calls the "occasion" of this journalism is also important. The columns and columns of detail in the newspapers, the public and profuse discourse on intimate subjects, generated a debate on censorship, the law, and the social effects of reading that exposed a deep anxiety about sexuality and the reconfiguration of the boundaries and categories through which the English defined themselves. The debate, in other words, responded to the *publicity* of the divorce court journalism and, once again, the representation of adultery was wedded to competing discourses on censorship.[19]

It is clear in the divorce court debates that a causal relation between the representation of divorce and the rise of divorce, between the representation of immorality and the rise of immorality, was feared. By focusing on the mimetic and contagious relationship between representations of sexuality and public immorality, however, debaters obscured the contribution that their own discourse made to the discursive publicity of adultery and the construction of legitimate forms of sexuality. It is not my purpose to pursue the question of whether or not divorce or immorality rose in response to these divorce court representations; instead, I want to interrogate the way in which the relationship between reading and social action was once again asserted and contested in the public sphere.

It is not surprising, given the widespread publication of intimate sexual details in these cases, that public opinion about the suitability of the divorce court column in the daily newspapers was both sharply divided and passionate. The most frequent metaphors employed by both sides in the debate—poison, disease, drugs, and garbage—recall the print censorship debates discussed in Chapter 1. Unlike the debates generated by French novels and obscene publications, however, these debates addressed newspaper reports rather than fiction, and a publication endorsed by the law rather than the contested category of literature. As such, they were at once more straightforward and more complicated. They were more straightforward because the category of aesthetics (its definition and its social value) was not a relevant concern, and more complicated because the divorce law that legitimated the divorce court columns was pitted against the law opposed to these ostensibly obscene publications.

I want to turn first to those critics who opposed the publication of divorce cases. A surprisingly wide and eclectic spectrum of the population voiced, sometimes articulate, sometimes hysterical, objections to these publications so precariously poised on the limits of the permissible in Victorian England. Indeed, Queen Victoria herself did not refrain from comment. In 1868 she made the following complaint: "the Queen wishes to ask the Lord Chancellor whether no steps can be taken to prevent the present publicity of the proceedings before the new Divorce Court. These cases, which must necessarily increase when the new law [the 1857 Matrimonial Causes Act] becomes more and more known, fill now almost daily a large portion of the newspapers, and are of so scandalous a character that it makes it almost impossible for a paper to be trusted in the hands of a young lady or boy. None of the worst French novels from which careful parents would try to protect their children can be as bad as what is daily brought and laid upon the breakfast-table of every educated family in England, and its effect must be most pernicious to the public morals of the country" (cited in Pearsall 220). The divorce court documentation was similarly objected to in an 1888 address to British Parliament delivered by Mr. S. Smith and subsequently published by the National Vigilance Association.[20] Smith deplored the "rapid spread of demoralizing literature" in England; and his "firm conviction was that all these evils [the corroded human character, the nation sapped of its vitality, the shocking state of the streets of

London (353)] had been greatly aggravated, greatly increased, in the last few years by the action of some of our newspapers with regard to the reports of low divorce cases which they had published with such fulness" (National 360).[21] Smith continued: "he believed that the reports of vile divorce cases, and others of an obscene character, published with loathsome plenitude, gave an immense impetus to the demand for indecent literature. They had created a taste for it; because there was this characteristic about this class of reading that the more a man read, the more he wanted to read.... If we, as a nation, decided upon new methods of stamping out this horrible disease, this pestilence, we must take some means of purifying the daily Press, and putting limitations on the power of publishing the details of Divorce Court proceedings" (National 360). Like the print censorship debates (and it is no surprise that Queen Victoria emphasizes her objection by stressing that divorce court publications are worse than French novels), the stakes here embrace the composition of the nation. Divorce publications are perceived to effect a kind of whittling away from within of national character and strength coupled with a fearsome permeability of national boundaries. For Queen Victoria, these publications were threatening because of the ease with which they crossed the thresholds of educated homes, like, one might say, an invisible poison within the folds of the daily newspaper. For Smith, these publications were the breeding ground for somatic reading desires that were closely linked with addiction and disease; reading divorce cases was said to produce not only a reading addiction to such materials (the insatiable desire to read more and more) but also an appetite for the behavior described therein and, as a consequence, a necessary decline in the state of national morals.

Like the contemporaneous debates related to French novels and obscene publications, the vulnerable reader was also a category of vital importance. The concern that young girls (and young boys) would be reading such reports motivated many of the objections to their publication. But this concern was not always limited to these categories of vulnerable readers; it was dispersed more evenly through the population. As the *Saturday Review* states: "Everybody reads it [the divorce court column], and everybody comes out of the reading with blushing cheeks and tingling ears" ("Divorce" 809). While this sense of a mass reading public intensified the publication debate and underscored the conservative demand for some form of censorship, it also made it more difficult to organize such censorship around a category of readers. Indeed the appeal to vulnerable readers in these debates was not compelling enough to withstand the competing categories of law and freedom. While the category of the young female reader was immensely persuasive in the context of the development and regulation of the English novel, it was much less persuasive in the context of divorce publications. If women, in some contexts, were contained and regulated by a category keenly alert to their "blushing cheeks and tingling ears," there were also places of cultural instability where these categories were tested and contested and where blushing cheeks and tingling ears were not limited to women's affective response but were extended to "everybody."

Nevertheless, the debaters relied on the category of the vulnerable reader (and in the process contributed to its construction) to make their claim for the pernicious relationship between reading and social action. One reviewer, for example, described divorce court publications as "unfit for the reading of any decent woman, and most dangerous stimulants to the prurience of the young" ("Purity" 657). Similarly, the letters and editorials in the daily London papers in response to the Dilke and Campbell trials charted a direct line from a young woman's reading to the erosion of sexual discretion, gender ideals, and the "private family" itself. These publications were perceived to erode the boundary between the public and the private in a manner that both threatened the conceptual integrity and the personal confidence of the individual subject. But what these critics also feared was an informed mass public and a true democracy of print; these publications would provide children, women, and the working classes with information better withheld. To have the power to censor publications would also be to have the power to control the dissemination of new and unpredictable forms of knowledge. The *Illustrated Police News*, for example, described the "demoralizing effects" of the case in terms of its publicity:

The influences arising from the promulgation of the amazingly objectionable evidence given in court have been as far-reaching as they are regrettable. To refer to one instance only. A bevy of High school girls were seen by one lady crowding about a railway book-stall and eagerly discussing the incidents of this trial. Beyond that we need not further go. When young girls of whom we naturally speak as "innocent" are bound to have had their minds polluted by the verbatim report of nearly all the newspapers published, the imagination will easily realize the avidity with which the most objectionable details given have been imbibed, further contaminating the partially bad, and adding evil ideas to minds already too familiar with depravity. ("Colin" 2)

The stress on the private family, moreover, underscores the often unstated, but powerful, fear that such public exposure of particular private families confused, in an irrevocable manner, the values of freedom, autonomy, and above all, privacy, by which the family itself was defined. Peter Gay notes that "the modern domestic setting [in the nineteenth century] offered unsurpassed protection from unwanted witnesses" (*Education* 445). The divorce court suggests the reverse. A 1909 discussion in the London *Times* on the value of publicity in divorce cases prompted the following comment: "Mr. Plowden, who opened the discussion, said his first instinct was to contrast the evils of publicity with the advantages of privacy. They had got to recognize that there was no such thing as privacy left in this country. There was no individual who was secure against having the most precious secrets of his life torn from him at the instance of an enterprising newspaper. There was no home, however high, however humble, that could successfully withstand the limelight of the halfpenny newspaper. (Laughter.) Publicity held the field: the Press had taken entire possession of the human race" ("Lord" 4 Feb. 1909: 4). Not everyone, however, laughed at the overwhelming publicity of modern life. Gilbert Murray in a 1909 letter to the London *Times* described such publicity as "an indiscriminate and degrading process of public torture," and he condemned "the assumption that it is desirable to make all parties to a divorce case, innocent and guilty, sensitive and callous alike, suffer as intensely as possible." He then offered an anecdote to illustrate his point: "In the Ukraine some time ago an adulteress, to improve her modesty, was flogged naked through the village. Our process is very similar, except that we apply it not only to the guilty, but to all who are accused" (17 Feb. 1909: 4). Murray argues that the divorce court publicity may operate as a form of punishment but because it is indiscriminate, because it punishes "all who are accused," because it uses suffering as a form of discipline, it should be eliminated. This argument supports Foucault's claim that the visibility of sexuality and the "new regime of discourse" with which it was associated produced unexpected and contagious spaces of sexual contact and possibility. Here the contagion is not only the product of reading about divorce cases — where one "catches" both a reading addiction *and* the immorality described in the reading material — but also of participating in them. For Murray is unwittingly right in his assertion that the innocent suffer as if they are guilty. Only the innocent *are* guilty. They just are not guilty of what Murray imagines. Their "guilt" is a product of speaking in a public space about sexuality; the discussion, the defense, and even the vindication, contribute to the participant's guilt. In this way guilt was instilled, diffusely and erratically but more or less successfully, in the divorce court participants and in the readers of the divorce court journalism.[22]

    Reading the divorce court publications, moreover, was perceived to carry exactly the opposite effect of reading a good English novel; instead of reading about marriage one read about adultery, and instead of finding one's values reinforced one found them collapsed. One letter to the editor of the *Times* is representative: "I hear everywhere loud complaints as to the grave mischief which is being caused by the details which some journals think fit to give the Campbell case, and of the effect which the reading of these reports has on servants, on the young, and on the working classes. Young lads may be seen devouring these details as they go home from work. Servants sit up through the night to read them." And, the writer concludes, "the freedom of the Press, invaluable as it is, does not extend to the publication of offensive details of evidence. It is little less than a scandal that the law officers of the Crown [should be] . . . unable to move on behalf of the public to prevent the unhappiness of a private family from being turned into the corruption of a whole nation" (10 Dec. 1886: 8). Another letter signed by over a hundred men (women were chivalrously exempted from exposure to this disagreeable issue) objected to the publications on similar grounds:

We, the undersigned, respectfully suggest to all those who have the control of the daily Press the desirability of some combined action by which they may minimize, if they cannot wholly suppress, the details of divorce cases and criminal trials, such as those which of late have occupied so many columns of the newspapers. . . . we have reason to fear that the full record of incidents in these cases ministers to a diseased appetite, and produces a most unwholesome effect on many minds. We desire further to call attention to the inevitable evils which must result from the familiarizing with vice the minds of tens of thousands of young persons of both sexes from whom, in these days, it is impossible to keep the daily newspapers. . . . we are sure that a combined effort to keep the pages of newspapers as free as possible from the stain of such impurities would be conducive to the public good. (*Times*, 3 Jan. 1887: 8)

The speed with which the signatures were collected (five days) reinforced the belief, on the part of the undersigned, that "there is a strong and general conviction of the necessity for combined action, to prevent, if possible, a repetition of the grave injury caused to public morals by the diffusion of demoralizing details" (8). The philosopher and historian W. E. H. Lecky was similarly troubled by such publications. The press, he argued in *Democracy and Liberty*, finds in these reports "a kind of literature which is, unhappily, as popular as it is degrading." "It is absurd," he observed, "to contend that this abuse is unavoidable, for the publicity of divorce proceedings is almost peculiar to England. It is, I believe, a nearly unmixed evil. . . . in addition to its effect in fomenting and gratifying an appetite for impure scandal, it seriously obstructs the course of justice" (169). Matthew Arnold also managed to incorporate a critique of the divorce court into his *Essay in Criticism*. In the essay he describes the divorce court as "hideous" and "a mire of unutterable infamy," and he laments its "crowded trials" and "newspaper reports" in which he finds the stamp of the Philistine (438). Scandal, as these positions suggest, was perceived to produce more scandal, to produce reading addictions, and, more disturbingly (although often the two were confused), sexual addictions inseparable from what was viewed as the rapid decline of civilized national values, "the public good," and "public morals."

Each of these arguments shares the belief that the divorce court documentation in the daily newspapers was demoralizing and likely to be dangerous to the public good. In short, it was feared that the very institution which regulated adultery also, indirectly but effectively, promoted adultery. These arguments opposed to divorce court journalism, however, did not go unchallenged. The countervoice in this debate granted the objections raised above — divorce cases, it was agreed, *were* disgusting — but argued that censorship of the cases was a greater evil than that which was censored. These debaters pitted public morals against a complicated argument that drew on the law, freedom of speech, and, most complexly, the value of visibility to maintain social order and the very boundaries perceived to be threatened.

For these debaters, freedom of speech did not denote an anarchic freeplay at odds with the law, but rather one of the most potent avenues through which the law could perform its ideological work. It was argued, for example, that publication facilitated the proper working of the law and that publication *extended* the law by working as a deterrent as well as a form of punishment (here "public torture" is turned to a positive end). To establish their authority these debaters made their position on the content of the divorce court unequivocally clear. *Pump Court* begins its defense of divorce court publications as follows: "The Colin Campbell divorce suit has proved to be all but an unmixed evil. . . . It has flooded the columns of newspapers with things that it is a shame to speak of even in secret" ("Balance" 121). *Lloyd's* newspaper similarly writes, "Of all the scandals of a scandalous year, the Campbell divorce case was the most protracted and the most odious" (26 Dec. 1886: 3). And the *Daily Telegraph* ironically asserts that "necessity of bringing a case so brimful of horrible suggestions and nauseating details before the world at all is one which cannot be too deeply deplored" (19 Dec. 1886: 5). Nevertheless, these newspapers quickly added, the "unmixed evil," the "odious" quality of the case, the "nauseating detail" should not prevent publication.

If the opposition to these publications argued that they posed a moral danger for readers vulnerable to somatic reading effects and, by extension, a political danger to the English nation, those in favor of the publications mobilized the audience in an entirely different direction. They argued that the audience, however it was composed, was a necessary component in the maintenance of the law. The reference to audience, as these debates make clear, was infinitely malleable. Who, after all, was reading the papers? Many commentators, of course, argued that young girls were reading the papers and that such reading had a pernicious effect. The *Pall Mall Gazette*, on the other hand, argued that, quite apart from who was reading the papers, the reader's participation in the divorce court trials was a commendable activity.

The *Times* eagerly swallows this latest nostrum [the reader's participation] of the advocates for hushing things up, and recommends it by some most extraordinary arguments. It actually adduces as an advantage the fact 'that people would no longer be able to compare one day's evidence with the next, or to weigh with scrupulous and lingering attention what a witness says in cross-examination with what he has said in his examination in chief.' From this it appears that it is a great desideratum in the eyes of our contemporary that people should not weigh with scrupulous attention the discrepancies of the evidence of witnesses, and should not compare one day's evidence with the next. To our thinking the fact that the new Rule would render this impossible is in itself sufficient to condemn it. (4 Feb. 1887: 1)

When the judge is called on to adjudicate between the different stories presented, the individual reader becomes both the judge and the jury at one remove, evaluating the stories of the parties involved *and* the verdict announced by the judge himself. Foucault's observation that the "judges of normality are everywhere" (*Discipline* 304) is particularly apt here: the judgment of normality is not a function of the trial's sentence—guilty or not guilty, abnormal or normal—but of its *process*, of the comparison between one day's text and another. *Pump Court* similarly argued that the "lords of ultimate appeal" are "the English public" ("Balance" 122); and the *Evening News*, in response to an obscene libel suit launched by the National Vigilance Association, issued a defense of their publication of divorce trials as follows: "publicity. . . . often brings forward witnesses (as happened once in the present case) who could not otherwise have known that their evidence was wanted. . . . It is well that the public should know the rights and wrongs of such cases, as public opinion will then be able to pronounce against the guilty party and in favour of the innocent. So, full and accurate reports in the newspapers of such cases have been declared to be privileged, as in the public interest, and so newspapers cannot be attacked for libelling an individual in its law reports, provided always such reports are accurate accounts of the proceedings in the Courts. What then do our accusers mean?" (20 Dec. 1886: 2). It was in the public interest, these commentators repeatedly claimed, that the record of divorce proceedings should be made visible; and this public interest, like the opposing arguments above, was often inflected by a sense of national distinction. A lawyer, for example, wrote the following to the *Times*: "It is of the essence of trial by jury that it should be public, and there is no precedent in the history of our country of any successful attempt to prevent publication of reports of such trials" (18 Dec. 1886: 8). But this argument could also be turned against itself. An opinion piece in the *Pall Mall Gazette* entitled "Pecksniff and Poison," for example, was unequivocal: the publication of divorce trials—denoted as "fetid filth" and "poisonous sewage"—"is the very prostitution of the press. The high and mighty seigneurs who preside over the daily newspapers have turned panders to the prurient curiosity of the multitude in order that out of the debauching of the public mind they may gain to themselves some filthy pence" (16 Dec 1886: 1).[23] Other commentators grudgingly acknowledged capitalism *qua* democracy: because there was a "great demand" and "eager purchasers" for the "fullest possible reports" their publication could not be arrested.

Justice, moreover, was not as straightforward as the *Pall Mall Gazette* and the *Evening News* hoped to demonstrate. J. Bayley described his participation in an earlier divorce case as follows: "we are bound, for the purposes of justice, to hear evidence in the judicial proceedings, the publication of which, at any distant period of time, or at any time afterwards, may have the effect of an utter subversion of the morals and religion of the people. The first time I had to consider this subject was in the case of some trials for adultery. It very often happens that, for the purposes of justice, our ears may be shocked with extremely offensive and indelicate evidence. But, though we are bound, in a court of justice, to hear it, other persons are not at liberty, afterwards, to circulate it at the risk of those effects, which, in the minds of the young and unwary, such evidence may be calculated to produce" (cited in "Balance" 122). Bayley is sensitive in a manner that most commentators are not to the tension between the "purposes of justice" and the "utter subversion of the morals and religion of the people." What does one do when justice is in conflict with social subversion? When the social subversion of "trials for adultery" leads to the social subversion of the entire country? How can the "revolting" material of the divorce court journalism be reconciled with a commitment to freedom of speech and the press? Most commentators in favor of such journalism necessarily negotiated these issues by highlighting the positive social effects of reading (in relation to the effective functioning of the law, for example) and downplaying the negative social effects of representations so vividly denounced by the opposition.

If publicity could further the functioning of the law, publicity was also understood to act as a deterrent to divorce in an argument that relied on the efficacy of scandal as a mechanism for social control (scandal, here, was not opposed to the law, but rather was an extension of the law in a different register). The pro-scandal argument ran as follows: the fear of publicity would encourage a couple to resolve their problems privately, within the form of their marriage, and better, would act as a powerful reminder not to generate marital problems in the first place. The confidence that publicity curbed divorce was expressed in *Hansard* as follows: secret or unreported divorce cases would remove "that check upon the violation of the marriage vows which the fear of publicity now supplied" (cited in Horstman 99). Scandal, so apparently subversive, was perceived to operate as a regulative mechanism through which the status quo would be at least minimally maintained.

Finally, one repeatedly reads the argument which Freud would articulate in "'Civilized' Sexual Morality" twenty years later: to suppress the divorce court publications would not destroy the desire for such publications but only redirect these desires in unhealthy and potentially devastating channels. The newspaper version of this argument is "Better a bad smell once in a while when the sewer is flushed than to allow it to generate undisturbed and unnoticed for ever its poisonous gas" (*Pall Mall Gazette*, 25 Jan. 1887: 7).[24] Freud's more sophisticated version may be cited as follows: "The damaging influence of culture essentially reduces itself to the harmful suppression of sexual life among civilized nations (or strata) by means of the 'civilized' sexual morality that prevails among them" ("Civilized" 185–86). Censorship, the pro-publication debaters argued, had its serious juridical cost; it prevented the circulation of information necessary for the adequate functioning of the law. And in a complicated negotiation of apology and desire, they asserted the central place of readers — not readers set apart in carefully defined categories tailored for censorship, but readers reading — in the regulation of sexuality. On the other side, the advocates of some form of censorship, with all the passion and rhetoric of the moral high road, asserted the need to regulate readers, to ensure that publications related to sexuality would not be read by members of the population susceptible to "blushing cheeks and tingling ears."

These debates document the struggle to define the terms through which the newspaper, reading, and adultery were perceived. If those opposed to the divorce court publications used mass readers to legitimate their appeal for censorship, those opposed to censorship used mass readers to support their appeals for freedom of speech. It was this latter argument that was, in terms of practice at any rate, most compelling. The divorce court publications were not censored and in this move, freedom of speech apparently displaced the category of the vulnerable reader to dictate the parameters of print regulation. Or did it? It could be argued that the category of the vulnerable reader did not command decisive attention because it was designed less to regulate print culture and more to regulate readers themselves. When it came to the serious claim on the censor's attention that the divorce publications posed, it was enough to consolidate the category of vulnerable readers, as the debaters do above. Social interest, as the publications and the debates make precisely clear, was already caught up in the dramatic, perplexing, and unquenchable "institutional incitement to speak about" sex (*History* 33) in the very spaces of power that the divorce court and its related discourses exemplified.

The divorce court, however, both used scandal *and* contributed to a necessary reconfiguration of the social space through which this use of scandal was understood and exercised. It makes a difference, after all, to introduce an intense, new discourse into the public sphere. Divorce court journalism unsettled received conceptions of normative sexuality (the *ménage à trois* referred to above, for example, bewildered readers and focalized the outrage aimed at this journalism); it challenged gender classifications by presenting articulate and sexual women in a public space defined by its scrutiny of sexuality (the double space of the courtroom and the newspaper); it disturbed class divisions by regularly relying on lower-class figures in court to present testimony that would incriminate the people for whom they worked; and finally, it redefined the institution of marriage. The divorce court made vividly clear one of the central contradictions of bourgeois ideology: the gap between the promised happy marriage and the very difficult struggle that marriage so often was. At the same time, it provided a new and entirely unexpected platform for self-expression, especially potent for women whose access to the public sphere was so restricted, that linked the establishment of the self to legal and sensational testimony. If the law and sensation often worked in tandem as the divorce court column demonstrates they also open a new space for representational possibilities from the inclusion of unfamiliar voices in the public sphere to the introduction of new narrative techniques in the English novel.

But to adopt topics like divorce and adultery for the novel — to capitalize on their popularity — is, Howells argues, too easy. The subject matter itself guarantees the interest of the reader, and the writer's real skills are not tested. Howells, moreover, captures the common current in the criticism of the divorce court reports when he associates the reports with a sophisticated trap for which most readers are unprepared: "The material itself, the mere mention of it, has an instant fascination; it arrests, it detains, till the last word is said, and while there is anything to be hinted. This is what makes a love intrigue of some sort all but essential to the popularity of any fiction.... But any author who will deal with a guilty love intrigue holds all the readers in his hand, the highest with the lowest, as long as he hints the slightest hope of the smallest potential naughtiness. He need not at all be a great author; he may be a very shabby wretch, if he has but the courage or the trick of that sort of thing. The critics will call him 'virile' and 'passionate'; decent people will be ashamed to have been limned by him; but the low average will only ask another chance of flocking into his net" (*Criticism* 71–72). Again an inability to make distinctions is clearly at issue here: the high is indistinguishable from the low, the great author from the shabby wretch. Howells' words situate scandal as a mechanism flexible enough to entwine both the parties involved and the curious onlookers in a mutually reinforcing dynamic.

Where George Moore looks to France and realism to revitalize what he sees as an impasse in English representation, English writers attempt to adjust the representation of adultery to the demands of their distinctively English audience. Moore attributes the "heaviness of thought" in English letters to the absence of "new subject matter." If only, he muses, "the Realists [by whom he means Flaubert, Goncourt, and Zola] should catch favour in England, the English tongue may be saved dissolution, for with the new subjects they would introduce new forms of language would arise" (*Confessions* 79).[25] It could be argued, however, that one needed to look no further abroad than the London newspapers for both the "new subject" and the "new forms of language" which Moore desired.

"A Theme for the Novelist": The Newspaper and the Novel

Queen Victoria's comparison between the divorce court documentation and the French novel makes an implicit connection between news and the novel, a connection which has been with the English novel since its origins.²⁶ But in the Victorian and transitional modernist periods there was also an understood distinction between content that was suitable (or at least permissible) in a newspaper and that which was suitable in the novel: French novel content—that is, adultery—was not suitable in the English novel, and the "scandalous" divorce proceedings were similarly inappropriate. George Moore, later in the century, described the situation with predictable sarcasm: "Turn your platitudes prettily but write no word that could offend the chaste mind of the young girl who has spent her morning reading the Colin Campbell divorce case; so says the age we live in" (*Confessions* 78).

What was the relationship between newspapers and novels, and more specifically between the divorce court proceedings documented in the newspapers and the representation of adultery in the novel? If the divorce court journalism introduced a new subject matter into mainstream English print culture, it introduced it in the context of a very definite *form*. Both the form of the divorce court journalism and the way in which this form was developed in the English novel are central to the cultural work—the relationship between reading and social action—that these representations performed. The journalistic documentation of legal trials, in general, has been crucial to the development of numerous English novelists as the novelists themselves are quick to point out. It is well known, for example, that Wilkie Collins and Charles Dickens read legal trials with real interest and a keen eye for literary insights, that Charles Reade and other sensation novelists often based their novels, at least in part, on plots borrowed from the crime columns in the newspaper, that Conan Doyle, Thomas Hardy, and even George Eliot perused the same columns, and that Joseph Conrad and Ford Madox Ford mined the newspaper transcriptions of trials for literary ideas. And yet a link between the form of these journalistic representations and formal innovations in the novel is rarely remarked. The fact that several of the formal innovations associated with literary modernism are also encountered in the journalistic transcription of legal trials, however, should give the critic pause. These innovations, moreover, are especially applicable to the divorce court journalism in which the crime recounted, unlike murder or theft, is also a crime that can only be represented by defying prevailing social views on print permissibility. Further, for the critic interested in the social function of representation, form is integral to interpretation; there are significant ideological differences, for example, between omniscient and unreliable narrators, causal and fragmented narrations, and closed and open texts.

By considering the form of the divorce court journalism, new relations between the newspaper and the novel emerge. Like the serial novel, the longer cases were carried in several installments and this staggered account produced not only a desire for more narrative, but also an elision between the world of the press and one's everyday life.[27] D. A. Miller describes this process in relation to the serial novel as follows: "Carefully cultivating our desire for a next installment or a future volume, the novel continually *promises* the totality it cannot, at any single moment deliver. . . . It is less likely that the novel's inherent discontinuities remove the reader from its control of his soul than that, distributed within a series of worldly interests, they allow this control to be broadened: beyond the temporal limits of the hours of perusal, and outside the spatial boundaries of the library or study" (*Narrative* 279). Mark Seltzer identifies this movement specifically with the relationship between the novel and news: "What is effected is not merely an ambivalent exchange between the private world of reading and the public world of news but also a publication of the private and domestic, and a privatization of the social." He further comments that "the later nineteenth-century novel is in part a history of the redefinition of the terrain of the 'novelistic' in relation to the rival, or alternatively, corroborative, discourses of journalism, sociology, and other reports on the world" (190). The divorce court documentation is a unique combination of the private subject matter of the novel (the family, marriage, sexual behavior, everyday activities) in the public genre of the newspaper. These documentations, moreover, with their summaries of the previous day's events at the beginning of each report and their abrupt breaks marked by the statement, "the court is adjourned for today," — the *Evening News*, always anxious to be dramatic, often ended their reports with the parenthetical comment "(left speaking)" — cultivate a desire similar to the novel's, for the next installment and for a resolution to the story/trial.

Four further interrelated characteristics of the divorce court journalism are relevant here: the disruption of narrative causality and linearity, the unreliability of the narrative itself, the multiple points of view, and the question of narrative closure. Not only do these characteristics stand in opposition to the dominant aspects of the eighteenth- and nineteenth-century marriage-plot tradition, but they also match several innovations now associated with modernism, or what Peter Brooks calls, "the detective story gone modernist: a tale of inconclusive solutions to crimes of problematic status" (238).[28] Adultery, as a crime of problematic status in the novels to which I will turn, is further complicated by a subtle shift in narrative evaluation in which closure — uncovering the secret, finding the solution to the crime — is not as important as a sense of doubt by which the narrator, the narrator's language, and the reliability of knowledge claims are informed. The possibility of confidently translating one's life into a transparent narrative form is replaced by a suspicion of the very way in which value-free evidence and conclusive endings were formerly trusted.

Causality is, of course, central to the novel genre. E. M. Forster defines plot as "a narrative of events, the emphasis falling on causality" (*Aspects* 93). Ian Watt also distinguishes the realist novel from its epic predecessor in terms of time and causality: "a causal connection operating through time replaces the reliance of earlier narratives on disguises and coincidences, and this tends to give the novel a much more cohesive structure" (*Rise* 24). And when John Bender asks, "Who could create and maintain the master narratives that would shape the social order?" (140) he is making a connection between narrative authority and effective sequence. The "aesthetic of isolation" — which Bender links with the penitentiary (as "psychological, sequential, introspective" [268]) and the realist novel — "takes shape when the spectator, the theorist, the artist, imagines and narrates structures of consciousness in reciprocation with social power" (203). The criminal, for example, is divested of her or his "narrative resources" and becomes, instead, a character to be formulated (202). The criminal as character follows the sequential, linear narrative of cause and effect and is reformulated. The divorce trials exemplify how causality is created: confused and scrambled accounts are forcibly reorganized according to causal narrative principles. In the novel, characters both subscribe to an implicit causality in their everyday lives, and everyday life is itself related causally as Watt and Forster suggest above. The traditional novel, unlike the legal trial, does not represent both the confused narrative and the imposition of narrative order. The modern novel, on the other hand, is often distinguished precisely by this feature of self-reflexivity.

Unreliable narration is a central feature of the divorce court journalism discussed above.[29] In addition to publicly acknowledged forms of social conduct like the code of honor, divorce cases were marked by the positions of *interest* from which the participants spoke. For the most part, the witnesses were deeply invested in the stories they narrated. When one turns to the testimony of the betrayed party, this question of narrative reliability becomes especially slippery. For the betrayed party is required to provide evidence for what is often experienced as an intensely painful, emotionally galvanizing act. How is it possible to give objective testimony on such an intimate subject? How is it possible to offer a reliable account of an event in which one is so inextricably involved?

This unreliable narration in the divorce court journalism finds an uncanny parallel in novels that represent adultery. In terms of the novel as a genre, unreliable narration challenges the claims to narrative authority on which the genre traditionally rests. The *assumption* of narrative fidelity which has been instilled in the novel-reading public since the genre's origins, moreover, means that manipulation of readerly trust is often missed (as the early critical reception of *The Turn of the Screw*, for example, indicates). Wayne Booth offers a comprehensive treatment of reliable and unreliable narrators in his *The Rhetoric of Fiction*, but his analysis has two shortcomings: he fails to attend to the reliability of language or representation itself (and reliability, as a consequence, is situated within the notoriously sticky problem of intentionality); and he is not interested in the specifically historical development of the unreliable narrator. But as the novels considered in this book testify, the development of unreliable narration as a literary strategy registers at the level of language itself and it is often worked out precisely in the context of representations of adultery.

Both the lack of linearity and the narrative unreliability are related to what is perhaps the most striking feature of these trials: the variety of perspectives from which the story is told. The case is illuminated from every possible angle, in every possible voice, and no single voice is privileged. Again, the manipulation of multiple points of view—while strongly evident in sensation novels of the 1860s—is one of the most compelling features of modernist novels and modernism itself. Anthony Giddens, for example, links what he calls "multiple sources of authority" and "multiple choice" to the institutionalization of "radical doubt" by which high modernity is marked (*Modernity* 3). And Fredric Jameson, in the context of Conrad, refers to such multiple perspectives "as the boiling emergence and disappearance of so many transitory centres, now no longer points of view so much as sources of language: each new detail, each new perspective on the anecdote, brings into being, as the very center of its whirlpool, another new speaker, himself for the moment the transitory center of a narrative interest which will quickly sweep him away again" (*Political* 224). A discordant chorus of often unfamiliar voices displaces the traditional center of authority in the construction of narrative integrity. If the cohesion of the narrative falters as a result, the force of this fractured text nevertheless contributes to the articulation of a new relationship between reading and regulation that severs reading from the social action with which it has previously been associated.

An absence of closure does not seem to be immediately relevant to divorce court journalism. The divorce trials, after all, usually produce a decisive judgment: someone is either guilty or not guilty of adultery. The divorce court journalism, however, challenges closure in three ways that are relevant to the English novel. First, the public notoriously distrusted the verdict of these trials. Arnold Bennett's novel *Whom God Hath Joined*, for example, illustrates exactly how fallible legal endings to divorce trials can be when one character refuses to testify and an act of adultery accordingly goes unproven. Second, distrust of legal decisions provoked public discussion that kept the divorce case alive long after it was legally resolved. And third, the closure that the divorce court affirmed did not in any way conform to the closure that traditional fictional narratives asserted. Instead it unsettled narrative closure by exposing the institution of marriage to critical scrutiny.

In terms of the novel, a great deal of attention has been paid to narrative closure.[30] Closure is read as an ideologically invested appeal to the reader's desire for narrative resolution; closure produces the impression that "just desserts" and "happy endings" are what one should expect in daily life. Such closure has the dual effect of warning the reader against wrongdoing (since the criminal is always suitably punished) and instilling in the reader the hope of better things to come (since after many trials and tribulations the protagonists receive their rewards, usually in the "good marriage"). This convention, however, was challenged in the late nineteenth century in the interest of verisimilitude. James, for example, deplored the convention of the "happy ending": "The 'ending' of a novel is, for many persons, like that of a good dinner, a course of dessert and ices, and the artist in fiction is regarded as a sort of meddlesome doctor who forbids agreeable aftertastes" ("Art" 48). Boone identifies the "modernist breakthrough" as, among other things, characterized by "thematic and formal irresolution" resulting in the reader's inability "to recuperate, hence naturalize, the text's manifold possible meanings or contradictions into a centrally unifying statement and [the reader] must therefore actively struggle to reach an even tentative judgment" (147, 146). The lack of narrative closure maintains the reading subject in a state of suspense particularly well-adapted to the "mystery and doubt" that the English novel, when it represents adultery, deploys.

I referred to the betrayed party in the context of unreliable narration above, but because the betrayed party is such a consistent focus in the English representation of adultery it is worth pursuing the implications of this focus in more detail. To be sure, the perspective on the betrayed party dictates an interested stance in the context of which it is difficult to determine the truth. But even more important than this position of narrative interest is the focus the betrayed party necessarily places on the truth. An adulterous spouse of course knows "what happened," and her or his goal will be either to hide this evidence or to report it with as little narrative embellishment as possible. To the extent that the adulterous spouse, moreover, does tell her or his story, it will be a story of adultery. Consider, for example, Emma Bovary's story of her adulterous liaisons (told, admittedly, in an omniscient narration) or Helena's story of her passion for Philip. The betrayed spouse, on the other hand, does not know what happened; he or she may suspect adultery or even stumble upon an incriminating scene but access to the whole story will, nevertheless, necessarily be limited. The story that this spouse tells, then, records the *discovery* of adultery. It is this story on which the divorce court journalism, by definition, focuses. The adulterous spouse's testimony is folded into a larger narrative structure driven by the attempt to accumulate proof of adultery. And this point has an important bearing on the English novel. When English novelists represent adultery, they repeatedly do so from the perspective of the betrayed party, a perspective that dictates the novel's obsessively legal and epistemological orientation. Each of the formal devices discussed here contributes to the novel of adultery's negotiation of print censorship. The novel adopts narrative strategies that are already legitimate in one arena of English print culture. These strategies both minimize the transgressive impact of representations of adultery by inflecting adultery as an epistemological, rather than a passionate, concern and by inculcating in the reader an attitude of wary regard and suspicion rather than rebellion and adulterous desire.

The divorce bill, Alfred Austin states in 1875, "familiarized the public mind . . . with conjugal infidelity" ("Novels" 179). But if adultery was "perfectly familiar," as Watson similarly claims above, it was also unsettling, strange, contradictory. The very visibility of adultery provoked doubt and indecision. Was it really adultery? How should one decide? It unsettled the central tenets of a bourgeois ideology committed to the purity of the middle-class woman and the integrity of the family. While it was the publications of the trials themselves that literally rewrote sexuality in the English public sphere, the debates related to the trials did little to dissipate the anxieties that these publications generated. They demonstrated social and narrative tensions, not fully articulated, certainly not familiar, that confounded the categories upon which Victorian critical commentators had learned to rely.

I have been arguing that the divorce court documentation mobilized the redeeming effects of scandal in its defense of the publication of what were considered to be obscene or indecent details relating to the cases. The representation of adultery, then, was not as subversive as critics like Tanner imagine; and it was definitely not unspeakable. At the same time, scandal was also conveniently lucrative: it sold papers as it exposed sexuality for the first time in a respectable channel. In short, sex was news. And to the extent that this news was incited by the betrayed party's intense desire to discover the truth of adultery, sexuality also defined the truth; it was *the* secret for which the reporters and the jury suspensefully waited. The courtroom and the newspaper made it not just legitimate, but also mandatory, to subject the most intimate details of one's private and sexual life to a comprehensive surveillance. It is in this context that Josephine Butler's comment on the publication of divorce cases defines a strategy which, for better or worse, regulates private discourse and sexuality in the Victorian and modernist newspaper and novel: "I believe we have arrived at that period of the world's history when we see with our eyes the fulfillment of Christ's words: 'Beware ye of the heaven of the Pharisees, which is hypocrisy. For there is nothing covered which shall not be revealed; neither hid that shall not be known. Therefore whatsoever things ye have spoken in darkness shall be heard in the light; and that which ye have spoken in the ear in closets shall be proclaimed upon the housetops.' . . . At the first glance we see only the horror and evil effects of such exposure, but I truly believe that full light shed upon these things is an essential element for their destruction" (12). The divorce reports promise complete narrative exposure; they recount private sexual details in the public press, they penetrate the subject's interior not only literally by describing floorplans, the thickness of one's carpets, where one's bed is located and what is done in that bed, but also psychologically, by exploring the minutest motivations behind an act of adultery, the sort of person to whom one is attracted, and the subject's ability to lie persuasively. The scandal of adultery was set in opposition to the sanctity of the family in a legal confessional charged with the task of determining the "true history" of adultery before the judge, jury, and fascinated public. One's innermost secrets were indeed proclaimed from the housetops and if this, as Butler suggested, inspired horror, one could be assured that a full light shed upon the most private sexual practices and desires was the means by which social ills would be corrected.

Adultery becomes — through a public, communal, and legal discourse — sensational, scandalous, *and* legitimate. The representation of adultery in the daily newspapers sparked a debate that not only contributed to the visibility of adultery but also set in motion a symbolic struggle that reconfigured the very terms of the censorship debate and defined, for the first time in this period, a valid arena for adultery's representation. These journalistic narratives of adultery produce a proliferation of discourses in pursuit of the sexual secret which is conflated with the truth and yet is also a secret-less secret, both always already known and never properly known, both familiar and radically unfamiliar. In the latter half of the nineteenth century there was in England a widespread attempt to regulate all discourse in the interests of normative sexuality and, indirectly, national identity. Print culture which did not operate to this end was censored, both covertly through the lending libraries and the regulative force of condemnatory reviews, and explicitly through legal and quasi-legal institutions. The one area which escaped was the newspaper transcription of divorce cases in which the law, democracy, and freedom were inextricable from sexuality, scandal, and narrative.

3

An Undercurrent of the Body

The Sensation Novel Debates

[M]any of our day, who make books their stimulants, think themselves at liberty to read anything that amuses them; and they take no account whatever of the time which they so employ. In the absorbing interest of literary dram-drinking, all higher studies are neglected, and the duties of life left unfulfilled. There are not a few young persons who seldom read anything but sensational novels, yet they are reading continually; — that is, in very plain language, they wallow from day to day, amid filth of the most defiling kind. The subjects which, of dire necessity, occupy the mind of the Judge of a Divorce Court, occupy theirs of free and deliberate choice. And their appetite grows by what it feeds on, just as the opium-eater requires stronger and stronger doses of the drug that destroys him.

Francis Paget, *Lucretia*

In 1868 Francis Paget wrote a long and erratic sensation novel, *Lucretia; or The Heroine of the Nineteenth Century*, to which he appended a polemical indictment of the sensation novel genre itself. The novel charts the adventures of a heroine who reads too much and, under the influence of her reading, engages in a number of thoughtless, but not ultimately harmful, actions. The conclusion, by contrast, is a direct appeal from the author to the reader; Paget is alarmed by the reading mania that he everywhere observes and disquieted by the damaging social effects following from such reading. If *Madame Bovary* was a "crime against the family," as Pinard claimed, the sensation novel perpetrated "crimes against civilized society" and as such, Paget insisted, demanded the most earnest and rigorous critical regard (299). Paget's conclusion, cited above, captures, in exaggerated terms, what most disturbed the critics. Reading, especially *addictive* reading, had become a social problem of real concern. The rhetoric of this conclusion obsessively equates reading with stimulants, dram-drinking, opium-eating, and drugs. The reader's appetite for reading grows; the reader wants more and more books. Addictive reading, moreover, is the product of particular types of books, books that treat "adultery as a social necessity" (304). Paget's novel and appendix illuminate what had become a central topic of the sensation novel debates of the 1860s: the female reader.[1] He begins with an ostensible interest in the sensation novel itself but his focus of critical engagement quickly shifts to an anatomy of the female reader in the form of his heroine, Lucretia (in the novel parody), and his construction of a distinctive category of gendered reading practices (in the critical appendix).

The sensation novel borrows from both French novels and divorce court journalism and, as a result, is the focus of many of the same critiques and condemnations. But two very obvious differences between these genres contributed to an intensified sense of urgency in the sensation novel's reception. The works were in English and they were fiction. For many reviewers, sensation novelists had managed to translate France's fascination with adultery into English terms and the divorce court journalism's real-life adultery drama into a fictional format. Unlike the divorce court journalism, moreover, where it could be argued that adultery was introduced into the public sphere by legal requirement, the sensation novel exploited adultery by "free and deliberate choice." It translated social and sexual anxieties into domestic detective novels that enjoyed a popularity inexplicable and disturbing in terms of prevailing ideologies.

Peter Brooks, following Susan Sontag and Roland Barthes, has opened up the question of an erotics of reading, a "reading," as he puts it, "of our compulsions to read" (*Reading* 36). What happens, however, when the psychoanalytic context of Brooks's analysis confronts the social and cultural context of the 1860s? What compulsions to read informed the enormous popularity of sensation novels as a specific genre in a specific time and place? The sensation novel debate addressed in the first section of this chapter does not come close to advancing the erotics of reading in which Brooks is interested, but it does make manifest both the power of reading and the strategies that were devised to subdue its effects.

If the social construction of the reader has been overlooked in studies of this period, the representation of adultery in the sensation novel has also received little attention.[2] Adultery, as sensation novel critics were quick to observe, played a key role in this new genre. I turn here to two infrequently discussed novels. Current criticism of the sensation novel has been limited by its repeated scrutiny of the same handful of texts; thus, in part, I want to broaden the ring of critical inquiry to include other texts equally deserving of analysis. These texts, however, also animate adultery in a manner that is central to the sensation genre and English literary history in general. The first novel, Caroline Norton's *Lost and Saved* (1863), has received surprisingly sparse critical attention given Norton's pivotal position in Victorian divorce law reform and agitation for women's rights.[3] When it was first published, *Lost and Saved*, with some exceptions, was applauded on the basis of its aesthetic merits and deplored for its bold exploration of social and sexual issues. This novel makes adultery visible, and problematically melodramatic, in a manner that is at once consistent with divorce court journalism (with which Norton had had first-hand experience) and condemnatory of current divorce law. The second novel, Mary Elizabeth Braddon's *The Doctor's Wife* (1864), has also received only limited critical attention.[4] Because her novel is a loose and very English translation of Flaubert's *Madame Bovary*, Braddon makes adultery visible in the context of censorship, readership, and nation discussed in Chapter 1. The French novel is not the only intertext for this novel, however; as one of the most popular and prolific sensation novelists of the period, Braddon also cleverly thematizes both the sensation novel and the sensation novel debate. Where Norton focuses on reading the body and the epistemology of adultery and addiction to which this reading is related, Braddon focuses on the reading of novels to engage a similar, but differently inflected, nexus of adultery and addiction.

How does adultery become visible, become a "social necessity" as Paget claims, in this period? How is this visibility related to somatic reading effects? What is the political impact of an addicted, reading *body*? And if there is an "undercurrent of the body" (Braddon, *Doctor's* 1:65) not only in the sensation novel but also in the criticism of the sensation novel, how can this body itself be made visible and intelligible? The 1860s reflect a volatile period in which sensation and reading were poised to reconfigure the social field. If English novels translated the passion of adultery as an epistemology of adultery, the brief decade of the sensation novel charts a transitional period in which both passion and epistemology coincide and tensely vie for critical attention. As detective novels, these novels have epistemology—a quest for knowledge—at their core and, as sensation novels, they represent a powerful anatomy of passion. If passion submits to epistemology with the advent of the modernist period, it owes an enormous debt to this brief period of critical tension.

"The Craving for Excitement": Fiction Addictions

How are we to understand the relationship between reading and social action in the 1860s? The very terms of the debate are unfamiliar. And the changing distribution of cultural authorities in the social field only accents this unfamiliarity. Mrs. Oliphant, a novelist and a critic, was one of the sensation novel's harshest critics and certainly no ally to feminist advances. George Eliot similarly disdained the vast majority of work produced by "lady novelists." In this period, men and women alike rallied to the support of established social boundaries, values, and prohibitions. They actively worked to restrict the new print culture, to return the strange and unsettling phantoms to the bottle from which they had sprung. The critical energy expended had a three-headed target: sensation novels; their authors; and the new, and still ill-defined class of readers to whom they appealed. The difficulty of the critics' task is immediately apparent. To stem the print production that they found so damaging, it was not enough simply to attack the novel; part of what was so disturbing was the shifting ground of the cultural field itself as it expanded to embrace new reading communities. While critics did tackle the problem in terms of the novelist, the novel, and the reader, the construction of the young female reader became the most compelling category through which the accelerated print production could be at least provisionally checked. I introduced this argument in Chapter 1 in the context of the widespread disapproval of French fiction and the national ideology that it was perceived to support. In what follows here I want to sharpen the earlier argument by turning to the sensation novel debate's contribution to this discourse on reading practices and the young female reader.

In the passage with which this chapter began, Paget compares the reader of sensation novels to an "opium-eater [who] requires stronger and stronger doses of the drug that destroys him." What this addiction metaphor stresses is desire: what the reader wants, what commands the reader's irresistible and restlessly craving interest. But what *does* the reader want? What, in anticipation of Freud's often-cited question, do *women* want? What *could* middle-class women possibly want when English society was so carefully syncopated to meet their emotional, spiritual, and material needs? The circulation of desire — the desire to read and the desires about which one read — disturbed this picture of satisfaction and domestic bliss. Bliss, as Mrs. Robinson recorded in her diaries, was beginning to take on a very different aspect. In sensation novels, moreover, adulterous desire was one of the most potent desires about which people could now read. As commentator after commentator declared, adultery was suddenly *interesting*. E. S. Dallas, for example, observes, "There is nothing half so interesting to the great mass of mankind as a mysterious murder in a street cab, or a full-blown adultery made patent in court" (*Gay* 312). A writer for the *Medical*

Critic makes a similar remark: "A heroine who was not an adulteress and a poisoner would disgust a modern novel-reader, and would prevent him from following, even as far as the second volume, the fortunes of a person so uninteresting" ("Sensation" 514).

Like W. D. Howells, the writer for the *Medical Critic* first suggests that precisely because adultery and poison are interesting in themselves they compensate for the lack of literary skill that the novelist might otherwise employ to capture the reader's attention. But then, the writer muses, why is adultery also the province of more talented writers? The broader answer to the reading revolution is located in the newspaper. The "columns of the daily papers," the *Medical Critic* argues, have become "formidable rivals to quiet novels" (514). The interest is then located in the "craving for excitement" that the daily papers generate and with which the new novel competes. The article continues: "If this be so, and if a popular craving for excitement is more fully satisfied now than at any former time, . . . it follows that the craving for excitement itself is the only element in the matter that presents much interest to the psychologist" (514).

The references to craving and addiction stress the relationship between reading and the reading body's desires. It is no surprise, then, that these comments are found in a medical journal concerned with the reader's body. But they are not limited to medical discourse. Greg also notes that developments in French fiction (and, implicitly, sensation novels) are "too extraordinary a psychological phenomenon to be ignored by any who desire to understand or penetrate the true aspect of their age" and, he asserts, they offer an illuminating example of "moral pathology" unparalleled in social history ("French" 401). Like the writer for the *Medical Critic*, Greg casts his examination of pathological reading in the language of craving and excitement: "The inspiration of French fiction . . . is the *craving for excitement*" ("French" 403). This craving conforms to the pattern of all addictions: it is an acute desire that cannot be satisfied and it is a desire to which one cannot say no (403). French history with its turbulent revolutions, religious discord, and general social unrest, according to Greg, shapes and fosters this desire for excitement. "Years spent in feverish expectation and in frantic jubilee demoralize the rest of life," he advises. And amid "excitement so tremendous as these [the immediate record of French history], what simple or quiet tastes could grow up and survive? After stimulants like these, how could the relish for a pure milk-diet be recovered?" (404). Leaving aside the advisability of a pure milk-diet, the development of the sensation novel forcefully demonstrated that the craving for excitement was not limited to French national boundaries.

Mrs. Oliphant articulates the renewed interest in French topics in her review of sensation novels a year and a half later. The lack of guns and drama across the channel, she argues, affects not only the French but also the English. The silence breeds a certain boredom and restlessness that encourages new inventions to regain public attention. In the absence of such drama, life is suddenly too "safe." If the French methods of meeting this small lull are perhaps overcharged, "we too," Oliphant notes of the English, "begin to feel the need of a supply of new shocks and wonders" (564). It is this French "stimulant," this demand for drama, that fires the English imagination and quickens public interest (565). The writer for the *Medical Critic*, Greg, and Oliphant share a fascination with the causes of this new revolution in reading. It is also a question that has been engagingly pursued by more recent critics. But it is a question that tends to obscure another approach to this period of English literary history. Instead of asking why a craving for fictional excitement developed at this particular historical juncture, I want to ask why a *language* of craving was used to describe a new class of reading habits.

A few examples will indicate the persistence of this rhetoric of addiction in the 1860s novel debates. W. R. Greg, as noted above, warns that reading French fiction leads to a fiction addiction, a "national craving for stimulants" that "has been fed and fostered without being quenched or cured — for that sort of thirst is never slaked" (405). For Greg, the addictive character of reading only escalates. In a frequently-cited passage, Greg's rhetoric too is burdened by the contagion to which he is clearly vulnerable even as he is repulsed: "The unhealthy appetite — ravenous because unhealthy — became clamorous for more; like the voluptuous despot, it offered a reward for a new sensation, a new pleasure, a new dish; and, as in that case, since the genuine and the natural was exhausted, the monstrous and the impure must be resorted to. . . . Voluptuous pictures of illicit love, in all its phases and in all its stages of progress, constantly approaching the limits of decency and often overstepping them, offered at once the most natural and the most vulgar source of excitement for the jaded appetite and the perverted taste" (405).[5] Greg's language, inflated, hyperbolic, and verging on the hysterical, also betrays a real concern with the addicted reading body. Henry Mansel argues that the "excitement" to which the sensation novel caters is one of the main "indications of a wide-spread corruption, of which they [sensation novels] are in part both the effect and the cause; called into existence to supply the cravings of a diseased appetite, and contributing themselves to foster the disease, and to stimulate the want which they supply" (Mansel 482–83). This "diseased appetite," like Greg's "unhealthy appetite," engenders the structure of addiction to which female readers were uniquely susceptible.

In Alfred Austin's "The Vice of Reading" the desire to read is interpreted as the disease of alcoholism: "[reading] has become a downright vice,—a vulgar, detrimental habit, like dram-drinking." "People," Austin claims, "rush to the circulating libraries for it [the new novel] the moment it is announced, apply for it, clamour for it, and never rest until they are devoting themselves to its perusal. Having finished it, they hunger for another. . . . If people cannot get novels, they will read anything rather than not read at all; just as the confirmed drunkard will drink spirits of wine, ink, or even water, rather than not drink. . . . people are not satisfied even with reading worthless novels; they must read still more worthless notices of them in the papers. It is the drunkard, not only draining his glass, but *licking it out*" (253–54, 256). Sensation novels, Mansel similarly writes, "act as the dram or the dose, rather than as the solid food, because the effect is more immediately perceptible." "The perpetual cravings," he continues, "of the dram-drinker or the valetudinarian for spirits or physic are hardly intelligible to the man of sound health and regular appetites" (Mansel 485). Mrs. Oliphant also discusses sensation novels in terms of the "public craving for its favourite food" ("Novels" 260). Adopting the rhetoric of addiction, she writes: "The feast [of penny dreadfuls] spread for them [young people] is ready and abundant, but every dish is a false one, every condiment vile. Every morsel of food is doctored, every draught of wine is drugged; no true hunger is satisfied, not true thirst quenched; and the hapless guests depart with a depraved appetite" (256). Again the focus is on appetite gone awry and desires that can neither be quenched nor satisfied. *All the Year Round* also argues that the desire for sensation novels indicates the "morbid failings and cravings of the grand outside Public. . . . This is a new and unhealthy greed—a diseased craving, an unwholesome fancy. This hungering after 'sensation' is a diseased and morbid appetite" ("Not a New 'Sensation'" 517). Finally, the *Christian Remembrancer* most sharply delineates the tension that sensation fiction generates between the mind and the body: sensation fiction works "by drugging thought and reason, and stimulating attention through the lower and more animal instincts" ("Our Female" 210). These comments describe a new genre that produces addicted and diseased appetites.

But is it really the sensation novels that are responsible for this radical shift in readerly response? Roger Chartier argues that new textual works "produce their social area of reception" (*Order* 14) and the novelty of the sensation novel, remarked by all contemporary reviewers, certainly demanded a modification of established understandings of narrative reception. But while characteristics unique to the genre (the blend of detection and everyday domesticity, the familiar geography and middle-class patterns of expectation and interaction, the tumultuous crash of incident and action, the obsession with hidden bodies) shaped the production of this new social area of reception, it did not automatically dictate that such reception be figured in terms of addiction and disease. These metaphors, like the metaphors of poison and nerves, highlighted the reviewers' anxiety with the reading body. More than this, the metaphors deployed by the reviewers *produce* a set of reading bodies — when thought and reason are drugged it is only the body that responds — that are pitted against a normative healthy and satisfied body. The repeated references to diseased craving and perpetual craving, after all, *assume* a desiring subject. Someone is there to experience the craving, to clamor for more. It would appear, then, that the social and cultural distress stems much more from newly ignited forms of desire than from the diseases and addictions that are so insistently named. It is important to stress that these references to craving are rhetorical gestures that not only reflect the enormous antipathy to the sensation novel (this point has often been remarked) but also construct a reader pathologically marked by the effects of disease and addiction. This translation of desire as disease performs the cultural work of regulating and delegitimating a new set of reading practices that, it should go without saying, only in the remotest ways resemble the picture of pathology and disease painted above.

This picture is given flesh and blood, so to speak, when one turns to specific references to the reader in these debates. Consider, for example, how Mrs. Oliphant constructs her version of the sensation novel reader. She highlights a particularly powerful moment in *The Woman in White* and observes how the reader shares the main character's somatic responses: the "reader's nerves are affected like the hero's" and the reader "too is chilled by a confused and unexplainable alarm" (572). This is a "simple physical effect" that resides in the contagion of sensation between character and reader. As Mansel so notoriously proclaims, these novels aim "at electrifying the nerves of the reader" by "preaching to the nerves" (488–89). Where thought and reason are drugged in the metaphors noted above, here they are short-circuited. The problem is that there are imperfect readers, that sensation novels appeal to "the unthinking crowd" ("Sensation Novelists" 93). An article entitled "Immoral Books" makes this point as follows: "it is necessary to have certain sanitary regulations in society calculated on the assumption that there are many persons highly susceptible of moral contagion. The sphere allowed to art is somewhat limited but this is a sacrifice which is necessary in the present imperfect condition of the world.... If the public taste were sufficiently enlightened to discriminate in all cases the healthy from the unhealthy handling of dangerous topics, no such rules would be necessary" (637). This susceptibility to moral contagion, only a short step from the moral pathology identified by Greg, is most pronounced in female readers (see also "Novels, Past and Present" 440). Robert Buchanan puts the problem as follows: "Erroneous notions of men, drawn from books, ruin many women yearly, paralyse the understanding, numb the faculty of insight just as it is going to accumulate its own wisdom, confuse the whole prospect of life at the very outset" (299).

As I will demonstrate, Isabel Gilbert, in *The Doctor's Wife*, is described as "dangerously susceptible of every influence" (2:117); she serves, in this context, as the stereotypical female reader who compromises her status as a wife for her fiction addiction and what Braddon calls her "phantasmal universe" (2:65). "As possible wives," Oliphant writes, in a review that opposes just the sort of sensation fiction likely to encourage such phantasmal universes, young women "ought to be taught to admire what is truly admirable in the opposite sex, and weaned as far as possible from the mere fetish-worship of money and a moustache" ("Novels" 439; see also "Lady Novelists," "Lotta," and "False"). The female reader is "impressionable and imaginative" and yet her imagination, if one follows the warnings of reviewers and novelists, is highly predictable: she will confuse the boundary between fantasy and reality; she will make inappropriate identifications; she will desire what she cannot have (the "money" and the "moustache"); she will become weak and enervated; she will neglect her husband and her family duties.

When Paget articulates the social problem generated by the sensation genre as a problem of reading, he is not alone. The *Saturday Review* similarly identifies a "popular passion for reading" that requires close scrutiny: "Nobody will care to deny — what is indeed self-evident — that novels may be, and are, the medium through which moral poison is frequently administered. A perceptible increase of depravity in popular writers will always be followed by a corresponding increase of injury to social and domestic manners" ("Novel-Reading" 196). Another reviewer writes that the "danger in this much written for age is of reading too much" and wonders "whether the craving for books may not be a disease" (Doubleday 110). The *Saturday Review*'s comments here are typical of the three-headed criticism that one encounters: there is a problem with readers; novels deliver moral poison;

and novelists are depraved. The second comment, by contrast, locates the problem primarily in the reader: the reader may have a disease. This construction of reading casts the reader in need (the reader is sick, the reader is unhealthy) of the critic's assistance (as the critic slips effortlessly into the role of social diagnostician and doctor). While references to the tangle of reader, novel, and novelist exemplified in the quotation from the *Saturday Review* are persistent throughout the 1860s, in 1875 Leslie Stephen clearly isolates the focus of critical concern: the "ethical question" addressing the relationship between print culture and social action "concerns the reader, and not the writer," he claims ("Art" 97). Indeed, expanding on the clinical metaphor, he argues that art may be a "poison or a medicine"; its action depends wholly "upon the condition of the patient" (98).

The language of addiction and disease constructs the young female reader as an unhealthy body, a "patient," in urgent need of medical intervention.[6] In her short essay "Epidemics of Will," Eve Sedgwick, following Foucault, argues that in the late nineteenth century the act of opium-taking began to accrue a new meaning: "what had been a question of acts crystallized into a question of identities" (582). The opium-taker becomes an opium addict. According to Sedgwick, "From being the *subject* of her [the addict's] own perceptual manipulations or indeed experimentations, she is installed as the proper *object* of compulsory institutional disciplines, legal and medical, which, without actually being able to 'help' her, nonetheless presume to know her better than she knows herself" (582). In the 1860s (that is, earlier than Sedgwick suggests) this shift from a set of practices to a pathologized individual were in the process of being worked out; both Emma in *Madame Bovary* and Isabel in *The Doctor's Wife* can be read as "case studies" in this context. The sensation novel debate reflects a deep concern with the agency exercised by a new class of female readers. These readers are contesting the image of passive quiescence and loving self-sacrifice that underwrites the domestic ideal. They are bored and they are restless. The sensation novel debate records the effort to translate female reading practices into "moral pathology" and to transform the female reading subject, with the aid of medical, legal, and literary institutions, into an object of cultural surveillance and investigation.

The ideological work performed by translating reading in terms of addiction, poison, or disease is twofold: it constructs the reader as an unhealthy patient in need of a doctor's assistance, and it uses this construction to consolidate a discourse on censorship. The young female reader's amazing innocence is only the flipside of her submission to the allure of fiction addictions and disease. She has neither the pedagogical instruction nor the physiological resources to withstand the somatic pull of the text. This condemnation of female reading practices participates in the condemnation of somatic reading practices central to both Victorian and modern cultural classifications. In the 1860s, the potential for articulating a powerful and positive erotics of reading is foreclosed as reading practices are instead pathologized in an effort to reduce the risks of more widespread social contamination. If critics and commentators, in response to sensation novels and readers, had celebrated the tremendous desire to read evident everywhere and forged an aesthetics to match, the period would look very different. Instead, this desire was reviled and the aesthetics that developed in its wake was an aesthetics of reading addiction and disease. Vulnerable readers, it was argued, could not withstand the craving for excitement (with all the connotations of excitement) that the sensation novel generated. And because vulnerable readers were female readers, the emerging agency of female readers was used as a pawn, allowed only its one small and predictable move, in the English discourse on censorship.

As the debates themselves make palpably clear, however, somatic reading practices were not, in fact, limited to women. I referred to the obsessive character of Paget's rhetoric, and the hysterical character of Greg's, but these adjectives could equally apply to most of the participants in the sensation novel debate. On the one hand, the obsession and the hysteria prove the point of the debaters: reading does have somatic effects. On the other hand, it also refutes the central tenet of the debates: these somatic effects are not limited to vulnerable—typically female—readers. Rather, they extend to all readers. Like the sensation novel reader, the debaters also seem to be reading sensation novels in an effort to discover the hidden body. Unlike the sensation novel readers, however, what these debaters find is the reading body and the reading subject, alive and actively shaping the mobile range of her desires. In their effort to still the force of this body they at once bring it to life as erotic and *unhealthy*. At the same time, they demonstrate that they are not exempt from the "simple physical effects" (Oliphant 572)—the thrill, the obsession, the hysteria—of reading itself, as somatic reading practices are more thoroughly distributed throughout the public sphere.

"A Practical Protest": Caroline Norton's *Lost and Saved*

Caroline Norton's *Lost and Saved* occupied an ambiguous cultural site in the years following its publication in 1863. Grouped with female sensation novelists, Norton's novel, it was argued, appealed to the reader's emotions and low "animal instincts" ("Our Female" 210), exploited a widespread, salacious interest in sex scandals, and indicted prevailing gender relations and the unjust social code that these relations promoted. But her novel also exceeded the category of the sensation novel: it was better written, it provided an acute scrutiny of the high society that Norton knew so well, and, as one contemporary reviewer remarked, it was written with a "purpose" (MacCarthy 46). Norton, moreover, was herself a prominent public figure. She had exercised her purpose in earlier political and legal writings with a relentless energy and keen critical eye. Her goal, ambitious and strange for a woman in the mid-Victorian period, was nothing less than to change the laws regulating marriage and divorce in England. Norton's political and legal writings have been perceptively analyzed by recent critics and her manipulation of melodramatic features in these works, in particular, have attracted attention.[7]

In what follows I want to consider how the political purpose of her earlier writings is extended and modified in *Lost and Saved*. Like her expository writings this novel draws on the melodramatic form associated with the sensation novel genre but it also deploys another competing framework, the genre of divorce court journalism, through which to make its dominant concerns visible. The tension between melodrama and the divorce court journalism contributes not only to an understanding of the ambivalent, uneasy early reception of the novel but also to the link between narrative protest, print censorship, and epistemology in the unfolding drama of mid-Victorian sexual relations.

When considering a topic for her second novel, Norton did not have to look far to find a sex scandal; her own experience provided ample material. The subject of divorce proceedings initiated by her husband, Charles, in 1836, the victim of spousal abuse both in her marriage and in the tumultuous years following the unsuccessful divorce petition, a mother separated from her children, and an author deprived of the earnings from her literary endeavors, Norton repeatedly appealed to the law to redress the injustices inflicted upon her by her husband. The letter of the law, if not the spirit of it, however, fully supported Charles Norton. And while the reform of marriage law was very much a focus of debate in the 1850s, Norton's grievances, like her later novel, did not always dovetail with the political goals of the Liberal government. Nevertheless, as Poovey argues, Norton's contribution to this debate probably did facilitate some of the legal reforms that she desired. As Poovey and Elaine Hadley also note, however, Norton's position as a prominent public agitator for legal reform conflicted with the figure of the private domestic woman celebrated in the period. To be a public woman—an intelligent, articulate, and fiercely committed public woman—was to excite reproof.

The challenge of her political writing was to find an acceptable mode—rather than only an acceptable man—through which to communicate wrongdoing. If women were restricted from publicly addressing questions of sexual injustice, then how could such injustices be legitimately articulated and redressed? Norton softens the force and challenge of her critique, as noted above, by relying on melodrama to carry her political appeal. Norton's reform, then, harkened back to an earlier period when "women were women" (innocent, quiet, dutiful, weak) and "men were men" (knowledgeable, resourceful, responsible, strong). The world had come to an impoverished pass when a woman was forced to rely on herself to pitch an appeal for justice, Norton, very persuasively and powerfully, lamented. Melodrama, with its stark celebration of virtue and expulsion of vice, was the ideal form through which to argue for a law that would allow a woman's virtue to remain unassaulted and a man's vice swiftly punished. The challenge posed by Norton's public voice was, therefore, tempered by the melodramatic tenor of her argument, the content of her proposed reforms, and her ostensible surrender to patriarchal social and sexual relations.

But Norton's political and legal writings were not her only attempt to challenge the law and the social norms that it endorsed. Her novel *Lost and Saved* offers another angle through which to approach her negotiation of Victorian sexual politics and the representation of adultery. *Lost and Saved*, not surprisingly, is even more melodramatic than her political writings; indeed the title itself encapsulates, in brief, the trajectory of the standard melodramatic plot.[8] This novel, however, also draws on the divorce court journalism with which Norton was personally familiar. While I would argue that the divorce court journalism informs Norton's political writings in a manner that has been overlooked, I want to focus here on Norton's novel where the implications of this journalism are more fully realized. The question posed at the outset can now be amplified. If Norton met the difficulty of publicly speaking as a woman with a recourse to melodrama, how did she meet the difficulty of writing explicitly about taboo sexual topics that only aggravated and compromised her already limited public authority? By providing a formulaic pattern through which the representation of sexuality was minimally tolerated, melodrama, as Poovey and Hadley argue, helped to advance Norton's aim. But it was the divorce court journalism and its quasi-legal authority that provided the most detailed and firmly, if contentiously, accepted format through which to approach adultery and divorce law reform.[9]

In the 1860s, novels afforded an excellent medium through which to communicate issues of political and social concern; as several commentators anxiously observed, they were rapidly surpassing even the sermon in their range of influence. But if they were read widely, they were also subject to limitations that more straightforward political writings did not encounter. *Lost and Saved* was, as Justin MacCarthy noted in 1864, "a practical protest" against restrictions placed on the range of representation in the novel (46). It was a protest, then, not only against systemic injustice but also against the implicit censorship to which the novelist was subject. These protests were themselves related to the novel's "purpose": Norton's writing is motivated by her intensely felt criticisms of divorce law and divorce law reform. And yet in *English Laws*, Norton is careful to distinguish her approach from what she perceives to be the limited political efficacy of fiction. If fiction derives its force from an appeal to sympathy, sympathy does not in itself translate into social change. As Norton notes, in a telling comparison between herself and an American slave, "sympathy could do no more for me than for Mr. Patterson's slave. It could not force open for me the iron gates of the LAW which barred out justice" (*English* 20). Indeed, sympathy and justice are diametrically opposed. Her narrative, she insists, is addressed "not to private sympathy, but to English justice" (*English* 23). Norton ostensibly separates two forms of protest that have received considerable critical attention: ideological protest that changes ideas and political protest that changes the law. Norton wants to draw clear lines between the two; nevertheless, as Poovey demonstrates, her narrative itself dramatizes the two as intertwined: it offers a personal account of Norton's history of suffering alongside a passionate appeal for political and legal change.

What is interesting here is that the melodrama on which Norton relied operated most powerfully through the register of sympathy; Norton's resonant record of Mr. Patterson's slave's struggles, the hardships of the impoverished and destitute, and her own fraught and lonely struggle, make visible and sympathetic the position of marginalized and oppressed social groups. In each of these examples, Norton uses the individual case—the story of a slave, a poor woman, and herself—to extrapolate larger social and political concerns. Her polemic is by no means limited to sympathy but it uses sympathy to make more urgent its political goals. In this context, Norton's critique of sympathy is disingenuous. The simultaneous disavowal and deployment of the sympathy garnered by melodrama is further complicated by the gender dynamics that melodrama typically supports. Melodrama may provide a framework through which women's grievances become legible, but it also advances the gender models endorsed by the prevailing ideology. And yet as MacCarthy notes above, Norton's novel works as a protest against restrictions placed upon the novelist, restrictions that have everything to do with the social construction of the Victorian domestic woman.[10]

Several critics have called for analyses that situate melodrama in its historical context.[11] Given the complexity and range of melodrama no single treatment, of course, can meet this demand, but I want to suggest here that part of the enormous appeal of melodrama in 1860s England was the challenge it posed to the implicit constraints on print culture. Melodrama, as Peter Brooks notes, represents a "victory over repression" and a "refusal of censorship" (*Melodramatic* 41). On the one hand, the genre's commitment to "saying everything" (42) broadened the discursive boundaries of the 1860s sensation fiction to which it was related. On the other hand, the "everything" was a highly moral everything; melodrama, again and again, with an unchecked thrill, staged the triumph of virtue over the forces of evil. In melodrama, it is a woman's nature to suffer and be saved. Norton—and several other writers too frequently dismissed as simply popular—questions this representation of female nature. In a sense she turns the genre of melodrama inside out: there is nothing natural about female suffering, and there is nothing fated about the cessation of such suffering. In real life, a hero does not always intervene to relieve the anguish of a woman's troubles. In real life, social and political relations are not immutable. In real life, women cannot pray and appeal to the inchoate heavens; rather, they must turn to the law. Critics have argued that Norton merely replaces the heroic manly man with the heroic manly law in her writings (see, for example, Acland 99), but such a critique sidesteps the enormity of Norton's claims. She rejects the comfort provided by a belief in a world mysteriously orchestrated to produce good and quell evil. Instead she emphatically insists that injustice is socially and politically (as opposed to fatefully and naturally) constructed. If the law is designed to produce and aggravate gendered injustices, then it is therefore within one's power to affect positive change. To be sure, Norton relies on melodrama to make this point, but in her novel she uses sympathy to move towards the law, rather than to elicit a cathartic release of tears.

The circumvention of censorship is related to a second aspect of melodrama important here: its clarity. The message of melodrama is vividly displayed in terms readily understood by even the most untutored reader. The sheer pleasure of melodrama, it is argued, derives in part from the genre's accessibility. But this point also demands reevaluation in the context of print regulation in the 1860s. On the one hand, as Brooks argues above, melodrama refuses to obey the restraints of censorship. On the other hand, in the 1860s, the topic that was most consistently subject to both explicit and implicit censorship was adultery. While melodrama could unequivocally announce that adultery was wrong, the representation of adultery itself was much less amendable to such epistemological clarity. How, after all, does one know that one's spouse has been unfaithful? How does one read the lived text of adultery in which the expressive signs of melodrama are obscured and uncertain?

It is here that the genre of the divorce court journalism is illuminating. Like melodrama, it provided Norton with a socially authorized vehicle through which to represent adultery. Like melodrama, the divorce court journalism challenged censorship, in this case by situating adultery as a crime within the purview of the law (and hence, following England's justice system, also within the purview of the public). Unlike melodrama, however, the divorce court journalism emphasized epistemological uncertainty. As I discussed in Chapter 2, divorce cases were always documented from the point of view of the betrayed party as the unhappy spouse and voyeuristic readers alike endeavored to discover the true story of marital infidelity. It is this point of view which foregrounds the epistemological questions with which English novels of adultery are concerned: not simply, how does one know when one's spouse is unfaithful? but also, on what criteria does one found knowledge claims in general? It is this point of view, too, which foregrounds the tension between melodrama and the divorce court journalism in Norton's novel: the moral clarity of melodrama confronts the epistemological uncertainty of the divorce court. Indeed, the genre of divorce court journalism, despite its avowed goals, was at odds with the melodramatic script grounded in the indisputable visibility of wrongdoing. To be sure, divorce cases made sex scandals visible, but ultimately these cases affirmed the unreliability of evidence and the evasiveness of domestic crimes confined to private spaces typically beyond the scrutiny of the law.

If melodrama and the divorce court journalism were arguably the two most available frames through which to represent marital discord and adultery in 1860s England, these genre frames were in radical tension with each other. The melodramatic recourse to excessive emotion vied tensely with the divorce court's promotion of reason and the law, and melodramatic confidence in the legibility of visible signs was challenged and often eclipsed by the suspicion and doubt that the divorce court itself staged. There was, in other words, an epistemological shift from scenes of certainty to scenes of doubt, from recognition scenes that stamped a character's virtue or villainy to "recognition" scenes that only triggered further forays of doubt. Norton's 1863 novel, not surprisingly, reflects this tension between emotion and reason, certainty and doubt, as it also participates in the refusal of censorship shared by both melodrama and the divorce court journalism. While Norton relies on the divorce court to stage her representation of adultery, she does nevertheless ultimately appeal to melodramatic clarity. At the same time, however, she also questions melodrama's most cherished maxims: the *natural* virtue of women and the maintenance of female innocence. She concentrates instead on the spectacle of the female reader to which both a woman's virtue and a woman's innocence are negatively related.

In *Lost and Saved* Norton offers an account of the female reader as a reader of the adulterous body. To be sure, the main character, Beatrice Brooke, often passes the time with a book in her hand, but her most engaged and passionate reading practices are not devoted to the printed page but rather to the more cryptic script of her "husband's" actions. Beatrice's suspicion of adultery provokes her to establish evidence to confirm her suspicion and to rebel against the censorship imposed upon the young female reader of the text and the world. Like so many later texts in the English tradition, informed by the conflicted tradition of melodrama and the divorce court, this novel translates adultery in terms of epistemology.

The story of *Lost and Saved* can be briefly summarized. Beatrice Brooke falls in love with Montagu Treherne. Their period of courtship is abbreviated by Montagu's desire for Beatrice, a desire that he feels in his "pulse," and motivated by this impatient desire, Montagu entices Beatrice to run away with him. What she imagines as a few hours together in Venice becomes, through coincidence and conniving, a week in Egypt. They talk of a real marriage. Beatrice falls ill. The possibility of marriage becomes more immediate and pressing. When it looks like Beatrice will die, Montagu stages a false marriage to bring her some measure of peace. But she does not die. Indeed, the security of her married state makes her stronger. Completely revived, she poses a problem for her still enamored but emotionally shallow lover/husband. Should he confide all? Or should he conduct himself with her as if they were truly married. Ever one to take the easiest and most agreeable route, Montagu opts for the latter approach. Beatrice agrees to keep the marriage a secret for two years in the interest of Montagu's inheritance, returns to England to live with her family, and to visit, when possible, her "husband's" apartments. This may be the perfect situation for Montagu's pulse, but when Beatrice becomes pregnant Montagu is suddenly confronted by the responsibilities he has thus far successfully evaded. She pleads with Montagu to acknowledge publicly the marriage. He tells her the truth: the marriage was a sham. Beatrice, enraged by the deception and its consequences, makes a break with Montagu. But she does not get far. She again falls ill and this time she recovers without the balm of marriage. Nevertheless, she chooses to consider herself married to Montagu. Her fortitude in this decision, thrust upon her by their baby's premature birth, provoked heated criticism from the critics and contributed to the novel's decline in sales once word of its contents spread. Beatrice's trials, however, were only beginning. Montagu becomes increasingly inattentive and cold. Beatrice begins to suspect that he is having an affair with Milly Nesdale, and her suspicions make her, for Montagu, an unpleasant and tiring companion. Beatrice repeatedly confronts Montagu and when she finally has irrefutable evidence, he leaves her. With a young child and no friends or supporters Beatrice struggles to support herself. This section of the novel includes some scathing critiques of high society—early readers of the novel read it as a *roman à clef*—and wrenching descriptions of Beatrice's impoverished condition and her desperation. The novel closes with Montagu accidentally poisoned and Beatrice free to marry a rich and sympathetic man who loves her.[12]

In what follows I focus only on the second volume of this novel in which Montagu's adultery slowly comes into focus. Beatrice is acutely aware of the deteriorating state of her relationship with Montagu. Indeed, the careful attention to detail devoted to courtship in other Victorian novels is here devoted to marriage. To be sure, Beatrice and Montagu are not really married and their socially unrecognized living conditions may have helped to make Norton's documentation of relationship miseries more acceptable. At any rate, the novel follows the lines of a melodramatic plot in which the woman apparently falls (in Norton's terms, is lost), painfully endures a series of trials while she awaits her prince, and then, with the reader's emotions finely wrought, in the final hour is saved and her innocence blazoned for all to see.

The contrast between Montagu's numerous social interactions and Beatrice's claustrophobic day-to-day existence within a cramped apartment is sharply delineated. As Montagu is increasingly away from home, Beatrice's resentment with respect to the disparity of their situations mounts. She *tries* to be the good Victorian wife, but her efforts are constantly frustrated by Montagu's indifference. And unlike the domestic ideal to which she aspires, Beatrice's capacity for self-sacrifice and loving regard has a limit. In *Lost and Saved* this limit finds its expression in Beatrice's failure to condone Montagu's adulterous actions. The second volume of the novel reflects Norton's own views and the "purpose" that Norton advances. Norton's 1855 "Letter to the Queen" vehemently contests the legally sanctioned sexual double standard that encourages women to turn a blind eye to their husband's adultery but harshly condemns wives for the same transgression (34–44). Her representation of adultery, then, is intertwined with her opposition to divorce law. As I noted above, the category of perception through which adultery becomes visible here also closely parallels the category of perception articulated by the divorce court. Adultery is translated as a question of knowledge, it generates suspicion and doubt, and it is recounted from the perspective, for the most part, of the betrayed party (in this case, Beatrice).

There are four stages to Beatrice's suspicions of Montagu's infidelity. First she is simply anxious and uneasy about Montagu's behavior. If he loves her, then why does he spend so much time away from home? If he plans on marrying her, then why is he flirting with other women? In this first period, Beatrice's suspicions are intensified by seeing Montagu and Milly at the opera together and later, in a passage that recalls *Madame Bovary*, seeing Montagu's hand emerge from Milly's carriage. The second stage is occasioned by a maid, Benson, who desires to exact revenge on Milly's cruel treatment of her by confiding in Beatrice. She discloses several unflattering aspects of Milly's character including the actions that cut Beatrice most deeply, Milly's "wicked intimacy" with Montagu (2:7). These words make intelligible what Beatrice has already witnessed: her lover is having an affair with Milly. But they also generate new and vivid scenes that she has not witnessed:

And other visions followed: things she had *not* seen; creations of disturbed fancy; tender looks and wooing words addressed by Montagu to her rival; summer walks in shady avenues (much Milly would have cared for such walks!); winter visits in warm hushed drawing-rooms, with the dying light of day, and sparkle of a cheerful fire, sole witnesses to laughing conversations, or earnest vows. Wild were the rapid pictures she drew, and wild, as she drew them, were the throbbings of her heart. She walked to and fro like a creature in a cage. She pressed her hands to her head, and dropped them, damp and clenched, by her side. Then she stood still again; looking at dumb surrounding objects with a vague stare of inquiry, as though they held a spell of answer to the question, "Is he false, or is he true?" (2:8–9)

It is these events that Beatrice cannot see, that adultery, by definition, baffles and evades, that the domestic detective in both the divorce court and the novel seeks to uncover and expose. The novel, therefore, participates in the process of making adultery visible. But its visibility occurs in the context of the confirmation of a domestic crime; it is interfused with the law. Adultery is made visible not only as a question of law but also as a question of knowledge and, melodramatically, an object of punishment. This pursuit of knowledge, however, is not without its passion both in the avid desire to find one's doubts confirmed and in the intense suffering and anguish that such doubts and such confirmation generate. The anatomy of passion and the unfolding of the peaks and plateaus of desire that are normally the province of the adulterous couple are here shifted to the reader of the adulterous body.

In the passage above, Beatrice is deeply disturbed by the maid's disclosures but she continues to harbor a faint hope that this new information is inaccurate. She does not suffer silently. She suffers and, like Norton herself, passionately speaks. She entreats Montagu to disconfirm Benson's words and renew his undivided commitment to her. Montagu, with his own desire to preserve domestic peace, obliges. He swears on the life of their son that he is not having an affair. Such an unequivocal denial would have set Beatrice's suspicions to rest if she trusted her husband. But, in this second stage, her suspicion is further aggravated by a visit from Milly herself. Milly, who does not know Beatrice and only wants to satisfy her own suspicion that Montagu has a mistress, assumes that Beatrice also does not know her. But Beatrice, of course, recognizes her at once and is on her guard. This interview, on the one hand, reassures Beatrice that Milly cannot be entirely confident of Montagu's affections and, on the other hand, indicates that Milly does have some claim to Montagu's attention. Both Benson's visit and Milly's heighten Beatrice's domestic vigilance. She dislikes the position in which she finds herself, a position that casts her, whether Montagu is true or false, as a suspicious and watchful wife: "She wandered and pondered, and adopted at length the fatal folly of watching his movements to help her to a decision" (2:20).

The third stage of Beatrice's suspicion provides an irrefutable confirmation of Montagu's treachery: a written record, in his own handwriting, of his relationship with Milly. What Beatrice discovers is a partial copy of Montagu's letter, impressed in her blotting pad, written to Milly on the previous day. Beatrice takes the damaging letter and locks it in her desk. This blotting pad retains the "trace," "the silent proof of perfidy" (2:33) of an infidelity that is more persuasive than the oral account of Benson or the strange fact of Milly's visit. Again this coincidence of adultery and evidence conforms to the dominant form through which adultery became visible in the Victorian period. It suggests that there is always an errant record—like the copy of Montagu's letter—of one's adulterous actions waiting to be read. On the one hand adultery is everywhere (Milly is unfaithful to her husband; Montagu is unfaithful to Beatrice); on the other hand, it will always be found out. And yet such discovery, as Beatrice's case records, is fraught with doubt, uncertainty, and hesitation. That night Beatrice dreams that she is happy again and this happiness bleeds into her first waking thoughts: "Quickly she rose, and passed like a white ghost from the inner to the outer chamber. She flung the shutter open; she seized her blotting-book—it was blank; he was true! But even while she laid it down, her eye fell on her desk; she ceased to dream—she remembered. Slowly she drew the desk toward her, unlocked it, and lifted out the packet containing the leaves she had put away. It was there—it was there—the SPECTER LETTER, the certificate of treachery, the seal of a thousand lies" (2:33). The suspicion of adultery shuttles Beatrice into a haunted world—she is a "white ghost," she reads a "specter letter"—poised between sleeping and waking, forgetting and remembering, the false and the true. Beatrice is "haunted," in particular, by what cannot be spoken in this novel, by "fantastic fancies and conjectures" (2:25). When she attempts to challenge Montagu, she is given a brief but crucially important space in which to refigure the Victorian norms dictating what counts as reasonable, in which to speak the unspeakable. But in the face of Montagu's calm authority and Beatrice's own position of utter dependence her own act of rebellion is quickly translated into the comfortable, because familiar, note of melodramatic excess. It is through melodrama that Beatrice's tumultuous feelings, her sense of loss and betrayal, and her real emotional pain can be most forcefully communicated. But it is a communication that undercuts her claim to reason and even to a stable position from which to assert her own moral and emotional authority. Before this final confrontation, however, there is one last scene to seal Beatrice's unwilling suspicions.

Beatrice chooses to exorcise the ghosts by which she is haunted, not by some magical act of banishment, but rather by making these ghosts more fully present. When the white sheet is abruptly pulled off and a "ghost" is revealed in all its living, breathing, imperfect humanity, its capacity to haunt evaporates. It may still retain a frightening aspect and it may enforce different, more painful, demands on the subject—demands that respond to worldly claims and values—but its occult power is lost. For Beatrice, and for the sensation novel in general, there is a certain perverse safety in keeping the ghost of adultery behind the scenes. The haunting might be disturbing but it is quiet—it speaks in a whisper—and, unnamed, it escapes explicit recognition. Beatrice, however, punctures this safety by tracking her ghost, pulling at the sheet, and naming her outrage.

She learns from the specter letter that Montagu and Milly plan to meet in three days. Instead of immediately confronting Montagu with her new knowledge she devises a plan. On the assigned day—the fourth of August—she follows Montagu to his appointed meeting place.[13] Hiding in the bushes she watches as Montagu and Milly flirt, walk together in the gardens close enough for her to overhear fragments of their conversation, and then return to the inn and ascend to their rooms. It is only after she has accumulated this new piece of information, this irrefutable proof of adultery, that Beatrice finally confronts Montagu. She explains to Montagu, "'I was with you—close by you, when you said to that most vile and wicked woman, "Come in, my fairy queen, and do not let us waste the hours in captious disputing." I was there—I saw you—I heard you'" (2:41).[14] Montagu counters passion with passion: "'You watched me!' he said, with inconceivable fierceness; 'you dared to watch me! wretched girl, take heed what you do. You had better beware'—" With her new knowledge and her moral, if not legal, claim to recognition as his wife, Beatrice does not submit to these threats. Instead she vehemently interrupts: "'No, it is you who had best beware—she who had best beware; that fine lady, with her safe home, her deceived husband, and her betrayed children. What hinders that I warn HIM: that I say to him, Fool! There is not a day you have not borne patiently the extremity of insult; the man you receive as a friend is your worst enemy; degradation and mockery are what he brings to your home; your wife and your friend are alike false! I will denounce her to Lord Nesdale. I will—I will, if I live to see tomorrow's sun'" (2:41–42). Beatrice's attempts to turn the tables on Montagu, however, are foiled by his social advantage over her—his name is not marred, as is Beatrice's, by their relationship, and he is not burdened with the responsibility of his son—and the latitude of emotional expression that follows from his lack of emotional investment. Montagu draws on both of these assets in his crafted attempt to console Beatrice and make amends: "'Beatrice, you don't know the world; all men, I am sorry to say, or most men, have these sort of adventures and liaisons to reproach themselves with. If you had not been so ill and jealous, I might have spoken more about it, and tried to make you comprehend my position. . . . Will it be any satisfaction to you that Nesdale should shoot me through the head, or that I should shoot him? Will it be any great comfort to you, to throw Lady Nesdale entirely on me, as of course, must be the case, if she loses home, and fame, and name for my sake. You quite mistake the value of the speech you overheard; what is there in it?.... Oh! my dear, be reasonable — be reasonable. Life is difficult enough already, for me; especially since our lives were united. Do not teach me to regret that we ever came together'" (2:45).[15] Beatrice, however, steadfastly refuses the logic of Montagu's words. Most importantly, she rejects his account of what is "reasonable." Equipped with a painfully gained knowledge of adultery and a resolute desire to act on that knowledge, Beatrice asserts her own claims to reason. "'I am reasonable, Montagu,'" she says. She then insists on reconfiguring the terms of the debate. It is not jealousy (her own mental state), she states, but treachery (Montagu's deception) that is most at issue: "'We do not understand each other,'" she tells Montagu. "'It is not only jealousy, nor all jealousy, though I admit that it is life and death to me to lose you. It is partly sorrow, and partly horror at the daily treachery which you, whom I once thought so noble and good, must daily practice in such a position'" (2:45–46). In this heated exchange on adultery Norton resists the easy translation of Beatrice's self-assertion as madness, and she refuses to reduce adultery to jealousy. Instead she provides a brief narrative space in which Beatrice can assert her own hard-won knowledge and her own categories of perception through which to interpret, and indict, adultery.

Beatrice's slow transformation from a loving and self-sacrificing wife to a wise and determined domestic detective is paralleled by her deteriorating physical state and the administration of drugs recommended by both Montagu and her doctor. Increasingly agitated by her suspicions of Montagu and already taxed by the uncertainty of her domestic situation in general, Montagu seeks the doctor's assistance for Beatrice. "And the more she fretted, and sickened, and wandered, and watched, the more Treherne absented himself from Stratton Street. Naturally waiting till the doctor had restored Beatrice; had calmed her nerves, and given 'more tone to her system'; and so enabled her to be once more cheerful and chatty, and fit to sing and amuse her husband-lover, and not bore and perplex him as she had done lately by her varying moods, causeless tears, flushings and fatigues, compelling him in the midst of all his occupations to 'wonder what the deuce ailed Beatrice" (2:23). Beatrice's failure to conform to the domestic ideal perplexes Montagu. Norton's novel, however, is surprisingly scathing and direct in its critique of a system designed to produce, whatever the cost, the perfect, passive, "cheerful and chatty" wife. When the wife does not slip into her assigned place as a matter of course, the doctor can aid her adjustment to domestic life by a careful program of drugs. The domestic ideal, in this case, relies on drugs for its successful enactment. And this option, from a woman's point of view, is less than enticing. After the confrontation discussed above, Montagu again urges Beatrice to take her drugs. She responds: "'Those draughts? I hate them, Montagu; they do not give me sleep or rest; they stupefy me. Don't you remember the last time I took them I could not be perfectly roused for a whole day afterwards. You have no idea how strange the sensation is: like floating in a pond full of summer lilies. Nothing seems to stir or signify'" (2:46). Montagu thinks that the pond and the lilies sound "pleasant" but Beatrice's, and Norton's, point is that her life is not pleasant. Montagu is not pleasant. Adultery is not pleasant. Beatrice's sense of entrapment is not pleasant. The discord between the real horror of her domestic situation and pleasant floating in a pond of lilies produces a strange sensation, an epistemological rupture, that Beatrice resists. But she does finally take the drugs and Norton closes the chapter with the comment, "Treherne did not go to sleep; nor did he seek the aid of opiates" (2:48).

If the drugs help Beatrice to enjoy the sleep of a child, it is certainly not a sleep that is represented as desirable in this novel. Like the naming of adultery, the waking state of the deceived woman, whatever the pain, agony, and acute despair, is privileged over an artificially induced pacifying of a woman's "reasonable" claim to be heard. While Beatrice sleeps the deep and "pleasant" sleep of the drugged, Montagu plots his escape. She sleeps and he writes three letters neatly orchestrating Beatrice out of his life, disclaiming his own affection for her, and severing his obligation and ties to her. When she awakens, he is gone.

I want to return now to MacCarthy's comments on *Lost and Saved* as a protest novel. The novel was enthusiastically received by general readers — it went into four editions — but harshly treated by the reviewers. The *Illustrated London News*, for example, called the novel "painful and repulsive" and unequivocally condemned its subject matter (cited in Acland 114). Norton defended her novel in a spirited letter to the London *Times*; not surprisingly, the young female reader was the focus of this defense. Her novel, Norton maintained, was not written for the young female reader and its contents should therefore not be accordingly delimited ("Letter" 8). In the following year, however, MacCarthy expressed a much stronger and, in the context of the novel's hostile reception, welcome position on this topic. First, he agreed with Norton's defense of her novel. But then he noted that to "condemn such a book [*Lost and Saved*] out of hand because it was not pretty reading for school-girls, is like condemning Mill's 'Political Economy' because it cannot be converted into nursery rhymes" (41). "There is no good end attained," MacCarthy argued, "by trying to persuade ourselves that women are all incorporeal, angelic, colorless, passionless, helpless creatures, who are never to suspect anything, never to doubt anyone, who regard the whole end and passion of life as ethereal, Platonic love, and orderly, parent-sanctioned wedlock" (48). This comment extends the critique of the young female reader in a direction too rarely voiced in the Victorian period. Beatrice suspects something, doubts someone, and passionately feels the rush of life, the pleasure and the pain, with a vehemence and a violence that leaves Treherne astonished and cowed. Both MacCarthy and Norton maintain that the young English woman needs to extend her knowledge in directions not standardly accepted by good society. She cannot, in short, rely on men or the law for protection.

The young female reader is not only a restrictive standard that delimits novelistic representation but also a category that itself needs to be questioned. Despite the fact that Norton only adopts the first half of this critique — her novel was not written for school girls — the entire tenor of the novel resonates powerfully with the bolder claim that perhaps women were not the incorporeal and angelic individuals that the domestic ideal announced.[16] For MacCarthy, the novel's protest is a protest against overly restrictive censorship *and* a protest against what effectively amounts to the social construction of women. In terms of censorship he writes that Norton's novel and three others considered in his review are "a practical protest, more or less direct and bold, against the tacit arrangement by which fiction in our day is expected to ignore all the perplexities, dangers, and sufferings springing from the relations between man and woman. We think the protest was needed. We can see no reason whatever why the novelist should be expected to shrink from taking into account one of the greatest sources of human trial, difficulty, and fall" (46). The second protest identified by MacCarthy takes issue with the representation of women as innocent and vulnerable, as readers who need to be protected: "The best justification for the adoption of such topics as the groundwork of novels destined for general reading assuredly is that women may perhaps be thus redeemed from the possibility of remaining in that imbecile and ignorant condition which the romancist [sic] commonly regards as innocence, and which woman is so generally encouraged to cherish as her special virtue, even by those who are so earnest in describing it as the principal cause of her ruin. . . . Women have especial need, as the world goes, to be shrewd, self-reliant, and strong; and we do all we can in our literature to render them helpless, imbecile, and idiotic" (45, 48). But if MacCarthy emphasizes the two-tiered "rebellion" in *Lost and Saved* — its protest against censorship and its protest against a radically impoverished representation of women — he overlooks the broader and more polemical engagements of Norton's novel. He neither mentions her critique of divorce law nor her critique of the sexual and social double standard. And while he is critical of her aesthetic style he does not acknowledge the framing strategies — borrowed from melodrama and the divorce court — that enable her multi-leveled protest in the first place.

As I have argued, however, the conventions of the divorce court permit, at least in part, Norton's complex exploration of adultery. The focus on domestic surveillance and detection, the fostering of suspicion and doubt, the suggestion that adultery nevertheless will always be discovered, that a hidden letter is always waiting to be read, that a compelling narrative can be attached to "things not seen" but suspected, inculcate in the reading subject a policy of watching for adultery and learning to read the signs by which adultery betrays itself. The novel works as a support for social order by extending the law into the home and encouraging a practice of domestic self-maintenance. It teaches the unwary spouse, and the reader who reads through this spouse's eyes, the painful lesson of reading the adulterous body. In terms of gender relations, to the extent that this lesson is directed to women, it contests the policy of censorship that the category of the young female reader advances. It teaches women to read the very text of adultery from which they have been protected. There is something to be gained, the novel insists, from learning to read and from expanding the range of one's reading skills. (Here, it should be noted, Norton shifts to the melodramatic text to insist that one can indeed read the expressive signs of sexual misconduct.) A woman's knowledge, rather than her innocence, is also the means by which she can assert her reason, intimately connected with a reading of the body, and recast adultery not as a woman's problem (madness or jealousy) but as a man's act of deception. Nevertheless, these gender revisions owe a debt to the extra-legal practices of social and domestic discipline through which social order was maintained.

Norton's protest is also advanced and delimited by the genre of melodrama from which she borrows. *Lost and Saved* recasts melodrama by insisting that evil stems not simply from one mean and misguided villain, but rather from a political and legal system that supports myriad forms of villainy. Norton takes this refiguring a step further by reversing the social values that organize and arrange moral actions; society, Norton starkly states, is bad and the outcast fallen woman is good. Like melodrama, the value judgments are in black and white; unlike melodrama, the victim and the victor are reversed.

Norton's critique of the medical establishment carries this protest still further. Couched in terms of melodramatic excess, *Lost and Saved* delivers a substantial blow to an understanding of women's "nature." If a woman needs drugs to remain docile in the face of domestic distress, then her self-sacrificing nature is called into question. This novel implies that women do not naturally accept their passive, domestic roles but rather are drugged, by their husbands and their doctors and the network of social authorities to which they are related, into quiet acquiescence.[17]

Caroline Norton's novel, while forgotten in English literary history, carries a significance that, like the hidden trace of a letter in Beatrice's blotting pad, is still waiting to be read. In terms of the novel of adultery in particular, *Lost and Saved* tells a story that is pivotal in English literary history. James's representation of adultery in *The Golden Bowl*, for example, owes an important debt to *Lost and Saved*. The old curiosity shop in which Milly and Treherne meet and converse in Italian, the representation of adultery from the perspective of the betrayed party, the strange moral flaw in the heart of a main male character too busy attending to superficial structures of happiness to notice deeper and more abiding emotional commitments and demands, all find important parallels in James's novel. If both *Lost and Saved* and *The Golden Bowl* are haunted by the ghost of adultery, *The Golden Bowl* is also haunted, in its most crucial moments, by Norton's novel.

To what extent, finally, was Norton's "practical protest" successful? The London *Times*, one of Norton's more positive reviewers, remarked that *Lost and Saved* "will greatly perplex its cooler critics to determine clearly the merits and defects" (6). The perplexity for Norton's contemporary critics and recent critics alike is heightened by tensions between the generic modes—melodrama (and sensation), the divorce court journalism, and, more generally, the novel—and the content of the protest itself. Norton negotiates the conflicted social space that she inhabits by drawing on, and adapting, the generic forms most readily available to her. Each of these forms, it can be easily demonstrated, operated as powerful supports to the systemic injustices that Norton herself so energetically opposed. But the tensions between generic forms and political protests, and the tensions within and between the generic forms themselves, could also be productive of unpredictable and unruly social outcomes. To introduce new reading styles and subjects to a community of young female readers carefully protected from such material, to reject the position accorded to the Victorian domestic woman, and to discount the prevailing discourse on censorship, was to confound a system devoted to the preservation of the innocent, docile, and apolitical domestic woman. Norton's work, in this context, deserves attention. Its very unevenness should encourage critics to return and scrutinize again the radical ambivalence, the "merits and defects," of her contribution to the lively intersection of protest and censorship, gender and politics, style and subject in mid-Victorian England.

In response to her detractors Norton writes, "so far from individual protests being worthless, they are the small hinges on which the great doors of change for ever turn" (8). Norton crafts her "small hinges" with care and passion; she initiates a dialogue that finds a response in the history of the novel and the history of feminist struggles for political change that persists today. Norton begins to develop an epistemology of adultery that has a crucial bearing on later representations of adultery in the English tradition. *Lost and Saved*, however, is also closely aligned with the sensation novel tradition. It is, as MacCarthy approvingly notes, "tried by the old passions and quivering with the old pains" (49). *The Doctor's Wife*, to which I will refer in the next section, with its intertextual adaptation of *Madame Bovary* and self-reflexive engagement with the sensation novel debate, does not explore the epistemology of adultery in quite the same way. Beatrice reads the text of her husband's adultery and requires drugs to subdue that disturbing vision. Isabel reads the texts of novels and sentimental poems that work like drugs to generate, instead of subdue, visions of adultery. To make one's practical protest, Norton suggests, it is necessary to be *awake* to pain, to learn how to name what ails one and contest a social construction that denies women a legitimate place from which to articulate such names and forcefully participate in social change. Braddon's novel explores a different form of drugs and offers a more extended and pressing analysis of addiction and a different means by which the sleeping body wakes.

"The Alcoholic Elements of Fiction": Mary Elizabeth Braddon's *The Doctor's Wife*

While early sensation novelists could not have been aware that they were participating in a new literary form, the genre was named and categorized remarkably quickly in critical reviews and commentaries. When I first read

The Doctor's Wife, however, I was surprised to discover that at least one novel also explicitly participated in this process: Braddon's novel thematized the sensation novel and the sensation novel debate in its representation of a sensation novelist, Sigismund Smith, and a sensation novel reader, Isabel Gilbert. Both Sigismund and Isabel seemed to operate as points of intersection between *Madame Bovary*, with its thematic interest in the doctor's wife's reading of light literature, and Braddon's own literary tradition. In 1862 Braddon had published *Lady Audley's Secret* to wide popular acclaim, and the 1863 publication of *Aurora Floyd* only consolidated her earlier success. *The Doctor's Wife* was published in 1864; by this time Braddon's skill as a clever, innovative, and bold writer of sensation fiction was already firmly established and, perhaps more to the point, critiqued.

The hostility directed toward the new genre, documented above, no doubt contributed to Braddon's own ambivalent relationship to the sensation novel: she earned her living by writing novels and was well received by her public but she longed to establish a reputation in the literary art world. *The Doctor's Wife*, with its ostensible departure from what Sigismund calls the "stimulant of bodies," is written to this end. In a letter to Sir Edward Bulwer-Lytton, Braddon explains that the "idea of the Doctor's Wife *is* founded on *Madame Bovary* the style of which book struck me immensely in spite of its *hideous* morality" (Wolff, "Devoted" 22) and she repeatedly expressed the hope that he would find this novel her best effort to date (Wolff, "Devoted" 19, 21). Braddon's attempt to distance herself from sensation novels is further emphasized in *The Doctor's Wife* itself when, toward the end of the novel, the narrator adamantly claims: "This is *not* a sensation novel. I write here what I know to be the truth" (2:227).[18] In these comments Braddon indicates that she is both adapting *Madame Bovary* for an English audience—drawing on its "style" but not on its "hideous morality"—and distancing herself from the genre that had secured her reputation.

Braddon chose an ambitious route for her aesthetic project. *Madame Bovary* might have aesthetic claims but it also had a reputation that rendered it difficult, if not impossible, for the English novelist legitimately to engage. Braddon's invocation of the sensation novel debate did not make this task easier. Unlike Norton, she did not draw on the authorizing frames of melodrama and the divorce court to bring adultery into the public sphere. Instead she chose the very genres—the French novel and the sensation novel—in which the representation of adultery had been most severely criticized. How, then, did she establish what MacCarthy calls "a middle place" (47) between the unrisky and bland English novel and the corrupt French novel?

The positive reception that *The Doctor's Wife* received suggests that she did manage to negotiate the spoken and unspoken constraints on representation with surprising agility. Indeed, her novel served as an example of an admirable and respectable balance between art and morality. In 1866 the *Saturday Review*, with *The Doctor's Wife* in mind, promoted the judicious "borrowing" and "translating" of French plots. When the French "heroes and heroines break through certain commandments which are observed more scrupulously in English novels than in English life, a very superficial alteration is often sufficient to reduce them within our conventional bounds. We can translate the morality as well as the language" ("French" 615). Like MacCarthy and others, this reviewer notes that the line between sensation novels and French novels is, in fact, less distinct than English moral self-congratulation implies:

Many of their [sensation writers'] stories are probably in effect quite as immoral as the common French novel, as the description of persons always saved from temptation by accidents beyond their own power is not much more edifying than that of the person actually yielding.... As, then, there is very little danger of the purity of some of our ingenious novelists being sullied by contact, they might very well take a lesson from the foreign practitioners of the art. The plan of adapting French plots has been extensively carried out in another department of literature, and is generally reviled as plagiarism. But the practice has certainly some merits to recommend it.... A very little alteration in the domestic relations of the parties [in French novels] would suit them for home consumption. ("French" 616)

The Doctor's Wife is an example of a French novel adapted for "home consumption." Mrs. Oliphant similarly endorses Braddon's "translation" as "perfectly allowable": "it is true that it [*The Doctor's Wife*] is to some extent plagiarized, as was pointed out at the time of its publication, from a French story; but the plagiarism was so far perfectly allowable that it clearly defined wherein the amount of license permitted by English taste differs from that which comes naturally to the French.... It goes against the seventh commandment, but does it *in a legitimate sort of way*, and is an invention which could only have been possible to an Englishwoman knowing the attraction of impropriety, and yet loving the shelter of the law" ("Novels" 263, emphasis mine).

But what *is* legitimate about Braddon's representation of adultery? How does she balance the appeal of adultery against the love of the law? If *Lost and Saved* conflates adultery and the law by showing how the representation of adultery *is* the exercise of the law, Braddon conflates adultery and reading and focuses her considerable narrative energies on an indictment of reading. In this context, she does not need to represent adultery because reading carries all of the passionate force and moral suspicion of adultery. This strategy fuses the French novel's representation of adultery with the sensation novel debate's indictment of reading to intensify the charges against reading. Reading here is just like adultery. Adultery and addiction merge in the young female reader whose desire for reading, figured as an addiction, occupies the space of what would otherwise be a desire for adultery. In a sense, then, Braddon thematizes the eroticization of reading that was only latent in the sensation novel debate. She uses it as a resource to extend her own analysis of the boundaries of aesthetic representation and the volatile position of the sensation novel in the shifting literary field of the 1860s. I will return to the implications of this strategy, this oddly constructed shelter of the law, after tracing more closely how this strategy unfolds in *The Doctor's Wife* itself.

The novel opens with George Gilbert, the country doctor of the title, going from his town of Graybridge to London to meet his friend Sigismund, the sensation novelist. Sigismund introduces George to Isabel, an inveterate and dreamy reader of novels, and George falls in love. Isabel lives with prankster half-brothers, a "shrewish" stepmother, and a father whose crude and mysterious ways even trouble George and Sigismund. One night this entire family disappears with only a brief note from Isabel explaining that their departure could not be helped. When Isabel later reemerges, apparently now an orphan, working as a governess for Sigismund's uncle, Charles Raymond, and still reading novels, George loses little time in proposing. Isabel accepts and they marry. Marriage, of course, is not what Isabel anticipated. A year later she meets Charles Raymond's cousin Roland Lansdell, a sometimes poet, wanderer, and wealthy man, the walking embodiment of the ideal man who inhabits her novels. She is delighted and does not hesitate, albeit tentatively, to cultivate his friendship. The two form a relationship based on the exchange of novels. Sigismund comes to visit and talk about novels. Roland realizes that he is in love with Isabel and asks her to run away with him. She is stunned and refuses. He, in turn, is stunned by her refusal and leaves Graybridge. Isabel cannot forget him but tries to be a good wife. She has a brief religious phase. She reads more novels. George dies of a fever. Roland dies and leaves his entire fortune to Isabel. Isabel apparently lives happily ever after. Sigismund continues to write his novels.

Isabel's most persistent fantasies involve marriage and death. In both marriage and death, moreover, heroism is always a constant possibility. While the thrust of the narrative is to suggest that her marriage fantasies are wildly out of line with the married life that she should expect (and the marriage that she, in fact, gets), the details of her life suggest otherwise. She does, after all, meet exactly the man of her novel-inspired dreams. He exists; he is not simply a dream. Unfortunately, he is also not her husband. In other words, this novel does not dispel the idea of a Prince Charming, it only warns against marrying too early and missing the opportunity to marry him. Isabel's death fantasies are equally ambivalent. Her terminal illness of choice is consumption, and she imagines countless scenarios where she stages her death by consumption to dramatic effect. Again, the death she gets does not correspond to the death she imagines. When she sits by the deathbeds of George and Roland respectively, she recognizes that death is not romantic but real and painful. Consumption also resonates in another way here. In a period when productivity was highly valued and increasingly challenged by new forms of production and a new shape to the marketplace itself, a fantasy of consumption, on the part of a young woman who constantly consumes novels to the detriment of her work, is by no means innocent as Paget's quotation at the outset of this chapter indicates. *The Doctor's Wife* both acknowledges that novel reading ill prepares the reader for marriage (that is, for George) or death (when reading and death are conflated in the metaphor of consumption) *and* suggests that the very desires that reading fosters may be satisfied (Prince Charming exists; death by consumption is not really death at all).

The reviewers typically read this novel as a critique of sensation fiction (and, as such, were apt to consider it Braddon's best novel), a reading which would also serve as a critique of her previous novels. But how does this critique work? Braddon condenses many of the most contentious aspects of sensation fiction in her key character of Sigismund Smith. He writes quickly, he responds to public demand, his novels are full of plot and incident, and his discussions of the writer's craft are closer to the deliberations of an assembly-line worker than an artist. Braddon writes, "Sigismund Smith was the author of about half-a-dozen highly spiced fictions, which enjoyed an immense popularity amongst the classes who like their literature as they like their tobacco—very strong. . . . he appeared in weekly numbers at a penny, and was always so appearing; and except on one occasion when he found himself, very greasy and dog's eared at the edges, and not exactly pleasant to the sense of smell, on the shelf of a humble librarian and news-vendor, who dealt in tobacco and sweetstuff as well as literature, — Sigismund had never known what it was to be bound. . . . he wrote for his public, which was a public that bought its literature in the same manner as its pudding — in penny slices" (1:11). Like Braddon herself, Sigismund had aspirations to write something better but in response to the market demand he "wrote romantic fictions by wholesale, and yet was as unromantic as the prosiest butcher who ever entered a cattle-market" (1:36). This prosy butcher, however, offers an acute description of the sensation novel. The only problem in writing for a demanding public, Sigismund confides to George, is the "tendency toward bodies" (1:65). George finds this remark "incomprehensible" and Sigismund responds as follows:

> the penny public require excitement . . . and in order to get the excitement to a strong point, you're obliged to have recourse to bodies. Say your hero murders his father and buries him in the coal-cellar in No. 1. What's the consequence? There's an undercurrent of the body in the coal-cellar running through every chapter, like the subject in a fugue or a symphony. You drop it in the treble, you catch it up in the bass; and then it goes sliding up into the treble again, and then drops down with a melodious groan into the bass; and so on to the end of the story. And when you've had recourse to the stimulant of bodies, you're like a man who's accustomed to strong liquors, and to whose vitiated palate simple drinks seem flat and wishy-washy. I think there ought to be a literary temperance-pledge, by which the votaries of the ghastly and melodramatic school might bind themselves to the renunciation of the bowl and dagger, . . . and all the alcoholic elements of fiction. (1:65)

The craving for excitement discussed above is translated here in somatic terms. One reads to discover the body, and the sense of a body waiting to be revealed invests each page with an "undercurrent of the body." The body does not have to be spelled out on the page to be felt as shivers of anticipatory excitement by the reader. But what if the body is not murdered but rather, although hidden, alive and adulterous? In this case, too, one reads for the body, but the reader's desire is not stilled by the murdered body that works like an emphatic finale to the novel's crescendoing sentences. The adulterous body incites a desire that is not set to rest, and a knowledge that is anxiously pursued but not typically resolved. Indeed, the fact that adulterers and adulteresses are murdered with such alarming predictability in nineteenth-century novels testifies to this point. The adulterous (and, as it happens, dead) body in the figurative coal-cellar of *The Doctor's Wife* is, of course, Emma Bovary. As the reviewer above observed, one does not have to represent adulterous actions to represent adultery. In Braddon's novel, the adulterous body exerts its pressure on the narrative like the undercurrent of the body to which Sigismund refers. Braddon's informed readers knew to expect adultery because they knew the story of Emma Bovary on which the novel was based, and her less informed readers could not have been unmoved by the accumulation of details signifying the slide toward adultery.

And yet the adultery does not happen. The undercurrent of the body remains but the adultery it signifies and teaches the reader to anticipate is not fulfilled. While at first glance this might appear to be a departure from the resolution offered by the body in the coal-cellar, it, in fact, only underscores what might be read as one of the immense pleasures of the sensation novel: the dead body in the coal-cellar is not really dead. If one reads for long enough one's reading will be rewarded, not with a confirmed murder, but rather with a walking ghost. This is the story told by Collins's *The Woman in White*, Braddon's *Lady Audley's Secret*, and Dickens's *Our Mutual Friend* to name only a few of the more prominent novels of the 1860s. If sensation readers could be assured of one thing, it was that the body in the coal-cellar, the body dropped in the treble and caught in the bass, had a pulse. It was simply waiting to be revived or awakened at the appropriate narrative moment. These "[d]ead, yet not dead" bodies, as the *Temple Bar* described them ("Sensational" 415), resembled nothing quite so well as the middle-class woman's social existence. Their powerful appeal to these readers sharply exposed the emerging faultlines in the domestic ideal: what Sigismund invokes, with uncanny precision, is the "dead" body that comes alive with reading, that makes itself a sensation, that makes itself *felt*. And while Sigismund identifies an "undercurrent of the body" informing the novel's interest, one can also locate an undercurrent of the body rippling through the sensation novel debate. It is this undercurrent that imbues the rhetoric of addiction and disease with its ability to signal danger. And it is this undercurrent that alerts us to the fact that female readers were beginning to experience their own, sometimes passionate, sometimes disturbing, but very awake bodies.

Sigismund's comments to George, however, would have conformed closely to the goals of Braddon's most hostile critics. Resist the recourse to bodies, they implicitly argued. But Sigismund hesitates. He reflects on his evaluation of the sensation genre and then modifies his comments as follows: "'But, you see, George, it isn't so easy to turn teetotaller, . . . and I scarcely know that it is very wise to make the experiment. Are not reformed drunkards the dullest and most miserable of mankind?'" (1: 66–67). Sensation novels are not dull, he says, and then muses, is not life more interesting with a little excitement? When the options are either temperance or the alcoholic elements of fiction, Sigismund opts for the alcohol, the addiction, and the undercurrent of the body. The resilience of the body persists in the sensation novel and in Sigismund's theories related to the sensation novel. These comments mark Braddon's departure from the mainstream criticism of the sensation novel. It is interesting, in this context, that when *The Doctor's Wife* was reissued in a yellowback edition several years later Sigismund's disavowal of his opposition to the "recourse to bodies" is deleted. Only his critique of the genre remains. In either case, however, it could be argued that Sigismund's marginal cultural authority does not command the force to significantly influence the fortunes of this genre.

But if Sigismund, with his marmalade and his toast and his enthusiasm for murders and passion fictionally wrought, provides an ambivalent, while perceptive, commentary on the sensation novel, the representation of Isabel Gilbert, the quintessential young female reader, seems to offer a much more straightforward indictment of the stimulant for bodies in which the genre trades. The bodies on which Braddon focuses here are not murdered but rather, on the one hand, reading and addicted, and on the other, adulterous. In part, Braddon's focus on the young female reader is prompted by Flaubert's own literary concerns in his depiction of Emma's reading practices. But Braddon's development of this theme also owes a great debt to her own literary and social context in which the young female reader's fiction addictions are a prominent focus. The Victorian discourse on censorship, in other words, is deployed in Braddon's depiction of Isabel as a young female reader who both underscores the need for censorship (reading, for her, produces addiction and disease) and ensures that the text will not overstep the boundaries of permissible representation (the young female reader operates as an internal constraint in the text as she also does in the social imaginary as a whole).

When the reader first meets Isabel, she is "so absorbed by the interest of the page before her that she did not even lift her eyes when the two young men went close up to her" (1:29). Sigismund quickly labels Isabel as a young woman who "'reads too many novels'" (1:39). After discrediting novels as opium—the novels that Isabel reads are described as "'beautiful sweetmeats, with opium inside the sugar'" (1:39)—he grants that they are fine in moderation, "'after a hard day's work,'" for example; and the point is clear: novels should not *replace* work; they should, rather, make it more bearable. Second, they should not fundamentally change the reader's psychology (Emma's decline via novel reading is documented to this end);

they should, rather, soothe a "tired soul to rest." Most important, the novel should not distract one from, or eclipse "the real world," what Sigismund calls "a healthy race on the barren moorland of life" (1:39).

But novel reading sometimes goes beyond relaxation after a day's work. This shift, if ultimately psychological, is again figured in terms of addiction and disease. Sigismund bluntly makes the point that is implicit in the reviews considered thus far: it is not the novel itself that is the problem but rather a distinction between the wise and the foolish reader. "'No wise man or woman,'" Sigismund claims, "'was ever the worse for reading novels. Novels are only dangerous for those poor foolish girls who read nothing else, and think that their lives are to be paraphrases of their favourite books'" (1:35). Isabel's "habitual reading" is sustained through her teenage years and when she is married, at the point where a young woman's fantasy husband is to be replaced by the real thing, she acutely feels the loss of her "opium." Her honeymoon, for example, is described in terms of the absence of books rather than the presence of a husband: "there were no books in the sitting-room at the family-hotel; and even if there had been, this honeymoon week seemed to Isabel a ceremonial period. She felt as if she were on a visit, and was not free to read. She sighed as she passed the library on the fashionable parade, and saw the names of the new novels exhibited on a board before the door; but she had not the courage to say how happy three cloth-covered volumes of light literature would have made her" (1:160). If the intensity of Isabel's fiction addiction only becomes palpable during the period of withdrawal that is her honeymoon, upon returning to her new home, "[s]he had given up novel-reading, and employed her leisure in the interesting pursuit of plain needlework" (1:157). But it does not take long for the "dangerous" habit to renew itself. The ennui of married life finds Isabel succumbing to the old cravings: "Isabel did as she liked; and this meant reading novels all day long, or as long as she had a novel to read" (1:174). Roland, her phantasmal lover, discovers "that she was perpetually reading the same books,—the dear dilapidated volumes of popular novels that were to be had at every circulating library" (1: 276). And her husband "grew to consider her only in her normal state when she ate her supper with an open volume by the side of her plate" (1:278).

Isabel's *reading* is the greatest crime against the family in *The Doctor's Wife*; it competes with her husband's tedious dinner-table talk and compromises her role as a wife. The focus on reading and eating takes its cue from *Madame Bovary* where Emma "read Balzac and George Sand, seeking to gratify in fantasy her secret cravings. Even at the table, she had her book with her, and she would be turning the pages, while Charles was eating and talking to her" (45). In *The Doctor's Wife* George is described as follows: "he took his dinner, or his weak tea, or his supper, as the case might be, and stretched his long legs across the familiar hearthrug, and talked to his wife, and was happy. If she had an open book beside her plate, and if her eyes wandered to the page every now and then while he was talking to her, she had often told him that she could listen and read at the same time; and no doubt she could do so. . . . She was satisfied as an opium-eater is satisfied with the common everyday world" (1:175–76). For both Emma and Isabel the first consequence of reading fiction is an elision of lived reality — the dinner table, the husband — and the bright, fantastic world of the novel. Isabel's reading tragically informs her role as a wife as many of the contemporary reviewers predicted. Graybridge gossip is quick to condemn Isabel for her habit observing that "a young person who spent so much of her time in the perusal of works of fiction could scarcely be a model wife" (1:174). While novel reading was most often described as a solitary activity — and as often disapproved of on precisely these grounds — Isabel's novel reading is, by contrast, both public and the subject of public debate. Even the most invisible addiction — the incorporation of words — betrays itself in its effects; in this case, Isabel's neglect of her domestic duties and her duty to join her husband as he eats. Isabel might look beautiful but she is, in fact, a sick and afflicted creature: "*look into* Mrs. Gilbert, and even this show of beauty vanished, and you only saw a sickly young person, with insignificant features and coarse black hair" (1:175). Braddon translates the widespread alarm about women's reading and the "diseased appetites" that it both creates and feeds into a fictional format: Isabel's reading addiction is written on her body. Thus far, Braddon's interpretation follows a course that tacks alongside the sensation novel debates.

But where Flaubert's analysis moves on to adultery, Braddon's stops with a simple addiction. There is something comical in all of this: the reader waits for adultery and in the very places where one most expects it to happen, there are only more and more books. When Gwendoline, Roland's cousin, warns Isabel that her reputation is in danger, Isabel contests the imputation by saying, basically, that it was "just books." "'I told George every — almost every — time I met with Mr. Lansdell . . . and George knows that he lends me books; and he likes me to have books — nice, in-st-structive books,'" (2:38). Isabel submits to the informing movement of her life which, while figured as a futile love for Roland, follows in fact what I have called a rhetoric of addiction. "Mrs. Gilbert abandoned herself to the dull monotony of her life, and solaced herself with the thought of Roland Lansdell as an opium-eater beguiles his listless days with the splendid visions that glorify his besotted stupor. She resigned herself to her life, and was very obedient to her husband, and read novels as long as she could get one to read, and was forever thinking of what might have been—if she had been free, and if Roland Lansdell had loved her" (2:33). This passage clearly describes a case not only of desires unmet but also of a monotony made palatable by a craving that is fed both by loose and reckless thoughts and a form of consoling novel reading. And, as reviewers knew, and as Isabel learned, this addiction like desire itself, by definition, could not be satisfied.

Braddon's novel, Oliphant implied above, subordinates "the attraction of impropriety" to the "shelter of the law." The law, specifically the *love* of the law, prevails. I agree with Oliphant, and yet her very terminology—the attraction of impropriety, the love of the law—introduces a fissure at the heart of this engagement with adultery and the law. For even as she endorses Braddon's approach to Flaubert's novel, Oliphant eroticizes her negotiation of censored subject matter. This point is made even more manifest in Braddon's novel itself. Both the attraction of impropriety and the love of the law are condensed in the figure of Isabel Gilbert, the young female reader. On the one hand, then, Braddon's representation of the female reader is perfectly consistent with the central tenets of the sensation novel debate; on the other hand, however, her minute interrogation of the reader renders real and visible many of the contradictions and complications in this figure. To be sure, Isabel reads too much, she craves her novels like an opium addict, and she experiences desires that her quiet country life cannot satisfy. Braddon forcefully demonstrates that she reads in an effort to redress the domestic tedium of the middle-class home. Like Beatrice she resorts to "drugs." But there is a crucial difference between the drugs that Beatrice takes and the "drugs" to which Isabel addictively turns. Beatrice takes drugs to put herself to sleep; Isabel takes drugs to wake herself up. For all of Braddon's condemnation of sensation novel reading, she does make this point sufficiently clear. While Isabel's fiction addiction is sometimes represented as an escape (her reading at the dinner table, for example, is a material escape from her husband's tedious talk, and the fantasies that her reading generates extend well beyond the act of reading), it is also represented as an addiction that generates desire. This desire animates the reading subject; she feels attraction, she feels love. Most important, however, it makes the reader painfully aware that there is something wanting, something that the domestic ideal does not provide, in Isabel's life.

Second, Braddon contests the category of the young female reader that stipulates a direct corollary between reading and social action. The reader who reads about moral depravity is depraved. The reader who reads about adultery commits adultery. Isabel's story, however, is much more complicated. She is addicted but her addiction escapes the implicit adulterous trajectory with which it flirts. Braddon borrows the rhetoric of addiction and disease but departs from the hysterical pronouncements that revile all women's novel reading. Isabel's reading may impede her grasp of the world in which she lives, it may make her sick, but it does not lead to adultery. The temptation is there, but while she cannot say no to reading, she can say no to adultery.[19]

Isabel may have a reading problem that recourse to plain sewing cannot correct, but she does not succumb to the temptations that it generates. Because her reading goes nowhere so to speak—it does not tip into diverting adulterous actions—the novel's focus remains on this reading and its peculiar bodily figuration. This is Braddon's third innovation. Again she makes explicit something that was implicit in the sensation novel debates: the eroticization of reading practices that the debate produces. Because Braddon is forced to avoid the representation of adultery (to work, that is, within the shelter of the law), the erotic energy that the text generates infuses the act of reading itself. Braddon implicitly conflates adultery and reading, the adulteress and the reader, and, in this conflation, invests reading with all the erotic passion and excitement denounced by the sensation novel's critics. The regulation of reading material, moreover, itself eroticizes, by making desirable, the forbidden object. It is in reading as opposed to adultery, for example, that the reader becomes aware of Isabel's body— its appetite, its craving, its desire.

One further point indicates the way in which Braddon writes against the grain of the sensation novel debate. I suggested above that critics of the sensation novel constructed the young female reader as a patient in need of medical attention. Braddon also constructs Isabel as a patient suffering, as her body indicates, from the ravages of her fiction addiction. But Braddon neatly slides the doctor off the scene. Where, in fact, is the doctor in this cultural imaginary? How does the doctor address what has been diagnosed above as a fiction addiction, a poison, and a disease? How does the doctor treat adultery? In *Madame Bovary* the doctor is entirely unaware of the problem; he is the picture of dull and smiling satisfaction. Similarly, in *The Doctor's Wife* the doctor is blind to Isabel's fever and deaf to her, albeit muted, delirious ravings. In *The Doctor's Wife*, as in *Madame Bovary* and other novels of adultery, it is the doctor—the body specialist, par excellence—who is described as the one who *does not know*.[20] But if the doctor does not understand this new reading body and the afflictions to which it is subject, who will? Flaubert, wary of remedies, desists from putting forward contenders, but Braddon has no scruples here. It is Sigismund—that is, the sensation novelist—who both immediately grasps Isabel's problem and, just as quickly, prescribes a remedy: Isabel should write a novel.

The Doctor's Wife closes, tellingly, with Sigismund himself writing a novel. The novel he writes deals with poison and an antidote. His heroine poisons herself with insect powder and the novel is finished. Sigismund's publisher, however, was pleased with the serial's popularity and wanted Sigismund to write a sequel. But what can he do? His heroine is dead. Unless she might perhaps come to life again: "You see there *might* be an antidote to the insect powder" (2:299). At the close of *Madame Bovary* Emma is dead from poisoning but perhaps for her too there is an antidote; for not only is she reanimated every time a reader picks up the novel but also another novelist, say Braddon, might some day write a sequel.

If we have been led to believe that sexuality was silent in the Victorian period, one finds a powerful undercurrent of the sexual body in both the sensation novel debates and the sensation novel itself. This observation is part of an ongoing revision of our understanding of Victorian sexual attitudes that offers a richer and more expansive picture of the social field. In sensation novels, sexuality is intertwined with epistemology; the novel's secret, fuelling and informing the reader's and the detective's desire for resolution, after all, is almost always a sexual secret. The narrative promise becomes a sexual promise of fulfilment. But because the English novel recoils in the face of explicit representations of sexuality, one encounters instead a distribution throughout the novel of the powerful sexual energies that lend the narrative its momentum. It is no wonder, in this context, that reading was so vigorously opposed by critics uneasy with what they quite rightly interpreted as the conflation of reading and the body.

I want to close this chapter by considering a short lecture delivered by Anthony Trollope in the same year that Paget wrote *Lucretia*. In this lecture Trollope also takes issue with women who read too much. He makes his point by way of an anecdote about a "fair, sweet-tempered, good-hearted, healthy girl" ("Novel" 82). This girl is seduced by novels. She compulsively reads the boxes of novels that arrive from Mudie's and is constantly requesting more. Indeed, she begins to resemble, as Trollope remarks, an "opium-eater" (85). Her health diminishes, she is "too languid for walking," and she shirks all physical and intellectual exertion. The story that Trollope tells is only a compressed version of what we have encountered in the sensation novel debates and the sensation novel itself: the woman who reads too much becomes addicted to her novels, her health declines, and, in Trollope's account, her marriage prospects evaporate. But Trollope's story also makes explicit the ideological work that such narratives perform: he does not assume the role of censoring problematic texts but rather, as he puts it, he assumes "the office of censor of young ladies" (87). By translating the reader's desire as an addiction or a disease, reading was defined as an activity that needed to be watched and, if not censored, at least carefully regulated. By limiting this translation to a specific segment of the reading community, however, the regulation of reading also became a regulation of women. Censorship in the 1860s, then, was never only about excluding certain books, but also about constructing and regulating certain targeted readers.

But it is too reductive, of course, to read this cultural moment as a simple confirmation of the hegemonic power of cultural practices. The relationship between the power of the female reader and the pathology of the female reader, for example, was much more dynamic than a cause-and-effect model would allow. A sequel could always be written, an antidote, in which the dead heroine is revived. By translating the reader's desire as addiction, the debates and the novels both named and contributed to the processes by which women increasingly gained forms of agency in the mid- and late-Victorian periods. If the desire for adultery suggested that there was something wanting in the middle-class woman's *married* life, the desire for reading, figured as an addiction, suggested that there was something wanting in the middle-class woman's life in general.

I want to return now to Paget's *Lucretia*, a parody that at least one critic interprets as a response to Braddon's novels. Lucretia, our "heroine of the nineteenth century," is bored and discontented. "I was not made for agricultural monotony," she writes, "and so my poor nerves are shattered; my spirits are quite broken. . . . I feel that the dulness of this place is destroying me" (1–2). Only sensation novels can redress the boredom that is destroying her. As Miss Stiffkey, from whom Lucretia later receives her books, remarks: "I do believe it was their [the circulating library's] provision, rather than the butcher's and baker's, that at times kept us alive" (239).

Paget is being facetious and funny in this novel as his appendix makes abundantly clear. But what happens when we take his novel seriously? Maybe the appendix is the joke and the novel is the serious document. Maybe Lucretia is truly revived and renewed by the novels she reads so compulsively.

This possibility suggests another approach to the question of the Victorian woman's compulsions to read broached at the outset. The sense of "something wanting" in Victorian women is often remarked in the sensation novel. Walter Hartright's perception of Laura Fairlie in *The Woman in White* in terms of "something wanting" (76–77, 86) and Braddon's similar representation of Lady Audley in *Lady Audley's Secret* in terms of "the sense of something wanting" (298) are only two of the more vivid and memorable examples of what is, in fact, a frequent trope. While the sense of something wanting is mysterious and foreboding, it is Braddon's *The Lady's Mile* that perhaps comes closest to identifying what is most disturbing in this trope and, indeed, in the sensation novel debates as a whole. The main character, Cecil Chudleigh, is wavering precipitously close to committing adultery. In an attempt to analyze her desires and her behavior, she states aloud to herself: "I read too much, and think too much, until I begin to feel that there is something wanting in my life" (207). It is reading that gives women the impression that there is something wanting in their lives. This impression is agitating for Cecil but, as Beatrice makes clear, it is preferable to feel and to know one's situation in all its painful complexity than to submit to stupefying drugs that put one to sleep. Indeed, the sense of something wanting becomes, instead, a sense of some*one* wanting. If this desire is typically translated as an addiction, it is also the indication of an emerging agency, very much alive and awake, only waiting to be felt and detected like the undercurrent of the body it ignites.

4

A National Habit of Repression

Henry James's Negotiation of Adultery in *The Golden Bowl*

Mr. Henry James is the wonderful artistic outcome of our national habit of repression. He has learned how to make repression a factor of art instead of an impediment.

Sir Francis Jeune, *Academy*, 1899

It is only one short step from Sir Francis Jeune's reference to England's national habit of repression to a consideration of England's national habit of censorship. As the print censorship, divorce court journalism, and sensation novel debates attest, this "habit" represents a chapter in England's history that has more often been written as a story of hypocrisy and psychological repression than a story of censorships tied to social, cultural, and legal institutions. To be sure, print censorship was obscured by persistent appeals to England's esteem for freedom of speech, the absence of censorship trials, and the general reluctance to apply the law to print culture infractions. Nevertheless, forms of implicit censorship were everywhere exercised (witness the antipathy to French representations and the subsequent print restraint discussed in Chapter 1 and the equally censorious response to English sensation fiction discussed in Chapter 3). By the 1890s, when Henry James was embarking on his later novels, the relationship between print censorship and the young female reader was firmly established, if also increasingly contested. In their different ways, for example, both Caroline Norton and Mary Elizabeth Braddon begin to rewrite this default reader in an attempt to gain greater representational freedom for the novel and greater cultural authority for its female readers and authors.

No author, however, has written as passionately on behalf of the novel's representational freedom as Henry James and, in this context, he admirably continues the work of Norton and Braddon. Like Norton and Braddon, moreover, his critical thinking on this subject is fraught with contradictions and tensions. For James, the novel is at once severely restricted and extravagantly free. This tension between a real, implicit censorship and a desired freedom, while clearly frustrating for the ambitious novelist, produces some of James's most important contributions to English print culture. Despite James's contempt for censorship in any form, the national habit of censorship is emphatically not an "impediment" for this novelist. It is instead transmuted into a "factor of art," a factor of English literary modernism, and a factor of modernist forms of knowing and seeing. More so than Norton and Braddon, James channels censorship into the service of his art; his success in this endeavor is marked by the fact that we no longer think of James as working within a cultural climate of censorship but instead simply imagine his strange silences, odd constructions, and reticences as embodying his art rather than as a studied and apt response to a "censorious world."

This analysis of James should by no means be understood as a celebration of censorship. Censorship, in any period, involves a complex series of competing interests, cultural demands, and national and political stakes that are difficult for the critic to make visible and comprehensible. In the Victorian period, this problem is exacerbated by the opacity of the censoring mechanisms and, for the late-twentieth-century critic, the difficulty is further deepened by an ingrained tendency to read censorship in the binary terms of law versus fantasy or freedom. As Foucault and others have made clear, and as I have already discussed, censorship cannot be reduced to the forceful exercise of the law over cultural freedom. This point is nowhere more evident than in the case of the young female reader. While Norton and Braddon begin a novelistic interpretation and revision of this figure, it is in James's later fiction, and specifically in his negotiation of adultery, that this project most fully, and problematically, unfolds.

In this chapter I turn to *The Golden Bowl*, James's last completed novel, to illustrate his approach to censorship, adultery, and the young female reader. It is in this novel that James stages what he increasingly perceived to be the central contradiction of English print censorship: the very cultural, political, and national politics that demand a young woman's innocence (in this case his heroine Maggie's) at the same time destroy it. For James, like MacCarthy and Norton before him, innocence is a danger. This view parallels, indeed is inseparable from, the cultural work that the novel itself performs: the social, political, and institutional pressures that enforce the novel's innocence also contribute to the corruption of that innocence. And yet if Maggie's innocence and ignorance are destroyed by the new reading culture that she is compelled to master, a similar claim was not typically made of James's novel itself. While early reviewers took issue with the novel's subject matter, they did not seem to fear that it posed any of the reading dangers that the representation of adultery was reputed to trigger so assuredly. But how did *The Golden Bowl*, a novel so centrally about adultery, escape such charges? On the one hand, James posits the possibility of the young female reader's intelligence and her resulting immunity to the causal link between novel reading and social or sexual perversion. On the other hand, *The Golden Bowl* did not seem to be a novel that young women would read; for James's critics, and in a complicated way, for James himself, the young female reader had been rendered irrelevant to the debate on print censorship because she, like Maggie before she learns to "read," has been "arranged apart" (331).

In what follows I will explore the ways in which James rewrites the figure of the young female reader and, in the process, challenges the system of print censorship by which he believed his own career as a novelist had been marred. James's novels and critical writings are especially illuminating for the history of print censorship in England because James's sense of consternation and frustration in the face of print restrictions is pressingly and immediately *visible*. Indeed it is odd that the tension between the visibility of censorship and the invisibility of restricted subjects has been so rarely remarked in his work. To refer to what is unnamable, after all, is also to refer to a process of censorship, however difficult to detect and understand, that renders the unnamable as such. But when critics have focused on the structure of unnamablity, they have tended to highlight the psychological implications of this structure — either, what impedes a particular character from naming? or what impedes James from naming? — instead of considering the fraught arena of social and cultural politics to which this structure of suppression was related.[1] In fact, James's novels are much less about filling in an invoked but absent content, than they are about what I will call the *event* of censorship itself.

For James the event of censorship deflects attention away from a discourse on repression; it does not so much seek to retrieve what is "behind" a given representation — "the horror of the thing hideously *behind*," as James puts it (*Golden* 471) — as to consider the way in which censorship produces a "behind" that resists established canons of reading and knowing. The melodramatic urge to voice evil and redress wrong, Peter Brooks astutely argues, is raised only to be disavowed in James's later novels. I believe these later novels, and here I depart from Brooks, are about something entirely different. Alive to the real institutional pressure imposed upon his art and anxious to avoid the already over-worked conventions for the English representation of adultery, James *confronts* censorship. Censorship—the unnamable, unutterable, unspeakable—is the drama of his text. Maggie will not say the word adultery, James will not say the word adultery, and yet, as *The Golden Bowl* demonstrates with such chilling precision, the absence of discussion and the absence of naming does not ensure the absence of sexual misconduct itself. It only shifts the stakes to a different level. Each of the characters works to hide not the adultery, but their knowledge of the adultery. James takes print censorship to its logical conclusion: it is not about preventing adultery, but rather about preventing the dissemination of knowledge. But if this is the case then its stated goal—the protection of the young female reader—is seriously misguided. The absence of knowledge, after all, reverberates most painfully for exactly the person that the system of censorship is designed to protect.

I noted above, however, that while James's novel suggests a critique of the young female reader as a standard for print censorship (she is a more capable and intelligent reader than her detractors allow), it also forcefully excludes the young female reader from the circle of readership that James imagines. It would not be an exaggeration to say that for many, certainly not only young women, *The Golden Bowl* is "unreadable." Indeed the stylistic innovations that impeded ease of reading in his earlier novels—the long, convoluted sentences, the slow pace of the plot, the closely mapped psychology of the central characters, the extended metaphors, and elliptical phrases—are most pronounced and developed in James's last completed novel.[2] The joke that James's language qualified for status as its own foreign language, recorded in Leon Edel's biography, comes to mind here. Edel writes: "Jokes became current in cultured circles about the lady who knew 'several languages—French, New Thought, and Henry James,' or the lady who boasted she could read Henry James 'in the original'" (*Master* 302). But we might also recall that early catalogues of pornography were always written in Latin to limit readerly access, that Boccaccio and other authors included in the 1857 obscenity debates were perceived to be less threatening because they did not write in English, and that many novels written in a foreign language were considered safe because of the obstacle that translation imposed.

James's revision of the young female reader in terms of the demand for and destruction of innocence goes hand in hand with his negotiation of adultery in *The Golden Bowl*. It is here too that he is assisted by an unlikely source: the divorce court journalism that continued unabated throughout his career as a novelist. If the representation of adultery was prohibited for the novelist, it was clearly not prohibited for the journalist. Could not the novelist, then, simply import some of the strategies discerned in divorce court journalism—strategies that apparently exempted these publications from the censor's control—for use in the novel? It is unlikely, of course, that James would approach the problem of adultery's representation in such literal terms but the strategies that he developed to represent adultery in *The Golden Bowl* nevertheless bear an uncanny resemblance to the form of the divorce court journalism. Where the divorce court always represents adultery from the perspective of the betrayed party, James represents adultery, for the most part, from the perspective of Maggie, the betrayed party; where the divorce court repeatedly tells the story of adultery from numerous and unreliable perspectives, James's characters, too, repeatedly tell the story of adultery from their differing, unreliable, perspectives; where the divorce court constructs a radically non-linear narration, James's narration, albeit to a lesser extent, circles on itself and consistently disrupts the narrative's linear progression; and where the divorce court was notoriously inconclusive (even when legal judgments were clearly made), James's novel also evades narrative closure. In the same move that James contests the category of the young female reader and the censorship with which it was related, he reinscribes its regulative function in the kinship between the betrayed party's quest for knowledge and her domestic policing activities. For James, the young female reader and the betrayed party come together in a remarkable negotiation of censorship and adultery that is productive of James's most lasting and important aesthetic innovations.

"The Woman Is the Public": James, Print Censorship, and the Category of the Reader

What can James's *The Golden Bowl*, exemplary high culture and famously difficult to read, have to do with current discourses on readership and audience, especially when these discourses take popular culture as their critical focus? In the last section of this chapter I will interrogate more closely the relationship between high and popular culture in terms of the division of reading communities that texts like James's novel effect. In this section, however, I want to consider the contribution that James's criticism makes to the ongoing debates related to censorship and print culture and the young female reader's overdetermined position in these debates.

Two points are crucial to my analysis. First, James dramatizes the relationship between the young female reader and censorship to challenge the restrictive representational economy of late Victorian and Edwardian England. It is no secret that James took vehement opposition to the content constraints imposed on the novelist's craft, but his dramatization of this struggle between author and perceived audience is less often recognized. The fact that this dramatization focuses on the young female reader, moreover, is telling. For James, it is the category of the young female reader that delimits his freedom of representational range; accordingly, it is this category that must be reworked and adapted to a changing and challenging literary landscape.

But it should be clear that to dramatize the young female reader, to thematically render the story of English censorship, is also to participate in the positive censorship effects that this story generates. This is my second point: censorship is productive of literary innovation and advances. Or, as Jeune notes above in the quotation that needs to be extended beyond a too-easy Freudian context, repression can produce art. Despite James's powerfully stated opposition in the face of print constraints, he warmly acknowledged the debt that the English novel owed to these very constraints. While I want to return to "The Future of the Novel" in more detail below, here I want to note that this essay captures the productive capacity of censorship succinctly. The often cited passage in which James takes issue with the novel's "mistrust of any but the most guarded treatment of the great relation between men and women" (107) is followed by a passage, less frequently cited, that reflects on the consequences of an "immense omission in our fiction" (108). Some of the consequences, James allows, are "altogether charming." "I cannot so much as imagine," he continues in a tellingly awkward formulation, "Dickens and Scott *without* the 'love-making' left, as the phrase is, out" (108). The next passage shifts again to assert the familiar Jamesian appeal for a greater latitude in representation to facilitate the novel's growth. But the fact that implicit print censorship could produce something good—a Dickens and a Scott that one would not want to change in any way—speaks to James's own tense location in English print culture. While he clearly desired to be on the cutting edge of novelistic production, to participate in the "future of the novel" and not simply to write about it, he was also indebted to the enabling constraints of his own history and social context. If the story that James tells of a young female reader challenges the category of the young female reader as a standard for censorship, the formal work of the figure of young female reader, especially as she relates to the divorce court's figure of the betrayed party, participates in the process of censorship that James otherwise contests.

A month before writing "The Art of Fiction" James visited Paris and spent at least one evening with Zola and others. He expressed his admiration for the naturalists in a letter to Howells: "Daudet, Goncourt, and Zola," he writes, "do the only kind of work, today, that I respect; and in spite of their ferocious pessimism and their handling of unclean things, they are at least serious and honest. The floods of tepid soap and water under which the name of novels are being vomited forth in England, seem to me, by contrast, to do little honour to our race" (cited in Edel, *Middle* 105). This is strong language in which the "unclean things" written by the French seem considerably less harsh than the "vomit" produced by the English.[3] How, then, could the English novel be transformed into a form of cultural production that garnered respect? The fact that James draws on the already compelling discourse of nation and race indicates the stakes at play in the shaping of the novel. These questions, as James demonstrates in "The Art of Fiction," moreover, are intimately bound up with the practice of censorship. On the one hand, censorship was perceived to uphold national morals and the multifaceted idea of domesticity to which such morals were related; on the other hand, as James and others increasingly argued, censorship inhibited the advance of sophisticated cultural productions and the positive sense of national identity and national pride that such productions instilled. In other words, soap and water novels might be "safe" in moral terms, but they would gain little national respect and credibility for a country keen to be competitive in broader cultural markets.

In this context, it is not surprising to find that "The Art of Fiction" couples its interest in art with an intense preoccupation with the language of prohibition and literary regulation. One encounters references to the wickedness of fiction (45), the "weight of proscription" (45), "the old evangelical hostility to the novel" (45), the novel's perceived "vaguely injurious effect" (47), the novel's capacity to hurt its readers (48), the novel's accessibility to "vulgarization" (49), the way in which the novel suffers "from being marked out or fenced in by prescription" (49), the importance of not imposing limits on fiction (50), the importance of granting the artist her or his subject (56), the importance of "freedom of choice" with respect to subjects (56), the importance of being inclusive (58), Mrs. Grundy (58), "little prohibitory inscriptions on the ends of sticks" (59),[4] an "index expurgatorius" (60), lawful and unlawful subjects (60), "the moral timidity of the usual English novelist" (63), and the "cautious silence on certain subjects" (63). I catalogue these references to emphasize the way in which James consistently returns to the novel's fraught position in the public sphere and its vulnerability to cultural regulation. It would not be necessary to insist on the novelist's freedom of choice, after all, if that freedom of choice was already an accepted fact. The essay as a whole is inflected by language of criminality, proscription, and the law more generally, but these references run alongside a consistent celebration of the novel's freedom, the flipside of the language of prescription and restraint, that prefigures the establishment of a separate aesthetic sphere to which James so signally contributes.

In the passages above, James argues against positions hostile to the novel and his frequent references to rules and prohibitions sometimes refer to the content (a question of social and political censorship) and sometimes to the form (a question of literary rules such as Besant advocates). But if this essay seems to argue against the law, it also participates in a disciplinary version of the law that asserts its own prohibitions and exclusions. Most pointedly, the domain of aesthetic freedom that James celebrates and desires excludes certain readers with every bit as much force as the English novel excludes certain subjects.

In the closing pages of "The Art of Fiction" James is explicitly impatient with the censorship of sexual relations. "In the English novel," he writes, "more than in any other, there is a traditional difference between that which people know and that which they agree to admit they know, that which they see and that which they speak of, that which they feel to be a part of life and that which they allow to enter literature" (670). In response to these gaps between knowledge and the admission of knowledge, James first invokes, to disregard, the view that novels pose a threat to society and morals, and, second, suggests that these gaps derive from the novel's traditional deference to the categories of readers who either lack knowledge (children) or are not supposed to know (women). James writes: "to what degree a purpose in a work of art is a source of corruption I shall not attempt to inquire; the one that seems to me least dangerous is the purpose of making a perfect work. As for our novel, I may say lastly on this score that as we find it in England today it strikes me as addressed in a large degree to 'young people,' and that this in itself constitutes a presumption that it will be rather shy. There are certain things which it is generally agreed not to discuss, not even to mention, before young people. That is very well, but the absence of discussion is not a symptom of moral passion" (63). This passage animates the tension between reading dangers and social unrest (the novel as a "source of corruption") *and* freedom of speech and aesthetic value (the "perfect work") discussed in Chapter 1. What is most interesting, however, is that print censorship is not linked with the police, legal authorities, or even the institutions responsible for printing, publishing, and disseminating the novel. Rather, it is associated with the perceived reader, "the young person." The circulating libraries, of course, contributed to the construction of this category of the vulnerable reader (the young person, young women, unmarried women, or women, in general) but what print institutions and cultural critics alike assume is that sexual knowledge (however minimal or mundane) should be restricted for vulnerable readers. Here James takes his critique of censorship a step further. It is not only that censorship prevents the development of a national identity grounded in healthy and vital cultural production, but also that censorship does not even accomplish the moral purity that it promises. The explicit representation of "certain subjects" may or may not be a source of corruption, but the cautious *silence* on these same subjects also may be a source of corruption. James himself is careful in his formulations here but like Justin MacCarthy, Fitzjames Stephen and others he suggests that silence by no means guarantees "moral passion." Indeed, in *The Golden Bowl* it will be the absence of discussion, and the censorship and regulation of discussion, that initially permits and subsequently assists the *immoral* passion that the novel records.

"The Art of Fiction" occupies an important place in the development of an aesthetics of the novel and very few anthologies of the novel exclude it from the provisional histories that such collections produce. But it also occupies, I am arguing, an important place in the history of censorship. If Robert Louis Stevenson responded to the aesthetic concerns of this essay, a host of other critics, most of them anonymous, responded to the article's subtext on censorship. Three months after its publication, for example, George Moore published "A New Censorship of Literature" in the *Pall Mall Gazette*. Moore's article is interesting both for the ways in which it responds to ideas already presented in James's earlier article and for how it anticipates the critique that James would also reluctantly make in his later, and more cranky, "The Future of the Novel." Moore writes the following:

> With the canons of art as laid down by Mr. Henry James and Mr. Besant I have no fault to find; I think them all excellent, but, while applauding the good counsel to "go to nature and study it," I cannot refrain from saying: "Yes, yes; but we cannot do as you advise.... What is nature but religion and morals? and the circulating library forbids discussion on such subjects." The subtraction of these two important elements of life throws the reading of fiction into the hands of young girls and widows of sedentary habits; for them political questions have no interest, and it is by this final amputation that humanity becomes headless, trunkless, limbless, and is con-

verted into the pulseless, non-vertebrate, jelly-fish sort of thing which, securely packed in tin-cornered boxes, is sent from the London depot and scattered through the drawing-rooms of the United Kingdom. (27–28)

This description echoes critiques of the English policy of implicit print censorship cited earlier, notably Justin MacCarthy's recognition of the English desire to render women as "incorporeal, angelic, colourless, passionless, helpless" (48). The body evaporates. Whether it is the women in fiction who are incorporeal or fiction as a whole that is stripped, piece by piece, of its body, the result is a literature that lacks vigor and vitality. The story of adultery, in particular, unlike the story of murder, requires a sentient body. To reintroduce the "political question," as Moore and others realized, was to reintroduce the body and either actively to participate in the censorship of young women's reading habits or to extend the range of young women's reading and thus to transform the category of the young female reader. Reading, in this context, becomes a political question of real concern in the final decades of the nineteenth century.

The politics of reading, however, was typically masked as the more legitimate question of the politics of aesthetic value. While the development of the novel was always linked with English national identity, in the mid-Victorian period this identity was grounded in the purity of the novel, its moral distinction from the French novel, and its cultivation of a private domestic sphere, guided by women, to enhance and inculcate the values of the nation. The link between the novel and national identity, in other words, relied upon an improvisational and reluctantly accepted print censorship. By the 1880s, however, English writers and cultural critics were becoming visibly restless, and sometimes rebellious, in the context of these constraints. As I noted in Chapter 1, the moral categories which distinguished the French from the English in the English's favor, were slowly displaced by aesthetic categories which distinguished the French from the English in the French's favor. It became increasingly difficult to derive national esteem and self-respect from a national ideology based on morality and imperial strength alone. As both James and Moore noted, the English novel became an embarrassment when it was forced to obey the dictates of the nursery rather than the drawing room. Another critic, in an article entitled "A Circulating Censorship" that directly links print censorship with the evisceration of English literature and the loss of national credibility, writes: "Novels are watered down into dreariness and vapidity. . . . literature is degraded, and the taste for really worthy books becomes obsolete in

England" (747). If earlier critics argued that immoral literature posed a threat to national stability, this critic turns the argument around and considers the threat that moral literature posed to an English national identity powerfully inflected and shaped by cultural formations. The essay closes, forebodingly, with a single question: "Who will save England?" (748).

James's critical writings afford an excellent opportunity to trace this relationship between print censorship, the category of the female reader, and the formation of a national culture. Once again, it is the middle term—the category of the young female reader—that is necessary to an adequate understanding of both print censorship and the English novel. James's specific comments on the young female reader are marked, first, by a definitional clarity—the young female reader presides over English novelistic production—and, second, by an analysis of the limitations of this form of internal constraint. When he refers to his imagined audience, as noted above, James repeatedly invokes the categories of youth and gender. In addition to "The Art of Fiction" references, James writes in his essay on Zola that the English novel "is almost always addressed to young unmarried ladies" ("Zola" 868). The most concise expression of this view, however, is found in the dramatic essay "An Animated Conversation" when one of his characters sharply remarks: "the woman is the public" (68). The very phrase "the woman is the public," of course, takes issue with the prevailing association of women with privacy; the claim that the woman *is* the public provides a subtle critique of the default female reader that challenges the underpinnings of domestic ideology in general.

The restrictions imposed by the female reader as default reader are self-evident in James's criticism. For example, in his review of Zola's fiction, James writes: "half of life is a sealed book to young unmarried ladies, and how can a novel be worth anything that deals only with half of life? How can a portrait be painted (in any way to be recognizable) of half a face?" (869). This restriction, this half-told story, is especially grievous when it impinges on the novel's relationship with knowledge and modes of knowing. "[I]t may be said that our English system is a good thing for virgins and boys," James writes, "and a bad thing for the novel itself, when the novel is regarded as something more than a simple *jeu d'esprit*, and considered as a composition that treats of life at large and helps us to *know*" ("Zola" 869). And in "An Animated Conversation" Darcy cautiously notes "that though they [women] are very welcome readers, it is fatal to write for them" (68). The literary consequences of this "damnable restriction" are repeatedly tabulated by James: the novel suffers from an incompleteness of picture; it is unable to exploit its epistemological strengths; it cannot compete in an international marketplace; and it is bland, predictable, and drearily conventional.

James, however, was by no means eager to alienate his reading public. The problem that he sought to resolve, as Anne Margolis has so nicely demonstrated, was reconciling his desire to write bolder, fuller fiction with his economic and personal interest in reaching the widest possible audience. If it was fatal to write for women, it was nevertheless possible to use the damnable restriction of the category of the female reader to develop aesthetic innovations that would sidestep censorious restrictions. James could challenge the default female reader in his criticism but he could not simply ignore this internal restraint in his fiction. His novels, novellas, and short stories, moreover, indicate that it was not as fatal to write for women as James's criticism implies. Indeed, I am arguing that James repeatedly thematizes print restrictions and the default reader to advance his own novelistic inquiry and development. As James was well aware, the national habit of repression and print censorship was bound up with the category of the reader; to turn censorship into a factor of art, the writer had to be attuned to the reader and reshape the reader in a manner that at once respected and defied novelistic limitations.

The default category of the female reader was most limiting and most potentially productive, however, when the novelist confronted the topic of adultery. It was this subject matter, after all, that was specifically prohibited in English print culture with the one flagrant exception of the divorce court journalism. It is when James speculates on the representation of adultery, therefore, that his recognition of the link between print censorship and the reading public is most pronounced. In his *Notebooks*, for example, James addresses the question of audience and national conventions in a manner that echoes Stack's reference to the "legal prose" of adultery in England: "if I were writing for a French public the whole thing [the plot of *The Wings of the Dove*] would be simple—the elder, the 'other,' woman would simply be the mistress of the young man.... But one can do so little with English adultery—it is so much less inevitable [than French], and so much more ugly in all its hiding and lying side. It is so undermined by our immemorial tradition of original freedom of choice, and by our practically universal acceptance of divorce" (103–4). Similarly, in his notes for *The Golden Bowl*, James summarizes the plot and then writes: "*Everything* about it qualifies it for *Harper's* except the subject—or rather, I mean, except the adulterine element in the subject. But may it not be simply a question of *handling* that?" (115). Margolis argues that in his post-theater fiction James "sets out to discover and perfect a strategy which will enable him to present sexual relations in general, and the 'adulterine element' in particular, as a legitimate subject for the Anglo-American novelist" (119). James recognizes, then, that the aesthetic crux lies not with the subject matter, strictly speaking, but rather with a question of "handling" it, a question, that is, of technique and form. As James later asks: *how* can the novelist handle adultery so that it is acceptable to the young female reader? His answer, given his deep commitment to the relationship between knowledge and the novel (the novel helps the reader "to *know*," as he notes above), is not surprising. Indeed, it is remarkably straightforward. Instead of presenting adultery as a story of criminal passion, James repeatedly presents it as a story of knowledge. More than any other English novelist, James develops an epistemology of adultery through which to make adultery palatable, even morally compelling, to his imagined audience. James translates the problem of strategy — which I have been arguing was a problem of censorship — into a problem of seeing and of knowing, and specifically seeing and knowing in the dramatic context of the deceived party. At the same time, however, he confronts the specificity of the novel itself and combines formal innovations with a theoretical attempt to negotiate an autonomous aesthetic realm, and, thus, to counter the claim that aesthetic representations — the representation of adultery, in particular — may be socially disruptive.

I want to close this section on James's contradictory response to the category of the young female reader with a consideration of his 1899 essay, "The Future of the Novel." More than James's other critical writings, "The Future of the Novel" directly engages the question of readership with respect to literary production. The classification of new readers, what James calls the "immense public" (100), in particular, creates a problem for the critic. Like Thomas Wright in 1883 and Wilkie Collins before him, James is concerned to identify and classify "the unknown public." In earlier decades the novel's dissemination could be more easily traced but in 1899 the book "is almost everywhere," and because the novel penetrates "easiest and farthest," its readers are almost impossible to determine. What one can be certain of is that this new public, "abysmally absorbent" (100), is cause for concern and "uneasiness" (101). At first this uneasiness is simply understood in terms of a levelling of taste: "the sort of taste that used to be called "good" has nothing to do with the matter: we are so demonstrably in presence of millions for whom taste is but an obscure, confused, immediate instinct. In the flare of railway bookstalls, in the shop-fronts of most booksellers, especially the provincial, in the advertisements in the weekly newspapers, and in fifty places besides, this testimony to the general preference triumphs" (101). James assumes that "good" taste — the good taste required to read and enjoy a Jamesian novel — has been displaced by the general preference advanced by the "millions." It is no accident, moreover, that the taste of millions is reduced to "instinct" and that it is reflected not just in the places that James records but also in the *public visibility* of the novel itself. In other words, the very fact that novels are so publicly and promiscuously available reflects the fact that good taste has been compromised. James is clearly unable to consider and value another definition of good taste, a definition that acknowledges the place of instinct, the emotions, and the body in the cultivation of a legitimate aesthetics. Similarly, he is unable to grant, with the exception of an elite few, the immense public's capacity to respond to art as he defines it. If, according to James, the new reading public contributes to a levelling of taste it also, more seriously, contributes to "the vulgarization of literature in general" (103). "The high prosperity of fiction has marched, very directly, with another 'sign of the times,' the demoralization, the vulgarization of literature in general, the increasing familiarity of all such methods of communication, the making itself supremely felt, as it were, of the presence of the ladies and children — by whom I mean, in other words, the reader irreflective and uncritical" (103). The irreflective and uncritical reader, the instinctual reader, becomes in this passage the source of the novel's evisceration (as Moore also noted above) and, consequently, the weakened state of the English nation. Like Pinard in the *Madame Bovary* trial, James assumes, in short, that women are guided not by reason in their reading practices, but rather by their "senses." While James at the outset of this essay was hesitant to classify the reader, referring only to "an immense public," he now confidently attributes the demoralization and vulgarization of literature not to the immense and rapidly growing public in general but rather to a crucial segment of that public, "ladies and children."

Once again, this focus on audience runs parallel to a focus on the novel's freedom; the novel "will stretch anywhere — it will take in absolutely everything" (102). The margin for "individual freedom" is "vast" (104); the novel "can do simply everything" and "it moves in a luxurious independence of rules and restrictions," James argues (105). There is a tension, then, between the evident restrictions imposed by an audience composed largely of female readers and the ostensible freedom that the novel enjoys. James himself acknowledges this tension; many novelists do not take advantage of the novel's freedom and the "form of the novel that is stupid on the general question of its freedom is the single form that may, *a priori*, be unhesitatingly pronounced wrong" (106–7). But while maintaining the novel's freedom, James locates the contemporary challenge for the novelist in the circumvention of censorship in terms of the young reader; the novelist should exercise her or his freedom, in other words, by challenging the print censorship that supports popular taste and the demoralization and vulgarization of literature. It is the category of the vulnerable reader, and the novelist's engagement with that category, that will vitally inform the development of the novel. Not surprisingly, the category of the vulnerable reader is most forceful, and hence most restrictive, when the question of sexuality, what James euphemistically calls the "delicate case," arises: "nothing . . . strikes me more as meeting this description [of the possibilities open to the novelist] than the predicament finally arrived at, for the fictive energy, in consequence of our long and most respectable tradition of making it defer supremely, in the treatment, say of a delicate case, to the inexperience of the young. . . . By what it shall decide to do in respect to the 'young' the great prose fable will, from any serious point of view, practically see itself stand or fall. What is clear is that it has, among us, veritably never chosen—it has, mainly, always obeyed an unreasoning instinct of avoidance in which there has often been much that was felicitous" (107). The result of deferring to the inexperience of the young, James notes, was a "mistrust of any but the most guarded treatment of the great relation between men and women" (107). While James grants that this strategy worked for Dickens and Scott, as I noted earlier, he argues that it no longer serves for the contemporary novelist. At this point James turns from the revolutionary impact of the new reading public to the revolutionary impact of the female author. Interestingly, the two are closely linked. James writes:

> It would be curious—really a great comedy—if the renewal [of the novel] were to spring just from the satiety of the very readers for whom the sacrifices have hitherto been supposed to be made. It bears on that that as nothing is more salient in English life to-day, to fresh eyes, than the revolution taking place in the position and outlook of women . . . so we may very well yet see the female elbow itself, kept in increasing activity by the play of the pen, smash with final resonance the window all this time most superstitiously closed. . . . It is the opinion of some observers that when women do obtain a free hand they will not repay their long debt to the precautionary attitude of men by unlimited consideration for natural delicacy of the latter. (109)

It is here that James comes closest to refiguring the characteristics through which the young female reader is typically defined. Young female readers themselves are deciding that they have had enough of an education based on avoidance, evasion, and silence; it is young female readers who are deciding to make the choice that James urges upon the writer in general, to negotiate the representation of a "delicate case" in the context of a young and female public. It is young female readers who, like James, are deciding that perhaps the limitations imposed by this readership no longer obtain. It is young female readers, finally, who, by redefining the range of the novel are also redefining the categories through which their reading has been previously restricted. It is ironic—a comedy—that the very category of readers for whom restrictions were imposed, is the category that most successfully rebels. Or is it? As James argued in "The Art of Fiction," the avoidance of prohibited topics did not guarantee, by any means, a morally pure literature. Indeed, print censorship might promote the very thing—in this case, the cultural authority of women—it was designed to prevent. While I noted above that James gives little credit to female readers in his critical writings (and, in this context, there is a real tension between his representation of female readers as "irreflective" and "uncritical" and his sense that they may be a positive source of cultural revolution), in his novels he is much more likely to rework the category of the female reader in a manner that resonates more closely with these final comments in "The Future of the Novel." And it is in relation to the topic of adultery—the visibility of adultery—that these issues are most fully worked out.

James's critical work clarifies his own views on the category of the young female reader: like Caroline Norton, in his criticism James repeatedly challenges the privilege accorded to the young female reader in English print culture. He does not challenge the category itself, but rather wishes for a different, less limited, projected audience. But, again like Norton, in his novels—and especially in *The Golden Bowl*—James launches a powerful invective against the *category* of the female reader: instead of arguing that young women should not read English novels, he suggests that young women are perhaps better equipped—less irredeemably innocent, more potentially knowledgeable—to deal with the novel than English cultural authorities imagine.

"Reading for the Trip": Maggie's Lessons

While many of James's novels and tales dramatize the young female reader in the context of adultery—one thinks of "The Author of Beltraffio," "A

London Life," "In the Cage," *The Awkward Age, What Maisie Knew*, and *The Wings of the Dove*, for example — *The Golden Bowl* provides the most complex and challenging approach to the English interweaving of readership, adultery, and implicit censorship. As in *What Maisie Knew* in which, as the title emphasizes, adultery is translated as a question of knowledge, in *The Golden Bowl* the *knowledge* of the female protagonist/reader becomes a subject of thematic urgency. How much knowledge (read: adultery) can the innocent young female reader be exposed to without danger? At what point is it dangerous for her *not* to know? It is this latter question that occupies James in *The Golden Bowl*. James not only demonstrates that innocence is a danger, but also that knowledge can work in the interests of dominant cultural concerns. In other words, female knowledge does not necessarily have to pose a threat to social stability and gender relations. His project, then, is at once strikingly radical and resoundingly conservative: James's version of the young female reader is educated, intelligent, and knowing (a radical revision of prevailing stereotypes) *and* a canny enforcer of domestic morality and the national culture to which such domesticity was related (a conservative revision of the link between women, domesticity, and national culture).

The Golden Bowl records a history of adulterous (and quasi-incestuous) relations in London's upper classes. Critics tend to interpret the novel's central character Maggie in terms of her skill as a reluctant, but ultimately successful, figural author (and as a double, in this context, for James himself). I want to consider instead what happens when we interpret Maggie as a reader and specifically a reader of the text of adultery. Maggie's position as a young female reader, a reader, indeed, who has not yet completed her intended reading assignments, is introduced early on. Like Beatrice, moreover, Maggie is first and foremost a reader of people rather than books. Initially her most pressing reading project is that of reading the story of her husband, a story that is told not only in old history books but also in his looks, movements, and conversation. It is Maggie's very status as a young female reader, however, that inhibits the success of this project. Maggie represents the paradigmatic young woman, innocent and vulnerable, for whom reading generates only "innocent pleasures, pleasures without penalties" (9). The fact that the novel opens with a reference to what Maggie has not read in books (the "rows of volumes" in the British Museum) and to what she has not read in the person because it is hidden (the part, the Prince says, that is "left out" of the books) puts an emphasis on the practice of reading. But how can Maggie read the Prince's public history of "the marriages, the crimes, the follies, the boundless *bêtises* of other people" (7), or his private history of a deep betrayal that hits much closer to home? Maggie is little prepared for the text of adultery that the Prince, however unthinkingly, delivers.

Maggie's initial inability to confront or comprehend betrayal is made clear. The Prince asks Maggie if she trusts him and she blushes; this is an area into which the young female reader does not typically venture. The Prince "had perceived on the spot that any *serious* discussion of veracity, of loyalty, or rather of the want of them, practically took her unprepared, as if it were quite new to her" (12). The possibility of betrayal is a "new" subject for Maggie as it also is for the stereotyped English female reader. But Maggie quickly recovers from her discomfort and assures the Prince that she believes him truthful and loyal. She is confident that he does not "dissemble or deceive" and this confidence will not be shaken; it is a "watertight compartment." Indeed, it is "the ship itself," what keeps one afloat. And then she takes the metaphor a step further to announce that this confidence is "one's reading for the trip" (12).

But while Maggie is busy reading the text of her husband's veracity, another text infiltrates between the lines of the expected story. It is the story of adultery that *The Golden Bowl* challenges Maggie as a female reader not only to understand but also to engage. James's point is simple but important: even when the young woman (as reader or otherwise) is protected from sexual betrayal she is also imbricated in it; it behooves her, therefore, to understand life in all of its messy complexity both more fully to understand her implication in the networks of sexuality from which she assumed herself exempt and consciously to act in a manner that advances her own interests. Where Maggie anticipates reading for the trip of her marriage that documents her husband's loyalty and nobility, she discovers instead a very different story that requires a refashioning of the categories through which she perceives her world. Because her society is so carefully orchestrated to protect her from such knowledge—a knowledge in this book that guards one against harm rather than incites danger—Maggie must learn to read a language that she does not at first understand, the language of betrayal and immorality, without the aid of a tutor.

To be sure, Maggie at first participates in the process—at once social, legal, and political—of maintaining her position of innocence embodied. She explains to her father: "I wouldn't in any case have let her [Charlotte] tell me what would have been dreadful to me. For such wounds and shames [Charlotte's poverty] *are* dreadful: at least . . . I suppose they are; for what, as I say, do I know of them? I don't *want* to know!" (138). It is only much later, after she has taken small reluctant steps toward the knowledge that is, notoriously, "a fascination as well as a fear" (402), that Maggie understands the ideological work that the category of the innocent young woman performs. Maggie is incredulous that Fanny thinks she may be happy when she is, in fact, "jealous, unhappy, tormented." Fanny explains, "I've never thought of you but as *outside* of ugly things, so ignorant of any falsity or cruelty or vulgarity as never to have to be touched by them or to touch them" (380); and Maggie's response smartly discloses the hidden assumption of Fanny's logic of censorship: "You've only believed me contented then because you've believed me stupid?" (381). But what implications follow from this construction of the innocent — or in Maggie's terms "stupid" — young woman?

While critics analyze Maggie's growing comprehension in the context of the struggle between innocence and experience, ignorance and knowledge, I am arguing that this drama also stages the social construction of the young female reader. The implication of the story, in this context, is twofold: innocence does not protect the young woman from evil; and innocence can, in some cases, aid and abet the evil it is designed to dispel. Maggie's knowledge does not simply expose her husband's and stepmother's affair, but also exposes the standard of female innocence, and the construction of the young female reader to which it is related, as a weak guarantee for moral passion. Indeed, the *intelligent* young woman who comprehends sexual misconduct introduces an anomaly into the organization of English domestic relations and the English novel. As Maggie says, her "screaming" cannot possibly conform to Fanny's perception of her innocence. And Fanny ruefully acknowledges her point: "Oh, your screaming," she says, "I've granted you, is something new. I must fit it in somewhere" (381). I want to turn now to the way in which Maggie's innocence is displaced by her slow accumulation of disparate facts that jar her epistemological confidence and compel her to take a stance as an active reader of her world.

If Maggie's introduction in Book First represents her radical failure to read (her failure to engage in her "reading for the trip" and her desire to avoid pleasures *with* penalties), Book Second represents Maggie beginning to read. This shift parallels another change in Maggie's outlook, recorded by the Assinghams in the last chapter of Book First. Maggie, Fanny tells her husband, "is beginning to doubt. To doubt, for the first time . . . of her wonderful little judgment of her wonderful little world" (278–79). Maggie has good reason to doubt of course: her husband is having an affair with her stepmother. Her "doubt of fidelity," as Bob Assingham aptly puts it, reflects the first testing of the Prince's "veracity"—his ability to deceive and dissemble—and launches, almost silently, the watertight compartment that figures Maggie's reading for the trip. Maggie's immediate response to her situation, indeed, is an avid desire to read *everything*: the Prince's conversation, the Prince's countenance, the small daily details of their lives, and the conversations of the people by whom they are surrounded.

The challenge for James, then, is to make adultery visible to the young female reader. If he can make adultery clear to her without too gravely challenging his period's representational economy, he will have fulfilled one of his stated goals: to write a novel of adultery that does not alienate his reading public. As Maggie waits for her husband, her own reading provides little consolation: "she couldn't help it if she couldn't read her pale novel—ah, that, *par exemple*, was beyond her!—but she could at least sit by the lamp with her book" (306). Instead, like Beatrice in *Lost and Saved*, she reads the more difficult text of the adulterous body. When the Prince finally arrives, Maggie is keenly alert to the physical signs through which he silently communicates: he is "*visibly* uncertain"; his uncertainty "was written in the face he for the first minute showed her" (308). And Maggie's desire to avoid the question of the Prince's veracity is put to the test: "it had been written only for those seconds, and it had appeared to go, quickly, after they began to talk; but while it lasted it had been written large, and, though she didn't quite know what she had expected of him, she felt she hadn't expected the least shade of embarrassment. What had made the embarrassment—she called it embarrassment so as to be able to assure herself that she put it at the very worst—what had made the particular look was his thus distinguishably wishing to see how he should find her. Why *first*?—that had, later on, kept coming to her; the question dangled there as if it were the key to everything" (308).[5] Maggie is startled. She reads the Prince's countenance and she introduces a new concept into her moral vocabulary: her husband's embarrassment. The fact that the Prince takes his cue from her in responding to the situation, moreover, disturbs her—it strikes her as the "key to everything"—and contributes to her sense of the "violence" of the situation (308). If the Prince takes his cue from Maggie and modifies his behavior accordingly then Maggie has reason to doubt his veracity (why, after all, does he need to apply to her before expressing himself? what does he have to hide?). This situation, moreover, provides a subtle allegory for reading in this novel as a whole. Like the Prince, the novelist must defer to the female reader—to what she knows and to what she can handle—before presenting her or his story.

Unlike Beatrice whose slow awakening to adultery follows a more legible path, Maggie's mistrust is triggered by only the minutest of events and her reading project accordingly proceeds by the smallest of steps. Nothing in particular, to her knowledge, has happened and yet Maggie is suddenly eager to know everything. Unwittingly, she pursues the story of adultery *before* any clear signs of adultery have emerged. She does not witness her husband in a compromising position, no maid knocks on her door with a story of betrayal, there is no trace of a letter sent, a conversation overheard. Everything is exactly as it always has been. And yet Maggie is suddenly alert, attentive, and sharply curious. If she has, in a sense, been sleepwalking through her marriage in the hope that if she does nothing then nothing will change, it could be said that she now wakes up. The structure of the novel contributes to this impression of Maggie's sudden swing into the world. In Book First, Maggie is a faint, almost absent, character moving quietly in the background of the novel's central events; in Book Second, by contrast, she moves to center stage as a powerful force with an active, voluble imagination, and a *presence* that cannot be ignored. When the Prince later returns after dressing for dinner, for example, Maggie makes her presence felt. She wants to hear a full account of his visit to Matcham—"she wished to hear everything about it" (315)—to hear, in other words, the story from which she has been protected in Book First. It bears repeating that she is not asking for the story of adultery. She is simply open to being a participatory audience to her husband's travels. With respect to Charlotte, Maggie demonstrates "the same show of desire to hear all her story" (319). She wants the "whole picture" (320). She thinks that the Prince, limited by his capacity as a husband, will not have told her everything and she wants "to miss as little as possible of Charlotte's story" (321). If the stated story is innocent enough—the Prince and Charlotte relate a pleasant visit in the country—the communication of it is much less so. Because the story of adultery cannot be openly communicated, Maggie must learn to be a super-subtle reader of the signs by which adultery betrays itself. Instead of the female reader "irreflective and uncritical" whom James scorns in his criticism, Maggie is the ideally sophisticated reader surpassing even educated male norms of readerly practice. She hears the ostensible story of Matcham but she is also sensitive to the register through which this story and subsequent stories are communicated: the Prince's and Charlotte's carefully syncopated responses, their excessive care, their practice of watching her, their small hesitations, and their telling silences.

Maggie, moreover, does not limit her reading only to the Prince's and Charlotte's stories. She reanimates her old desire to know her husband better through his history—the "reading for the trip" of her marriage to which she earlier referred. To this end, she extends her reading of the Prince's countenance and conversation to her reading of the "rows of volumes" in the British Museum. Her reading sharply departs from an English national culture (and the brand of English imperialism to which it was related) to embrace the older and more unsettling tradition of the Roman empire. Fanny, however, assumes an easy annexation of Roman history with English cultural values. Maggie has only visited the museum on one previous occasion and Fanny imagines Maggie's resulting reading experience as "enlarging and inspiring" (408), replete with "lessons" on how to be a heroine (409). Maggie's reading, Fanny assumes, should more firmly secure Maggie's position as dutiful wife, as mute heroine befitting her position as a princess glowing in the established glories of the past. It is no accident, however, that on the same day that Maggie seeks out new reading experiences she also discovers the golden bowl. After visiting the museum, Maggie visits some shops—"an old bookseller's, an old printmonger's"—and the antique store where she purchases the golden bowl. Like the Prince's cryptic body language, like his country's history, the golden bowl will tell a story, not of fairy-tale princes and princesses, but rather of adultery. It is a story that Maggie discovers, with shock, that she can read.

The equation between the golden bowl and adultery is not, of course, instantly made. Indeed, Maggie buys the golden bowl, loaded emblem of adultery that it is, and innocently carries it home as a present for her father. Struck by Maggie's simplicity, however, the shopkeeper is unable to rest easy with his knowledge that Maggie has purchased a gift with a flaw, and several days later he pays Maggie a visit in her home. In the midst of explaining his exceptional visit, the shopkeeper notices a photograph of the Prince and Charlotte and tells another story of a much more damaging flaw. The Prince and Charlotte were once intimate, Maggie learns, they shopped together, they considered buying the bowl but did not do so. Maggie knows how to read this story in a manner that the shopkeeper could not possibly have imagined. The signs by which adultery betrays itself—a flawed bowl, a fragmented story—require the most exacting attention.

A quasi-legal model, never remote in this novel, is most evident when Maggie tries to fill in the pieces of the missing story. But even before Maggie has the "proof" or "evidence" of the bowl she is deeply suspicious. In a series of exchanges between Maggie and Fanny, for example, at first Fanny is unwilling to be interrogated by Maggie and counters Maggie's questions with her own. The result is a barrage of questions as the two women refuse to relinquish the role of interrogator. A brief example will suffice. Maggie opens the dialogue: "What awfulness, in heaven's name, is there between them [Charlotte and the Prince]? What do you believe, what do you *know*?" Fanny: "'Between them?' What do you mean?" Maggie: "Anything there shouldn't be, there shouldn't have *been*—all this time. Do you believe there is—or what's your idea?" Fanny: "Do you speak from a suspicion of your own?" (378–79). Fanny eventually gains the upper hand in this conversation, but as her discussions with Maggie advance in Book Second, Maggie's knowledge of the adultery undermines Fanny's authority and she finally submits to Maggie's questions and accepts her own responsibility in the domestic arrangements.

Maggie's interrogation of the Prince in chapters 34 and 35 is even more direct, however, in its approach to the story of adultery. Nevertheless, explicit articulation of this story is what all the characters scrupulously avoid. Unlike countless Victorian novels in which characters approach the very edge of adultery only to avert it at the last minute, this novel approaches the edge of articulation only to retreat before the word is spoken. Like Beatrice who, with proof of adultery, is nevertheless challenged by her husband, Maggie's proof is also subject to the Prince's scrutiny. It should be incumbent upon the Prince to provide his supplement to the shopkeeper's story; instead, he obsessively focuses on Maggie's story. The Prince's desire for a "straighter telling" resembles a "cross-examination" (460) to which Maggie responds with her own story of a cross-examination: she asked the vendor "question upon question" (462), she tells the Prince, and if her explanation was "weak," it adhered, nevertheless, to the "facts" (460). The story of adultery figures, of course, an important moment in Maggie's shift from innocence to what she calls "real knowledge" (447). When Maggie questions the Prince about the bowl, for example, the word knowledge and its cognates are repeated twenty-three times in two and a half pages (446–48). Maggie had doubted and suspected; now she knows. It is as if she is suddenly thrown into a giddy, new world filled with the knowledge that has been denied her. Here all the passion and erotic intensity derived from an adulterous affair is transferred to the sheer epistemological thrill of discovering adultery.

The tables have turned. The story of adultery from which Maggie was excluded is now the story from which she excludes others. If the father, thematically and figuratively, prohibits certain texts from young women's reading programs, in *The Golden Bowl* it is the young woman herself who chooses not to communicate the story of adultery to her father. The shopkeeper only intended that the golden bowl should be purchased in full knowledge of its flaw, that a loving daughter should not give such flawed gift to her father. Maggie, however, not only withholds the golden bowl, she also withholds the story of adultery that it signifies. Similarly, while she tells her husband the story of the bowl, she does not tell him how she plans to respond to it. The Prince's lack of knowledge, his "sense of uncertainty," threatens his "dignity"; Maggie "had handed him over to an ignorance that couldn't even try to become indifferent" (517). The Prince struggles and his struggle is intensified by the calculated ignorance to which he is subjected.

When she discovers the story of adultery, then, Maggie also learns something important about the way that knowledge works. She learns that to withhold or censor knowledge is to occupy a position of power. The young female reader's powerlessness is accordingly assured through a concentrated collusion between novelists, printers, and cultural authorities to withhold vast areas of knowledge—the great relation between men and women—from these readers. It is no accident that Maggie is obsessed not only with the possibility of adultery—the "awfulness" between the Prince and Charlotte—but also with the manipulation of knowledge. James thematizes the category of the young female reader and the culture of print censorship to which it is related, while he also displays a series of literary strategies that both make Maggie's reading lessons more demanding and register the forms of self-censorship that allow James himself a greater authorial freedom.

Maggie, in a sense, is required to learn a new language, a language that will give her entry to the privileged places already enjoyed by the Prince and Charlotte. As David Hall notes in a very different context: "Literacy connoted cultural authority; illiteracy, cultural inferiority and exclusion" (153). Against other critics who stress that the unabashedly materialistic values of Adam Verver and Maggie were also shared by James and his disappointing position in the literary marketplace, I would argue that this novel advances cultural capital over economic capital. Charlotte's evident literacy in things European gives her an advantage over Maggie; it allows her, for example, to invent "a different and inferior" standard for Maggie (307) and to fine tune the process by which Maggie is excluded from intimate conversations with her own husband and with Fanny, from dances and dinners, and from social gatherings like the weekend in the country. The fact that these exclusions are chosen by Maggie herself does not diminish her reduced cultural authority in the context of the more practiced social decorum of Charlotte and, to a lesser degree, the Prince. As Maggie later learns, and as a capitalist market culture has long known, the ability to produce in one "the sense of highly choosing" (525) was the most accomplished reflection of cultural authority. It is only when Maggie endeavors to produce this sense in Charlotte and succeeds that the tables have indeed turned (524). By this time—when Maggie tellingly pursues Charlotte with the book—Maggie has finally gained a degree of cultural literacy, a fluency with the world she inhabits, that marks her as a young female reader who can learn. More importantly, Maggie's necessary literacy also opens the possibility that one of James's strategies is to write a difficult book, to shift the burden of censorship from the young female reader to the work of the language itself.

The scene in which Maggie pursues Charlotte demands closer scrutiny. When Maggie wants to talk with Charlotte she needs a "pretext" and the pretext she comes upon is a book. This book, moreover, is not just any book but rather an old novel "in the charming original form of its three volumes" (523). What we find here is Maggie *using* the novel in the very manner that it has been used against her; by making explicit and material the novel's social function as a pretext obscuring larger ideological goals, James indicates the more subtle ideological work that the genre of the domestic novel performs. The three-decker novel, of course, signifies the proper Victorian novel tailored to the restrictive dictates of the young female reader. In this context, the fact that Maggie brings Charlotte the "right" volume—Charlotte accidentally has the second volume when she thought she had the first—is not only about Maggie's control of the story, of what gets read, but is also about the attempted construction of Charlotte as a young female reader. If Charlotte turns from the text of adultery in which she participates to the old Victorian novel in which such stories are always carefully excised, Maggie insists that her turn will not be in form only. At the same time, neither the Victorian novel nor the readers for whom it is ostensibly written are as innocent as they appear. Maggie has learned this lesson only too clearly. The novel is a sign of both eros (it hides in the folds of Charlotte's dress) and deception (it disguises—or covers—her purpose): "She had caught a glimpse, before Mrs. Verver disappeared, of her carrying a book—made out, half lost in the folds of her white dress, the dark cover of a volume that was to explain her purpose in case of her being met with surprise" (523).

Maggie's pursuit of Charlotte, her replacement of the wrong volume with the right, is usually interpreted by critics in terms of her narrative authority. Leon Edel, for example, argues that the "final artifact is the work of a printer, a book, a three-decker novel. . . . Order, sequence, and chronology are restored. Each has the right volume" (5:222). And Jolly similarly notes that Maggie restores the traditional order and, in the process, exercises the "tyranny of three volumes" over Charlotte "with an irresponsible but despotic power" (191). But neither critic considers that the volumes, correctly ordered, remain unread and untouched at the end of the chapter. Indeed, Charlotte exercises her right to dismiss this form of cultural authority: she picks up the first volume and then she puts it down again and walks away. This refusal to be tethered to the restraints and the imposition of ignorance dictated by the three-decker novel cannot, of course, free Charlotte into the deeper, more complete knowledge that she desires. But it does affirm her consistent negotiation of the fraught cultural location that she occupies as she actively, if unsuccessfully, fights the "bath of benevolence" by which Maggie's freedom of movement was restricted (330). Maggie's willingness to play Charlotte's game, moreover, indicates the distance she has traveled from the "soothing" effects of such a bath. Immersed now in a different bath of lies, deceit, and denials, Maggie finds her world expanded — these new fictions, after all, broaden her arena of action — and she welcomes the role that she can play here. When she lies and asserts that she has "failed" in her attempt to separate Charlotte and Adam, she, like Charlotte, also rejects the standard of readerly innocence that the three-decker represents: "Maggie waited; she looked, as her companion had done a moment before, at the two books on the seat; she put them together and laid them down; then she made up her mind. 'I've failed!' she sounded out before Charlotte, having given her time, walked away" (531). The fact that Maggie's lie coincides with putting the traditional novel down signals her departure from the conventional and gendered reading practices dictated by the novel as it also signals James's own development of different writing strategies that demand different, more strenuous and more accomplished, reading skills. Maggie may attempt to restore a traditional order, but this order is accepted neither by Charlotte nor, ultimately, by Maggie herself. Instead, James's novel requires and constructs a different sort of reader.[6]

 James's thematics of censorship, then, represents censorship as, at best, ineffectual, and, at worst, enabling the very representations and situations it is designed to prohibit. In other words, at worst, this novel demonstrates that censorship, instead of eliminating adultery, produces the possibilities for its enactment. To put it crudely, had the Prince and Charlotte's prior relationship been "represented" to Maggie, then their subsequent adulterous affair would not have been possible. It should be noted that this is a narrative, moreover, that positively thrives on denials, deceptions, and obfuscations. From the Prince's and Charlotte's adulterous deception to Maggie's blatant denial of knowledge of the deception to the staggering number of euphemisms for adultery, *The Golden Bowl* can almost be read as a celebration of the restrictions by which it is ostensibly most shackled. It turns its impediment, its handicap, into a restless, exuberant, and certainly aesthetic energy. The denial or censorship of adultery, moreover, not only facilitates acts of adultery but also renders impossible the legal function of appropriate punishment. Instead, adultery is accommodated by a narrative apparatus that closely resembles the narrative techniques of the divorce court journalism. The law no longer works most forcefully in the register of condemnation and punishment but rather in the display of the *possibility* of adultery. Denials, after all, are often the opposite of reassuring, and in *The Golden Bowl* the rhetoric of denial only inflames Maggie's suspicion and sharpens her desire to know.

What is denied does not disappear. This point is perhaps made most clear in the unlikely example of Adam Verver and the haunted text. What exactly does her father know? Maggie painfully wonders. She is unable to discern the exact degree of his knowledge and critics have been no more successful in this enterprise. Adam's somewhat cryptic desire "to conjure away the ghost of the anomalous" (365) — to eliminate or deny what does not fit into prevailing categories of perception — corresponds to the studied avoidance of problematic topics exhibited throughout the text while it also testifies to the ghost-like persistence of such topics even in the absence of discussion. It is interesting, then, that this rhetoric of haunting informs Adam's discussion of their situation: "What it comes to, I daresay, is that there's something haunting — as if it were a bit uncanny — in such a consciousness of our general comfort and privilege. Unless, indeed . . . it's only I to whom, fantastically, it says so much. That's all I mean, at any rate — that it's 'sort of' soothing; as if we were sitting about on divans, with pigtails, smoking opium and seeing visions. 'Let us then be up and doing' — what is it Longfellow says? That seems sometimes to ring out; like the police breaking in — into our opium den — to give us a shake. But the beauty of it is, at the same time, that we *are* doing; we're doing, that is, after all, what we went in for" (366). There *is* something haunting in their general comfort and privilege. But what haunts here is less the anomaly of adultery than the profit of censorship. Indeed, the haunting is conflated with the soothing as Adam adjusts his terminology to describe his perception of the situation. At this point, two metaphors are introduced that, I want to argue, shift the passage from a consideration of Maggie's and Adam's situations to a consideration of the novel, censorship, and the law. The first metaphor describes their situation: "as if we were . . . smoking opium and seeing visions." The second metaphor describes the disruption of this situation: "like the police breaking in." The reference to opium and visions, of course, recalls the Victorian anti-novel debates. If novels were like opium in their generation of visions and addictions, *The Golden Bowl*, a novel of adultery, would be especially disruptive in this respect. Like opium addictions, then, fiction addictions require police intervention. But Adam as quickly shifts away from this necessity, in effect, noting that the work of the police is *already* being done. It is to the accommodation of adultery in the novel, then, that I now turn.

"Like the Police Breaking In": The Drama of the Divorce Court

The hostility to the novel was motivated, in part, by a fear that novelistic representation was contagious. This fear itself presupposed the novel's potent position in the public sphere; the novel, after all, was only perceived to be dangerous because it was so integrally woven into the fabric of everyday life. While James thematized this hostility in his extended meditations on censorship and the young female reader in *The Golden Bowl*, he also developed stylistic devices designed to either shape a more subtle reader or alienate less subtle readers and thus render his novel less open to reproach. But if his novel registers a sensitive negotiation of the *prohibition* against the representation of adultery, it also registers a careful mobilization of the one arena in which there was a *proliferation* of discourses related to adultery, the divorce court journalism. Indeed, in *The Golden Bowl* James negotiates the representation of adultery in a manner that bears a striking resemblance to the popular genre of divorce court journalism. The second half of the novel is told from the perspective of Maggie, the betrayed party in the adulterous triangle; the story of adultery is told repeatedly; the reliability of evidence is questioned and challenged; and the narration, overall, is thoroughly informed by legal structures and language (conversations are "cross-examinations," objects and subtle actions are "evidence," subjects are "judges" and "witnesses," and so on).[7]

The word adultery may not once be mentioned in this novel, but adultery itself is certainly represented and it is represented in a particularly English form. The reader is encouraged to share not the turbulent passions of adulterous desire, but the galvanizing anxiety of a character who uncertainly watches her husband for signs of adulterous betrayal. It is this focus on the betrayed party which foregrounds the epistemological questions with which *The Golden Bowl* is most concerned. It is this perspective, too, which foregrounds what interests me here: the novel's accommodation of adultery in terms of what I am calling domestic surveillance. The choice of point of view is a rhetorical *and* a political choice, as Susan Lanser illustrates, and it inescapably structures the concerns which a narrative will engage (101). If the censorship of adultery enables the practice of adultery, Maggie's pursuit of the truth, her encounters with sexual tensions and ambiguities, and her ultimate desire to avoid confrontation contribute to a representation of adultery that works in the service of domestic regulation and stability. Maggie reads the text of adultery and revises the legal construction of the female reader in the process, but this revision is, at the same time, circumscribed by the law. If the prohibition against the representation of adultery, in other words, encourages adultery, the proliferation of the representation of adultery serves to regulate and discipline it. This regulation works by way of the visibility of adultery, a visibility which stages sex and the law as intertwined in the service of knowledge. The law, however, does not entirely break in (and here the equivocal metaphor is important); rather, the law works by simply staging and restaging the quest for (a never fully grasped) truth, the staging, in other words, of the epistemology of adultery.

My reference to domestic surveillance and regulation clearly borrows from Foucault's elaboration of surveillance as regulation (as opposed to more visible forms of punishment) in the context of what he calls disciplinary power (as opposed to contract or law). There have been at least two Foucauldian readings of *The Golden Bowl*. In "The Subject of Power" Leo Bersani argues that "James's novels are model demonstrations of the definition of power proposed in *La valonte de savoir*" (10), specifically in James's fascination with the intimacy between discourse and power and the "equivalence . . . between exercising power and knowing" (10). Unlike most Foucauldian readings, however, Bersani argues that the power/knowledge matrix does not subdue Maggie to its inscrutable, but nevertheless powerfully normative, boundaries. On the contrary, Maggie "escapes" the normalization which the novel, both thematically and formally, embraces. "Resistance to power could be attributed to the *unlocatability* of the point of resistance," Bersani argues (11), and Maggie as an over-determined heroine, cannot be pinned down.

Mark Seltzer, by contrast, approaches the novel as a considerably more conservative vehicle through which normalization is successfully effected. He argues that "Maggie's actions in the second half of the novel represent an almost diagrammatic institution of the rule of the norm" (90), and he treats the novel, accordingly, as a disciplinary mechanism, an uncanny enactment of the Foucauldian disciplinary dynamic. He extends Bersani's argument to draw an equivalence between knowledge, power, language, *and* love. "Far from being opposed," he notes, "love and power in *The Golden Bowl* are two ways of saying the same thing" (66, 94). And he contradicts Bersani's argument in stressing that Maggie in no way escapes this network. Rather, she controls the other characters through a process of "sympathetic identification" (71) which bears a striking resemblance to British imperial policy. Indeed, Seltzer labels her loving manipulation of the relations by whom she is surrounded (her husband, her father, and her mother-in-law) "domestic colonialism" (72).

What these readings convey, however, is a certain abstraction of literary culture and literary production.[8] The point which neither Bersani nor Seltzer considers, for example, is the extent to which the act of *adultery* itself mobilizes disciplinary strategies in a distinctive manner. The fact that the most prominent discursive genre for the representation of adultery was the divorce court journalism with its energetic and voluminous transformation of sex into a legal and sensational discourse is clearly important in this respect. Equally absent from Bersani's and Seltzer's accounts is a consideration of readership and print censorship. How can explorations of social transgression and containment make sense without an understanding of the political resonance of the novel as a genre, its designated and constructed readers, and its dialogue with other discursive formations? I do not want to reduce literary production and aesthetic innovation to popular or material sources, but I do want to animate the always charged and fertile interplay between these different arenas of diverse cultural activity.

James was a consistent participant in the debates on print censorship and his own narrative innovations are clearly informed by, and at times resistant to, the central issues raised by these debates: the default young female reader; the prohibition against the representation of adultery; the conflict between morality and freedom; and the role of the novel in the articulation of national ideology. James was also keenly interested in the drama of the divorce court. Where else could he find a public and legitimate display of the central topics—adultery, sexuality—denied to him as a serious novelist? For James, and for countless other cultural commentators, the divorce court not only confirmed the open secret of the presence of adultery in English life, but also provided a set of strategies through which adultery could be legitimately represented. In addition to vividly displaying the fact of adultery, then, it also circumvented the taboo against the *representation* of adultery.

At first glance, it will seem misguided to suggest that James's work is in any way informed by newspaper journalism. James's dislike of the press and what he calls a "newspaperized world" (*Notebooks* 42), after all, is well-known. And yet the apparently contradictory position that he "privately enjoyed public scandals" has only been recently remarked by Adeline Tintner (253). Tintner draws a connection between the 1891 Card Scandal and "The Real Thing," between a divorce case for which James was a juror and "The Given Case," and between the Dreyfus Affair and both *The Ambassadors* and "Mora Montravers." I find Tintner's comparison between "A Given Case" and the divorce court too literal, but with one reservation my argument below accords with her claim that the "form of presentation [of the story] is determined by the procedure in an actual divorce case" (262). My reservation is that one does not need to base such a claim on an "actual" case; Tintner's argument is considerably more compelling if James's form of presentation is compared to the *journalistic* documentation of divorce cases and not simply to one particular case in which he was involved.[9] This consideration would explain why the form of presentation which Tintner finds in "A Given Case" is not unique to that story, but rather is a central feature of James's style when he represents adultery. The "virtual 'courtroom' procedure" and the "quasi-legal terms" (Tintner counts over seventy) which Tintner identifies in this story are in fact found in much of James's later work (which invariably deals with some version of infidelity).

Tintner's recognition that the atmosphere of such scandals informed James's work, however, is central to my argument here: the divorce court column represented one legitimate method of representing adultery as it, at the same time, generated discussions related to press censorship and literary censorship. When Henry James writes to his brother William that doing "British Juryman threw lights — and glooms" (*Treacherous* 180), he suggests that this duty was not wholly unprofitable for himself as a writer. In addition, he attended the Parnell divorce trial in 1889 and, as Edel points out, used the words "thrilling" and "throbbing" to describe it (*Treacherous* 168). From the American perspective, Sara Davis also notes that James was in New York when the Beecher-Tilton divorce scandal was exposed (Theodore Tilton accused the minister Henry Ward Beecher of misconduct with

Tilton's wife, Elizabeth), and the *Nation* for which James was then writing, covered the trial each week (575). It seems undeniable that James was thoroughly engrossed in the climate of the divorce court at a time when he was beginning to explore the representation of adultery in the novel. His first *Notebook* entry for *The Golden Bowl*, for example — 12 January 1887 — follows directly on the heels of the Dilke and Campbell divorce scandals.

But while James was fascinated by divorce cases, he also deplored the publicity with which they were so often associated. James's depiction of the press's failure to respect personal privacy is reflected by the "publishing scoundrel" in "The Aspern Papers" and by Flack in the short novel *The Reverberator* (titled, tellingly, after the newspaper on which the narrative is focused), both of which were published in 1888. In the same year James also published "A London Life" which deals explicitly with divorce and scandal. *The Reverberator* was inspired in part by May Marcy McClellan's exposure in the American press of, in James's words, the "personal domestic arrangements and secrets" of the Venetian families with whom the young woman was staying (*Notebooks* 40). James's response to this small scandal reflects both the atmosphere of the period and his own aesthetic attitude: "One sketches one's age but imperfectly if one doesn't touch on that particular matter: the invasion, the impudence and shamelessness, of the newspaper and interviewer, the devouring *publicity* of life, the extinction of all sense between public and private" (40), and he further remarks on the "mania for publicity which is one of the striking signs of our times" (42). This mania for publicity, moreover, is explicitly associated with the divorce court in James's essay on Robert Louis Stevenson. Novelists, James argues, must find a way of grappling with the "extraordinary" and the "next report of the next divorce case (to give an instance) shall offer us a picture of astounding combinations of circumstance and behaviour" ("Stevenson" 1249).

There is perhaps no more astounding combination of circumstance and behavior than the Prince's affair with his stepmother and Maggie's careful struggle to conceal this extraordinary fact from her father. But to a much greater extent than the divorce court, this novel *suspends* explicit punishment. Even in the divorce court the specific punishment allotted to the participating parties is much less important than the way in which the institution of the divorce court in general produces a sense of being constantly watched. In *The Golden Bowl* James demonstrates how an attitude derived from the divorce court can effectively work to discipline adultery. It is enough, in this novel, to know simply that one is watched, and the consequences of adulterous discovery are much more enduring and penetrating precisely because direct confrontation and explicit punishment are avoided. At the same time James borrows narrative strategies from the divorce court journalism the better to legitimize his own approach to prohibited subject matter.

To recognize the extent to which adultery was automatically associated with publicity is to clarify one of James's specific concerns in *The Golden Bowl*. Fanny's panic in response to the Prince and Charlotte's adultery is expressed in these terms. Musing on the implications of their affair and her own complicity in its development, she thinks that the world would not know "sooner or later what she had done, or would know it, at least, only if the final consequence should be some overwhelming publicity" (202). Fanny fixes this "possibility" hard, sees "the straight shaft from the lamp of a policeman in the act of playing his inquisitive flash over an opposite housefront," and feels "incriminated" (202). The policeman's light upon housefronts and upon Fanny's carriage, like evil lurking in the corridors of home, catches Fanny by surprise and she feels "blind terror." The police do not break in; rather, they have, in a sense, always already been there. Publicity clearly works in the service of the law: it contributes to the prevention of crime (the policeman's light might catch the criminal) and, more important, it makes visible the participants in criminal activity and it uses this visibility as both a punishment and a deterrent.

As Maggie's sense that "there may be something—something wrong and dreadful, something they [the Prince and Charlotte] cover up" (379) sharpens into the reality of adultery, her energy shifts from the discovery of adultery to the disciplining of adultery. The divorce court, the "straight shaft from the lamp of a policeman," is rigorously avoided in this novel; but to avoid the publicity of the divorce court that so alarms Fanny, a form of this publicity must be exercised within the protected space of the home. To this end, Maggie puts into play her own form of "precaution and policy" to match, and override, the precaution and policy she has already witnessed between the Prince and Charlotte. To avoid the specific work of the law she becomes an agent of the law in a much deeper and more unsettling sense. And it is here that the divorce court with its reviled publicity can most emphatically blazon its success. For the publicity works. To avoid the court Maggie carries the court—gingerly, expertly, respectfully—into her home.

It is Maggie's divided position as at once betrayed wife surprised into a deep love for her husband and domestic detective coolly cleaning up the mess of adultery to reestablish the legitimate couples that has excited such controversy. Is Maggie a "saint or sinner"? Or as Seltzer puts it, a character of love or a character of power (65)?[10] By situating the criticism in the context of love and power, Seltzer can persuasively collapse the distinction between these two terms: "Maggie controls precisely through the power of sympathy" (71). This form of control—a form of domestic surveillance that misses nothing precisely because of its keen capacity for identification—bears a close resemblance to the novelistic practice of James himself, as many critics have remarked. Maggie, for example, confides to Fanny that she "goes about on tiptoe, I watch for every sound, I feel every breath" (380). And James describes his novelistic practice in similar terms: "I track my uncontrollable footsteps," he writes in the Preface, ever vigilant not to let them escape "even on the stealthiest tiptoe" (1323). Maggie, other characters in the novel (Fanny, for example, who comments to Bob: "we must go on tiptoe. We must simply watch and wait" [281]), and James practice a policy of domestic surveillance to maintain domestic stability. It is not, however, simply the characters and the author who participate in this process. The formal design of the novel engages the reader too in the practice of domestic policing and close watching. Point of view, as noted above, had ideological consequences; the reader shares Maggie's growing uncertainty, her gripping desire to know, and the tentative steps by which she learns to read the text of adultery. This scrutiny of the adulterous plot, moreover, does not unsettle domestic stability. James's revision of the young female reader as the reader of adultery only binds her more tightly to the domestic sphere and her moral role within it.

It is through sympathy, compassion, and, privacy—all qualities associated with the genre of the novel itself—that Maggie succeeds in at once testing and securing her position within the domestic sphere. There is, of course, a long tradition from George Eliot to Richard Rorty praising the novel's cultivation of sympathy and compassion. In 1866 one critic, for example, deftly links such sympathy to justice and benevolence. "Deficiency in the two great social virtues, justice and benevolence," this critic writes, "is less often due to conscious dishonesty or heartlessness than to an inability to 'enter into the mind and circumstances' of the suffering or the injured—to look at the matter not exclusively from your own, but also from his, point of view" ("Uses" 324). And it is fiction, in particular, that contributes to "the power of enlarged and ready sympathy" (324). Indeed, such sympathy is one of the "practical effects of the imagination"; reading, in this context, is advocated as an antidote to discrepancies in class relations and a deterrent to crime. Criminals, this writer argues, are unable to imagine vividly enough the consequences of their crimes.

But if sympathetic identification promotes justice and benevolence, if it deters criminals and fosters instead a loving and compassionate regard for others, it can also be used to opposite ends as Maggie amply demonstrates. Maggie tells her father that "one must always . . . have some imagination of the states of others" (486), and it is precisely her ability to exercise this imagination that allows her to exact such a cruel and lasting punishment for Charlotte and such humiliated submission from her husband. How can one rest easy in one's adulterous affair if one feels that the walls have eyes? Unless one is erotically inspired by this possibility of being watched — and it could be argued that this is one of the directions that the novel of adultery and its descriptions of desire take — this sense of being watched, controlled and, in a perverse sense, authorized in one's adultery will detract from the erotic freedom that adultery otherwise promises. Sympathetic identification, however, is also interesting in another way. Inverting or twisting the connection between reading and the sensual body, sympathetic identification establishes a connection between reading and the disciplined body. Consider, for example, the way in which sympathetic identification involves an abstraction of the reader's body (and in this sense conforms more to the taste of reflection than to the taste of sense) to enable the occupation of another's body (and it is here that the abstracted body forcefully returns). Maggie's sympathetic identification uses the novel's engagement with the body to curtail rather than incite acts of adultery.

The lamp of the policeman, then, is replaced by Maggie's much more sophisticated figurative "telescope." The telescope, like Maggie's policy overall, must be concealed; her "unremitted rule" is still not "under any provocation to produce it in public" (449). The "special point" in Maggie's awakening consciousness is "the necessity of concealing excitement" and of "keeping the thing born [her suspicion] out of sight" (302). Maggie wants "to bring about a difference, touch by touch, without letting either of the three, and least of all her father, so much as suspect her hand. If they should suspect they would want a reason" (322). The crucial thing Maggie realizes is not to let the others see that she sees, she must not let herself be "suspected of suspicion" (372, 383).[11] Maggie's suspicion inescapably situates her in the vicious circle — the whole vertiginous game. Her position resembles that of Helen in *The Tenant of Wildfell Hall* who, when she discovers her husband's adultery, feels "like a criminal" (347), or Basil's in *Basil* who, when he discovers his wife's adultery, characterizes her seducer as "a wretch as guilty as himself" (160). Now Maggie too finds that adultery implicates even the most apparently "innocent" parties.

Where the policeman's light illuminated the facades of houses, moreover, Maggie's telescope penetrates these facades to enter the private spaces of the home and, more complexly, the psyche. Maggie puts herself in Charlotte's shoes to the point where Charlotte cannot escape; as a domestic detective she controls Charlotte's actions with the deft moves of a subtle and stealthy spy. Maggie "breathed Charlotte's cold air":

> [She] turned with her, in growing compassion, this way and that, hovered behind her while she felt her ask herself where then she should rest. Marvellous the manner in which, under such imaginations, Maggie thus circled and lingered — quite as if she were, materially, following her unseen, counting every step she helplessly wasted, noting every hindrance that brought her to a pause . . . she absolutely looked with Charlotte's grave eyes. . . . There were hours of intensity, for a week or two, when it was for all the world as if she had guardedly tracked her stepmother, in the great house, from room to room and from window to window, only to see her, here and there and everywhere, *try* her uneasy look, question her issue and her fate. (504–5)

Similarly, Maggie's "imagination tracked" the Prince (513). As a domestic detective Maggie tracks the criminals, experiencing, through the force of her sympathetic imagination, their anxieties and tensions, anticipating their evasions, their retreats, and their questions. The absence of apparent violence in this approach — there are no angry exchanges — belies the deeper symbolic violence to which both Charlotte and the Prince are subjected.

While this practice of seeing through another's eyes — in both coercive and corrective terms — seems to be the special province of the female reader, it is not, in fact, limited to Maggie's domain. To a minor extent, both the Prince and Fanny also have a desire to occupy, in a sense, the body of another. The Prince admits to Fanny his fear of "being 'off' someday *without* knowing it" and solicits a policy of sympathetic identification to correct and clarify his own vision: "I shall always want, your eyes. Through *them* I wish to look — even at the risk of their showing me what I mayn't like" (23). But it will be Fanny herself who later uses this technique to correct her vision of happy domesticity. She confides to her husband: "it was as if I were suddenly, with a kind of horrible push, seeing through their [the Prince's and Charlotte's] eyes" (272). It is Charlotte's inability, by contrast, to practice such sympathetic identification that sends her reeling in Book Second. She tells Fanny, "I can't put myself into Maggie's skin — I can't" (228).

More important, however, Maggie's father, the other betrayed party in this novel, also demonstrates a facility for domestic surveillance, hardened by an apparent absence of sympathy. Interestingly, the person from whom Maggie has most desperately tried to keep the story of adultery, is the person, figuratively speaking, who withholds that same story for generic female readers. If a watchful attitude is useful in orchestrating adultery as both the Prince and Charlotte suggest, it is even more useful in controlling adultery. The most vivid, and chilling, deployment of domestic surveillance describes Adam's "indescribable air of weaving his spell" as if he were "mildly and modestly" "holding in one of his pocketed hands the end of long silken halter looped around her [Charlotte's] beautiful neck. He didn't twist it, yet it was there; he didn't drag her, but she came" (510, 508). This "silken halter" is later extended as Adam's figure, "constantly crossing, in its regular revolutions, the further end of any watched perspective," maintains Charlotte's subdued and utterly wretched state: "the thing that never failed now as an item in the picture was that gleam of the silken noose, his wife's immaterial tether, so marked to Maggie's sense during her last month in the country. Mrs. Verver's straight neck had certainly not slipped it; nor had the other end of the long cord — oh, quite conveniently long! — disengaged its smaller loop from the hooked thumb that, with his fingers closed upon it, her husband kept out of sight" (539–40). Adam's power then is kept "out of sight" (like Maggie's telescope) and his manner has the "marked peculiarity of seeming on no occasion to *have* an attitude" (559). What is distinctive about Adam's control is its lack of specificity: Maggie "felt him still simply weave his web and play out his long fine cord" (559).

Father and daughter work together to subdue, if not eliminate, adulterous desire. Maggie's success as a domestic detective resides in her ability to create the impression of a constant, but unidentified, threat; a constant, but unidentified, surveillance. The Prince and Charlotte experience the "crisis . . . after the fashion of the established ghost, felt, through the dark hours as a constant possibility" (452); they are haunted by what cannot be spoken but also by what cannot be entirely suppressed. Maggie, by simply "watching and waiting," produces her desired effect. The "strain of the perfunctory" is the element in which they all live to the point that it takes on the "likeness of some spacious chamber in a haunted house" (509) from which escape is impossible; and for the Prince it is like "being sent to prison" (513).

And yet unlike Charlotte, who similarly seems as if she is caged or imprisoned (465–66), the Prince is "lurking there [in his prison] by his own act and his own choice" (545). The Prince has taken Maggie's "inspecting gaze," to borrow Foucault's terminology, and interiorized it to the point where "he is his own overseer . . . exercising . . . this surveillance over, and against himself" (*Power* 155). Maggie belies the equivocal note of freedom, the breakdown of the opposition between captivity (the prison) and freedom, when she draws on the French Revolution as a ready analogy for their relationship:

It was every moment more and more for her as if she were waiting with him in his prison—waiting with some gleam of remembrance of how noble captives in the French Revolution, the darkness of the Terror, used to make a feast, or a high discourse, of their last poor resources.... She might have been losing her head verily in her husband's eyes—since he didn't know, all the while, that the sudden freedom of her words was but the diverted intensity of her disposition personally to seize him. He didn't know, either, that this was his manner—now she *was* with him—of beguiling audaciously the supremacy of suspense. For the people of the French Revolution, assuredly, there wasn't suspense; the scaffold, for those she was thinking of, was certain—whereas what Charlotte's telegram announced was, short of some incalculable error, clear liberation. Just the point, however, was in its being clearer to herself than to him; her clearnesses, clearances—those she had so all but abjectly laboured for—threatened to crowd upon her in the form of one of the clusters of angelic heads, the peopled shafts of light beating down through iron bars, that regale, on occasion, precisely the fevered pitch of those who are in chains. (547)

Maggie's domestic translation of the divorce court works by way of suspense rather than the scaffold. It is slow and attenuated rather than quick and dramatic. It looks like freedom and yet it is something else: the Prince suspensefully *waits*. He waits to be told what to do; unable fully to command the situation, he defers to the judgment of his wife—her clearnesses, clearances—and lets her words and actions weave a spell which is as tightly binding and imprisoning as the spell through which Adam entraps Charlotte. Once an active player in the game of adultery (although the rules, admittedly, were dictated by Charlotte) the Prince now waits for a punishment, the scaffold or otherwise, that will not come. It is not surprising, moreover, to find adultery linked with the French Reign of Terror. This image also completes a subtext which has threaded through the novel since its opening: James's implicit dialogue with the French novel and its association with adultery.[12] In the first conversation between Maggie and the Prince the reader is told that the Prince speaks English "too well" and he cannot speak it worse. "'When I speak worse,'" he tells Maggie, "'I speak French.'... intimating thus that there were discriminations, doubtless of the invidious kind, for which that language was most apt" (5). And Maggie's dream "of making good, of making better" her own French ironically foreshadows the "French revolution" to come. And yet the real social and political turmoil that Paget and others imagined would follow from representations of adultery is averted. There is no scaffold, no real revolution, no reign of terror; there is only the devastating, paralyzing "supremacy of suspense" as the Prince quietly waits in his prison built of words, watching eyes, and careful silences.

If Maggie and her father practice a policy of domestic surveillance that parallels and privatizes the disciplinary work of the divorce court, the form of *The Golden Bowl* similarly echoes the form of the divorce court journalism. To be sure, the form and the content here are intertwined. The perspective of the betrayed party, for example, dictates a focus on domestic detection, discovery, and surveillance. The absence of closure, similarly, upholds the supremacy of suspense. Nevertheless, because the form of the divorce court journalism so closely resembles narrative innovations associated with the modernist novel, I want to isolate three formal strategies (in addition to the point of view of the betrayed party already discussed above) on which James draws to represent adultery in the English novel.

First, *The Golden Bowl*, as a story of adultery, is by no means straightforward. Despite its apparently linear structure this is not a linear narration. Thematically, the narrative is obsessed with causality but structurally it tends toward repetition and circularity. And, indeed, even its thematic interest in causality shades into a privileging of circles that defy causality. Fanny, for example, claims somewhat vindictively that it was Maggie who "*began* the vicious circle" (289). In another exchange between Fanny and Bob, however, Fanny names Charlotte as the cause (205–7). And earlier Fanny considers herself uneasily as the "producing cause" (202); Charlotte's sense of security also rests on the fact that she had come to the same conclusion. Fanny is "helpless," Charlotte tells the Prince, because it "all began with her" and she cannot, therefore, condemn the lovers without condemning herself (250). Instead of determining causes (the three origins cited above do not permit of reconciliation), James is concerned to illustrate not who began the vicious circle (as Fanny tries to) but rather how the vicious circle does not have, by definition, an origin. In the second *Notebooks* entry for the novel James writes: "the whole situation works in a kind of inevitable rotary way—in what would be called a vicious circle.... the rotary motion, the vicious circle, consists in the reasons which each of the parties give[s] the other" (74–75). And this rotary motion is a much better description of the novel's formal structure than its loose linear plotting.

Consider the story of Charlotte and the Prince's failure to purchase the bowl. It is related to the reader in five different versions. At the beginning of Chapter 33 the shopkeeper tells Maggie about his encounter with Charlotte and the Prince; Maggie relates this account, in part, first to Fanny (in Chapter 33) and then to the Prince (in Chapter 34). In the following chapter, the Prince and Maggie return to the incident, or "anecdote," again. And there is finally the first description, related in Chapter 6, of the Prince and Charlotte's encounter with the vendor. Similarly, Fanny and Bob's exchanges, while conforming to a linear time line, repeat and reinterpret previous events in the text. Because so much of the novel is devoted to reflections of the principal characters, moreover, a sense of linear flow is disrupted. Like the golden bowl itself, this story is a story that is told and retold in fragments.

Second, the narrative is much more unreliable than one might at first imagine. When Fanny notes that neither the Prince's nor Charlotte's "word in such a matter [of adultery] would count" (269), she highlights a degree of unreliability, if not blatant deception, that applies to all of the characters. And yet we are disarmed by a narrator who gives the impression that, despite the enormous number of lies told in the text, the narrative itself is untainted by this tendency toward evasion and distortion. If characters and actions are untrustworthy in the extreme, the narrative itself at least seems highly trustworthy. But is it? On one level, the sheer number of euphemisms, circumlocutions, and ambiguous phrases contribute to a sense of unreliability. With James's passion for the unspecified "it," the narrative evades decisive summary. What exactly happened? After reading 567 pages, many of which are preoccupied with the quest for knowledge, it is impossible for the reader to answer this question.

On another level, the structure of the novel is misleading. It is divided into two parts and this division implies that half the narrative will be devoted to the Prince, after whom the first part is named, and half to the Princess, after whom the second part is named. Indeed, many critics persist in reading the novel in this way despite the fact that the first part by no means focuses on the Prince. The second part, on the other hand, is much more exclusively devoted to Maggie and is much more consistent, although not wholly so, in telling the story from Maggie's limited perspective. James, of course, contributes to this misperception by declaring in the Preface that the two parts convey "the consciousness of but two of the characters [the Prince and the Princess]" (xlii). And in this divided text, James notes, the narrator's stance is also unavoidably divided and unreliable. There is the "pretense" of detached authorship which seems, James declares, to "*ostensibly* reign" (xlii). James's stress on "ostensibly" underscores the pretense by which the unwary reader might be deluded (like Charlotte, least canny and subtle of readers, whose "deluded condition" is what the novel aspires, at all costs, to avoid). It would be more accurate, James insists, to understand the narrator as interested, involved, *near* to his characters. As James famously puts it: "I get down into the arena and do my best to live and breathe and rub shoulders and converse with the persons engaged in the struggle" (xlii). But how, then, can this narrator tell a reliable story? The only reliable account that the narrator can give is a reliable account of unreliability, as the Preface itself avows. A lot more could be said here about unreliability in *The Golden Bowl*; but I only want to indicate that James refines and extends a limited narrative point of view, introduced in his earlier narratives of adultery, in which the pretense of detachment renders his novel at once "safe" and radically unreliable.

Finally, the novel closes on a note of suspense rather than decision. Several critics have commented on *The Golden Bowl's* conclusion which is central to this study insofar as I am arguing that the novel ends on a note of unresolved suspicion which animates both Maggie's response to her husband and the reader's response to the text. This absence of closure, moreover, again parallels formal characteristics associated with the divorce court journalism. The final paragraph of the novel reads as follows: "'that's our help, you see,' she added—to point further her moral. It kept him before her therefore, taking in—or trying to—what she so wonderfully gave. He tried, too clearly, to please her—to meet her in her own way; but with the result only that, close to her, her face kept before him, his hands holding her shoulders, his whole act enclosing her, he presently echoed: 'See? I see nothing but *you*.' And the truth of it had, with this force, after a moment, so strangely lighted his eyes that, as for pity and dread of them, she buried her own in his breast" (567). The debate addresses "the end" for which Maggie has so patiently (and ruthlessly, and lovingly) worked as either affirmative (Maggie's marriage, after all, is still intact) or negative (who would want such a marriage?) In short, is the fact that Maggie and the Prince are finally alone together and embracing a good thing or a bad thing? Why can't Maggie look her husband in the eyes? Why does she feel pity and dread?

Marianna Torgovnick, like Joseph Boone, reads the ending as complicating the novel's commitment to the traditional marriage plot. Several critics read in the reference to pity and dread a reference to Aristotle, and Torgovnick provocatively situates this reference in the context of *Oedipus Rex*. I would suggest, however, that the reference to Aristotle indicates the extent to which James's novel *departs* from tragedy, and especially tragedy in relation to the representation of adultery by which the Continental tradition was marked. Even a summary consideration of Aristotelian tenets should make this point clear. Tragedy, following Aristotle, is an imitation of a complete action and a series of events inspiring pity and fear; the events should come as a surprise and follow as cause and effect (what Aristotle refers to over and over again as "*probable or necessary* sequence"); and the pity and fear should be cathartic. James, however, goes to considerable trouble to illustrate exactly the opposite of each of these points: the action is not complete (neither in terms of a comprehensive point of view nor narrative closure), it defies causality, and it would be difficult to argue for the novel's carthartic effect.

James's translation of Aristotle's pity and fear into pity and *dread* is not, I would argue, gratuitous. No critic to my knowledge has discussed this conclusion in a Kierkegaardian context, and indeed Kierkegaard had not been translated at the time of James's writing, but his comments on dread and the possibility with which it was associated are apt in terms of James's text: "dread is by the aid of faith absolutely educative, laying bare as it does all finite aims and discovering all their deceptions. And no Grand Inquisitor has in readiness such terrible tortures as has dread, and no spy knows how to attack more artfully the man he suspects, choosing the instant when he is weakest, nor knows how to lay traps where he will be caught and ensnared, as dread knows how, and no sharp-witted judge knows how to interrogate, to examine the accused, as dread does, which never lets him escape, neither by diversion nor by noise, neither at work nor at play, neither by day nor by night" (275). William Spanos places the distinction between dread and fear described by Kierkegaard at "the heart of the existential/phenomenological critique of positivist humanism" (165). He cites Heidegger's distinction between dread and fear, borrowed from Kierkegaard, as follows: "We are always *afraid* of this or that definite thing, which threatens us in this or that definite way"; whereas dread has no object. The "indefiniteness of *what* we dread is not just lack of definition: it represents the essential impossibility of defining the 'what'" (cited in Spanos 165).[13]

In this context, James's substitution of dread for fear captures the tenor of his novel as a whole; dread permeates not only the final embrace between Maggie and the Prince, but also the other domestic relationships, each of which is marked, as I have indicated, by a domestic surveillance always sensed but nowhere explicit. For Kierkegaard, however, dread is not wholly a thing to be regretted. "He who is educated by dread is educated by possibility, and only the man who is educated by possibility is educated in accordance with his infinity. . . . If at the beginning of his education he misunderstands the anguish of dread, so that it does not lead him to faith but away from faith, then he is lost. On the other hand, he who is educated by possibility remains with dread, does not allow himself to be deceived by its countless counterfeits, he recalls the past precisely; then at last the attacks of dread, though they are fearful, are not such that he flees from them"

(276–78). When the terms of the case are dread and possibility, doubt and suspicion, there are no easy answers. No criminal may be placed under arrest because the limits of representation do not permit of definitive judgment and because *everyone* is in some sense a criminal: the vicious circle has no origin. In *The Golden Bowl* there is no solution to the mystery, no resolution to the novel, and society does not, therefore, emerge exempt from the domestic crimes in which all the characters are implicated. There may be "evidence" of the Prince and Charlotte's affair "up and down London" (397), but the evidence resides in the context of mutual implication and, as such, figures the flipside of a policy of surveillance, equally diffused, which maintains the "supremacy of suspense" (547) without the authority of arrest. As Fanny recognizes, Maggie's "doubt of fidelity" produces an atmosphere of unrelenting "suspicion and dread." Toward the end of the novel Maggie couches her suspicion of infidelity in the context of unexpressed dread and unbounded possibilities: "there were yet other possibilities, as it seemed to Maggie; there were always too many, and all of them things of evil when one's nerves had at last done for one all that nerves could do; had left one in a darkness of prowling dangers that was like the predicament of the night-watcher in a beast-haunted land who has no more means for a fire. She might, with such nerves, have supposed almost anything of anyone; anything almost of poor Bob Assingham . . . anything, verily, yes, of the good priest" (517). But Maggie's pervasive suspicion should come as no surprise. Fanny has warned the reader early on: "One can never be ideally sure of anything. There are always possibilities" (65).

"A Little Community of the Elect": Redefining the Reading Public

In *The Golden Bowl* the popular genre of divorce court journalism is adapted for the serious novel. While James distances his writing from the aspects of this journalism that he despises, the structural affinities—especially the inculcation of suspicion and doubt and the practice of domestic surveillance in the context of adultery—are nevertheless remarkable. The parallels between the divorce court journalism and James's literary representations of adultery reinforce the central arguments that I am making in this book: first, that in the English tradition adultery was translated as epistemology and represented in the service of the law; and second, that English modernist innovations are inextricable from the social and historical conditions of literary production, specifically the discourse on censorship and the divorce court journalism. As the epigraph to this chapter asserts, James used the discourse on censorship to fuel his aesthetic innovations, he turned repression into art. But for critics interested in the social function of art an obstacle immediately presents itself. A Foucauldian argument claims that the novel upholds social norms and values however apparently contestatory or subversive it may claim to be; indeed, as I have suggested above, the novel, like the divorce court journalism, uses the socially inflammatory subject of adultery the better to cement and bind social norms.

But this argument assumes a wide reading public. How relevant is it to *The Golden Bowl*, a novel that for all its interest in reading was read by only, as one reviewer put it, "a little community of the elect" (cited in Gard 381)? The very modernist strategies that James developed to extend the range of his subject matter, also contributed to the radical contraction and redefinition of his reading public. In 1932 Gertrude Atherton recalled her perception of James's audience: James "lost his large public during his second phase and was little read" in the early 1900s "save by intellectuals" (cited in Gard 362). The woman, above all, is no longer the public. Maggie may read the text of adultery in *The Golden Bowl*, but *The Golden Bowl* itself was not a novel that appealed to the typical female reader of Braddon, Norton, and others throughout the Victorian and modernist periods. In the absence of a large reading public, the cultural work that this novel performs shifts registers. *The Golden Bowl* is political not in its complex negotiation of the circulation of power (although it does undeniably do this, it just does not have enough readers for this strategy to tell in any meaningful way upon social order) but rather through the classification of readers that is part, inadvertently or not, of the project of modernism.

Even a cursory glance at the critical reception to James's novels testifies to his success in confronting censorship and representing the subjects he desired. As usual, this point is made in the context of French fiction. *Maisie*, one reviewer writes, "ranks . . . with the worst schools of French fiction" (cited in Gard 272). And another reviewer argues that James's novels "are as full of the covert suggestion of foulness as the worst French novel" (333). F. M. Colby's 1902 review essay on James, however, captures what is most baffling about James's challenge to the implicit censorship by which his choice of subject was delimited. While James has "written furiously against the proprieties for several years," the censors have "let things pass" in James's work that "in other writers would have been immediately rebuked" (cited in Gard 336). Colby's speculations on this subject correspond closely to my argument above: an elaborate stylistic smoke screen, or as Colby puts it, "fig-leaf," enabled James both to represent adultery and evade censorship. Colby writes, "A year ago, when Henry James wrote an essay on women that brought to our cheek the hot, rebellious blush, we said nothing about it, thinking that perhaps, after all, the man's style was his sufficient fig-leaf, and that few would see how shocking he really was. And, indeed, it has been a long time since the public knew what Henry James was up to behind that verbal hedge of his, though half-suspecting that he meant no good, because a style like that seemed just the place for guilty secrets.... His impunity is due to the sheer laziness of the expurgators. They will not read him, and they do not believe that anybody else can" (335). Although James enjoyed a broad and enthusiastic readership in the early and middle stages of his career, by 1902, his writing, despite its engagement with prohibited subject matter, was not perceived to pose a threat to social or political stability. First, his readership was too small to merit concern; and second, even among that small group of readers, only a "few" shared the cultural competence required to comprehend James's stylistic code and see the "shocking" material that it obscured. Literature could be regulated, in other words, without "the police breaking in." While Colby contemplates the anomaly of James's freedom from censorious constraint, the fact is that James is already performing the work of the police. Colby writes that "in a literature as well policed as ours, the position of Henry James is anomalous. He is the only writer of the day whose moral notions do not seem to matter. His dissolute and complicated Muse may say just what she chooses. This may be because it is so difficult to expose him. Never did so much vice go with such sheltering vagueness" (337). To be sure the vice in James's work is difficult to expose, but this point alone does not explain the anomaly to which Colby refers. The difficulty in exposing James's infractions of social norms and values is linked to the larger and more important point of *difficulty* itself. Because James's works are so difficult to read, they exclude the young female reader with whom the discourse on censorship is most concerned. James's practice of self-censorship, then, does not result in the censorship of vice, but rather in the regulation of female readers. Unlike the restraint exercised by cultural authorities and institutions in the mid- to late Victorian period, however, James inscribes this restraint within his novels themselves. If the goal of print censorship, after all, was to restrict the reading of vulnerable readers, James's novels perform this function almost too well.

To better understand the cultural work of reader classification that James's later writing performs, it is helpful to consider Ortega y Gasset's analysis of modernist fiction. The distinction between elite and popular readers, the educated and the so-called masses, is of course familiar to critics of modernism. Ortega y Gasset argues that modern literature "divides the public into two groups: one very small, formed by those who are favorably inclined towards it; another very large—the hostile majority.... It is not that the majority does not *like* the art of the young," he continues, "but that the majority, the masses, do not *understand* it" (5–6). This division, moreover, "implies that one group possesses an organ of comprehension denied to the other.... Through its mere presence, the art of the young compels the average citizen to realize that he is just this—the average citizen" (6). Conversely, the new art also serves the function of helping "the elite to recognize themselves" (7). As one critic writes, "Mr. Henry James writes for the few, and belongs to the few. It is, indeed, almost a pity that so many dunces have been banged, bullied, and frightened into saying that they like the work of Mr. Henry James, but that he is really too subtle" (cited in Gard 266). And Stopford Brooke notes in 1897: "[James] has now arrived at so involved and tormented a style that I find the greatest difficulty in discovering what he means. I read and read again his sentences, and it is like listening to a language I do not know. I read his last novel but one, and I was in the same helpless condition. I believe this style is the fine flower of modern culture at present, and that not to appreciate it is to be in the outer darkness, but I prefer outer darkness" (cited in Gard 263). The fact that James's writing is like a language that this critic does not know reflects two points: first, to make adultery speakable and visible James institutes new and unfamiliar categories of perception (that are, nevertheless, closely wed to the popular pattern of the divorce court); and second, that the strangeness and foreignness of James's "language" works as an impediment to comprehension. This critic and many others are in the dark. "The readers of the story [*Maisie*]," another critic writes, "will probably never understand exactly what any one concerned said or did or meant" (cited in Gard 273). In the critical reviews it is repeatedly noted that James's style is "difficult"; the phrases are "tortured and obscure" (275).[14] And the following comments are typical: "[t]he honest reader in search of a story will stare dazedly through perhaps a third of James's new book [*The Awkward Age*], and then shut it with a snort" (292). To "keep up with Mr. James in this story [*The Sacred Fount*] strains even a willing intelligence to the breaking point" (307). *The Wings of the Dove* "is not an easy book to read" (319): "it will not do for short railway journeys or for drowsy hammocks, or even to amuse sporting men and the active Young Person. The dense, fine quality of its pages — and there are 576 — will always presuppose a certain effort of attention on the part of reader; who must, indeed, be prepared to forgo many of his customary titillations and bribes" (319). *The Golden Bowl*, similarly, is "not built for popularity" (377), and most readers will not be able to appreciate it (379). James's novels may work within the boundaries of the law defined by the divorce court, but they do not exploit the divorce court journalism's popular and accessible style. On the contrary, James seeks a more refined and sophisticated reading public, a reading public that he is obliged, in many ways, to shape himself. If James's novels do not appeal to "the majority of readers" (289), then, on what conception of the reading public does he rely?

It is perhaps no accident that in the Preface to *The Golden Bowl* James attempts to define a new reading public by first offering his own exemplary reading practices and then expanding this illustration to imagine a broader reading community. He invites his reader to "dream" with him, to have "fun," to experience a "contagious" beauty, a deep "pleasure," to be "led captive by a charm and spell" (lviii–lix). And yet this dream, this pleasure, and this fun bears no similarity to the intoxicated reading practices of the undiscriminating public for whom James expresses such disdain. Instead James borrows the terminology of mass reading appeal to make a pitch for his own, more singular, approach. This approach requests two things from its reader: the reader should be a meticulous and close *re*reader, alive to the vibrations rather than the explicit statements of a given text; and the reader should read out loud. This latter stipulation requires the reader to read so carefully that no word is missed, no nuance is left unregistered, no rhythm is broken. It is to this reader, a reader like himself, that he pitches *The Golden Bowl*.

Like so many other writers, James finds, the cost of circumventing censorship is to become irrelevant and unreadable; James's social impact is now limited and hostility to his fiction, while it may occasionally be mentioned, is hardly taken seriously. It would, of course, be absurd to argue that James was once a socially vital and political writer who, in an effort to gain some measure of literary freedom, emptied out the very material that contributed to his vitality and to his politics. But there is certainly no doubt that James's earlier work was more accessible and more relaxed and that as he became increasingly interested in taboo subject matter his work, accordingly, became increasingly, detached, remote, and difficult to read.

It is ironic that James's later novels provoked praise for censorship. Sir Francis Jeune, for example, shifts from the national habit of repression to the "genius of repression": "Let us thank the proprieties, the conventions of this land, the genius of repression, which have created that need for a new realism, delicate as a silver-point, to which his [James's] works make so satisfying a response" (cited in Gard 288). But it is not simply repression that produces literary innovation, it is repression and adultery. James's negotiation of censorship takes place in the context of his desire to represent adultery; and like the novels in the Continental tradition "canonized as great" to which Tanner refers, James's later novels contribute to a distinctively English tradition of the novel of adultery. To circumvent censorship he both rewrites the central category of the young female reader and adapts narrative strategies from the divorce court journalism, consonant with literary modernism, to translate his stories of adultery as stories of epistemology and abysmal knowledge. Where, in this context, is the undercurrent of the body? James's fiction, one critic writes in 1904, "is a land where the vices have no bodies and the passions no blood, where nobody sins because nobody has anything to sin with. Why should we worry when a spook goes wrong?" (cited in Gard 337). And indeed, on the one hand, there is no longer anything to worry about. In his effort to write serious books designed for the drawing room James refined his central audience out of existence; his novels, even his most vivid novels of adultery, could "be left wide open in the nursery" (337). On the other hand, however, as *The Golden Bowl* demonstrates, a "spook" has a way of making itself felt. It exerts its unspoken pressure — a haunting, uncanny vibration — and exacts its cost. For if Maggie is shocked by the ghost of adultery, she is also awakened to the captivating spell of reading the adulterous body.

5

A Good Read

Ford Madox Ford's *A Call* and *The Good Soldier*

"A tale of passion" Mr. Hueffer [Ford Madox Ford] calls it, but there is no more passion in it than in an entomologist's enthusiasm over his drawer of pinned and varnished beetles. The characters are specimens, their story is a "case." . . . Our exposition of Mr. Hueffer's novel is quite fair in respect of the readers to whom, in essence and manner, it will be simply detestable. It will have no indifferent readers. To the residue, . . . [it] will afford immense entertainment.

Morning Post, April 1915

You must have your eyes forever on your Reader. That alone constitutes . . . Technique!

Ford Madox Ford, "Technique"

Toward the end of Ford Madox Ford's *The Good Soldier* Nancy Rufford finds a newspaper article recounting a divorce trial to prove adultery (or "guilty intimacy" as the case also puts it); she retires to her room anticipating a "good read" (237). But Nancy, we have been informed by John Dowell, does not understand the word *adultery*, and the case perplexes her: "she could not understand why a chart of the bedroom accommodation at Christchurch Old Hall should be produced in court" (237). In fact, it makes her laugh. To her mind the case seems to be suggesting something that cannot possibly exist. Marriage, for Nancy, precludes loving anyone except the person to whom one is married. Mr. Brand, the defendant, therefore, does not love Miss Lupton. What then does the conclusion mean? "Yet there it was—in black and white. . . . Mr. Brand was adjudged, in two or three brief words, at the end of columns and columns of paper, to have been guilty of cruelty to his wife and to have committed adultery with Miss Lupton. The last words conveyed nothing to Nancy—nothing real, that is to say" (238).

Neither the sensation novels of the 1860s nor the novels of Henry

James allegorize the categories of perception through which adultery becomes visible quite so vividly as this account of Nancy Rufford reading a divorce case. Before Nancy reads the case, she cannot see adultery. After she reads the case, adultery becomes stark, frightening, and very real. The "last words"—the accusation of adultery—open a sickening possibility: "the whole effect of the reading upon Nancy was mysterious, terrifying, and evil. She felt a sickness—a sickness that grew as she read" (239). Nancy's "good read" has exposed the very thing that she has been trying to escape. It opens the "unthinkable" possibility that Edward Ashburnham—a married man—might love *her*.

In this short anecdote Ford, with uncanny precision, conflates the two most persistent categories of perception through which adultery was made legible in the Victorian and modernist periods: the divorce court journalism and the young female reader. Both of these categories of perception, I have argued, relate to the larger question of print censorship and the symbolic struggle over the competing appeals to aesthetics and morality. The divorce court debates and the recent reanimation of the print censorship debates in 1910 and 1913 only heightened these concerns when Ford was writing *A Call* and *The Good Soldier*. It is not surprising, then, that the account of Nancy's reading experience captures, in a condensed form, concerns related to Ford's novel as a whole. The reading of a legal case in which the personal affairs of the Brands are made very public coincides with the reading of a novel in which the personal affairs of the Dowells and the Ashburnhams are also made very public and are, ultimately, adjudged. The reader of *The Good Soldier* is in a position not unlike Nancy's. After reading pages and pages of paper the accusation of adultery is there in "black and white" but what, really, does it mean?

But if the reader is in a position like Nancy's, does the reader also share her reading responses? Does reading about adultery make one laugh? Does it make one sick? In the words of the *Morning Post* reviewer cited above, does it produce an "immense entertainment" or is it "simply detestable"? In fact, these and similar somatic or political reading responses were precisely what literary modernists like Ford and James, increasingly sensitive to the implicit censorships by which the literary field was constructed, were concerned to circumvent. Ford's strategy, shared widely by other literary practitioners, was to highlight a novel's formal concerns and in the process to deflect attention away from the socially contentious and politically inflammatory questions of problematic content. When Ford turns to the reader, for example, his emphasis is resolutely placed upon "technique" and the aesthetic considerations raised by new narrative innovations or as Ford, never modest, puts it, a "new form" for the novel ("Techniques" 297). While early critics of Ford's *The Good Soldier*, like the reviewer for the *Morning Post*, were quick to notice Ford's subject matter—the "book is unpleasant" (cited in "Contemporary" 225), it has a "sordid theme" (225), its "plot is most unsavoury" (226), it has a "distorted, sex-morbid atmosphere" (221), it reflects an "unpleasant imagination" (221), it is only of value "to the specialist in pathology" (235)—the body of Fordian criticism that has emerged later in the century has almost always followed Ford's lead and devoted itself to questions of technique and of form.[1]

As a result, a number of key aspects related to *The Good Soldier* and Ford's writing in general have been overlooked. First, the relationship between Ford's formal innovations and the social and political pressures to which he was subject in the Edwardian period, particularly the divorce court journalism's articulation of adultery and the print censorship debates, has not been addressed. Ford, in fact, was an ardent reader of legal trials and in this chapter I want to illustrate the ways in which the journalistic format of divorce trials shaped his own approach to taboo subject matter and informed his modernist narrative innovations. Second, because Ford's focus on technique, while genuine and committed, has not also been understood as a strategy through which to circumvent censorship, the ideological investments of this focus on technique have also been missed. On the one hand, like other novels of adultery considered in this book, *The Good Soldier* represents adultery through the prism of the betrayed party's always partial and incomplete perception. This narrative choice once again produces the translation of adultery in terms of epistemology rather than passion (and renders problematic and jarring the subtitle of Ford's novel). On the other hand, the focus on technique also carries implications for a more general understanding of the social function of reading and the social function of the novel that has been equally neglected. This point deserves some elaboration.

The focus on form, as I have suggested above, deflects attention away from content; it also contributes to the social construction of new reading communities. Perhaps the best example of the way an emphasis on form may be systematically used to avoid issues related to content is found in the 1985 effort to prevent the Cincinnati Museum from exhibiting the photographs of Robert Mapplethorpe. During the trial the art critic Janet Kardon evaluates Mapplethorpe's graphically explicit and disturbing photograph of "fisting" in terms of the "centrality of the forearm" and the photographer's manipulation of light and shadow (cited in Merkel 47). In this way, attention is elided from the homosexual imagery and only the form or technique is presented as important and worthy of comment. To be sure, Ford's content is neither as explicit nor as contentious as Mapplethorpe's (even allowing for the many decades that separate these two figures) but in Ford's work a similar elision of the content, nevertheless, obtains. The social construction of new reading communities, moreover, is related to this elision of content. As Bourdieu argues, and certainly as Kardon's remarks confirm, the attention to form is a learned disposition that divides audiences and limits interpretations. It highlights the aesthetic stance defined by disinterestedness and detachment—as opposed to laughter, sickness, and distress—most closely aligned with the advent of literary modernism.

But Ford has no desire to alienate his reader. Indeed his focus on technique is always concerned to arouse the reader's interest. And, unlike James's later novels, his writing style is neither difficult nor forbidding. In fact there is a real tension in Ford's novel between narrative strategies designed to circumvent censorship and the narrative qualities that these strategies, in many ways, disavow. This tension is then repeated in the Fordian criticism without any sense of the material contexts that illuminate the situated and conflicted position from which Ford writes. In *The Good Soldier* Ford wrestles with the competing demands of morality and aesthetics, passion and detachment, sympathy and ironic detachment. The focus on form allows him to sidestep, without nevertheless entirely preventing, criticisms directed to his "unpleasant" content; and yet, like Mapplethorpe's photographs, the novel only works when that content is understood to be an integral part of the narrative as a whole.

"It Goes On and On": Divorce Court Journalism and *A Call*

Like James, Ford was deeply interested in divorce court journalism and its social implications; and like James, Ford both decried the public scandal that the journalism necessarily provoked and demonstrated an acute awareness of the way in which the divorce court journalism, nevertheless, could be mobilized by the serious novelist. Ford's first novelistic treatment of this journalism is found in his 1910 novel *A Call*, in which he deals explicitly with one man's fear of the divorce court. *A Call*'s subtitle, The Tale of Two Passions, prefigures the subtitle to *The Good Soldier*, A Tale of Passion, and in many ways this novel may be read as an introduction to Ford's later novel.² Before turning to *A Call*, however, I want to consider briefly some divorce cases with which Ford may have been familiar.

While Ford was intrigued by material presented in newspaper cases and urged Conrad to take advantage of this resource in the composition of his novels, it seems unlikely that any single divorce case directly influenced his writing. And yet Ford's interest in divorce law, like Norton's, was deeply personal. In 1909 his wife, Elsie Martindale, threatened a divorce. At first Ford was alarmed by the potential scandal a divorce case would provoke, but given his increasingly intimate relationship with Violet Hunt, the possibility of divorce began to look promising. In the meantime, Elsie, encouraged by family and friends, hesitated about the divorce and finally dropped the topic altogether after first being granted a separation decree. Ford was enormously disappointed; he pursued a divorce in Germany and after several years of legal stalling and apparent turmoil announced that it had been successful. Violet and Ford then announced their marriage. This move opened them to challenges of bigamy in England and one of the worst scandals of Ford's career.³ If Norton translated her frustration and outrage with divorce law reform into vigorously argued political documents outlining her grievances, Ford's experience with English divorce laws emphasized his own conflicted social position poised between a desire for the respectability conferred by marriage and a disdain for the social conventions that circumscribed passionate expression. Most important, however, it made him wary of and disenchanted with the English laws governing marriage and divorce.

The persistent concerns related to divorce court journalism — its association with publicity, personal exposure, and scandal, its engagement with reading and censorship, and its ostensible role as a deterrent to adultery — figure centrally in the conduct of Ford's "good people." A consideration of several of the divorce trials published in the month before Ford ostensibly began *The Good Soldier* should clarify these points. The transcriptions are representative of a mood (suspicion and the need to accumulate evidence of adultery) and a tone (judicial and sensational) in relation to adultery which, I have argued, was persistent throughout the Victorian period and into the early decades of the twentieth century. In addition, both the language ("shock," "suspicion," "saying things") and the content (the intimate relationships between sets of couples, the naiveté of key parties, the gambling and blackmail) of several of the cases also recur in Ford's *The Good Soldier*.

On 23 October 1913, for example, Florence Collinge was accused by her husband of committing adultery with Harold Edward Harker. The Collinges and the Harkers had been on intimate terms for about seven years, visiting each others' homes, taking trips together, and so on. "About 1910," the *Times* newspaper report relates, "the respondent and the co-respondent began to go about together more than they had previously done, and they went on motor-car rides, to golf courses, and elsewhere. The petitioner had no suspicion of anything wrong, as he had the utmost confidence in his wife" (24 Oct. 1913: 4). In a different case, on 15 October 1913, a divorce was granted to a woman on the grounds of her husband's adultery, incurred gambling debts for which she had to pay, and consistent cruelty. The debts include the implication of blackmail which he conceals from his wife. In another two-day case, the husband fears his wife will commit suicide if he leaves her; his sisters report that his wife "said things" about one of his other sisters and that evidence of his wife's adultery "came as a thunderbolt upon the petitioner" (23 Oct. 1913, 3). Indeed, the discovery of adultery is typically described in terms of thunderbolts or tremendous shocks (it "was a great shock to the petitioner" [30 Oct. 1913, 3]) and, in part, this strategy is deployed, as I noted earlier, as a technique to mitigate the culpability of the petitioner and to elicit sympathy on the part of the jury and judge. Dowell develops such a strategy of innocence and ignorance into a fine art of naïve bewilderment. "I had never the remotest glimpse, not the shadow of a suspicion, that there was anything wrong as the saying is," he claims (74). Finally, a four-day divorce case involving a retired army officer began 17 December 1913, the day on which Ford states that he began to write *The Good Soldier*, and again the case involved cruelty, drinking, unexpected revelations, and unsupported counter-allegations.

In addition to these divorce cases, in late November 1913 an English vicar was accused of committing adultery with his ward Hannah. This story was extremely sensational and it was reported widely in the daily newspapers. The vicar was found guilty of four charges of immoral conduct. He was acquitted of the accusation of adultery, however, because, while the Chancellor and the Court "regarded the case on the charge of adultery as one of the gravest suspicion," the "evidence" itself—the terms of endearment he used with Hannah, the fact that he sometimes ate food off her plate and sipped from her teacup, that she had been seen sitting on his lap, and that he had spent a considerable amount of money on "the girl"—was not considered decisive. The counsel for the prosecutor, Millward, "endeavoured to persuade the Court that the evidence did amount to proof of adultery. It had been held, he said, that when there was inclination coupled with opportunity they might infer that adultery had been committed. The fact that the defendant was always arranging for a third person to be with the girl was in itself significant: it was not the action of a stepfather, nor of a man who adopted a girl" (3 Dec. 1913, 4). In *The Good Soldier* Ford takes details of a similar nature—Nancy Rufford is the ward of Edward and Leonora and she too is caught in a triangular plot of ambiguous proportions—and reworks the legal pursuit of proof within the context of a domestic tribunal.

Ford's earlier novel, *A Call*, develops a thematic interest in the divorce court that will be amplified and modified in *The Good Soldier*. The novel focuses on Dudley Leicester, "one of those men who are essentially monogamous" (34), for whom "a man was a man, a woman a woman; the leader in a newspaper was a series of convincing facts, of satisfying views, and of final ideals" (30). Dudley lets his respect for the newspaper trigger a "dread" that the newspaper—and, in particular, the newspaper's documentation of divorce—may destroy him.[4] His fears derive from one indiscreet, but possibly innocent, evening spent with an old girlfriend, Etta Stackpole Hudson, while his wife, Pauline, is away in the country. While at Etta's he answers her telephone and is subsequently paralyzed by the possibility that the calling party, who hangs up and remains unidentified until the end of the novel, may have recognized his voice. Etta's reputation is well known but she has, she proudly confides to Dudley, avoided scandal despite a conspiracy of women who would delight to see her fall: "If ever my name got into the papers they'd [the women] manage it [Etta's fall] too. But that will never happen. You know women are quite powerless until your name does get into the papers" (42). After his evening with Etta, and his discomposure over the phone call, Dudley rehearses all of the predictable responses the divorce court was designed to provoke in a fearful public. "How long does it take things to get in the newspaper?" he asks his friend Grimshaw the following morning. He then "looked feverishly under the heading of Court and Society [in *The Times*], and under the heading of Police Court and Divorce Court. But his eye could no more than travel over the spaces of print and speckled paper, as if it had been a patterned fabric. And suddenly he asked: 'Do you suppose the servants spy upon us?'" (52). Grimshaw responds in a round-about fashion but concludes that the servants "are always on the watch" (54) and that "it's an advantage to have no vices in particular, and to have committed no crimes. . . . You can't conceal things. It's a perpetual strain" (55). His comments, needless to say, do little to relax Dudley's anxiety. Dudley's dread of being discovered develops quite suddenly into a catatonic retreat from the world: worried friends and blundering doctors attempt to assist his recovery but Dudley moves only as an automaton and remains silent. The response to his condition is interpreted as society's sentence on the English household: "these three [visitors] seemed to be a small commission sent by Society to inquire into the state of a household where it was suspected something was 'wrong.' He [Dudley] realized that it was probably only the state of his nerves; but every new word added to his conviction that these were not merely 'people,' bland, smiling, idle, and innocuous—good people of social contacts. They were, he was convinced, inquisitors, representing each a separate interest. . . . And outside there seemed to be—he seemed to hear them—the innumerable whispers of the tongues of all Society, canvassing the results of the report that would be brought back by this committee of inquiry" (111). There was a strong sense in English culture of what authors, objecting to censorship, called "secret tribunals," select groups of people evaluating either literature or public morals and finding them wanting.[5] As Dudley's comments indicate, these groups could be anywhere and they could be composed of anyone. The possibility of this insidious "committee of inquiry" instills in Dudley a sense of caution and suspicion as well as a sense of guilt. The language of the law is powerfully deployed here but the work of the law cannot be substantiated. Instead, the law is folded into everyday discourse and it exercises its force even in the most protected of spaces, the domestic sickbed. The "tongues of all Society" will return in *The Good Soldier* when Dowell summarizes social good as the impulse toward a tedious and enervating normality. This normality, moreover, is instilled through the very practice of surveillance and exposure which both the "inquisitors" and Dowell embrace in their production of reports for a "committee of inquiry" which may be considered as either a jury or the reading public.

Pauline's response to her husband's assumed adultery further signals the disintegration of moral values and personal integrity with which the novel is concerned: "I haven't made a scandal or any outcry about Dudley Leicester. That's our day and that's our class. But look at all the difference it's made in our personal relations! Look at the misery of it all! That's it. We can make a day and a class and rules for them, but we can't keep any of the rules except just the gross ones like not making scandals. . . . We haven't learned wisdom: we've only learned how to believe. We cannot avoid tragedies. Tragedies! Yes, in our day and in our class we don't allow ourselves easy things like daggers and poison-bowls. It's all more difficult. It's all more difficult because it goes on and on" (149). Pauline's recognition of the paramount rule — not the rule against adultery, or cruelty, or blackmailing, or even general misbehavior, but the rule against *making scandals* — is consonant with Leonora's "dread of scandals" (196), a concern also shared by Edward, in light of which both Leonora and Edward maintain the form of a happy marriage in the midst of agonizing unhappiness. The fear of public scandal serves its purpose: the misery "goes on and on" as the form, even if it is empty or, in Dowell's metaphor, rotten at the core, is perpetuated. And again this lack of conclusiveness in terms of narrative form promotes social regulation; punishment is not exercised and the reader is maintained in her or his suspense.

Unlike *A Call*, Ford's *The Good Soldier* illustrates the English novel's tendency to focus on the betrayed party and, as such, it concentrates several of the issues with which I have been concerned. In this novel Ford aims "to do for the English novel what in *Fort comme la mort* Maupassant had done for the French" ("Letter" xxii); as a result, Ford's novel provides a telling contrast to the French manipulation of the same subject matter, adultery.[6] In outline the novels are similar but the point of view from which the story is told differs entirely: Maupassant's novel is told from the point of view of the adulterer whereas Ford's novel is told from the point of view of the betrayed party. It is this reformulation of the European tradition in terms of point of view which is one of the trademarks of the English novel of adultery.

"Gross Stories": A Tale of Seduction

The Good Soldier is fascinated by seduction. Not only does it relate, with only a partially suppressed exuberance and envy, the serial seductions of Edward Asburnham, but it is also captivated by the seductive potential inhering in storytelling itself. Like Balzac's "Sarrasine" this is a story keenly and self-consciously attuned to the link between seduction and narration. At the same time, *The Good Soldier* interrogates a central set of questions in the print censorship debates: what is the relationship between storytelling and social action? What are the "practical effects of the imagination"? Does the story of adultery promote acts of adultery? Does the story of seduction, in turn, seduce the reader? These questions are especially pertinent, of course, to *The Good Soldier* itself and its own obsessive account of adulterous liaisons. The story opens with Dowell's bewildered, jangled narration. The many breaks, interruptions, repetitions, and stutterings in the first pages of the novel indicate that our narrator has undergone some sort of crisis or trauma and yet the exact nature of this crisis is left undescribed. Instead, toward the end of this chapter Dowell tells his reader two stories about seduction and adultery.

The first story is an anecdote related to Dowell by Leonora. She confides that she tried to take a lover but that once she was "in the man's arms" she recoiled; she could not do it (11–12). What does this anecdote mean? Dowell wonders. His response, predictably, is: "I don't know; I don't know" (12). This first story of adultery is a story of adultery averted. As any reader of the Victorian novel knows, however, to entertain, and especially to *speak* of, the possibility of adultery, however ultimately innocent one's actions, is to be irreparably tainted; and to *listen* to illicit stories, as Dowell's second anecdote will imply, is also to be implicated in the story told. It is no wonder that Dowell is nervously troubled by Leonora's anecdote. The fact, moreover, that the first story of adultery is related by the one character, with the exception of Dowell, who is most free from adulterous practices similarly disturbs the narrative's credibility. If this novel reads in many ways like a divorce court transcription in which the star witness (Dowell) offers evidence for a series of adulterous tangles, it also exposes at every turn the severely compromised nature of such evidence.

The second story of adultery relates even more directly to the storytelling process itself. Dowell speculates on the relationship between listening to "extraordinarily gross stories," stories that are so bad they "will give you a pain" (13), and sexually illicit behavior. It would seem to follow, he thinks, that the same men who enjoy such stories would also be likely to engage in adulterous activities. Is there not a relationship, after all, as the Victorian discourse on censorship maintains, between listening to or reading illicit stories and performing illicit actions? As Dowell puts it, "if they [the listeners] delight so in the narration, how is it possible that they can be offended . . . at the suggestion that they might make attempts upon your wife's honour?" (13). But Edward's behavior reverses this theory; he intensely dislikes "gross stories" and yet this dislike is no guarantee for the purity of his actions; on the contrary, despite his apparently flawless narrative interests his actions are adulterous in the extreme. This very discrepancy between stories and actions, moreover, make Edward dangerous; his actions cannot be predicted, his whole demeanor, as a result, becomes untrustworthy and unsettling for a character like Dowell who seeks clear signs by which to order his world. For as soon as Dowell inverts the equation— dislike of gross stories generates illicit behavior—then he confronts the apparent anomaly of himself: "if poor Edward was dangerous because of the chastity of his expressions—and they say that is the hallmark of the libertine—what about myself? For I solemnly avow that not only have I never so much as hinted at an impropriety in my conversation in the whole of my days; and more than that, I will vouch for the cleanness of my thoughts and the absolute chastity of my life. At what, then, does it all work out? Is the whole thing a folly and a mockery? Am I no better than a eunuch or is the proper man—the man with the right to existence—a raging stallion forever neighing after his neighbour's womenkind?" (14). The content of this passage, of course, is itself undercut by the form. Did not Dowell just tell his reader the "gross story" of Leonora's adultery averted? And what about his speculations on Edward, storytelling, and adultery, not to mention, the numerous stories of adultery recorded in *The Good Soldier* as a whole? Ford would have been well aware that Dowell's narration would be interpreted as a "gross story"; the early reviews of the novel, for example, are quick to focus on the narrative's sordid themes as illustrated above. The first chapter of *The Good Soldier*, moreover, is nothing if not filled with "hints of impropriety." There is a tension, in other words, between the form of the telling—Dowell's claim to the absolute chastity of his expressions—and the story that is told. This short passage suggests one way to contest arguments in favor of print censorship. As soon as the causal link between gross stories and immoral actions is broken, an appeal for censorship cannot be maintained. After all, following Dowell's thoughts, an obsession with seduction and stories of sexuality should promote moral actions, sexual *disinterest*, an absence of passion, a life as cool and hard as a beetle's in a case.

These two stories are instructive in other ways as well. For by telling a story of Leonora's adultery averted and Edward's pursuit of adulterous pleasures, Dowell diverts attention from his own story of adultery. And Dowell's story of adultery, regrettably for him, has nothing to do with turning down adulterous passes, on the one hand, or accumulating adulterous conquests, on the other. His story instead is a very English narrative of adultery. He obsessively and repetitively relates the story of adultery discovered. Once again, the passion of adultery is translated as the epistemology of adultery in *The Good Soldier*. Indeed, this novel claustrophobically intensifies the relationship between adultery and epistemology. As Samuel Hynes argues, this "novel of doubt" (228) addresses "epistemological" questions which introduce "uncertainty about truth and reality," an uncertainty that the unreliable first-person narration only complicates (Hynes 226).[7] But in the absence of strong epistemological claims and highly skeptical of a law that works by way of scandal, Dowell (like Ford) interposes a law that works by way of seduction. It is seduction and pleasure that spurs this story and it is seduction and pleasure by which the reader is entrapped. While the question of Dowell's passion may be impossible to settle it is clear that Dowell's storytelling goals are motivated in large part by a desire to seduce his reader. In his excessive eagerness both to tell and to suppress the story of adultery Dowell's "hints of impropriety," his gaps and silences, his ellipses and his euphemisms, his fractured and faltering narrative, contribute to an erotics of reading generated by the very censoring mechanisms designed to inhibit such expression.

Dowell's two early stories of seduction and adultery can be contrasted to another story of seduction that is repeatedly told in this novel. In a sense, this other story conflates the two stories referred to above: it tells a story about a story that adulterously seduces a married man. The story to which I refer is Dowell's account of Florence's seduction of Edward at M——. Ironically, the character who is the greatest talker in the novel, Florence, a "queer, chattery person" (15), is the only character whose point of view is not recorded as part of Dowell's story. At the same time, she represents for Dowell a complete and devastating sort of knowledge. By contrast to Dowell's confounded "I don't knows" repeated throughout the text, Florence exerts a narrative authority through the very pressure of her ready and various knowledge. Bewildered, Dowell addresses his reader: "But how could she have known what she knew? How could she have got to know it? To know it so fully" (10). Characteristically Dowell does not specify exactly what the "it" is here and this ambiguity only heightens the sense of a cloistered, almost accessible, certainly powerful, knowledge that Florence holds.

Her knowledge, however, is nowhere better demonstrated than in her manipulation of storytelling to advance the seduction plot. Like most scenes in this novel, the day of the visit to M—— is told repeatedly, from different perspectives and with different details.[8] Dowell begins the story, he digresses, he turns to something else more pressing and immediate, he returns to the story, he tries again, he digresses and so on. It is clear that the details of this day are sharply inscribed on Dowell's consciousness and that he is pulled in two directions: he wants to tell the story, and he is deeply distressed by the telling of the story. The story that he tells, in fragments, is itself an account of a story that Florence tells and the day excursion that serves as its backdrop.

The Ashburnhams and the Dowells take a day trip to M—— on Florence's urging. The train ride parallels in many ways Strether's train ride in

The Ambassadors: the country side is tranquil, the colors are bright, and Dowell placidly looks out the window. He is certainly not paying attention to his wife. Leonora, by contrast, is keenly alert to Florence. "Florence was imparting information so hard," Dowell writes, "and Leonora was listening so intently that no one noticed me" (46). And as Dowell relaxes, Florence's subtle seduction of Edward advances. When they arrive at M—— the group visits a castle and enters what was ostensibly Martin Luther's bedroom and here Florence opens the "heavily-shuttered windows," against the custodian's wishes, to illuminate the room in the center of which is a large glass case which contains a piece of writing. And it is here that Florence begins to tell her carefully practiced and polished story. The writing, Florence claims, is Luther's Protest. The "piece of paper" was "like the half-sheet of a letter with some faint pencil scrawls that might have been a jotting of the amounts we were spending during the day" (48). But what is the Protest doing in the center of Luther's bedroom?

Reading this novel we walk into a bedroom, open the windows, and discover the piece of paper, encased in glass, which was instrumental in the rise of the affectionate family: "It's because of that piece of paper that you're honest, sober, industrious, provident, and clean-lived," Florence says to Edward (48). Not only is this the standard definition of the Protestant subject, but it is also exactly the opposite of who Edward is and who Florence wants him to be. The Protest allows him to be one thing under the guise of something else. This is not a "gross story," it is a history lesson (filled, as several critics have pointed out, with very dubious history); and yet Florence's whimsical tale has a forceful effect. She continues: "If it weren't for that piece of paper you'd be like the Irish or the Italians or the Poles, but particularly the Irish." Here Dowell perks up somewhat. He notices that Florence "laid one finger upon Captain Ashburnham's wrist" and he senses "something treacherous, something frightful, something evil in the day. . . . It was as if we were going to run and cry out; all four of us in separate directions, averting our heads. I was horribly frightened and then I discovered that the pain in my wrist was caused by Leonora's clutching it" (49). At first glance the level of fear and foreboding seems entirely out of proportion with the events in question: Florence's finger on Edward's wrist; Leonora's hand on Dowell's wrist. But Dowell quite rightly finds Florence's story of Luther's Protest menacing. For by the end of it Dowell is no longer with his wife and Leonora is no longer with her husband. Dowell and Leonora run out of the room effectively redistributing authorized partners. Dowell is with Edward's wife, Florence is with Leonora's husband and the early stages of a seduction are accomplished.

Like Caroline Norton's practical protest, moreover, the account of Luther's protest in this novel invokes a double protest related to print censorship and divorce law reform. Luther's writings, for example, incited some of the most flagrant acts of censorship in history. As Annabel Patterson records, in 1535 Francis I launched an intensely hostile response to the new print culture: "all printing of any kind was to cease on penalty of hanging; all bookshops were to be closed; and a list was published of suspected Lutheranists who were immediately condemned to banishment, without trial, from French territory" (4). And if the Protest makes possible who Edward ostensibly is, it also ultimately enables English divorce laws. Divorce, of course, was still a topic of lively debate in the period during which Ford was contemplating his novel. An article in The *Times* entitled "Lord Halifax's Protest" reads, in part, as follows: "Lord Halifax said that the recommendations of the majority of the Commission [on Facilities for Divorce] could be shown to be a danger to morality, the security of the family, and the well-being and happiness of individuals, and, so far as they were founded on any principle at all, led to the spread and promotion of divorce by mutual consent, which did not differ from the promotion of free love" (21 Oct. 1912: 4).[9] These comments at first appear consonant with Dowell's own position (and Egg's painting): adultery poses a danger to morality, the family, and individuals. But if Florence sheds light on a previously censored document to advance her adultery plot, Dowell sheds light on Florence's adultery plot in a manner that overlaps with Edwardian narratives on censorship and adultery; he illuminates an area better left in the dark, and he makes the private story of the bedroom public and visible through his writing.

These stories of seduction find a parallel in Dowell's own approach to storytelling. Despite his claim that his expressions are always chaste, and his conduct impeccable, his narrative, perhaps not surprisingly, exhibits the same desire to seduce that we have already seen above. First, Dowell describes a scene of close intimacy between himself and his reader. Imagine, he writes, that it is just the two of us alone in a country cottage. A fire burns. The sea sounds. Outside there is a great moon. In many ways, this narrative strategy recalls another central novel of adultery, *The Scarlet Letter*. Hawthorne's narrator, the Surveyor, disapproves of the indiscreet writers who "indulge themselves in such confidential depths of revelation" suitable only for the "one heart and mind of perfect sympathy" (6–7). The Surveyor himself prefers a happy medium between indiscreet revelation and detached observation: "it may be pardonable to imagine that a friend, a kind and apprehensive, though not the closest friend, is listening to our talk; and then, a native reserve being thawed by this genial consciousness, we may prate of the circumstances that lie around us, and even of ourself, but still keep the inmost Me behind its veil" (7). Ford's narrator Dowell also imagines a talk and a friend but without the Surveyor's equivocations: "So I shall just imagine myself for a fortnight or so at one side of the fireplace of a country cottage, with a sympathetic soul opposite me. And I shall go on talking, in a low voice" (15). The ostensible goal behind Dowell's method of narration is to enlist the sympathy, and accordingly, the love, of his reader and it is the clear promiscuity of this goal that sits uneasily with the narrative's competing interests in subduing and regulating transgressive desires.

Ford's quotation of Novalis in one of his short propaganda books — "It is certain that my conviction gains immensely as soon as another soul can be found to share it" (*St. Dennis* 7) — is consistent with Dowell's attitude regarding the relationship between an author and her or his readers. Ford defines the act of reading as creating precisely this sort of fusion between writer and reader: the novelist "must address himself to such as be of good will; that is to say, he must typify for himself a human soul in sympathy with his own; a silent listener who will be attentive to him, and whose mind acts very much as his acts" (*Critical* 78). But this approach is not without its difficulties as Laura Tracy recognizes: "A writer proposing to establish an intimacy with his reader similar to that of two lovers is really proposing to make a private affair public, to bring love into the marketplace" (68). But it is also about the "practical effects of the imagination." For what does the story *do* here, if not seduce? And if this seductive potential is alluring, it also introduces the entangling politics of print censorship pitted against an aesthetic detachment that this novel, despite itself, always frustrates.

If Dowell's narration imagines a bond between the narrator and the reader that is at once about sympathetic identification and seduction, his descriptions of love and adultery are also strikingly similar to this construction of the reader/author relation. Dowell summarizes his attitude to adultery, which will later be modified, exactly halfway through the novel. In the same move, he offers one of the many justifications of adultery which are considered and rejected during the course of the narrative: "As I see it, at least, with regard to man, a love affair, a love for any definite woman, is something in the nature of a widening experience. With each new woman that a man is attracted to there appears to come a broadening of the outlook, or, if you like, an acquiring of new territory. A turn of the eyebrow, a tone of the voice, a queer characteristic gesture — all these things, and it is these things that cause to arise the passion of love — all these things are like so many objects on the horizon of the landscape that tempt a man to walk beyond the horizon, to explore. He wants to get, as it were, behind those eyebrows with the peculiar turn, as if he desired to see the world with the eyes that they overshadow" (126–27). The "sympathetic soul" to whom Dowell refers above is someone with whom he identifies; this scene of desire, then, resembles the form of narration that Dowell privileges. Like the ideal listener, the lover "wants to get, as it were, behind those eyebrows . . . to see the world with the eyes that they overshadow." Not only is Dowell tapping a long tradition of male rationalizations of a possessive (and consequently, by definition, constantly unsatisfied) sexuality, but he is also defining the possessive matrix of his own loss of Florence. The woman is a piece of "new territory," her characteristics are "like so many objects"; in the act of sexual conquest a man gains a new territory and new objects which he experiences, profits by — "in the nature of widening experience" — and discards.

The lover in this account, it is important to note, is a promiscuous lover and also, by implication, an adulterous lover. It is an account that should generate mistrust and suspicion (in both love relationships and the idealized scene of reading) rather than trusting regard. Dowell continues: "But the real fierceness of desire, the real heat of passion long continued and withering the soul of a man, is the craving for identity with the woman he loves. He desires to see with the same eyes, to touch with the same sense of touch, to hear with the same ears, to lose his identity, to be enveloped, to be supported" (127). This shift is revealing: from a possessive sexuality which sees women as constantly reinstated boundary marks beyond which a man wishes to explore (and by which he may define himself) to a love which is not a recognition (seeing oneself in the eyes of another) or an addition (another conquest) to one's identity but a *loss* of identity, a loss of identity which then confirms one's "own worthiness to exist" (127). The logic of adultery equates identity with a loss of identity; one does not exist until one loses one's identity in another. How can there be a difference of opinion if one is so completely a part of another person? How can one be betrayed if one is always seeing through the other's eyes? And yet this ideal is never realized. The "real heat of passion" here is about an absolute epistemological confidence (where one is in the mind of another and sees with her or his eyes) that evaporates in the moment that it is realized (insofar as one's identity evaporates). And *The Good Soldier* translates this "passion of love" as an epistemological problem; for what the novel demonstrates above all is the impossibility of the sort of interpersonal knowledge that Dowell describes. What Dowell does not know, *cannot* know, is that his wife is unfaithful.

Because Dowell is confronted by his abysmal inability to know, he privileges a form of complete knowledge, a merging and overlapping of sensibilities, in love relationships. And yet it is precisely this form of idealized love that is so completely outside the range of Dowell's experience. He can only look wistfully at the experience of others, namely Edward, to imagine what love might be. But perhaps his failure in love relationships can be redeemed by his narrative. The narrative of *The Good Soldier*, its intensely intimate confession related in a "low voice" to an imagined "sympathetic soul," may be Dowell's last hope to participate in the seductions from which he has been excluded. If this technique bears a similarity to seduction it also bears a similarity to sympathetic identification and domestic surveillance to produce a much more conservative reading of Ford's novel.

Under Arrest: A Tale of Epistemology

I want to expand further on the relationship between adultery and epistemology in *The Good Soldier* by way of a lengthy digression involving a Victorian narrative painting and four recognition scenes in the novels of James that take place specifically in the context of visual art. Victorian narrative painting may seem remote from Ford's aesthetic concerns but the painting I have in mind both clarifies one of the most persistent puzzles posed by *The Good Soldier* — its focus on the date 4 August — and illuminates Ford's dialogue with melodrama, narrative, and Victorian representations of adultery. The four recognition scenes in James's novels extend this analysis in a modernist context. Each of these scenes challenge realist representations of adultery by highlighting the way in which the spectator (or reader) is implicated in what she or he sees.

The narrative painting that interests me here is Augustus Egg's 1859 triptych, *Past and Present*. I have already discussed this painting in some detail in the context of the new divorce legislation and its symbolic representation in the public sphere (see pages 73–76 of this book). The reader will recall that the painting represents a husband's discovery of his wife's adultery, its effects on the family, and its social consequences for the erring woman (as she is pictured first in the bourgeois parlor and then in the streets). The narrative features of the painting alone invite a comparison to

Ford's representation of adultery in *The Good Soldier*. Like Egg, Ford is concerned to address the discovery of adultery (as opposed to the practice of adultery) and his approach is marked by a rich symbolism. In Egg's painting, for example, a halved apple, lying on the floor, is revealed to be rotten at the core; two children build a house of cards precariously balanced on a Balzac novel; and one of the paintings on the wall charts Adam and Eve's exile from paradise. Ford's novel echoes each of these symbols with a twist. Dowell asks in the first few pages of *The Good Soldier*: Is the apple really rotten? Is the house of cards really so fragile? Is paradise really lost?

The title of this painting, moreover, captures an important aspect of Ford's novel. Critics have frequently remarked on Ford's interest in the relationship between past and present (see, for example, Moser 49), and Saunders discusses Ford's writing in terms of a desire not only "to relive the past" but also "to superimpose it on the present" (68). "'Rembrance now,'" he writes, "could be taken as Ford's literary motto" (69). But if the narrative aspects of this painting and its title suggest a productive dialogue with Ford's novel, the journal entry affixed to the painting is even more provocative: "August the 4th. Have just heard that B— has been dead for more than a fortnight, so his poor children have now lost both parents. I hear *She* was seen on Friday last near the Strand, evidently without a place to lay her head. What a fall hers has been!" It seems clear that Ford was *inviting* his reader to make this connection between Egg's painting and his novel by selecting August 4th not only for Dowell's own discovery of Florence's adultery but also for many of the novel's most momentous events.

The fact that 4 August 1914 was also the date that England entered the First World War, however, has limited critical speculation to the question of whether Ford was intentionally invoking the war in his choice of dates. This possibility is appealing to critics because it nicely situates *The Good Soldier* in a modernist context, on the eve of the war that would so dramatically change English history. But this explanation of the date does not correspond to the facts of Ford's composition of the novel. Ford states that he began writing *The Good Soldier* on his fortieth birthday, 17 December 1913, and finished it in July 1914. When he was writing, then, Ford could not have possibly known when the war would begin. But Ford was also a notorious exaggerator and enormous critical energy has been expended in an effort accurately to fix the date of the novel's completion in a manner that does not rely on Ford's word.[10] Nevertheless, the issue remains unresolved. Reference to Egg's painting, however, provides a plausible extratextual source for the contested date which emphasizes Ford's novelistic treatment of adultery without, at the same time, precluding the possibility that he was also invoking the First World War.

The plausibility of this source is further underscored by Ford's fascination with his grandfather, the painter Ford Madox Brown. Brown was a contemporary of Egg's and one of his more famous paintings, "Take your Son, Sir!," also addresses the theme of the fallen woman encountered in *Past and Present*. Ford's own interest in Pre-Raphelite art combined with the fact that he wrote his grandfather's biography make it unlikely that Egg's painting could have escaped his attention. But if Egg's painting resonates powerfully with Ford's novel, Ford novel's also departs from its treatment of adultery in several important ways. The painting's straightforward chronology, for example, underscores a causal and a moral point—adultery leads to ruin—that the form of Ford's novel challenges. As I noted above, moreover, Dowell *questions* the prevailing symbols through which the knowledge of evil was communicated. The symbol of the apple is perhaps the best example here. Where the apple in Egg's painting clearly signals the wife's sexual transgression—she has eaten from the tree of knowledge, the fruit is rotten at the core—in Ford's novel, the apple occupies a much more equivocal position. Dowell writes: "If for nine years I have possessed a goodly apple that is rotten at the core and discover its rottenness only nine years and six months less four days, isn't it true that for nine years I possessed a goodly apple?" (9). Is it not true, Dowell asks in other words, that everything depends on the position of the observer, on what the observer sees ("a goodly apple"), indeed, on what an observer *can* see?

Past and Present highlights the fact that Dowell can no longer rely on a Victorian model of narrative coherence with respect to the representation of adultery. The knowledge of adultery destabilizes the ground of knowledge itself, it challenges and supplants old categories of knowing (in particular, the imagined transparency of realist representations), without providing new models through which to organize the world. In part, this challenge to ways of knowing and seeing one's world was implicit in the divorce court journalism, but it is the English novelists of adultery who develop its implications most extensively. Mary Douglas suggestively describes the role that ritual, in the context of framing, carries to render the world knowable and legible: "ritual focuses attention by framing; it enlivens the memory and links the present with the relevant past. In all this it aids perception. Or rather, it changes perception because it changes the selective principles. . . . It [ritual] can permit knowledge of what would otherwise not be known at all. . . . There can be no thoughts which have never been put into words. Once words have been framed the thought is changed and limited by the very words selected. So speech created something, a thought which might not have been the same" (64). If Ford manipulates the divorce court journalism to render adultery visible in a manner that resonates with Douglas's more general discussion of ritual and the effects of framing here, he also generates a dialogue, at once playful and rigorous, with Egg's painting that similarly illuminates adultery for the English audience. I have argued that Egg's chronological presentation of adultery departs from the divorce court format, but his presentation of adultery from the perspective of the betrayed party and his appeal to the epistemology of adultery is consistent both with this format and with Ford's novel. *The Good Soldier* gives a voice to the betrayed husband; the silent, stricken man in Egg's painting is animated and speaks from within the frame that has both circumscribed and defined English adultery. At the same time, as I will illustrate below, Ford's narrator speaks from a position *on* the frame and accordingly destabilizes the epistemological guarantees that the frame has previously ensured.

Like Ford, James needed to develop a form through which adultery could be *seen* in the English novel and to do so he both used and radically contested the reflection model to which most of his peers were still committed. I have already discussed how James's negotiation of the female reader and his manipulation of the divorce court journalism contributed to the visibility of adultery in his later novels, but his explicit framing of infidelity or adultery from the perspective of the betrayed party in *The Ambassadors*, *The Wings of the Dove*, and *The Golden Bowl* also served this purpose effectively. The betrayed party directly addressed epistemological issues of deep concern to James as she or he, at the same time, and by means of the same inquiry, challenged the very epistemological principles upon which this inquiry was based. James explicitly interrogates the question of framing: of distinguishing between an outside (the stance of the detached spectator) and an inside (the framed picture); the subject (who recognizes something) and the object (which is recognised). A sexual transgression, infidelity, is described in the context of a transgression between representation and "reality," or, more literally, a confusion between representation (the framed picture) and "reality" (the everyday life in which the picture is seen). What demands attention in these novels is that the "reality" with which the characters confuse the representation is itself a representation, is itself specifically textualized. This is not to pursue the familiar, but unhelpful, slogan that "there is nothing outside the text" but rather to show how the line demarcating the representation from the represented — the frame — becomes a condition of possibility that upsets the safety it was initially employed to ensure; the "honesty" of "a gilt frame" ("Art" 47–48) to which James refers is accordingly destablized.

The Portrait of the Lady offers a striking introduction to the relationship between the frame, adultery, accurate representation, and the epistemological questions that each of the above novels engage. Isabel recognizes that her husband's relationship with Madame Merle is not what it appears to be, and this recognition is presented pictorially. While this image — Gilbert Osmond sitting, a "familiar silence," "the mutual gaze" — is not directly equated with a literal painting as the scenes to which I will presently turn are, it nevertheless bears comparison. Isabel, James writes, "received an impression" from her position "just beyond the threshold" to the room in which Madame Merle and Osmond are located. There is "nothing unprecedented" about this impression but "she felt it as something new"; and there is nothing to "shock" in this and yet it "arrested her," the "thing made an image," "struck her as something detected" (408). There is a remarkable coincidence in event, diction, and structure between this scene and similar recognition scenes in the later novels. In each of the scenes a betrayal is recognised and subsequently dealt with.

Marianna Torgovnick makes two observations with respect to this passage. First she notices that "the moment ends before she [Isabel] had fairly seen it," before she can "read" its meaning (168). But it is this scene (in large part) that prompts Isabel's all-night vigil, a vigil concluding on a note of at least partial recognition: Isabel "stopped again in the middle of the room and stood there gazing at a remembered vision — that of her husband and Madame Merle unconsciously and familiarly associated" (435).

The second point that Torgovnick makes concerns the place of the observer. Do "we include Isabel in the 'painting' or do we omit her, presenting just the two individuals she beholds?" (170). This issue is crucial to the way in which James modifies his approach to representation and, in particular, the specificity of the perceiving subject. Isabel sees what she sees because of her involvement in these domestic relations, and her position before the threshold — on the border distinguishing the inside from the outside — signals her involvement as it, at the same time, complicates the very possibility of detached observation. There is, then, a double invocation of adultery: *what* Isabel sees suggests conjugal infidelity, while *how* she sees suggests narrative infidelity. This double vision also recalls Dowell's narrative: he relates a complicated history of adultery and deception; and his own narrative is forcefully implicated in a similar nexus of deception and unreliability. The perception of adultery, in other words, puts pressure on the form through which adultery is itself represented and rendered intelligible. Isabel may gain knowledge of adultery, but she does not do so in terms of epistemological realism — an accurate representation of an external event — but in terms of a network of relations, of her involvement in what she sees, and of her resulting interpretation.

James writes within the conventions of the realistic novel, and yet his desire to represent adultery requires a shifting of his own aesthetic frame; he resists an explicit presentation of the relation between Madame Merle and Osmond and instead chooses to represent Isabel "motionlessly *seeing*" ("Prefaces" 1084). The story itself, moreover, describes a woman who sees herself as implicated in a certain situation (indeed she can only see the situation *because* she is implicated) and her interpretation belies both her complicity and her distance. Chapter 42 thus serves to challenge the conventions of the realistic novel, and at the same time allows Isabel to deal with the situation in a way that both holds the image in her mind, and permits critical reflection upon it.

The passage to which I will refer in *The Ambassadors* is the celebrated scene by the river in which Strether sees what he has been, throughout the novel, scrupulously avoiding. He inadvertently stumbles upon a clandestine meeting between Chad and Madame de Vionnet and he tries to treat the situation as normal. But the modification from the "monstrous oddity" (382) of their accidental meeting to some semblance of normalcy does not occur without both tension and violence. The countryside into which Strether leisurely travels by train recalls for him a painting by Lambinet he had seen many years ago in a Boston gallery. In fact Strether has never explored the country except "through the little oblong window of the picture frame" (374). But the frame does not recede now that Strether is about to step into the "real" thing. Rather the frame accommodates even this move. As Strether walked through the country "the oblong gilt frame disposed its enclosing lines" (375). Indeed he remains bounded by the frame for the entire day: "he really continued in the picture — that being for himself his situation — all the rest of this rambling day" (378); "he had all the while not once overstepped the oblong gilt frame. The frame had drawn itself out for him, as much as you please" (379).

At dusk as Strether stands in a pavilion which "almost" overhangs the water at the garden's edge — in other words, on the border between land and water, day and night — there is an addition to his picture that ultimately tests and transgresses the frame circumscribing realistic fiction; and, at the same time, the reader is made aware of the frame as frame. At first the image is innocent enough: two figures, a man and a woman, in a boat on the river. "It was suddenly as if these figures, or something like them, had been wanted in the picture, had been wanted, more or less, all day, and had now drifted into sight" (382). What is it, exactly, that is "wanting"? It is this sight of two figures in a boat which, despite Strether's weariness, excites him with "a sharper arrest" (381). The idyllic quality of the perception is punctured, however, by Strether's recognition that the figures in the boat are Madame de Vionnet and Chad Newsome, and that Madame de Vionnet too feels the "shock" of recognition. Strether's surprise is deepened by his awareness that Madame de Vionnet and Chad, believing themselves unobserved, do not wish to acknowledge him: "It was a sharp, fantastic crisis... it had only to last the few seconds to make him feel quite horrible" (383). The violence of recognition is replaced by a second violence, "the violence of their having 'cut' him," and to avert this violence Strether breaks this silence with a wave and a call (383).

The illicit nature of the relationship between Madame de Vionnet and Chad is clear to Strether. Nevertheless, nothing is said about this affair and every effort is made to maintain normal relations. "[T]hey were blinking it, all round, and that they yet needn't, so much as that, have blinked it— though indeed if they hadn't Strether didn't quite see what else they could have done" (386). Infidelity is alluded to but it is not labeled: "He kept making of it that there had been simply a *lie* in the charming affair—" (386). The entire scene, however, is marked by an already inscribed textuality (the Lambinet to which Strether compares the "natural" countryside, the volume by Maupassant that Strether carries in his pocket and which he looks forward to reading, and the description of his recognition as a "wild fable" [384]), and it is dealt with both in terms of the reflection model and this model's epistemological limitations. In other words, the very epistemological model on which Strether relies to understand the appearance of Madame de Vionnet and Chad is undercut by what the appearance of these two figures means. The scene stresses the fact that the apparent border between picture and play (theater) cannot be maintained: "the picture and play seemed supremely to melt together" (326). The frame then is tested (each party was "*trying* the other side" [329]) as the picture passes from a representation informed by the Lambinet to a representation which must account for Madame de Vionnet and Chad, from Strether's "sharper arrest" to the "shock" of recognition, the sense of something "quite horrible," the "violence," and the unsaid which dictates the terms of social intercourse between the three characters.

Like Strether in *The Ambassadors*, Milly Theale in *The Wings of the Dove* also experiences an exceptional "arrest" that instigates a shift from painting to "life" when she unexpectedly recognizes Merton Densher, a gentleman whom she knows and likes, in London's National Gallery. Milly has been sitting down to rest after spending a number of hours looking at the pictures. In front of her a mother and two daughters discuss the paintings behind Milly's back. "'Handsome? Well, if you choose to say so.' It was the mother who had spoken, who herself added, after a pause during which Milly took the reference as to a picture: 'In the English style'" (176). Milly's curiosity is piqued and when the women leave she turns around to see the picture to which they referred. Instead of seeing a painting in the English style, however, she sees paintings from the Dutch school. Disappointed, she gets up to leave. But standing a short distance from her is a man whom she recognizes as the subject of the mother's comment.

The English style of the "handsome" gentleman in question holds her with an "arresting power." "This arresting power, at the same time—and that was the marvel—had already sharpened almost to pain, for in the very act of judging the bared head with detachment she felt herself shaken by a knowledge of it" (177). The gentleman is Merton Densher. Milly would prefer not to acknowledge his presence and likely would have turned around and left before he too recognised her, had not "a perception intervened that surpassed the first in violence" (177). The "shock" of recognition occurs this time when she recognizes her good friend Kate Croy with Merton Densher.

The subsequent interaction between these three characters—they leave the gallery and go to Milly's for lunch—is marked specifically by what is not said. The predicament in which they find themselves "wasn't definite or phraseable—and the way they let all phrasing pass was presently to recur to our young woman as a characteristic triumph of the civilized state" (178). And "she was to wonder in subsequent reflexion what in the world they had actually said, since they had made such a success of what they didn't say" (178). The "subsequent reflexion" parallels Isabel's reflection on the image of Osmond and Madame Merle together and betrays the conflict between two different versions of what is happening. Milly's method of dealing with the situation is, however, to become "as spontaneous as possible" (179), an American reflex in which Maggie will also seek refuge. I want to leave *The Wings of the Dove* here, again with the shift from "handsome" picture to handsome person, with the "arrest," the "violence," the "shock" of this transition, and with the "unsaid" that structures the subsequent communication, and motivates the movement beyond the initial "arrest."

The scenes in *Portrait of a Lady*, *The Ambassadors*, and *The Wings of the Dove* to which I refer above find a more complicated parallel in *The Golden Bowl*. Because James focuses on the betrayed party (Isabel, Strether, Milly, and Maggie respectively) he is able to explore the epistemological questions — the "philosophical bearing" — which he considered missing in representations of adultery as he, at the same time, sidesteps the difficult question of "handling" adulterous passion explicitly. Like *The Ambassadors* and *The Wings of the Dove*, a similar network of knowledge, situated subjectivity, and infidelity is explored in the context of visual art in *The Golden Bowl*. But in this novel the stakes are raised as the adulterous dynamic is more deliberately focused as the theme of the novel. Unlike Strether and Milly, moreover, Maggie Verver knows about her husband's affair. Nevertheless she too finds herself arrested by a certain picture that conveys to her more than she has been willing to admit. Again real characters are framed as in a picture. Again when the frame betrays its limitations the visual picture deteriorates and the protagonist tries to avoid, and then to face, what cannot be said. Again this recognition occurs on the literal border between an outside and an inside. The scene to which I refer is well known. The Prince and Charlotte are playing bridge with Fanny and Bob Assingham. Maggie herself does not participate in the card game, but instead tries to read a French magazine. Tiring of her reading, she leaves the room and walks outside. As she walks along the terrace — the "old smooth stones" (469) which border the house and separate it from the darkness beyond — she discovers that she can see into the rooms and, like Milly and Strether, what she sees arrests her attention: Maggie "stopped afresh for the look into the smoking-room, and by this time — it was as if the recognition had of itself arrested her — she saw as in a picture, with the temptation she had fled from quite extinct, why it was she had been able to give herself so little, from the first, to the vulgar heat of her wrong" (470). The picture calls to mind "horror" and "evil," but with the intention of a careful avoidance: "The sight, from the window, of the group so constituted, *told* her why, told her how, named to her, as with hard lips, named straight *at* her, so that she must take it full in the face, that other possible relation to the whole fact which alone would bear upon her irresistibly" (471). But the hard lips, the necessity of taking knowledge full in the face, obviates the freedom of naming and the knowledge arising from the picture that the passage suggests. It is not surprising, then, that this sense of control is radically undercut moments later.

The contentment that Maggie feels when she stares at the figures in the window is destroyed when one of those figures exercises her capacity to move beyond Maggie's vision, to step beyond the enclosing frame. (It should be clear, of course, that to step beyond one frame is not to escape framing all together.) When Maggie discovers that Charlotte has removed herself from the card game, she sees it as "a breaking of bars." Above all, Maggie desires the reassurance that Charlotte will be again circumscribed and contained by the frame: "The splendid shining supple creature was out of the cage, was at large; and the question now almost grotesquely rose of whether she mightn't by some art, just where she was and before she could go further, be hemmed in and secured" (472). To go further will be to meet with Charlotte and it is exactly this, like Milly and Strether before her, that Maggie wishes to avoid. Maggie entertains the possibility of closing the windows — which would amount to a conscious desire not to know — and "giving the alarm" (472); but as quickly as she considers this she rejects it. Instead she braces herself for a confrontation with Charlotte.

Charlotte finds Maggie on the terrace and the two exchange trivialities as they walk back toward the door. Before they enter Charlotte hesitates in front of the lighted window. "Side by side, for three minutes, they fixed this picture of quiet harmonies, the positive charm of it and, as might have been said, the full significance — which, as was now brought home to Maggie, could be no more, after all, than a matter of interpretation, differing always for a different interpreter" (476). The sense of revelation, of recognition and arrest, that Maggie experienced when she first glanced in the window is no longer operative. But James does not simply dismiss the frame; he does not entirely replace the frame or the picture with the performative force of his scenic principle. Instead, he demonstrates how the frame is both the condition of possibility for seeing (the recognitions above only come into focus in the context of the frame) and the limit that frustrates any claim to the fidelity of the representation. The frame at once generates and undercuts vision. It initially confers safety and distance and, as James notes in "The Art of Fiction," it warns one to be on guard. As the examples above demonstrate, however, the frame lulls the viewer into a false complacency; the picture, in fact, is much more real and menacing than one imagines. James's representation of infidelity in his late novels illustrates that the truth does not step forward with a warning but rather sneaks up from behind, framed and messy, subdued and shocking, pastoral and violent, silent and loquacious. It speaks and it does not say a word.

Charlotte's search for Maggie was motivated by a specific question that she wished to ask her. It amounts to asking: do you know about my relationship with your husband? But is posed in somewhat less direct terms: have I done anything to displease you of late? Maggie lies and answers no. Maggie's persistent avowal of normalcy denies the deep unrest that troubles her thoughts. Neither the visual picture at the window nor the prose picture that James writes can faithfully reflect the *knowledge* of infidelity and the need for fidelity with which her mind struggles. James's concern to represent adultery with a "philosophical bearing" invites the epistemological focus which emerges most coherently in his later work. Adultery in the English novel is not, strictly speaking, about marriage or desire (although it is about these things too), but about *knowing*. And what the representation of adultery inevitably calls for is a new account of epistemology. James's discourse on the frame allows him to represent adultery without incurring the wrath of his audience, delimited as it is within the safety of the frame, as he at the same time challenges the very integrity of that frame in terms both of sexual infidelity and the fidelity of narration itself.

In 1896 James was frustrated with *Century Magazine*'s prudish rejection of his article on Dumas; Dumas, he writes in his *Notebooks*, "is famous because he wrote certain things which they [*Century Magazine*] won't for the world have intelligibly mentioned" (154). The challenge for James in his later novels is to find a way to translate scenes of adultery so that they may be intelligibly mentioned. If, in these novels, the observers begin by standing, more or less, *on the frame* — Isabel on the threshold, Strether on the water's edge, Maggie on the terrace — then they, as observers, as framers, are what make the recognition scenes possible. But what becomes clear in the subsequent action is that they are not just *on* the frame, they are also *in* the frame, part of the picture: the frame is folded into the picture of what they see. Oddly, the crimes of adultery and deception are not themselves "arrested" so to speak (the responses are in each case marked by what is not said and there is no "sounding of the alarm"), but instead it is the observing parties themselves who are "arrested." They stop. They are taken aback. And here James, with his fine sensitivity to the social and sexual dictates of his time orchestrates an important move: he at once complicates the representation of adultery (by sidestepping the conventional forms while remaining within the boundary of the permissible) and the genre of the novel (by self-reflexively, or pictorially, undoing realist conventions). In a sophisticated and consistent manner he illustrates the following simple idea: adultery becomes a crime, not when it is committed, but when it is seen, when it is publicly recognized. Accordingly, and this is James's perceptive innovation, it is the character who *sees* adultery, and not the character who commits the act itself, who is placed "under arrest." It is the frame on which James invariably writes as his "privileged observers" hover on the line between the picture and their own perilous worlds. There is no crossing to safety. The "accurate representation," upon which so much relies, is a lie, a "lie in the charming affair." In *The Good Soldier* Dowell figuratively stands on the same frame or border as Isabel, Strether, Milly, and Maggie; as a reader/spectator his narrative addresses the epistemological questions to which Hynes refers above as it also self-consciously grapples with the priority accorded to the spectator or reader in scenes of adultery.

Bedroom Secrets: A Tale of Sexual Trauma

I have argued that one of Dowell's goals in telling his story is the hopeful, slightly sad, desire to seduce his listener. A victim himself of the seductions of others he is at once a bewildered and astonished husband repeatedly betrayed by his wife, and a storyteller who imagines that this history of betrayal might, perversely, tempt his listener into love. But to this end he confronts real obstacles. For how does one tell the story of adultery? One can easily imagine this story from Edward's point of view: there would be passages of acute psychological anguish and long convoluted rationalizations of his behavior but there would also be descriptions of intense physical passion and fabulous, expansive desire. Dowell's story of adultery, by contrast, is bluntly summarized by a closed bedroom door. And if the story of adultery imposes distinctive narrative obstacles for Dowell, these obstacles are only aggravated by a degree of trauma that Dowell also communicates in the telling.

Max Saunders relates what he aptly calls Ford's "aesthetics of suppression" (2:87) to the difficulty of recounting the trauma produced by war experience, but it can just as productively be linked to Ford's pre-war narratives and the sexual traumas that they record. Indeed, the difficulty of recounting sexual trauma is compounded by the fact that not only are there psychic barriers to the reiteration of painful experience but there are also social and political prohibitions against such expression. In this context, *The Good Soldier* works on two levels at once: Dowell's account of his traumatic discovery of adultery records a psychological struggle both to tell the story of adultery, however agonizing, *and* to avoid and suppress this same story; and Ford's account of Dowell's account must respond to the social prohibitions exercised on novelistic representation without sacrificing its appearance of spontaneous and unstudied confession. Needless to say, Ford himself was preoccupied with these issues. He spoke often and openly about the English habit of repression; and, as Vincent Cheng notes, the English "discouragement of open and free expression," especially with respect to "things" (read: sexual things), became increasingly central to Ford's writing (305).[11]

Ford's commitment to representing adultery in particular, the paradigmatic "thing" restricted from civilized conversation and the serious English novel, was facilitated by recourse to the divorce court journalism. In *A Call* he had explored this journalism in terms of its exploitation of scandal and its capacity, quietly but forcefully, to regulate sexual behavior. In *The Good Soldier* Ford is also concerned to address the way in which the divorce court and the divorce court journalism manipulate scandal to perform the work of the law. Here the closed bedroom door is, in fact, an asset. For the novel traces the means by which adultery becomes visible, the closed door opened, while conforming, at least on the surface, to the tenor and logic of the divorce court journalism. In this domestic detective story, Dowell and Leonora, like Maggie and her father, practice a form of domestic surveillance through which adultery may be regulated without the interference of the court.[12] To this end, the law is carried into the home. In addition to this thematic link between Ford's novel and the divorce court journalism there are also several formal parallels between the two genres. *The Good Soldier*'s development of the betrayed party, narrative reliability, disrupted chronology (what Ford calls the "time shift"), and problematic closure all closely resemble narrative strategies associated with the divorce court journalism.

Before turning to Ford's formal innovations, however, I want to consider his development of domestic surveillance. While the strategies of surveillance common to the detective story also intensely, even obsessively, prevail in this modernist narrative, what Dowell's narration emphasizes is that they do not work. *The Good Soldier* belabors the spectator's epistemological limitations, the *failure* to see. Leonora sees too much; Dowell does not see enough. The epistemology of vivid display common in realist narratives, the lifting off of the housetops and the scrutiny of previously private spaces, is replaced by questions, doubt, suspicion, and epistemological crisis. What really happened? In the absence of first-hand testimony, how can one possibly know?

The epistemological crisis at the heart of Dowell's narrative is paralleled by the two forms of domestic surveillance in which he engages: the inept, but blandly amusing, surveillance of Florence at the level of the story's content; and the excessive, meandering surveillance of the four characters to whom he is closest at the level of the story's structure. Dowell returns to the scene of the crime, in other words, and not only fills in missing pieces, correcting earlier interpretations, but also radically extends the range of his scrutiny. Florence's narrative control, her brazen assertion of desire, is usurped by Dowell and his own story, a story that has him listening in the places where he only daydreamed and understanding in the places where he was bewildered. At first, Dowell is not trying to prevent or control adultery but rather to prevent *talk* of adultery. To "protect" Florence from her alleged heart condition, Dowell observes, for "twelve years I had to watch every word that any person uttered in any conversation and I had to head it off what the English call 'things' — off love, poverty, crime, religion, and the rest of it" (18).[13] Dowell's scrupulous attention to his wife's conversational environment does not, however, extend into the bedroom: "I believe that for the twelve years her life lasted, after the storm that seemed irretrievably to have weakened her heart — I don't believe that for one minute she was out of my sight, except when she was safely tucked up in bed" (10). The shift in this sentence from "I believe" to "I don't believe" structures the development of the novel itself. Later Dowell modifies his report, no longer believing his own account: "But looking over what I have written, I see that I have unintentionally misled you when I said that Florence was never out of my sight. Yet that was the impression that I really had until just now. When I come to think of it she was out of my sight most of the time" (97). Dowell's narrative vigilance forces him to confront the lack of domestic vigilance he exercised in his own life. Perhaps Dowell's most amusing exposure of his failure to see is the ingenuous assurance he offers to Leonora: "well, Leonora, a man sees more of these things than even a wife. And, let me tell you, that in all these years I've known Edward he has never, in your absence, paid a moment's attention to any other woman — not by the quivering of any eyelash. I should have noticed. And he talks of you as if you were one of the angels of God'" To which Leonora responds, "'Oh, . . . I am perfectly sure that he always speaks nicely of me'" (106). Again the division between talk and action is telling. If Dowell has to avoid "things" with Florence, the purpose of his narration is to offer a report on precisely those things which previously escaped his notice, the things which he did not, in fact, see.

It is striking that Dowell faults Leonora with exactly what he fails to do himself: "She should have gone eavesdropping; she should have stood outside bedroom doors. It is odious, but that is the way that the job is done" (203). While Leonora does, in fact, stand outside bedroom doors (in this way she discovers Maisie leaving her husband's room and later knows when Florence and Edward are having an affair), Dowell not only is excluded from his wife's bedroom but also should he want to enter he has to knock, and should Florence not answer he has been supplied with a crowbar to break the door down. Dowell's writing, however, situates him in the bedrooms from which he has previously been excluded. Dowell the husband watches his wife with a protective trust while Dowell the narrator approaches others with what Hynes describes as "compassionate doubt" noting that "by an act of perfect sympathy" Dowell "has known what Ashburnham was" (234). But this claim is overstated: Dowell's sympathy with Edward is seriously flawed and, if anything, demonstrates the *limits* of love, trust, and narration.

The figure of the domestic detective and the exercise of domestic surveillance, however, are most fully realized in the character of Leonora Ashburnham. Her exacting scrutiny of her husband, her regulation of his affairs, brings the law into the domestic spaces of the home (as Dowell's narration intertwines the law with the domestic space of the novel) with a rigor and unflinching attention to the events most painful to witness and record. But Leonora's narrative, as it is related by Dowell, also does more than simply locate the law in the home; it suggests that domestic peace — the norm of the domestic space — *relies* on both adultery and its quasi-legal regulation. The home is not an enclave remote from criminal activity and the public institution of the law but rather is the very locus of the law as D. A. Miller has so cogently argued in the context of the Victorian novel.

In an attempt to control both Edward's incessant lies and his marital affairs Leonora justifies first having "his secrets at her disposal" (54) and later practicing a policy of blatant "spying": "Leonora describes herself as watching him as a fierce cat watches an unconscious pigeon in a roadway. . . . she watched and watched, and uttered apparently random sentences about Florence before the girl, and perceived that he had no grief and no remorse" (144). And Dowell later explains: "For, watching Edward more intently and with more straining of ears than that which a cat bestows on a bird overhead, she was aware of the progress of his passion for each of these ladies. She was aware of it from the way in which his eyes returned to doors and gateways; she knew from his tranquillities when he had received satisfactions" (194). And at "dances she was in a fever of watchfulness" (195). Leonora's urgent need not to be surprised, to create what Dowell refers to as a "shock-proof world" (53), overrides her desire flatly to prohibit Edward's affairs (along contractual lines, for example). She expresses this preference for knowledge to Florence: "Yes, you would give him up. And you would go on writing to each other in secret, and committing adultery in hired rooms. I know the pair of you, I know. No. I prefer the situation as it is" (77).

It is only, however, when Leonora no longer has to watch and control her husband that their domestic economy disintegrates. Leonora's sanity is inseparable from the necessity of her alert domestic scrutiny. Edward, it appears, is not going to pursue his desire for Nancy and Leonora realizes that she can "relax some of her vigilance" (146). But later we recognize the extent to which she depends on the necessity of this very vigilance: "And then Leonora completely broke down.... She felt that she could trust Edward with the girl and she knew that Nancy could be absolutely trusted. And then with the slackening of her vigilance, came the slackening of her entire mind" (148). It does not matter what Leonora sees — if she sees too much or if she sees the wrong thing — as long as she does not renounce her role as a domestic control. Surveillance is not then a means to an end (say, the discovery of adultery) but a means *and* an end: the domestic equilibrium is maintained in the Ashburnham household through Leonora's constant vigilance and Edward's constant need for vigilance.

In this context, the home becomes a domestic tribunal in which Edward is judged. The law may enter the home with the black-and-white decisiveness of the judge's ruling on the Brand divorce case but, like all black-and-white judgements in this novel, the case is not closed. Indeed with the inclusion of Nancy, the exercise of the law becomes as mysterious, as terrifying, as evil as Nancy's reading experience. The following passage, for example, illustrates the tension between earlier forms of the law — the poison bowls and the daggers on which one can no longer rely in *A Call* — and the relentless, searing effects of a law that uses publicity and "talk" to exact its results:

> Those two [Leonora and Nancy] women pursued that poor devil [Edward] and flayed the skin off him as if they had done it with whips. I tell you his mind bled visibly. I seem to see him stand, naked to the waist, his forearms shielding his eyes, and flesh hanging from him in rags.... It was as if Leonora and Nancy banded themselves together to do execution, for the sake of humanity, upon the body of a man who was at their disposal. They were like a couple of Sioux who had got hold of an Apache and had him well tied to a stake. I tell you there was no end to the tortures they inflicted upon him.

> Night after night he would hear them talking; talking; maddened, sweating, seeking oblivion in drink, he would lie there and hear their voices going on and on. . . .
> They were like judges debating over the sentence of a criminal; they were like ghouls with an immobile corpse in a tomb beside them. (259–60)

Edward hears "their voices going on and on." It is the sound of these voices that works like torture on him; the words, the "endless talking" (264), work like wounds upon his body, and they prefigure Edward's final suicide with a *pen*knife. The domestic crime of adultery may be discovered but in English novels of adultery the "criminals" are rarely arrested; rather, they are disciplined through a process that perpetually suspends the relief of a sentence. Dowell writes that it would "have been better in the eyes of God if they had all attempted to gouge out each other's eyes with carving knives" (270), but, as Foucault argues, it is precisely the "interrogation without end" (*Discipline* 227) that most effectively realizes the law's goals.

It is a desire to avoid the law, to avoid scandal, moreover, that both enables Edward's adulteries and motivates Leonora's domestic surveillance.[14] Mrs. Basil's husband blackmails Edward "with threats of the divorce court" (63), a threat which works on Edward's own distaste for publicity. Along "with his passions and his shames there went the dread of scenes in public places, of outcry, of excited physical violence; of publicity, in short" (66). And when Leonora discovers that Edward is being blackmailed, her doubt about what is really happening is sharpened as her fear of publicity mounts: "her road had again seemed to stretch out endless: she imagined that there might be hundreds and hundreds of such things that Edward was concealing from her—that they might necessitate more mortgaging, more pawnings of bracelets, more and always more horrors. She had spent an excruciating afternoon. The matter was one of a divorce case, of course, and she wanted to avoid the publicity as much as Edward did, so that she saw the necessity of continuing the payments" (69). Leonora's ruthless vigilance does not ensure epistemological confidence. If her vigilance is exercised with the goal to curb Edward's adulteries it only accentuates and inflates Leonora's imagination of them and, accordingly, her need to maintain a vigilant watch. Like Beatrice and Maggie, Leonora imagines things that she does not see—"hundreds and hundreds of such things"—and she is on her guard; the knowledge of her husband's adultery only heightens her tendency to suspect. As Dowell on another occasion notes, "At times she imagined herself to see more than was warranted" (194). The visibility of adultery produces an imaginative excess: because adulterous practices are so difficult to prove, the smallest details incite alarm and suspicion. It is, to borrow a resonant phrase from Peter Brooks, an "hallucinated consciousness" that propels the grim cycle of the Ashburnham's marriage. In a disciplinary world that does not permit poison or daggers, the quiet scrutiny and the manic hallucinations ensure that the domestic tragedy "goes on and on."

The Good Soldier's focus on domestic surveillance is linked to one of the novel's most contested formal features: the reliability of its narration. Is Dowell simply a clinical observer, admittedly baffled by his experience, who dispassionately relates a story of adultery? Or is he, in fact, deeply invested in this story that, after all, recounts his wife's affair with his best friend? Is Dowell's narrative surveillance—his account of the last nine years—filled with as many gaps, missing moments, closed doors, and blank stares as his attempted domestic surveillance of Florence? Critics, however, have been concerned with the question of Dowell's reliability to the exclusion of what he is reliable or unreliable about: the very question of reliability—sexual reliability—itself. Laura Tracy notes that the form and the content, for example, contradict one another: "The novel is about a tale of violent passion and betrayal; Dowell narrates it from the perspective of detached observation" (87). And Mark Schorer situates the novel's irony in the same context: "the book's controlling irony lies in the fact that passionate situations are related by a narrator who is himself incapable of passion, sexual and moral alike" (ix). But if the discrepancy between form and content is accurate on the level of passion, it is not necessarily accurate on the level of infidelity or unreliability. Carol Jacobs is the only critic who makes explicit the lack of reliability described in the text and the narrative unreliability: "As the narrative rolls along . . . we begin to suspect that the text itself is a kind of adulterer, continually turning form the straight line of narration in which it might remain true to what is said before. It promiscuously betrays not only itself, but also us, its intimates, enticed as we are to a two-week honeymoon in a country cottage only to find that our own text is unfaithful" (35). What Jacobs does not remark is that this narrative betrayal, its incitement of suspicion and doubt, is fully consonant with the divorce court journalism which the novel both explicitly invokes and implicitly draws upon to develop rhetorical strategies uniquely suited to the English representation of adultery.

There is no doubt that Dowell's famously quirky narration is limited. Indeed, this limited narration reflects Ford's attempt to create a "new form" for the novel. Ford writes:

That we [Conrad and Ford] did succeed eventually in finding a new form I think I may permit myself to claim, Conrad first evolving the convention of a Marlow who should narrate, in presentation, the whole story of a novel just as, without much sequence or pursued chronology, a story will come into the mind of the narrator, and I eventually dispensing with a narrator but making the story come up in the mind of the unseen author with a similar want of chronological sequence.... We evolved then a convention for the novel and one that I think still stands. The novel must be put into the mouth of a narrator—who must be limited by probability as to what he can know of the affair that he is adumbrating. ("Techniques" 297–98)

This "new form" will also recall, of course, James's third-person limited narration. For both James and Ford, this point of view facilitates the representation of adultery otherwise informally prohibited to the English novelist. And in both cases, the point of view also underscores a central motif of the novels themselves: when one tells the story of adultery from the perspective of the betrayed party this story will always be fractured, incomplete, and distorted. In a word, unreliable. The betrayed party is on the frame, so to speak, neither inside nor outside the picture of adultery that slowly comes into focus.

If the narration of *The Good Soldier* resembles the form of the divorce court in its focus on the betrayed party, it also resembles the divorce court in its repetition and its "want of chronological sequence."[15] In a narrative that is about characters who are not in their proper places it is worth noting that the narrative too is out of its proper place; Dowell, for example, forgets to mention events "in their proper places" (201). While this lack of propriety is essentially Dreiser's complaint when he faults the novel for failing to provide the appropriate beginning, middle, and end (14) it is a technique that Ford values. In his study of Conrad he notes: "It became very early evident to us [Ford and Conrad] that what was the matter with the Novel, and the British novel in particular, was that it went straight forward" (*Conrad* 129–30). The movement back and forth—"one goes back, one goes forward," as Dowell observes (201)—is more explicitly foregrounded in the divorce court journalism when headlines announce "The Case for the Husband," "The Case for the Wife," "Evidence of the Petitioner," "Servant's Evidence," "Detective's Evidence," "Cross-Examination," and so on.

In the divorce court documentation the repetition involves both denial of factual evidence and fluctuations as to the chronology of events; and it is always particularly urgent to determine the exact date of the reported events. Dowell's persistent reference to August 4th, for instance, is typical of the legal demand to fix dates. The *Phillips* v. *Phillips* divorce case reported in

The *Times* in early December 1913 offers one representative example of the attempt to fix dates and the repetitive quality of such cases.

While there [at Paignton] in 1910 Mr. Phillips used to go to see Mrs. Goldschmidt when she was ill and play cards with her when she was in very scanty attire. Mrs. Phillips's suspicions were aroused, nor were they allayed when on their return to town, at an evening party, Mrs. Goldschmidt stood up, looked fixedly at Mr Phillips and exclaimed, "I am the happiest woman in Hampstead; don't I look it?" (28 Nov. 1913: 3)

She [Mrs. Phillips] saw her husband kiss Mrs. Goldschmidt there [at Paignton] on two occasions. On the latter of these two occasion she taxed her husband with it. He said, "Thank God, I am free. This is my birthday." He then went out to Mrs. Goldschmidt's house. (29 Nov. 1913: 4)

Mr. Goldschmidt and her [Mrs. Phillips's] husband became friends, and six or seven years ago the Goldschmidts moved to Hampstead. She denied that she herself formed one of party who played cards with her husband and Mrs. Goldschmidt after the latter's confinement. She could not remember the name of the person who told her that Mrs. Goldschmidt and her husband had played cards together when the latter was "scantily attired." The witness was cross-examined at length as to the alleged incident of her husband's kissing Mrs. Goldschmidt at Paignton when (the witness) was concealed behind a hedge. (4 Dec. 1913: 4)

Mr. Henry Allan Phillips denied that he had ever committed adultery with Mrs. Goldschmidt. He, his wife, and the Goldschmidts were on perfectly friendly terms until 1911. He had never played cards with Mrs. Goldschmidt in his wife's absence when the former was ill. He never remembered that Mrs. Goldschmidt at a party gave him a "peculiar look" and exclaimed, "I am the happiest woman in Hampstead." . . . Her evidence [Mrs. Phillip's] as to when she was in Paignton in August, 1911, was all untrue. (5 Dec. 1913: 4)

Ford employs this repetitive technique to his advantage in Dowell's references to the day at M——, the Kilsyte case, his constant repetition of small details, and contradictions. In this way, Dowell disrupts traditional narrative order and the authority such order confers.

Finally, in addition to disturbing chronological sequence, Ford also parodies the traditional ending of the novel and the "sentence" of the divorce/adultery trial. His "real" story, like the traditional story, has a happy ending: "well, that is the end of the story. And, when I come to look at it, I see that it is a happy ending with wedding bells and all. The villains — for obviously Edward and the girl were villains — have been punished by suicide and madness. The heroine — the perfectly normal, virtuous, and slightly deceitful heroine — has become the happy wife of a perfect normal, virtuous, and slightly deceitful husband. She will shortly become the mother of a perfectly normal, virtuous, and slightly deceitful son or daughter. A happy ending, that is what it works out at" (273). But this is not the ending. Ford identifies such closure with the traditional novel, and the failure to provide this "very natural human desire" with a new novel form: "To the theory of Aloofness added itself, by a very natural process, the other theory that the story of a love should be the history of an Affair and not the invention of state in which a central character with an attendant female shall be followed through a certain space of time until they come to a happy end on a note of matrimony or to an unhappy end — represented by a death. The latter — the normal practice of the earlier novelist and still the normal expedient of the novel of commerce and of escape — is again imbecile, but again designed to satisfy a very natural human desire for finality" (*English* 131–32; see also the Epilogue to *A Call*). The happy ending referred to above is followed by four pages which detail both Nancy's madness and Edward's suicide. Edward's suicide, moreover, affirms the complete success of Leonora's surveillance on both formal and thematic grounds. Whereas Dowell earlier claimed that there "is not even any villain in the story" (179), he has now identified some villains and manipulated his story into the traditional mold: a happy ending, wedding bells, and a clear distinction between the villains and the perfectly normal heroine.

But the "normal" is a sleight of hand: virtue breeds deceit, the normal produces the abnormal, order creates disorder. The lost world — or Florence's "world well lost" (130) — which Dowell initially laments is, in fact, exactly the world he does not want. Because the normal and the abnormal are inextricably caught up in one another one should be wary of Dowell's shift from moral confusion to moral clarity, from black to white. Earlier Dowell could not identify any guidepost by which to orient his moral decisions, and now he has no apparent difficulty in outlining the conventional desires suited to a conventional program as it is practiced by the "heroine" Leonora: "Leonora, as I have said, was the perfectly normal woman. I mean to say that in normal circumstances her desires were those of the woman who is needed by society. She desired children, decorum, an establishment; she desired to avoid waste, she desired to keep up appearances. . . . But I don't mean to say that she acted perfectly normally in this perfectly abnormal situation. All the world was mad around her and she herself, agonized, took on the complexion of a mad woman; of a woman very wicked; of the villain of the piece" (260).

Dowell finds to his dismay, however, that this situation is no longer what he wants: the conventional program breeds exactly the deceit which he bemoans as the outcome of a loss of a conventional program. That Dowell's search for knowledge would lead to this form of distasteful knowledge, exactly the opposite of what one would expect, has in fact been hinted at in the text from the "beginning." The authority conferred by the law — by the legal narration of the divorce court — is undercut as each of the formal principles through which the divorce court establishes its evidence is demonstrated as unreliable or fallible. It is important to recognize that Ford's formal innovations are linked to his desire to represent adultery (to counteract, in other words, the national characteristic of restraint that he finds so appalling) and, accordingly, to circumvent the censoring mechanisms by which he believed the English novel was limited. And it is this double goal that is *productive* of narrative innovation. If Ford, then, develops formal traits linked to the divorce court both to criticize the dominant institution through which adultery was rendered visible in English print culture and to legitimate and more fully enable his own explorations of adultery in an aesthetic register, he also unavoidably engages the epistemological and narratological questions that this exploration invites. This narrative which turns on bedroom secrets, unread and illegible letters, chronological confusion, and eavesdropping, finds a convergence of its epistemological and its sociohistorical threads, its form and its content, in literal, literary, and legal cases. It is to the "case," then, that I now turn.

Cases: A Tale of the Law

The link between prohibition and production, so vital to an understanding of the representation of adultery in English print culture, is elaborated in a typically idiosyncratic manner in *The Good Soldier*. In this novel, the law does not, in fact, succeed in curtailing adultery, redirecting the appropriate desires in the appropriate direction; on the contrary, it produces adultery. The two legal cases recounted in the text — the Kilsyte case and the Brand divorce case — illustrate this point. The Kilsyte case is a product of Edward's desire to comfort a young kitchenmaid whom he meets on a train. Her distress takes the form of tears and his comfort takes the form of an arm around her shoulder and a kiss. The kitchenmaid, however, draws the line at sympathetic talk (for which Edward is well suited being the sentimentalist he is) and not physical contact (for which Edward is unfortunately also well suited, not because he is a sensualist, like Florence, but because he cannot distinguish between talk and sex.).[16] Nevertheless, a kiss does not denote adultery, or even necessarily a serious violation, and Edward's kiss is presented in terms of his innocent desire to comfort the distraught girl. At this point in the narrative, moreover, Edward has been strictly faithful to Leonora and has not even entertained the possibility of adultery. It is, in fact, the court case itself—designed to punish Edward for his transgressive behavior and restrict further actions of a similar nature—which *generates* a shift in attitude: "he assured me that, before the case came on and was wrangled about by counsel with all the sorts of dirty-mindedness that counsel in that sort of case can impute, he had not had the least idea that he was capable of being unfaithful to Leonora. But, in the midst of that tumult— he says that it came suddenly into his head whilst he was in the witness box—in the midst of those august ceremonies of the law there came suddenly into his mind the recollection of the softness of the girl's body as he had pressed her to him" (171). As a result, he "saw himself as the victim of the law" and maintained that "it had put ideas in his head" (171–72). In two of his subsequent affairs he uses the case to his advantage. In his seduction of La Dolciquita he "took her into the dark gardens and, remembering suddenly the girl of the Kilsyte case, he kissed her" (174); and in his attempt to gain the affections of Maisie he "awakened her attention by swearing that when he kissed the servant in the train he was driven to it" (55).

Between the Kilsyte case and the Brand divorce case which more or less closes the narrative, Dowell refers to several literal cases which, like the legal cases, produce exactly the opposite of their intended effect. For example, Dowell's knowledge of Edward is, for nine years, limited to superficial details, such as the fact that Edward owns several fancy cases. The privilege this detail is given in the text is worth noting:

And that [details about birds, bits, boots, etc.] was absolutely all that I knew of him until a month ago—that and the profusion of his cases, all of pigskin and stamped with his initials, E. F. A. There were guncases, and collar cases, and shirt cases, and letter cases, and cases each containing four bottles of medicine; and hat cases and helmet cases. It must have needed a whole herd of the Gadarene swine to make up his outfit. And if I ever penetrated into his private room, it would be to see him standing with his coat and waistcoat off and the immensely long lie of his perfectly elegant trousers from waist to boot heel. And he would have a slightly reflective air and he would be just opening one kind of case and just closing another. (29)

It is one of these "fascinating cases containing fifteen different sizes of scissors" (71) which gets Maisie in trouble with Leonora and in fact leads to the intimacy between the Ashburnhams and the Dowells. Maisie is returning the borrowed case to Edward's room (because she is poor and cannot afford a maid) a few hours after Leonora has discovered that Edward is being blackmailed by the husband of one of Edward's previous lovers. When Leonora sees Maisie leaving Edward's room she assumes the worst and boxes her ears; Florence, however, happens along the hall at this point and sees what looks like a jealous contest between two women, thus giving Florence a "hold over" Leonora which Leonora decides to reduce by keeping Florence "under observation" (71). And so begins the nine-year friendship. The incident in the hallway following the return of the case, moreover, precipitates Maisie's own contact with a case when she falls dead into her trunk fleeing Edward, Leonora, and the adulterous plot they had planned for her.

If Maisie's return of Edward's case led to unexpected results, Edward's cases themselves did not produce their intended effect. Leonora tried to please Edward but failed because she did not understand "his way": "She was always buying him expensive things which, as it were, she took off her own back. I have, for instance, spoken of Edward's leather cases. Well, they were not Edward's at all; they were Leonora's manifestations. He liked to be clean, but he preferred, as it were, to be threadbare. She never understood that, and all that pigskin was her idea of a reward to him for putting her up to a little speculation by which she made eleven hundred pounds" (183). The case is not closed here, so to speak; on the contrary, it is open and productive. And like the law that seeks to prohibit crime and redress wrongdoing, in this novel it produces exactly the opposite of its intended effect.

I want to consider, finally, the literary case. What is the "whole effect of the reading" (239) on the reader of *The Good Soldier*? Nancy's act of reading the Brand divorce case converges, as I have noted, with the reader's act of reading this novel. Nancy approaches the case—as the reader also first approaches Dowell's story—in a chronologically reversed order: "The case occupied three days, and the report Nancy first came upon was that of the third day" (237). The first effect upon Nancy is confusion: "she could not understand why one counsel should be so anxious to know all about the movements of Mr. Brand upon a certain day. . . . She did not even see why they should want to know that, upon a certain occasion, the drawing room door was locked. It made her laugh: it appeared senseless that grown people should occupy themselves with such matters. It struck her, nevertheless, as odd that one of the counsel should cross-question Mr. Brand so insistently and so impertinently as to his feelings for Miss Lupton" (237). The confusion which Nancy experiences is again paralleled in the reader's response to *The Good Soldier*. Why is Dowell telling us "all about the movements" of everyone "upon a certain day," the visit to M—, and the events which conspired there? Why is Florence's door always locked? What are Edward's real feelings—feelings to which Dowell returns insistently, if not impertinently—about Nancy? And if "chasing a scrap of paper [Florence]" is "an occupation ignoble for a grown man" (134), is it as "senseless" as grown people occupying themselves with transcriptions of the divorce court, or for that matter reading the scraps of paper that constitute *The Good Soldier*? Nancy's reading promotes a certain solidarity between Leonora and Nancy, moreover, which allows them to produce their own verdict on the events within a distinctly domestic tribunal. "They were like judges debating on the sentence of a criminal" (260), Dowell tells us. And the verdict is responsibly recorded by Dowell in black and white: guilty of adultery.

Adultery has been unavoidably exposed, and it has been exposed not only to the naïve American, Dowell, but also to the innocent Catholic convent "girl," the young female reader, Nancy. The press is, as Florence asserts in a different context, in the bedroom: Dowell has stood outside bedroom doors and entered bedrooms previously prohibited to him to record, however incompletely, carefully guarded bedroom secrets. Both Dowell and Nancy, moreover, find themselves (like Beatrice and Maggie before them) implicated in what they see and hear. Peter Brooks uses de Maupassant's "Une Ruse," a short story dealing with adultery, to illustrate how listening to such a tale also "implicates the listener" (*Reading* 217). "Does not reading," he asks, "—having read—put him [or her, the listener], like it or not, on the side of fallen knowledge?" (218). Like Leonora's brief story of adultery averted, Dowell's tormented story of adulterous discovery and belated desire inextricably weaves the reader into its narrative design. So that for even the most innocent of readers a new possibility may arise: perhaps, the narrative invites the reader to think about love and seduction. Perhaps, like Nancy, the reader may wonder: could she or he be the object of a married person's desire?

But *The Good Soldier* also suggests that the opposite reading effect is just as likely: perhaps this story will encourage the reader to follow Nancy's example in her ruthless retreat from Edward and her chilling regulation of his adulterous desire. For if the divorce court journalism inflames Nancy's erotic imagination it also as quickly subdues it to the service of the law. Again the young female reader learns to read the adulterous body only to adopt the strictest and cruelest forms of domestic control. To gain a degree of cultural authority, then, this reader must ardently support the social order that holds her in place. *The Good Soldier*, however, does not stop here. Nancy reads the divorce court journalism and learns a new word: adultery. And this knowledge shatters her world. Beatrice's bold reason and Maggie's cool domestic authority are replaced by a young woman who reads and learns about adultery to the detriment of her language and her sanity. For when the novel closes, Nancy's language is pared down to only a handful of words and her reason is lost.

It is important, I have been arguing, to read *The Good Soldier* as a novel that is *about* adultery and the categories of perception—the divorce court journalism and the young female reader—through which adultery is uneasily rendered visible in the modernist period. This reading not only illuminates Ford's debt to both the Victorian tradition (the law, novels, journalism, and visual art) and his contemporary context (the novels of James and Conrad and the print censorship debates), but also situates Ford's formal accomplishments, the modernist narrative innovations for which he is best known, in a material context. As a result it becomes possible to see *The Good Soldier*'s ideological investments and its exploration of the social function of reading despite the powerful narrative mechanisms that deflect interpretations in different and safer directions. If Ford's novel is poised uneasily between the "tale of passion" and the "case" study, its treatment of the relationship between the teller and the listener further complicates both the novel's epistemological claims and its increasingly attenuated social function in English print culture. Ford entices his reader with the promise of a "good read" but, in the end, it is precisely this good read that can no longer be realized.

Conclusion

The Narrative of a Waking Body

[Our philosophies of language], products of a leisurely cogitation removed from historical turmoil, persist in seeking the truth of language by formalizing utterances that hang in midair, and the truth of the subject by listening to the narrative of a sleeping body—a body in repose, withdrawn from its socio-historical imbrication, removed from direct experience.

Julia Kristeva, *Revolution in Poetic Language*

When I read this passage from Kristeva's *Revolution in Poetic Language* I was immediately sympathetic. Despite my reservations with Kristeva's argument as a whole I too wanted to embrace the recalcitrant historical turmoil so often absent from studies of language and studies of the novel. I too wanted to avoid the narrative of a sleeping body. And yet how does one write the narrative of a waking body? It is a difficult task, constantly subject to faulty interpretations and overlooked contexts and, like the divorce court journalism and the novels I have discussed here, always in an important sense incomplete. While this is a project concerned to address the fraught interplay between the prohibition and the production of the story of adultery, I am aware that I also sometimes replicate the very prohibitions I am attempting to document. The most glaring omission here is the voice of the adulteress, neatly excised from most English novels of adultery and similarly absent in these pages, but no doubt others also exist. I want to stress, then, that this is the beginning of a project that could profit enormously from further archival research, challenging counter interpretations, and different inflections on the story of adultery.

Nineteenth-century novel reviewers had long argued that the representation of adultery did not belong in the English novel. If the novel was supposed to represent life, after all, what excuse did the English novel have for representing adultery, a subject, many argued, that had almost nothing to do with English domestic relations? And yet there were many cultural commentators—novelists, reviewers, and critics alike—who took issue with this impoverished and incomplete picture of English sexual life. Increasingly, English novelists petitioned for a greater freedom in their choice of subject matter. Like their European counterparts, they too wanted to represent adultery, to test and enlarge the boundaries of the novel, to carve out their own distinctive spaces in literary history. Eager to engage the tensions and contradictions of the period in which they lived and frustrated by the persistent disavowals of adultery in English life, many English novelists turned to the European novel as a literary model for the representation of adultery. French novels, in particular, were a source of great inspiration for all of the novelists considered in this book. But as reviewers were quick to point out, and as the novelists themselves knew, the French practice of adultery was very different from the English. The representation of adultery in the English novel too often strained and faltered when it sought to transport a French or European sensibility to the English landscape.

This book has accordingly sought to document a distinctively English history of the representation of adultery. Both the discourse on censorship (which in turn generates the category of the female reader and the category of nation) and the divorce court journalism are categories of perception that shape the representation of adultery in decisive ways. They allow us to *see* a history of the English novel of adultery that has otherwise been obscured. I have focused on the way that adultery becomes visible in English print culture to illustrate that the prevailing categories of perception through which an idea or practice becomes visible dictate how a particular thing can be seen and to counter the claim that adultery is irrelevant to the development of the English novel. To understand the representation of adultery in English print culture, in other words, one cannot rely on the narrative of a sleeping body, the narrative that hangs in midair, and is immutable to change. Rather, one must attempt to grapple with the lively, contradictory, dynamic narratives, at once exuberant and tedious, sensational and mundane, as they exist, in all of their complex mutability, to approximate as closely as possible what I am calling the narrative of a waking body.

I want to turn to one last story of adultery that differs from the stories I have related thus far. At first this story will sound familiar. It is told from the perspective of the betrayed party and the narration is fragmented, non-chronological, and incomplete. Its focus — while providing scrupulously detailed accounts of the sexual landscape from the placement of bedrooms to the perversion of bodies — is intensely epistemological. The central character in this story is an attractive, articulate, and perceptive young woman who is propositioned by an older, married man. She objects to his overtures—he tries to kiss her as they walk along a lake in the country—and complains to her father. But her father is having an affair with this man's wife. He accordingly prefers that his daughter placate the older man's amorous intentions to deflect attention away from his own adulterous actions. To complicate matters further it is possible that the daughter is both jealous of and in love with her father's lover. This story, of course, is famous and by now many readers will have recognized the text to which I refer: Freud's case history of Dora. Indeed, the broader story of psychoanalysis and Oedipal drama to which Dora's story is related is perhaps the most familiar story of adultery in Western culture.

In 1900 Dora begins analysis with Freud in an effort to cure her nervous hysteria. Dora's father is having an affair with Frau K and Herr K clearly expresses his own desire for Dora. Dora recoils from her position as an object of exchange in these adulterous triangles, but Freud translates her stated sexual aversion to Herr K into his own normative model of bourgeois sexuality. Several critics have justifiably objected to this effort to rewrite feminine sexuality as a version of patriarchal clinical psychoanalysis. But what interests me here is the striking thematic and formal parallels between the vastly different, and intentionally anomalous, psychoanalytic cases with which Freud deals, and the legal and literary cases to which I refer in this book. As such, Freud's case study of Dora condenses several of the issues pertinent to my argument and serves as an appropriate point from which to conclude.

In the introduction to his case study Freud confronts the problem of the reader and the appropriateness of his frankly sexual text. Who will read this case study and what will his readers think? What excuse can he offer for such open and unashamed discussions of sexual matters? A case history, he writes, is all too often read by other physicians as, on the one hand, a "*roman a clef* designed for their private delectation" (*Dora* 3); and, on the other, as cause for "astonishment and horror" (41). Freud vehemently disclaims any intentions to titillate or dismay his reader, appealing to his "rights as a gyneacologist" and to the disrespect to his profession implied by accusations of unnecessary salaciousness (3). Freud was rightfully worried that his intentions would be misinterpreted. His comments register an attempt to articulate different ways of imagining and comprehending the representation of sexuality in the public sphere. So familiar to us now, Freud's early struggles with a severe and judgmental public suggest that the representation of sexuality may be cause for neither titillation (the private delectation of the reader who simply enjoys sexual subjects) nor approbation (the astonishment and horror of the reader who is deeply offended by sexual subjects). To meet this challenge Freud offers the medical frame of reference; surely one can talk about sexuality if such discussion will enable a curing of the body.

And this talk is distinctive in ways that its familiarity in our culture has obscured. Freud asks Dora to talk about herself, to give "the whole story of [her] life and illness" (10), however difficult and disjointed. It is impossible to recover completely Dora's talk both because it is framed by Freud and because the case study itself is only Freud's remembered paraphrase of Dora's words. Nevertheless, Freud's comments on the difficulties imposed by the "whole story" merit attention. There are enormous obstacles to hearing the whole story; patients may be quite clear about one part of their lives but in others "their communications run dry, leaving gaps unfilled, and riddles unanswered" (10). It is precisely these silences, gaps, and riddles, however, that will prove so profitable for analysis. To this interpretative puzzle is added the problem of sequence: "The connections—even the ostensible ones," Freud writes, "are for the most part incoherent, and the sequence of different events is uncertain" (10). Steven Marcus attributes these formal characteristics to the content, sexual and otherwise, of the psychoanalytic case: "[The case history's] narrative and expository course . . . is neither linear nor rectilinear; instead its organization is plastic, involuted, and heterogenous and follows spontaneously an inner logic that seems frequently to be at odds with itself; it often loops back around itself and is multidimensional in its representation of both its material and itself. Its continuous innovations in formal structure seem unavoidably dictated by its substance, by the dangerous, audacious, disreputable, and problematical character of the experiences being represented and dealt with" (64). Specific narrative issues emerge, in other words, when one tries to represent discourses typically prohibited in one's society: the narrative is filled with pauses, descriptions are broken off midstream, the story is composed of riddles and it is fragmented not only in its telling but also in its absence of closure.

Freud draws attention to the incompleteness of Dora's analysis in his introduction; it is one of the case's persisting frustrations that he tries to address by regaining his narrative control. First, the title "Fragment of an Analysis of a Case of Hysteria" indicates that the results are inconclusive; Dora breaks off her analysis before she is "cured." Freud then adds three other ways in which the case is incomplete: the method of his analysis is itself fragmentary; he does not include the transcriptions of his discussions with Dora; and finally, even if the case were "complete and open to no doubt" it "cannot provide an answer to all questions arising out of the problem of hysteria" (7). No case history, in other words, is truly complete and the fragmented nature of Dora's narrative only heightens this general point.

I mentioned at the outset that this story of adultery is told from the perspective of the betrayed party. As both an object of exchange in a sexual triangle and a canny observer of her father's adultery, Dora's role is complicated. To be sure, Dora is a sophisticated and "sharp-sighted" (27, 29) reader of the adulterous body; she is keenly alert to the signs by which adultery betrays itself. But while a good deal of Dora's story is driven by the desire to know who has been unfaithful to whom (she has, after all, amassed an extraordinary amount of evidence with which to indict her father), it is also quintessentially unreliable. For how can one *know* the story of adultery? By Freud's account Dora's story of adultery tells as much about *her* adulterous desires as it does about her father's, Herr K's, and Frau K's. She tells the story of adultery and she finds herself implicated in the crime that she relates.

But it also bears remembering that we have access to Dora's story only through Freud's remembered, and reworked, account of it. And if Dora's mediated narrative is unreliable, Freud's narrative is arguably even more so. Again Marcus identifies a key aspect of this case study: "like some familiar 'unreliable narrator' in modernist fiction," he writes, "Freud pauses at regular intervals to remind the reader . . . that his understanding of it [the case] remains in some essential sense permanently occluded" (66). Freud, of course, is deeply invested in the narrative that he seems only to observe and record (see Hertz 234–35; and Moi 196). He listens to Dora where others had refused to hear her story but his cavalier translation of her "no's" into "yes's" (51), his excited disclosure of "a symbolic geography of sex!" (91), his shocked "discovery" that Dora loves not only Herr K, her father, and Frau K but also Freud himself, all suggest a desire for the linear narration at the expense of the messy complexity of the story of adultery and the narrator's reliability in communicating this story to his reader.

In terms of both the form and the content there is clearly a striking resemblance between Freud's case study of Dora and the English novels of adultery addressed in this book. It is not surprising, then, that Freud's case has been compared to both sensation novels and modernist novels. Nancy Armstrong, for example, compares Dora's case to a sensation novel which competes with Freud's attempt to gain interpretative authority over the unruly text (234). But Armstrong also refers to *Dora* as "the prototype of the modernist text" (227), Steven Marcus treats *Dora* as "a modern experimental novel" ("Freud" 64; see also Rieff ix), and Neil Hertz posits a connection between Freud and James or, as he puts it, between what Dora knew and what Maisie knew (224; see also Brooks, *Body* 235). Indeed, each of the novels that I have discussed in this book could profitably be interpreted through a psychoanalytic lens. At the same time, if there are thematic and formal parallels between the case study and the novels studied here, there are even more pronounced parallels between the case study and the divorce court journalism.

More restrained and conventional than the case study, the divorce court journalism nevertheless provides an account of sexual passions and practices otherwise absent in English print culture. While purporting to be scandalized by these unabashedly public displays of private acts, this journalism relishes in the minutest details by which transgressive sexuality betrays itself. The divorce court journalism also resembles the case study in its narrative unreliability, its disruption of linearity, and its lack of narrative closure. If at the turn of the century most English readers (and no doubt Freud himself) were familiar with the divorce court journalism and its massively detailed representations of adultery, most readers now are probably much more familiar with the Freudian case study and its similarly voluminous representations of adultery and sexuality. While both of these discourses — the divorce court journalism and the psychoanalytic case study — are stunning examples of the institutional incitement to speak about sex to which Foucault refers, only one, the case study, retains its critical purchase today. To be sure, Freud's case studies were part of a much larger project to rethink subjectivity and to provide an interpretative framework through which questions of human agency and desire could be better understood. The divorce court, by contrast, attempted only to adjudicate between conflicting claims related to adultery and to legislate in favor of one side or the other. Nevertheless, it was the divorce court journalism that was most available to writers of Victorian and transitional modernist novels and if psychoanalysis often commands critical attention, this journalism remains crucial to an understanding of the English novel of adultery.

The case study of Dora also animates the other category of perception that has intimately informed the representation of adultery in English print culture: the discourse on censorship and its construction of the young female reader. Dora, like Florence in *The Good Soldier*, has a mysterious and wide-ranging knowledge of sexual matters. At first Freud is puzzled. The "question of *where* her knowledge came from was a riddle," he writes (24). The mystery is soon solved, however, when Freud learns of Dora's secret reading habit. But if her reading accounts for her knowledge of sexuality — she "used to read Mantegazza's *Physiology of Love* and books of that sort" (19) — it also makes her vulnerable to sexual fantasies. Herr K denies his own seduction of Dora, for example, by blaming Dora's story of seduction on her reading of books that have inflamed her imagination. He assumes that she became "over-excited by such reading" (19) and, like Mrs. Robinson, imagined the adulterous scene that she described to her father. Herr K.'s inappropriate behavior is displaced by Dora's reading practices; a certain construction of female reading practices, in other words, is *used* to turn a real seduction into an easily dismissed hysterical fantasy. When it comes to a young woman's reading about sexuality, moreover, the clear connection between reading and knowledge is obscured by the more troubling, less tangible, sense that reading prompts fantasies — as if there is something erotic and tantalizing in the act of reading — fantasies that are only intensified when the subject matter also happens to be related to sexuality.

While this spur to fantasy may be damaging for Herr K and Dora's father — Dora makes an accusation that contradicts both men's accounts of what has happened — it is, in most respects, even more damaging for Dora herself. For Dora's account is easily dismissed and her moral authority and general desirability are destroyed. Herr K makes the point with cruel comprehensiveness: "no girl who read such books and was interested in such things could have any title to a man's respect" (55). Like the vulnerable reader who Lord Cockburn imagines when he frames the Hicklin standard, Dora's reading is perceived to suggest "thoughts and desires which otherwise would not have occurred" to her (*Law Reports* 371). And it is only one short contagious step, following the English discourse on censorship, from these thoughts and desires to social action. Reading, in other words, carries social consequences. If these consequences fall most severely on the female reader herself, impairing the reliability of her voice and marring her reputation, they also have consequences for the nation. Without a powerful moral center and a space free from public commerce, without, in other words, an "angel in the house," the English nation itself could be rocked by a political turmoil that, for the time being, it nervously located only beyond the country's borders.

In his essay on authorship Foucault makes a provocative connection between authors, transgression, and censorship. "Texts, books, and discourses began to have authors," he writes, "to the extent that authors became subject to punishment, that is, to the extent that discourses could be transgressive" ("Author" 148). And he asks: "How can one reduce the great peril, the great danger with which fiction threatens our world? One can reduce it with the author" (158). It is this view that has more or less dictated critical responses to literature and transgression. The English discourse on censorship, however, suggests a different way to reduce the "great danger" that fiction poses to a newly democratic print culture. One can construct a category of readers through which to restrict perilous representations. Indeed this focus on the young female reader as an implicit restraint on English print culture is part of the way that censorship works. And yet as both betrayed party and reader of the text of adultery, this figure also manipulates rhetorical strategies from the divorce court to counter restrictions imposed on the reading subject.

The divorce court journalism, the novel, and the case study all struggle to articulate the categories of perception through which sexuality may be legitimately discussed and made visible. In each case, established ways of knowing falter in the face of efforts to describe adultery and new models must be tentatively advanced. The attempt to represent adultery puts pressure on the traditional form of the novel: the development of third-person limited narration in James's novels; the uneasy translation of adultery as a domestic detective story; and the attention to multiple and unreliable points of view, disrupted causality, recalcitrant evidence, and resistant closure in most English novels of adultery. On the one hand, censorship seems to work without the aid of the law; after all, the representation of adultery is folded so tightly into the law itself, it is so relentlessly legal and epistemological, that it hardly looks like adultery at all. Its "charge" is, in a sense, absorbed by the structure through which it is articulated. In a different context, I think of my students who read Dora's case study anticipating the "first-rate detective novel" and the exposure of "forbidden sexual desires" promised on the back cover. But it is so tedious, many of them complain, and all those difficult medical words make it impossible to read. One does not need legal censorship, in other words, to dispel and discourage readers. In the context of adultery, novelists will either avoid the representation of reviled subject matter or they will represent it in such a way as to make it look like "nothing." In the last volume of his *History of England* Thomas Macaulay captures this point with characteristic concision and flare: "From the day on which the emancipation of our literature was accomplished, the purification of our literature began" (607). As the law relaxes, in other words, the restraint imposed upon print culture intensifies.

On the other hand, adultery *was* represented. And it was precisely the discourses and institutions designed to subdue adultery that contributed most forcefully to the categories of perception through which it was rendered legible. The discourse on censorship, for example, tenaciously linked the representation of adultery to questions of nation and gender. But it is the divorce court journalism with its daily scrutiny of marital infractions, its close tracking of allegedly adulterous spouses, its massive accumulations of the everyday details by which adultery betrays itself, its righteous legal commentary, and its generation of a vast array of critical responses, at once breathless and bottled, that testifies to the public visibility of adultery and shapes the way in which adultery is perceived and experienced. These categories of perception do not just make adultery visible, then, they make it visible in a certain way. It is not surprising, moreover, that when English novelists wanted to represent adultery they relied on the categories of perception most readily available in their culture.

If the divorce court journalism relied on the authority of the law to legitimate its public representations of sexuality in much the same way that Freud appealed to a medical discourse to authorize his own transgression of discursive boundaries, novels of adultery developed strategies from this journalism to authorize and legitimate their own approaches to prohibited subject matter. They translated adultery in terms of epistemology and the law rather than passion and pleasure. But the novelists on whom I have focused here do not simply reflect the prevailing discourses related to adultery. They also adapt and revise them. The category of the young female reader looks very different and is approached with different interests and investments in the novels of Collins, Norton, Braddon, James, and Ford. Similarly, when the novel borrows rhetorical strategies from the divorce court journalism it also modifies them. And when the novel translates adultery as epistemology it does so to confront the questions that the divorce court journalism confidently assumes it has already answered: not simply, how does one know if one's spouse is unfaithful? But also, on what criteria does one found knowledge claims in general? And these questions, like the English novel of adultery's formal innovations, speak most centrally to modernist concerns and interests. English novels of adultery also contribute to modernism in another way. If one way to avoid censorship and please one's audience was to adopt the "legal prose" and ruthlessly epistemological perspective of the divorce court, another way was to sever the connection between reading and social action (from the reader's blushing and eroticized body to a similarly compromised body politic) articulated by the discourse on censorship. And it is this approach that both James and Ford, in their different ways, couple with their inventive and supple manipulation of the divorce court journalism. The connection between reading and social action — at once sensational, somatic, and political — so important to the mid-Victorian period is occluded by these modernist writers concerned to establish a degree of print freedom. It is a connection, nevertheless, that current criticism would do well to reestablish and rework in different, more positive, directions.

I have illustrated how adultery became visible in the public sphere between 1857 and 1914 and how this visibility contributed to the development of the English novel. In the process, I have tried to introduce adultery back into English culture. Both the divorce court journalism and the category of the young female reader, I have argued, contribute to a specifically English version of adultery that links representations of adultery to the law, epistemology, and censorship. The narrative of the waking body is difficult to pin down, it moves, it is unpredictable and evasive. In my account it involves not only the body of language — the materiality of the word, the structure of the work — but also the body of the reader animated by this language. Narratives do not hang in midair. It is not possible, in other words, to understand fully the representation of adultery in English print culture in isolation from the historical context that shapes and conditions its representation. And if this context secured adultery to prohibition and the law — through the discourse on censorship and the divorce court journalism, respectively — it also incited extraordinary commentary. Adultery was, as critics in the 1860s repeatedly remarked, *interesting*. Or as the Colonel says in *The Golden Bowl*: "Oh, about that particular crime [adultery] there is always much to say. It is always more interesting to us than any other crime" (99). And despite adamant claims to the contrary, in English print culture there was always much to say about adultery.

I want to close with two very ahistorical references — fragments from Dora's dreams — that nevertheless resonate with the arguments I have made here. In the first dream Dora describes a house on fire, a hurried exchange between her mother and father, and an attempt to retrieve a jewel case. The dream is related to Freud as follows: "*A house was on fire. My father was standing beside my bed and woke me up. I dressed myself quickly. Mother wanted to stop and save her jewel-case; but Father said: 'I refuse to let myself and my two children be burnt for the sake of your jewel-case. We hurried downstairs, and as soon as I was outside, I woke up*" (56, italics in original). I want to focus here on two lines: "*My father was standing beside my bed and woke me up* [*weckt mich auf*]" and "*We hurried downstairs, and as soon as I was outside I woke up* [*wache ich auf*]" (56). Freud offers clever speculations on both passages but he never comments on what is most obvious and discordant here: Dora wakes up twice. The two references to waking should prompt some important questions: does Dora fall back to sleep after she is woken by her father? Or does she not fully awake? And what is the difference between these two formulations of waking? I want to make only two brief observations. The dream reflects, in the context of waking, a shift from a non-reflexive to a reflexive verb, from the agency of the father to the agency of the daughter and it is odd that neither Freud nor subsequent critics have remarked on this transition. It is also notable that the dream must imply either that the father is unable fully to wake his daughter or that the second reference to waking inflects the word somewhat differently. First, she is physically woken and then she — psychologically? spiritually? — wakes up. She realizes herself; she is alert, awake, alive.

The second dream records Dora's movement from outside to inside, from a strange town in which she finds herself, to the house where she lives, and the discovery of a letter from her mother announcing her father's illness. The majority of the dream is then devoted to Dora's attempt to return home to her parents and her discovery that her father has died. The passage on which I want to focus is a remembered addendum to Dora's second dream: "*she [Dora] went calmly to her room, and began reading a big book that lay on her writing-table.*" Ascertaining that the book is like an encyclopedia, Freud comments on Dora's "guilty reading": "Now children never read about forbidden subjects in an encyclopedia *calmly*. They do it in fear and trembling, with an uneasy look over their shoulder to see if someone might be coming." But if Dora's father is dead, Freud muses, the reading scene might be different. Dora "might calmly read whatever she chose." And struck by this idea he elaborates on it: "If her father was dead she could read or love as she pleased" (92). Freud, however, overlooks a significant element in Dora's dream: the relationship between Dora's reading of forbidden books, always important in Freud's analysis, her reading of letters, and her writing of her life. Again I will offer only a few brief observations. After the first dream Freud catches Dora concealing a letter from her grandmother in which the grandmother expresses the desire for Dora to write (70); in the second dream Dora reads a letter from her mother prefiguring her father's death (86); and in the addendum Dora reads a large book that is on her writing-table. From the grandmother's letter, to the mother's letter, do we then encounter Dora's "letter" in the shape of a dream? Is this geneaology of women's writing one way that Dora might rewrite Freud's own attempt to write the story of her life? If Freud speculates that the death of Dora's father might free her to read what she desires, it is also clearly the case that the absence of Freud—actively desired by Dora, reflected in the anonymous man's offer to accompany her in the dream and Dora's flat refusal ("I refused and went alone" [86]), and effected soon after the dream when Dora abruptly ends her therapy—might free Dora to realize better her incipient desires and aspirations. He grandmother wants her to write, her mother writes of her father's illness, and Dora tells Freud about a dream where a young woman reads.

But these are only dreams. The dynamic relationship between censorship and adultery that Freud seeks to comprehend cannot simply be superimposed on the broader social field of nineteenth- and early twentieth-century England. As the examples in this book demonstrate, the death of the father, figurative or otherwise, does not guarantee for the reading daughter a sudden freedom, at once calming and intoxicating. English print censorship is much more inchoate and clever, much more subtle and devious, and much more pervasive and multifaceted than the simple image of a repressive father implies. Dora's dreams may reflect a transition from being woken on her father's terms (complete with the exposure of adulterous desires that Freud believes he uncovers) to waking herself, from the angel in the house to the woman outside the house, but this transition, like the fantasy of the dead father, also belies a different less hopeful story. For Dora's dramatic story of adultery and attempted seduction ricochets most severely on Dora herself and her dream of waking is swiftly contained by a psychoanalytic framework that is unable to hear what she says: *I woke up.* The representation of adultery in English print culture is similarly shaped by the categories of perception through which it becomes visible, categories that at once enable and restrict its articulation. These are only dreams. And yet perhaps the dream too has its place in a cultural history of the novel. Somatic reading pleasures may be thwarted, "guilty reading" punished, novels severed from politics, and yet at the same time forbidden subjects are represented and somehow, somewhere the sleeping reader wakes.

Notes

Introduction: Censorship and Adultery

1. I use the term *transitional modernist novel* to indicate those novels that do not fall easily into either realist or modernist categories. Instead, these novels — by Henry James, Ford Madox Ford, Thomas Hardy, and earlier novelists like Mary Elizabeth Braddon and Wilkie Collins — register, formally and thematically, a sense of transition between set categories: an uneasiness with the limitations of realist form, and an uncertainty about the direction in which the novel will next develop.

2. In 1857 the new Matrimonial Causes Act redefined the social and legal resonance of adultery by shifting divorce settlements from canon law to secular law, and in 1914 the advent of World War I profoundly altered the formation of the English novel.

3. See Ronald R. Thomas's *Dreams of Authority* for a more extended discussion of this connection (28–30).

4. Freud's work, of course, has provided a basis for some of the most stimulating developments in twentieth-century thought. Both Jacques Lacan and Jacques Derrida, in entirely different ways, develop Freud's theories in directions that he probably would not have anticipated. In the context of the novel, Peter Brooks's Freudian criticism is both provocative and illuminating.

5. Hunter et al., for example, develop a theory of pornography that is based on a rejection of the repressive hypothesis and they criticize a position that equates censorship laws with repression. See also Michael Levine's *Writing Through Repression* for a study of the productivity of censorship in the context of Freud and Derrida.

6. Judith Butler has analyzed identity politics in terms of its necessary exclusions in considerable detail (see *Bodies* 111–19 for one example).

7. It should be noted that Foucault does address these issues; indeed, a related set of questions underscores his critical orientation in *The History of Sexuality*. But, in the absence of any real consideration of class (both in the traditional Marxist sense and in Bourdieu's sense, important for this study, of cultural capital as a class indicator), his analysis lacks the critical tools with which these questions could most effectively be answered.

8. Because this book is interested in censorship the dominant liberal tradition in England, articulated most forcefully by John Stuart Mill, is not the focus of my attention. This liberal tradition, and the enormous influence it has exercised over English cultural development, has too often obscured the work of censorship in English culture and the myriad forms of social regulation in which any social group participates. For a nuanced critique of the liberal position see Hunter et al.'s *On*

Pornography and for a reading of censorship in the context of the liberal position see Richard S. Randall's *Freedom and Taboo*.

9. Samuel Hynes discusses implicit and explicit forms of censorship in *The Edwardian Turn of Mind* (254–306). Tzvetan Todorov relates self-censorship to social taboos in *The Fantastic* (158–62), Michael Levine similarly discusses self-censorship in psychoanalytic and social terms in *Writing Through Repression*, and Christopher Prendergast reads mimesis in terms of censorship in *The Order of Mimesis* (52–57).

10. It should be noted that James is discussed as an English novelist in this book; his later novels, on which I focus, were written after he had moved permanently to England and were informed by his English experience.

11. See Carolyn Porter ("After"), Carolyn Dean, and Terry Eagleton (*Aesthetic*).

12. Keating offers an excellent and detailed overview of the fraught terrain on which the English censorship debates were played out in *The Haunted Study*.

13. Levine, admittedly, grants the political nature of the articulation of such a space: "the 'free space' of the university [and, by association, the aesthetic sphere] is, of course, constantly contested; part of its politics is the attempt to resist simple partisanship" (15).

Chapter 1. The Democracy of Print

1. The mid-century print censorship debates were multi-faceted. In a legal context, the debates over the Obscene Publications Act and the *Regina* v. *Hicklin* case, discussed in section two, address the question of print censorship. The Indecent Advertisements Act in 1889 is also relevant here. Hunter, Saunders, and Williamson provide a good overview of these debates in *On Pornography* (57–91). The 1888 Vizetelly trial for the publication of Zola's *La Terre* also generated debate and controversy. The circulating libraries were infamous for the restrictions that they informally imposed on print culture. These restrictions generated lively and voluminous debate that extended well beyond the legal framework invoked by specific acts and statutes. For good overviews of this form of print regulation see Greist and Hiley. The question of print censorship also informed newspaper representation and incited debate as section three of this chapter and Chapter 2 as a whole illustrate. As section one of this chapter illustrates, the question of print censorship occupied considerable attention in the mid-century novel debates. This point is taken up in greater detail with respect to the sensation novel in Chapter 3. Finally, as I was completing this book, Joss Marsh's fascinating study of blasphemy and related print infractions in the Victorian period was published. *Word Crimes* provides an excellent account of an area of print censorship not treated here and is a welcome addition to the field.

2. The trial of Madame Bovary has been admirably treated by Dominick LaCapra in *"Madame Bovary" on Trial*.

3. I do not mean to suggest that no attempts were made in the Victorian period to educate female readers, to teach them to read rationally rather than sen-

sually. On the contrary, a vast amount of time was spent trying to determine effective ways by which women could be educated and their reading habits improved. Nevertheless, most of the literature devoted to this topic discusses ways of restricting women's reading and channeling it in "safe" directions. The category of the vulnerable young reader as female, therefore, worked to regulate women's reading even when it sought to improve their education and reading practices.

4. See also Armstong, Cvetovich, Flint, and Matlock.

5. The powerful opposition between the literary and the obscene becomes increasingly more pronounced as censorship laws are modified into the twentieth century. The current United States law, for example, dictates that if a given work has aesthetic value then, by definition, it cannot be prosecuted as obscene.

6. This reviewer continues: there is "room enough for descriptions of life and character without running foul of the Seventh Commandment; and it is not always the worse for a writer to be compulsorily debarred from the easiest way of snatching an illegitimate success" ("Immoral" 637). Frederic Harrison similarly derides "the monotonous variations on its [French literature's] one string of adultery — adultery without love, sentiment, or excuse. . . . To be addicted to it, is a vice; to manufacture it, is a crime. They are not books, these things. To imbibe this compound, is not to read" (*Choice* 70). See also "Recent," Oliphant, "Novels," "Novel-Reading," and "Claptrap."

7. Stang, however, notes that Mrs. Oliphant's observation is inaccurate. "The English novel," he writes, "for almost twenty years [since the publication of *Jane Eyre*] had been in a seriously tainted condition; that is, novelists had felt free to deal with transgressions of the code governing sexual morality" (191–92). While this claim is also not entirely accurate, what is interesting, and what he does not pursue, is the insistence with which claims like Mrs. Oliphant's were made in the face of evidence to the contrary. It is this "logic of censorship" that I am interested in here.

8. For two very different discussions of reading and the French Revolution see Sandy Petrey's *Realism and Revolution* and Roger Chartier's *The Cultural Origins of the French Revolution*. The highly charged, and sometimes baffling, rhetoric in these print culture debates can also be usefully situated in the context of rapidly developing imperialist expansion. While the Indian Mutiny of 1857 alerted the English to the fragility of imperialist enterprises, the completion of the Suez Canal in 1869 and an increasingly sophisticated imperialist discourse reinforced the importance of a national identity that, in these debates, was perceived to be related, in part, to reading practices. Edward Said's *Culture and Imperialism* gives an excellent and long overdue account of the relationship between literary production and British imperialism that provides a fascinating intertext for the Victorian print culture debates.

9. The role of the reader in Victorian England has received considerable critical attention. For general discussions see Amy Cruse's *The Victorians and their Books*, Richard Altick's *The English Common Reader*, Richard Stang's *The History of the Novel in England*, Peter Keating's *The Haunted Study*, and Raymond Williams's *The Long Revolution*. For studies that focus specifically on the female reader see Sally Mitchell's *The Fallen Angel*, Mary Jacobus's *Reading Women*, Kate Flint's *The Woman Reader*,

and Andrea Vrettos's *Somatic Fictions*. For two studies of the female reader in France see Jann Matlock's *Scenes of Seduction* and Janet Beizer's *Ventriloquized Bodies*.

10. I have not illustrated the many ways in which both Flaubert and Collins invoke the category of the young female reader only to invert it. Instead I am interested here in how they draw on an increasingly familiar and predictable catalogue of characteristics to describe female reading practices.

11. For a more detailed consideration of the early British reception of Flaubert see Pacey's "Flaubert and His Victorian Critics." Pacey notes that no article on Flaubert appears in English periodicals until 1878 and the focus of his study is, accordingly, on the 1880s and 90s. This range, however, both overlooks English reviews of *Madame Bovary* like Stephen's here and the way in which English literature was informed by Flaubert in explicit borrowings (for example, *The Doctor's Wife*) and implicit influences.

12. These comments are also informed by the implicit censorship exercised by the circulating libraries. See, for example, Guinevere Griest's *Mudie's Circulating Library and the Victorian Novel*.

13. Robert Buchanan similarly notes: "the immorality [in English novels] is of a different kind, but it works quite as perniciously in its own sphere as the immorality of modern French writers of the avowedly immoral school" (298).

14. It is interesting to note that the novel was published by Vizetelly and Company, the same company that would be prosecuted for publishing an English translation of Zola's *La Terre* four years later.

15. MacKinnon writes, "Sooner or later, in one way or another, the consumers want to live out the pornography further in three dimensions. Sooner or later, in one way or another, they do" (*Only* 19).

16. Countless critics and novelists complained about the standard of the young female reader but they did not contest her social construction; instead, they argued that literature should be written for men instead of women, that it was unnecessarily limited when it was written for women, and so on.

17. It is interesting that while Dumas's novel was considered obscene, the opera based on this novel, *La Traviata*, was well received and enjoyed great popularity in London.

18. Linda Williams makes a similar point in *Hard Core*: "It is not surprising . . . that I should want to protect myself against the perceived contaminations of a 'filthy subject' — lest I be condemned along with it" (xi).

19. In this context it is interesting to consider *The Lancet*'s rationale for not acknowledging Havelock Ellis's *Sexual Inversion*: "What decided us not to notice the book was its method of publication. Why was it not published through a house able to take proper measure for introducing it as a scientific book to a scientific audience? . . . . we considered the circumstances attendant upon its publication suspicious. We believed that the book would fall into the hands of readers totally unable to derive benefit from it as a work of science and very ready to draw evil lessons from its necessarily disgusting passages." A book becomes indecent, the writer continues, not because it addresses an indecent subject, but because it is "offered for sale to the general public with a wrong motive." The article closes with a "moral of the story": "It is — be careful about the publisher" (1345).

20. Madeleine Smith, strictly speaking, does not commit adultery—she is unfaithful to her lover only in sentiment and not in action—but because contemporary reviewers interpret her case in the context of adultery I also follow their terminology here.

21. A series of journal articles in the mid 1850s record "a strange habit of eating arsenic" (Jesse 391) in Lower Austria. This trend suggests the double inflection of poison discussed above: at times, it was deadly and at other times it was used in the service of good health. "The poison-eaters," *Chambers' Journal* writes, eat arsenic to look more healthy and in the villages where this is the practice they do have the appearance of "exuberant health" (391). But, the journal warns, for the arsenic to continue to be effective in this manner, higher and higher doses are required, to the point where the intaker constantly gambles with her or his life.

Chapter 2. Columns of Scandal

1. See Mary Poovey's "Covered but Not Bound: Caroline Norton and the 1857 Matrimonial Causes Act" in *Uneven Developments* for a detailed discussion of the debates related to this Act. For contemporary responses to the Divorce Act see the *Quarterly Review*'s 1857 review article "The Bill for Divorce," the *New British Review*'s 1857 "The Marriage and Divorce Bill," and the *New British Review*'s 1861 "Marriage and Divorce—The Law of England and Scotland." For a discussion of the Commission created to modify this Act in 1911 see the *Quarterly Review*'s 1913 "The Majority Report of the Divorce Commission." Lawrence Stone's *Uncertain Union: Marriage in England, 1660–1753* and *Broken Lives: Separation and Divorce in England, 1660–1857* provide a history of divorce in England before 1857. Finally, for a popular history of divorce in the period about which I am writing see "History of Divorce" in the London *Times* (1912).

2. In fact, it was argued that obscene publications would be reduced by the new divorce bill. The *Saturday Review* comments on this argument seven months after the bill came into effect and then describes the bill's effects in terms of obscene publications: "It was urged that whereas, under the old system, the unsavoury details of a divorce case were placed under the public eye at least three times, they would under the new system, be dismissed into obscurity after a single publication. There was a considerable degree of audacity in the argument, inasmuch as there was no conceivable reason, either of public duty or of expediency, for ever publishing the details of such proceedings at all; but if we are to judge from the stream of filth which almost daily flows through the columns of most of our contemporaries, the single cable of the new system is thicker than the three-fold cord of the old one" ("Purity" 656–57).

3. Keith Thomas records the Lord Chancellor's response as follows: "'It had ever been the feeling of that House, indeed, it was a feeling common to mankind in general that, although the sin in both cases was the same, the effect of adultery on the part of the husband was very different from that of adultery on the part of the wife. It was possible for a wife to pardon a husband who had committed adultery; but it was hardly possible for a husband ever really to pardon the adultery of a wife"

(202). Thomas further cites Gladstone's analysis of the divorce bill debate: "I believe that a very limited portion of the offences committed by women are due to the mere influence of sensual passion. On the other side, I believe that a very large proportion of the offences committed by men are due to that influence" (207). See also *The Woman Question*, vol. 2 (15–17, 24–27) and Gail Savage's "The Operation of the 1857 Divorce Act, 1860–1910."

4. Under the old divorce law, divorce cases were also published, although much less frequently, as a form of scandalous literature. See, for example, *Trials for Adultery; or, the History of Divorces, Being Select @ Doctor's Commons, For Adultery, Fornication, Cruelty, Impotence &c.*, a seven-volume set of divorce cases published in the late eighteenth century. See Peter Wagner's "The Pornographer in the Courtroom" for a sociological study of the literature on divorce before 1857. See Anne Humpherys's "Coming Apart" for a study of divorce court journalism after 1857.

5. This chapter takes its title from a headline in the *New York Times*. The article counts the columns in eight London newspapers devoted to divorce cases and then asks: "How is it that the eloquent and impassioned moralists who waxed so indignant when they denounced the Apocalypse of evil in July, 1885 [the Maiden Tribute case in which the *Pall Mall Gazette* exposed child prostitution], have not uttered a single word of protest against the flooding of London by this deluge of obscenity?" (26 Dec. 1886: 2).

6. While there are several accounts of the novel and adultery, Tony Tanner's *Adultery in the Novel: Contract and Transgression* provides the most extended and thoughtful consideration of the role which adultery plays in the novel's development. But in his acknowledged "absence of historical and sociological material" (368) and in his failure to distinguish between the Continental and the English tradition, Tanner grounds his argument on two claims that misrepresent the latter tradition. First, Tanner posits the adulteress as outside the dominant social forms and adultery as outside of social descriptions. This position is based on Tanner's assumption that adultery was "unspeakable" in nineteenth-century society; in other words, he repeats the claims of the nineteenth-century reviewers and critics discussed above. Second, Tanner argues that if adultery is unexposed, secluded in an unspoken realm of society, then to represent it in the novel will be to threaten a social stability which is dependent on marriage as "the structure that maintains the Structure" (15); the entire edifice crumbles and "adultery as the gap, or silence, in the bourgeois novel . . . finally leads to its dissolution and displacement" (14). The distinctive "historical and sociological material" relating to adultery in the English tradition, however, cannot be overlooked and it tells a very different story.

7. This case is interesting insofar it is less a trial for adultery—the "adultery" was openly admitted and it was instead the validity of the Yelverton's marriage that was contested—than a trail of a woman's honor. The opening remarks focus on the Irish public's ability to judge a woman's virtue: "If the moral sense of the Irish people is sound and true upon any subject, it is sound and true with regard to woman's virtue; and we do not believe it possible that a woman of sullied honour, still less of utterly impure, could command their sympathy" (*Yelverton* v). It then argues that because Mrs. Yelverton captures the sympathy of her public she is innocent. The Preface closes by translating the Yelverton divorce case not in terms of

law but of literature: "Wherever her romantic story has been told, the recital of her wrongs has thrilled all hearts; and there are few families in the land that do not rejoice in her victory" (vi).

8. The divorce court is also described in the Preface to the *Mourdaunt* v. *Mordaunt* case as follows: "The Divorce Court is generally acknowledged to be a dim, dark hole, without comparison in the metropolis, possessing accommodation which is both scanty and bad, and ventilation in which considerations as to health and life can never have been entertained. It has scarcely room for those who have business there, much less for strangers" (*Mordaunt* 1–2).

9. Similarly, in the Campbell case discussed below, "barriers had to be placed in the corridor leading to the Court to stay the pressure of the crowd" (Fenn 121).

10. A writer for the London *Evening News* in 1886 also comments on the powerful social commentary that the divorce court provides for the interested observer: "to the student of human nature, willing to forgo for a time a purely contemplative attitude, a divorce suit frequently offers material absorbing enough to induce him to struggle with the crowd at the doors, and sit within the ill-ventilated Court, while the drama of human life, human passion, and human suffering is unfolded before his eyes. . . . No wonder, then, that the Divorce Court is a place of fascination" (24 July 1886: 2).

11. It is worth noting that the French newspapers did not subscribe to the practice of printing divorce court proceedings, and as a result their modes of discursive sexual definition developed differently.

12. The sexual double standard finds its concrete embodiment in several of the laws passed in the nineteenth century. The Matrimonial Causes Act to which I will refer below is one example. The Contagious Diseases Act, passed in 1864, forced prostitutes to be subjected to medical inspections and met, somewhat later, with violent objection from feminists. And the Infant's Custody Act, passed in 1839, gave women unequal rights to their children. See also Mary Poovey's *Uneven Developments* and Judith Walkowitz's "The Politics of Prostitution."

13. Divorce trials in the United States were also recorded in the American newspapers. Sara Davis refers to the Beecher-Tilton scandal in 1870 in which the minister Henry Ward Beecher was accused of committing adultery with Elizabeth Tilton. Davis notes that the "trial received sensational coverage in the newspapers" (575), including *The Nation* for which James was writing at the time. But because the divorce laws varied from state to state it is more complicated to use their documentation as a register of the times.

14. Jenkins notes that this case was the first since 1857 involving a politician of Dilke's stature although he also cites the Mordaunt case (1870) in which Lady Mordaunt identified the Prince of Wales as co-respondent. She told her husband, in the sensational and morally charged language by which these cases are typically marked: "Charlie, you are not the father of that child . . . Lord Cole is the father of it, and I am the cause of its blindness" (215). For a detailed account of the Dilke case see Jenkins's *Victorian Scandal* (215–370).

15. This desire to blame men for women's adultery clearly conformed to the dominant views of the period. Consider the following comments, for example: "Our own opinion is, that very few good husbands are ever deserted by their wives. . . . Under the old system, the law recognized an injury done to the husband

whose wife was unfaithful to him; but, the non-existence of the woman being complete, the wife whose husband was taken from her by another woman, was not compensated for her loss. And yet it is true, that although, as before said, good husbands rarely lose their wives by infidelity, good wives often lose their husbands" ("Marriage and Divorce" 169).

16. Jenkins argues that the sheer wealth of detail that Mrs. Crawford provided contributed to her verisimilitude: "Her account of changing cabs, of passing messages, of arranging meetings—the whole paraphernalia of deceiving her husband—carried a note of conviction" (325). It is this quality of detail too that lends to the trial a sense of novelistic form.

17. This case, like others, generated a plethora of related writing. Several penny pamphlets outlining the details of the case were published, a full-length bound volume of the case is recorded as being a part of James Joyce's library, and Hector Malot's novel *Josey* (1887) is loosely based on the case. For other treatments of divorce and adultery in Victorian novels see Wilkie Collins's *The Evil Genius* (1886) and Florence Marryat's *On Circumstantial Evidence* (1889).

18. *Lloyd's* draws attention to the class confusion that such cases generated: "It has been the fashion of late for the higher classes to organize missions to the masses; but, judging by recent revelations of the manners and customs of polite Society, the process ought to be reversed. When mothers who wish to marry their daughters to advantage see no harm in the intimate friendship of unmarried girls with notorious aristocratic profligates. . . . [and here the reviewer gives a long list of equally suspect practices amongst the aristocratic classes] it would be lamentable if there were not a widespread feeling of disgust, indignation, and contempt. . . . The vile story of pride and meanness, selfishness and hurt, cruelty and treachery, is hardly relieved by a single touch of manly generosity or womanly tenderness. The very atmosphere is mephitic—it is earthly, sensual, revolting" ("Divorce," 26 Dec. 1886: 3). Here, as in many other commentaries on divorce cases, the "sensual" and the "revolting" are used as synonyms.

19. It is interesting to compare these debates, with their concern for publicity, to the 1857 Obscene Publications Act debates in which the infraction of privacy was a central critique of the proposed legal changes. Lord Lyndhurst, for example, condemned the Act as follows: "at any hour of the day, or any hour of the night, an officer may go into the house, search every room, every bedroom, even the beds in which women are lying, because they may conceal improper publications" (*Hansard* 146:1358–59).

20. Smith had been instrumental in attempting to pass a bill, introduced into the House of Commons in May 1887, forbidding the publication of obscene or indecent material specifically relating to divorce trials.

21. The Secretary of State, Mr. Matthews, also confirms Smith's position: "it was not only French literature that ought to be condemned, much harm was also done by . . . the penny dreadfuls, the quack advertisements, and the full reports of divorce cases which appeared in the daily Press. All such classes of publications were pernicious in the extreme, and they ought to be brought within the reach of the law in every civilized country" (National 364).

22. Based on his experience as a divorce court journalist Henry Fenn writes: "A

most deplorable feature in a fashionable case is the presence day after day of numbers of these women. To them it is the same thing as going to the theatre, only more exciting.... They listen to the unsavoury evidence that is given, and by prurient curiosity, they carry their curse with them — a diseased and blackened mind" (102).

23. And the London *Times*, reporting on a Divorce Commission, records Mr. Plowden's comment as follows: "He considered, for instance, that the publicity given to proceedings in the Divorce Court was a public evil. (Cheers.) He quite understood that from a business point of view newspapers were obliged to do it, but he would like to see a stand made by the leading journals of the day against the publication of these things. He could not imagine anything worse for public morality than the terrible details which were now being sent from Edinburgh day by day. (Cheers)" ("Lord" 4 Feb. 1909: 4B).

24. Another version of this point is found in the *Saturday Review* (1859): "The great law which regulates supply and demand seems to prevail in matters of public decency as well as in other things of commerce. Block up one channel, and the stream will force another outlet; and so it is that the current dammed up in Holywell Street flings itself out in the Divorce Court" (cited in Trudgill 138). Eric Trudgill comments as follows: "Theoretically the pure young miss would be debarred from encountering this pollution but in fact, it was said, prohibition encouraged her to often read the papers on the sly" (138).

25. The *Sporting Times* repeatedly made fun of divorce cases by contrasting them with realist literature. The divorce cases inevitably were exposed as more daring and more provocative than their French competition. "Since the Colin Campbell case has been on, the parting words of wifey to hubby on his way to the City, have varied from: 'Please bring home something nice for dinner' to 'For goodness sake don't forget the *Standard*'" (4 Dec. 1886: 1). And one ballad entitled "Othello's Occupation Gone" begins: "There was once a young disciple of the realistic school" who admires Zola and wants to write a novel in his style. Upon its publication he goes to the newspapers to see how it has been received: "On the eve of publication he perused with eager zest / All the columns of 'The Ev'ning' — last edition — / From his pallid lips at length there broke a wild, despairing wail: — / 'All my fictions fade to nothing. These veracious / Social 'Chronicles of Campbell' show that 'tis without avail / That a realist attempts to be salacious" (11 Dec. 1886: 1).

26. See for example Lennard Davis's *Factual Fictions*, Michael McKeon's *The Origins of the English Novel, 1600–1740*, and J. Paul Hunter's *Before Novels*. Davis articulates a direct causal relationship between journalism and the development of the novel and while both McKeon and Hunter, quite rightly, pose the relationship in considerably more complex terms, they both define "the journalistic context" as significant in the novel's development.

27. E. S. Dallas criticized the serial novel — what he called "a hazardous experiment" — for the way in which it accustomed readers to fragmentation and encouraged a focus on plot to maintain the reader's interest (cited in Skilton 31).

28. Joseph Boone outlines this narrative tradition as follows: "the use of developmental and perspectival structures to inscribe erotic 'meaning' into the body of the text, the differing valences of male and female forms of bildungsroman, the deployment of various techniques . . . to create an impression of the novelistic world

as a hierarchically ordered 'whole,' and especially the valorization of the closed ending" (71).

29. This unreliability also extended to other trials, of course. In a letter to Edmund Gosse, Henry James writes the following: "Did you see in last evening's halfpenny papers that the wretched O. W. seems to have a gleam of light before him (if it really counts for that), in the fearful exposure of his (of the prosecution's) little beasts of witnesses? What a nest of almost infant blackmailers!" These comments are glossed by Edel: "An allusion to some of the Crown witnesses in the first trial of Oscar Wilde, one of whom was characterized by the judge as 'a most reckless, unreliable, unscrupulous and untruthful witness'" (*Letters* 291–92).

30. See for example Marianna Torgovnick's *Closure in the Novel* and J. Hillis Miller's "The Problematic of Ending in Narrative."

Chapter 3. An Undercurrent of the Body

1. There are several rich and perceptive, if conflicting, analyses of the sensation novel genre to which this chapter is indebted. See, for example, Cvetovich, Brantlinger, Fahnestock, Hughes, Loesberg, D. A. Miller, Showalter, and Tillotson.

2. In the extensive body of critical work devoted to sensation novels only one short newspaper article, Margaret Maison's "Adulteresses in Agony," actually focuses on adultery. And yet the representation of adultery was central to the development of the novel in the 1860s. In addition to the novels that deal with adultery specifically in the context of divorce, adultery also figures in George Meredith's *The Ordeal of Richard Feverel*, Mrs. Henry Wood's *East Lynne*, Mary Elizabeth Braddon's *The Lady's Mile*, Guy Lawrence's *Anteros*, Dinah Mulock Craik's *A Life For a Life*, Charles Reade's *Griffith Gaunt*, Trollope's *He Knew He Was Right* (and to a lesser extent in Trollope's *Can You Forgive Her? The Small House at Allington*, and *The Last Chronicle of Barset*) as well as in the novels central to this chapter, Caroline Norton's *Lost and Saved* and Braddon's *The Doctor's Wife*.

3. The text of *Lost and Saved* was reissued, with an introduction by S. Bailey Shurbutt, in 1988. In addition to this introduction, two biographies on Norton, by Alice Acland and by Alan Chedzoy, contain minimal commentaries on this novel. Mary Poovey's analysis of Norton's political activities offers the best account of Norton's contribution to divorce and marriage law reform in the context of an emerging, and conflicted, feminist orientation.

4. Christopher Heywood has written two critical essays comparing Flaubert and Braddon in this context. See "Flaubert, Miss Braddon, and George Moore" and "A Source for *Middlemarch*: Miss Braddon's *The Doctor's Wife* and *Madame Bovary*." See also Kate Flint's *The Woman Reader* (278–84) and Wolff's *Sensational Victorian* (161–64).

5. Critics of the sensation novel often complained of the uniformity of language and plot in these works but the same charge could also be delivered against these critics themselves. Compare this passage from Greg to the following from Mansel (in addition to the many echoes in the discussion below): "There is something unspeakably disgusting in this ravenous appetite for carrion, this vulture-like

instinct which smells out the newest mass of social corruption, and hurries to devour the loathsome dainty before the scent has evaporated" (502).

6. In her study of the tension between medical discourse and sensation novels Sally Shuttleworth argues that "[m]asculine reason and control are implicitly set against female sensation and nervousness and bodily disorder" (Shuttleworth 193; see also Vrettos 98). While she notes that sensation novels themselves demystify medical authority, she does not construct this argument in the context of doctors/cultural critics and pathologized readers/patients. She does not, in other words, consider how female nervousness and bodily disorder are constructed by the medical and cultural discourses.

7. See Mary Poovey's *Uneven Developments* (51–88) and Elaine Hadley's *Melodramatic Tactics* (133–79).

8. For an overview of the relationship between sensation novels and melodrama see Winifred Hughes's *The Maniac in the Cellar* (5–37) and Martha Vicinus' "'Helpless and Unfriended': Nineteenth-Century Domestic Melodrama." See also Patrick Brantlinger's "What is 'Sensational' About the 'Sensation Novel'?" in which he states: "As with melodrama, so with the sensation novel" (5).

9. The fact that Norton intensely disliked this sensational genre does not, of course, prevent her from drawing on its form to develop her own more literary ambitions.

10. See also Judith Walkowitz's analysis of Josephine Butler's recourse to melodrama to mobilize social change with respect to the Contagious Diseases Acts of the 1860s.

11. See, for example, Elaine Hadley's *Melodramatic Tactics* and the introduction to Michael Hays and Anastasia Nikolopoulou's edited collection entitled *Melodrama: The Cultural Emergence of a Genre*.

12. Norton's biographer notes the loose relationship between this novel and Norton's own life. For other novels that draw more closely on Norton's life, see Anthony Trollope's *He Knew He Was Right* (1868) and George Meredith's *Diana of the Crossways* (1885).

13. August 4th is a resonant date in the English representation of adultery. It was the date of the adulterous wife's exposure in Augustus Egg's triptych entitled *Past and Present* (1858), it is the date of Treherne's exposure here, and it is the date of Florence's exposure in Ford's *The Good Solider* (1914).

14. This passage echoes Wilkie Collins's *Basil*, first published in 1852 and reissued in 1862. Basil suspects that his partner is unfaithful and when he tracks her and her lover to out-of-the-way lodgings confirms "the awful thrill of suspicion": "I listened; and through the thin partition, I heard voices—*her* voice, and *his* voice. I *heard* and I *knew*—knew my degradation in all its infamy, knew my wrongs in all their nameless horror" (160). Anne Brontë's *The Tenant of Wildfell Hall*, first published in 1848 and reissued in 1863, also stages a similar scene. Helen follows her husband into the garden and overhears a discussion that confirms her "torment of suspense" related to adultery. She confronts her husband with this newfound knowledge: "I have trusted to no third person. I was in the shrubbery this evening, and I saw and heard for myself" (243).

15. Similarly, in Dinah Mulock Craik's *A Life for a Life*, Penelope Johnston

discovers that her fiancé has a lover in the country. He responds: "I have done no worse then hundreds do in my position . . . and the world forgives them, and women too" (245).

16. Norton's equivocal position on these issues is expressed in a review, published a few months after *Lost and Saved*, that addresses "The Angel in the House" and "Goblin Market." First, Norton contrasts the "skeleton in the cupboard" (a theme made popular by the sensation novel) to "the angel in the house." While praising Patmore's poem she hints, obliquely, that even the angel may have a skeleton in her closet. Despite the enormous differences between these two poems, however, Norton applauds both.

17. The complexity of Norton's challenge to melodramatic principles is brought into relief when one compares *Lost and Saved* to Mrs. Henry Wood's *East Lynne* written two years earlier. East Lynne has often been discussed as an exemplary melodramatic text (see Cvetkovich, Kaplan, and Mitchell among others). Like Beatrice, the novel's heroine, Isabel, suspects her husband of adultery. Unlike Beatrice, Isabel is incorrect in her suspicions and, also unlike Beatrice, she runs away with a lover of her own. But in this novel Isabel very rarely speaks for herself (the novel, interestingly, stages a discourse of self-censorship that would be worth pursuing), quickly feels acute remorse, is disfigured in a horrible accident, and finally dies after extended and anguished suffering. This final passage of suffering, moreover, calls for a silence even more harsh and harrowing than the earlier restraint of the dutiful wife.

18. It is interesting that this was one of the lines later deleted (or censored) from the cheap reissue of Braddon's novel. The deletion no doubt was driven by a desire to profit from Braddon's reputation as a sensation novelist.

19. It is worth noting that, also on the level of theme, Isabel never renounces her love of Roland. She never says that her love was a mistake and she never really stops thinking about him. Isabel, moreover, is left Roland's fortune upon his death, accepted openly by the community that earlier chastised her, and allowed to live happily (and richly) ever after.

20. *The Scarlet Letter*, *The Woman in White*, and *Middlemarch* also interrogate the doctor's ability or inability to "read" sexual misconduct.

Chapter 4. A National Habit of Repression

1. Critics have, of course, often discussed James's avoidance of taboo subjects. His novels are read as models of narrative reticence and indirection which frustrate even the most sophisticated readers' hermeneutical goals. (See, for example, John Auchard's *Silence in Henry James*.) Only two critics, however, situate this reticence and indirection in the context of the implicit and explicit forms of print censorship with which James grappled. Roslyn Jolly provides an excellent overview of James's negotiation of the hostility to the novel expressed by cultural authorities in *Henry James: History, Narrative, Fiction* (1–19). And Anne Margolis's equally excellent *Henry James and the Problem of Audience* also tabulates the print censorship to which James was subject. Both Jolly and Margolis insist on James's need for some strategy,

or set of strategies, by which to circumvent print censorship. I have benefited enormously from both of these books.

2. For interesting accounts of James's stylistic complexities and his representation of homosocial desire see Eve Sedgwick's *Epistemology of the Closet* and Kaja Silverman's *Masculinity at the Margins*. For an account of James's representation of scandal (in the context of homosocial desire and sexuality more generally) see William Cohen's *Sex Scandal*.

3. Roslyn Jolly and John Goode are the only critics, to my knowledge, specifically to situate Besant's and James's essay in the context of literary censorship and naturalism.

4. W. D. Howells similarly scorns "that little sign to keep off the grass . . . at one point only" (*Criticism* 76) although he is more explicit than James and identifies that "one point" as adultery.

5. While Maggie is disturbed by the Prince's blush — "the red mark of conviction flaming there in his beauty" — she will, herself, later blush with the same burning sense of dismay and discomfort when she begins to read the meaning of the golden bowl: a "bright red spot, red as some monstrous ruby, . . . burned in either of her cheeks" (410). For a different interpretation of the blush see Sedgwick ("Queer" 8).

6. In many ways, this scene with Charlotte serves as a counterpoint to the French novel-reading scene in *The Awkward Age*. The French novel symbolizes a young woman's loss of innocence and forcefully indicates that a woman can indeed be seduced by a book. Where Maggie puts forward acceptable reading material for Charlotte that is rejected, the French novel in *The Awkward Age* represents tabooed reading material that is accepted. (For a subtle and interesting reading of *The Awkward Age* see Julie Rivkin.) If a French novel does not itself circulate in *The Golden Bowl* it is because the events described, and the novel, approximate as closely as possible for the English audience, the French novel itself. This point illuminates the Prince's fluency in French and Maggie's own limited capacity to read and speak the language.

7. The focus on the betrayed party is a persistent feature in James's novels that address adultery. Consider, for example, *The Portrait of the Lady*, *What Maisie Knew*, *The Ambassadors*, and *The Wings of the Dove*.

8. Joseph Litvak also makes this charge while proceeding to make his own rather abstract, albeit interesting, contribution to the James debate (196).

9. Neither Edel nor Tintner seem to be aware of the fact that divorce cases were transcribed in the London newspapers. In respect to James's jury duty, Edel writes that "all we know of the experience is recorded in Henry's remark to William [cited below in the text]" (*Treacherous* 180).

10. The "saint or sinner" debate recapitulates the sexual double standard written into the British divorce laws. Maggie is either a saint for tolerating her husband's adultery and redeeming her marriage or she is a sinner because of the means by which she chooses to do so. What critics do not question, however, are the terms of this debate. They take for granted that it is the wife's duty to rectify a faltering relationship; she may do it well, or she may do it callously, but the assumption is that she should do it. See, for example, Judith Armstrong (143). For a summary of this debate see Walter Wright's "Maggie Verver: Neither Saint Nor Witch." See also

R. B. J. Wilson's *The Ultimate Narrative* (13–39). Joseph Boone, on the other hand, is unusual in his recognition of Maggie's position: "Maggie inhabits one feminine stereotype after the other. Despite gains in self-assertion, she remains trapped in limiting social definitions of her role" (191).

11. Fanny, similarly, does not want to be suspected by the Prince: "To prove to him that she wasn't really watching him—ground for which would have been too terribly grave—she had followed him in his pursuit of pleasure: so she might, precisely, mark her detachment" (247).

12. James's humor with respect to the French tradition of adultery is frequently overlooked. In *What Maisie Knew*, for example, Maisie confides almost everything to her dolls but there were some things "she really couldn't even tell a French doll" (55).

13. These references to Heidegger are from "What is Metaphysics?" See also *Being and Time* (228–35).

14. See also 299, 333, 340, 342, 366–67, 373, 391, 396 in Gard's *The Critical Heritage*.

Chapter 5. A Good Read

1. It should be noted, however, that almost all early reviews of Ford's novel also remarked on his clever manipulation of narrative form and on his formal innovations. Denis Donoghue, like most critics, minimizes the sociological context of this novel. "The ordinances of society are not invoked. The main conflict is not between self and society but between type and morality, and finally the blame is laid upon Fate, the force of nature that ordained the type in the first place" (561). Charles Hoffman's (updated) study of Ford acknowledges this absence of social and historical studies related to Ford's work: "Little that is 'new' has been discovered or written about Ford's fiction since the 1960s. What is needed is a greater sense of an overview of Ford's fiction and its relationship to Ford's intellectual and historical milieu" (xiii). Max Saunders' recent biography of Ford does begin to provide some of this overview; Saunders, for example, considers the womens' movement, divorce law reform, the relationship between sexuality, religion, and morality (1:414). See also Robert Green's *Ford Madox Ford: Prose and Politics*, Gene Moore's "The Tory in a Time of Change: Social Aspects of Ford Madox Ford's *Parade's End*" and Brian May's "Ford Madox Ford and the Politics of Impressionism."

2. Most critics agree that *A Call* is Ford's best novel before *The Good Soldier*. It is striking that no critic seems to recognize the significance of the call to which the title refers, despite the fact that it is clearly linked with the divorce court in the novel and functions as a catalyst to Dudley's mental illness.

3. For an account of the Throne trial scandal, initiated by the publication of Violet Hunt's claim that she was Ford's legal wife, see Saunders (1:372–78).

4. Ford writes, "Dudley Leicester had entered into a world of dread" (50). And later Dudley's wife says to Grimshaw: Dudley's "done something—with Etta Hudson. Well, and ever since he's been dreading that it should get to my ears—and me in mourning for dear mother, and he alone and dreading—oh, dreading" (83).

5. The National Social Purity Crusade was easily the most active and ener-

getic new organization for the improvement of morals; in the space of only five years, between 1908 and 1913, they put together at least ten substantial publications related, directly and indirectly, to print censorship.

    6. In this context, Ford relates an amusing anecdote again indicating the extent to which adultery was perceived as a French theme: "I happened to be in company where a fervent admirer exclaimed: 'By Jove, *The Good Soldier* is the finest novel in the English language!' Whereupon my friend Mr. John Rodker, who has always had a properly tempered admiration for my work, remarked in his clear, slow drawl: 'Ay yes, it is, but you have left a word out. It is the finest French novel in the English language!'" ("Letter" xxii).

    7. Since the publication of Schorer's "An Interpretation" in 1951, and Hynes's "The Epistemology of The Good Soldier" ten years later in 1961, questions of narrative reliability have been inevitably linked with questions of epistemology. Arnold Weinstein, for example, refers to the novel as an "epistemological funhouse" (14). See also Richard Hood and Paul Armstrong.

    8. See Carol Jacobs for an excellent reading of this scene that differs from mine.

    9. For a further discussion of this Commission see the *Times*, 12 November 1912.

    10. See Mizener, 252, and Note 21, 565; Moser xxxiii; Saunders 436–37.

    11. In relation to one of the sources for *The Good Soldier*, for example, Ford writes that the "decency" of a lovers' parting — they are very "civilized" — is "a manifestation of national characteristic that is almost appalling" (*English Novels* 339). The challenge for Ford was to stage this event of censorship — in the tense and quietly controlled parting between Edward and Nancy — without at the same time fully subscribing to the implicit censorships by which he too felt constrained in his novelistic practice.

    12. Ford claims that "the great novels of the world . . . have all — and this is no paradox — been mystery stories" (*March* 832), and he credits the detective story with several of the aesthetic innovations associated with modernism.

    13. The significance of "things" is conveyed indirectly by Ford in his discussion of James's *The Turn of the Screw*: "I have stripped this episode [in James] of all its descriptive passages save one in order to reduce it to the barest and most crude of bones, in order to show just exactly what the hard skeleton is. And it will be observed that the whole matter — the whole skeleton or the only bone of it — is the one word 'things' — 'I said things'" (*James* 156).

    14. A letter to the editor of the *Times* on 20 May 1913 is indicative of the sentiments expressed here: "In a notorious divorce suit a young girl, who had been a guest in a country house, found herself unexpectedly confronted with an unpleasant incident and her name and the nature of the evidence . . . were uselessly published broadcast. Publicity is capable of being amongst the severest forms of punishment, although least controlled, and in relation to minor offenses (especially those of young people) the punishment may be wholly disproportionate to the actual culpability involved" (11). Nevertheless Leonora does occasionally succumb to the desire to expose the others: "at moments she almost yielded to denounce Mrs. Basil to her husband and Maisie Maiden to hers. She desired then to cause the horrors and pains

of public scandals" (194). And Edward finds himself willing to face the divorce court—"the publicity, the papers, the whole bally show" (70)—when relations with Leonora are strained beyond apparent tolerance. But the thrust of the narrative is to avoid exactly this sort of scandal.

15. Several critics have attempted to restore chronological order to this otherwise disjointed and disrupted text. See Roger Poole, Patrick McCarthy, James T. Adams and Vincent Cheng, among others.

16. Christopher Tietjens in *Parade's End* makes a similar equation between talk and sex: "You seduce a young woman in order to be able to finish your talks with her. You could not live with her without seducing her; but that was the by-product. The point is that you can't otherwise talk. You can't finish talks at street corners; in museums; even in drawing-rooms. You mayn't be in the mood when she is in the mood—for the intimate conversation that means the final communion of your souls" (629).

Works Cited

Primary Sources

"Act to Amend the Divorce and Matrimonial Causes Act of Last Session." *English Woman's Journal* 2 (1859): 119–22.
Alcott, Louisa May. *Moods: A Novel*. Boston: Roberts, 1884.
Arnold, Matthew. *Culture and Anarchy*. 1869. Ed. Samuel Lipman. New Haven: Yale University Press, 1994.
———. *Poetry and Criticism of Matthew Arnold*. Ed. A. Dwight Culler. Boston: Houghton Mifflin, 1961.
[Austin, Alfred]. "Our Novels: The Sensational School." *Temple Bar* 29 (July 1870): 410–24.
[———.] "The Vice of Reading." *Temple Bar* 52 (1874): 251–57.
Baedeker, Karl. *London, A Guide for the Traveler*. London: Baedeker, 1901.
"The Balance of Advantage." *Pump Court* (January 1887): 121–22.
Bennett, Arnold. *Whom God Hath Joined*. 1906. London: Methuen, 1919.
Besant, Walter. *The Art of Fiction*. London: Chatto, 1884.
"The Bill for Divorce." *Quarterly Review* 102 (July and October 1857): 251–83.
Braddon, M. E. *Lady Audley's Secret*. 1862. New York: Virago, 1985.
———. *The Lady's Mile*. 1865. London, Maxwell, n.d.
———. *The Doctor's Wife*. 2 vols. Leipzig: Tauchnitz, 1864. Reissued: London: Kent, n.d.
"The British Press: Its Growth, Liberty, and Power." *Quarterly Review* 30 (1859): 367–402.
Brontë, Anne. *The Tenant of Wildfell Hall*. 1848. Ed. G. D. Hargreaves. Middlesex: Penguin, 1984.
Buchanan, Robert. "Immorality in Authorship." *Fortnightly Review* 6 (15 Sept. 1866): 289–300.
Butler, Josephine. "Should Divorce Cases Be Reported?" *Pall Mall Gazette* [London] (25 Jan. 1887): 12.
"Charge Against a Vicar." *The Times* [London] (28 Nov. 1913–3 Dec. 1913): 4–8.
"A Circulating Censorship." *Saturday Review* (13 Dec. 1884): 747–48.
"Claptrap Morality." *Saturday Review* (28 July 1866): 104–5.
"The Colin Campbell Case." *Illustrated Police News* (1 Jan. 1887): 2.
Collins, Wilkie. *Armadale*. 1866. Oxford: Oxford University Press, 1989.
———. *Basil*. 1852. Ed. Dorothy Goldman. Oxford: Oxford University Press, 1990.
———. *The Evil Genius*. 1886. Ed. Graham Law. Peterborough, Ontario: Broadview, 1994.

———. *The Legacy of Cain*. 1888. New York: Fenelon, [n.d.].
———. "Letters of Dedication." In *Basil*. Ed. Dorothy Goldman. Oxford: Oxford University Press, 1990. xxxv–xl.
———. *The Woman in White*. 1860. London: Penguin, 1974.
———. "The Unknown Public." *My Miscellanies*. 1859. London: Chatto, 1885.
"Contemporary Reviews." In *The Good Soldier*. Ed. Martin Stannard. New York: Norton, 1995. 219–238.
"Culture and Anarchy." *Quarterly Review* (1892): 337–40.
Dickens, Charles. *Bleak House*. 1852–53. London: Penguin, 1978.
———. *Dombey and Son*. 1847–48. London: Penguin, 1971.
———. *Our Mutual Friend*. 1864–65. London: Penguin, 1985.
"Disclosing Proceedings Heard in Camera." *The Times* [London] (6 May 1913): 4–6.
Divorce Court. *The Times, Pall Mall Gazette, Divorce News and Police Reporter, Illustrated Police News, Daily Telegraph, Sunday Echo, Sunday Express, Reynolds Newspaper, Lloyd's Weekly Newspaper, Evening News* [London] 1858–1914.
"The Divorce Court at Work." *Saturday Review* (31 Dec. 1859): 809–10.
"The Doctor's Wife." *Saturday Review* (5 Nov. 1864): 571–72.
Doubleday. "Books and Their Uses." *Macmillan's Magazine* 1 (1859–60): 110–15.
Doyle, Arthur Conan. "A Case of Identity." *The Original Illustrated Sherlock Holmes*. Secaucus, N.J.: Castle, 1978. 41–52.
Egerton, Hugh. "The Scientific Novel of Gustave Flaubert." *National Review* 1 (1883): 894–907.
Eliot, George. *Adam Bede*. 1859. New York: Penguin, 1980.
———. *Daniel Deronda*. 1874–76. Clarendon: Oxford University Press, 1984.
———. *Middlemarch*. 1871–72. Ed. Bert Hornback. New York: Norton, 1977.
"*Evening News*' Defence: Publicity *versus* Privacy." *Evening News* [London] (20 Dec. 1886): 2.
Fenn, Henry Edwin. *Thirty-five Years in the Divorce Court*. London: Laurie, [n.d.].
"Fiction and Its Uses." *Fraser's Magazine* (December 1865): 746–60.
Flaubert, Gustave. *The Letters of Gustave Flaubert*. Ed. and trans. Francis Steegmuller. 2 vols. Cambridge: Harvard University Press, 1980.
———. *Madame Bovary*. 1857. Trans. Lowell Bair. Ed. Leo Bersani. Toronto: Bantam, 1981.
"Flaubert and His Work." *Saturday Review* (10 Sept. 1889): 378–79.
Ford, Ford Madox. *Between St. Dennis and St. George, A Sketch of Three Civilizations*. London: Hodder, 1915.
———. *A Call: The Tale of Two Passions*. 1910. Manchester: Carcanet, 1984.
———. *The Critical Attitude*. London: Duckworth, 1911.
———. "Dedicatory Letter to Stella Ford." In *The Good Soldier: A Tale of Passion*. 1915. New York: Vintage, 1989. xix–xxiv.
———. *The English Novel: From the Earliest Days to the Death of Conrad*. 1929. Darby: Arden, 1979.
———. *The Good Soldier: A Tale of Passion*. 1915. New York: Vintage, 1989.
———. *Henry James*. 1913. New York: Hippocrene, 1964.
———. *Joseph Conrad: A Personal Remembrance*. 1924. New York: Hippocrene, 1965.

———. *The March of Literature from Confucious to Modern Times*. London: Allen, 1939.
———. *Parade's End*. 1924. New York: Random House, 1979.
———. *The Shifting of the Fire*. London: Fisher Unwin, 1892.
Ford, Ford Madox, and Joseph Conrad. *The Nature of a Crime*. New York: Doubleday, 1924.
Forster, E. M. *Howard's End*. 1910. New York: Bantam, 1985.
"French Novels." *Saturday Review* (26 May 1866): 615.
Galsworthy, John. "The Library Censorship." *The Times* [London] (3 Oct. 1913): 4.
Gamma. "Divorce A Vinculo; or, The Terrors of Sir Cresswell Cresswell." *Once a Week* 2 (25 Feb. 1860): 184–91, 205–11, 227–32, 247–55, 270–77, 297–305.
Gard, Roger. Ed. *Henry James: The Critical Heritage*. London: Routledge, 1968.
Gosse, Edmund. "The Censorship of Books." *The Times* [London] (2 Oct. 1913): 5.
[Greg, W. R.]. "False Morality of Lady Novelists." *National Review* 8 (1859): 144–67.
———. "French Fiction: The Lowest Deep." *National Review* 11 (October 1860): 400–27.
"La Griffe Rose." *The Spectator* (13 Sept. 1862): 1029–30.
"Gustave Flaubert." *Fortnightly Review* 29 (1878): 573–95.
Hannigan, D. F. "The Tyranny of the Modern Novel." *Westminster Review* 143.3 (March 1895): 301–6.
Hansard's Parliamentary Debates. 356 vols. 3rd series.1857–58.
Hardy, Thomas. *Jude the Obscure*. 1895. New York: Signet, 1961.
Harrison, Frederic. *The Choice of Books*. London: Macmillan, 1866.
Hawthorne, Nathaniel. *The Scarlet Letter*. 1850. In *The Scarlet Letter: An Annotated Text, Backgrounds and Sources, Essays in Criticism*. Ed. Scully Bradley, Richmond Croom Beatty, and E. Hudson Long. New York: Norton, 1961.
Heidegger, Martin. *Being and Time*. 1927. Trans. John Macquarrie and Edward Robinson. New York: Harper, 1962.
"History of Divorce." *The Times* [London] (8 Nov. 1912): 10.
Howells, W. D. *Criticism and Fiction and Other Essays*. Ed. C. M. Kirk and R. Kirk. New York: New York University Press, 1959.
Hugo. "Which Perjury?" Reply to letter of Sigma. *Paul Mall Gazette* [London] (24 Dec. 1886): 2.
[Hutton, Richard Holt]. "Sensation Novels." *Spectator* (8 Aug. 1868): 931–32.
"Indecent Literature." *Daily Telegraph* (2 Sept. 1885): 3.
"Immoral Books." *Saturday Review* (24 Nov. 1866): 636–37.
James, Henry. *The Ambassadors*. Ed. S. P. Rosenbaum. New York: Norton, 1964.
———. "The Art of Fiction (1884, 1888)." In *Henry James, Literary Criticism: Essays on Literature: American Writers, English Writers*. Ed. Leon Edel. New York: Library of America, 1984. 44–65.
———. "The Future of the Novel (1899)." In *Henry James, Literary Criticism: Essays on Literature: American Writers, English Writers*. Ed. Leon Edel. New York: Library of America, 1984. 100–110.
———. *The Golden Bowl*. 1904. Oxford: Oxford University Press, 1988.
———. *Henry James: Letters*. Ed. Leon Edel. Cambridge: Harvard University Press, 1974.

———. "A London Life." In *The Complete Tales of Henry James*. Ed. Leon Edel. Philadelphia: J. B. Lippincott, 1963. 87–212.

———. "Louisa M. Alcott: *Moods* (1865)." In *Henry James. Literary Criticism: Essays on Literature: American Writers, English Writers*. Ed. Leon Edel. New York: Library of America, 1984. 189–94.

———. "Mary Elizabeth Braddon: *Aurora Floyd* (1865)." In *Henry James. Literary Criticism: Essays on Literature: American Writers, English Writers*. Ed. Leon Edel. New York: Library of America, 1984. 741–46.

———. "Nathaniel Hawthorne (1804–1864) (1896)." In *Henry James. Literary Criticism: Essays on Literature: American Writers, English Writers*. Ed. Leon Edel. New York: Library of America, 1984. 458–67.

———. "The New Novel (1914)." In *Henry James. Literary Criticism: Essays on Literature: American Writers, English Writers*. Ed. Leon Edel. New York: Library of America, 1984. 124–59.

———. *The Notebooks of Henry James*. Ed. F. O. Matthiessen and Kenneth B. Murdock. New York: Braziller, 1955.

———. *The Portrait of a Lady*. 1881. London: Penguin, 1983.

———. "The Prefaces to the New York Edition." In *Henry James. Literary Criticism: French Writers, Other European Writers, The Prefaces to the New York Edition*. Ed. Leon Edel. New York: Library of America, 1984. 1035–1342.

———. *The Question of Our Speech and the Lesson of Balzac*. Boston: Houghton, 1905.

———. *What Maisie Knew*. 1897. London: Penguin, 1985.

———. *The Wings of the Dove*. 1902. Norton Critical Edition. New York: Norton, 1978.

Jesse, F. Tennyson, ed. *Trial of Madeleine Smith*. London: Hodge, 1927.

Jeune, Sir Francis. Rev. of *The Awkward Age*. In *Henry James: The Critical Heritage*. Ed. Roger Gard. London: Routledge, 1968. 286–88.

Jones, Henry Arthur. "To Miss Grundy." *The Case of Rebellious Susan*. 1909. London: Folcroft, 1973. 7–11.

———. "The Case of Rebellious Susan." In *Representative Plays by Henry Arthur Jones*. Ed. Clayton Hamilton. Vol. 3. Boston: Little, Brown, 1925.

Kennard, N. H. "Gustave Flaubert and George Sand." *Nineteenth Century* 20 (1886): 693–708.

Laclos, Choderlos de. *Les Liaisons Dangereuses*. Trans. Richard Aldington. New York: Simon, 1962.

"Lady Novelists." *Eclectic Magazine* (December 1868): 1500–1509.

"The Law of Divorce." *Times* [London] (12 Nov. 1912): 9–11.

Law Reports. "*Regina* v. *Hicklin*." Queen's Bench Cases. Vol. 3. London: William Clowes, 1867–68. 360–79.

Lawrence, Guy. *Anteros*. London: Chapman, 1871.

Lecky, W. E. H. *Democracy and Liberty*. 2 vols. London: Longman's, 1896.

"The License of Modern Novelists." *Edinburgh Review* 106 (July 1857): 124–56.

Lilly, W. S. "The New Naturalism." In *Documents of Modern Literary Criticism*. Ed. George J. Becker. Princeton: Princeton University Press, 1963. 275–95.

"Lost and Saved." Rev. *Illustrated London News* (7 June 1863): 4.

"Lost and Saved." Rev. *The Reader* 1 (23 May 1863): 501–2.

"Lost and Saved." Rev. *Times* [London] (22 May 1863): 6.
MacCarthy, Justin. "Novels with a Purpose." *Westminster Review* 82 (1864): 24–49.
"Madeleine Smith." *Saturday Review* (11 July 1857): 26–27.
"The Majority Report of the Divorce Commission." *Quarterly Review* 218 (1913): 230–54.
Malot, Hector. *Josey*. London: n.p., 1887.
[Mansel, H. L.] "Sensation Novels." *Quarterly Review* 113 (April 1863): 481–514.
Maritus. Letter. *The Times* [London] (21 May 1856): 9.
"The Marriage and Divorce Bill." *North British Review* 27 (1858): 162–93.
"Marriage and Divorce: The Law of England and Scotland." *North British Review* 35 (1861): 187–218.
"The Marriage Law of the Three Kingdoms." *Cornhill Magazine* 16 (1868): 432–39.
Marryat, Florence. *On Circumstantial Evidence*. London: n.p., 1889.
Marx-Aveling, Eleanor. Introduction to *Madame Bovary* by Gustave Flaubert. Trans. Eleanor Marx-Aveling. London: Vizetelly, 1886.
[Masson, David]. "Three Vices of Current Literature." *MacMillan's Magazine* 2 (May 1860): 1–13.
"Matrimonial Divorce Act." *English Woman's Journal* 2 (1859): 56–62.
Maxwell, Herbert. "The Craving for Fiction." *Nineteenth Century* (June 1893): 1046–61.
Meredith, George. *The Ordeal of Richard Feveral: A History of a Father and Son*. London: Dent, 1935.
Mill, John Stuart. *On Liberty*. 1859. London: Norton, 1975.
"A Month in the Divorce Court." *Saturday Review* (8 Jan. 1859): 36–37.
Moore, George. *Confessions of a Young Man*. New York: Modern, 1925.
———. *Esther Waters*. 1899. New York: Duffield, 1953.
———. "A New Censorship of Literature." 1885. In *Literature at Nurse, or Circulating Morals: A Polemic on Victorian Censorship*. Ed. Pierre Coustillas. Hassocks, Eng.: Harvester, 1976. 27–32.
Mordaunt v. Mordaunt, Cole, Johnstone, and Others. London: Savill, n.d.
National Vigilance Association. "Pernicious Literature." In *Documents of Modern Literary Realism*. Ed. George J. Becker. Princeton: Princeton University Press, 1963. 350–82.
Norton, Caroline. Reviews of "The Angel in the House" and "Goblin Market." *Macmillan's Magazine* 8 (September 1863): 398–404.
———. *Caroline Norton's Defense: English Laws for Women in the Nineteenth Century*. [1854]. *Selected Writings of Caroline Norton*. Ed. James O. Hoge and Jane Marcus. New York: Scholars' Facsimiles, 1978.
———. Letter. *Times* [London] (28 Jan. 1857): 8.
———. "A Letter to the Queen on Lord Chancellor Cranworth's Marriage and Divorce Bill." [1857]. *Selected Writings of Caroline Norton*. Ed. James O. Hoge and Jane Marcus. New York: Scholars' Facsimiles, 1978.
———. *Lost and Saved*. 2 vols. Leipzig: Tauchnitz, 1863.
———. *Selected Writings of Caroline Norton*. Ed. James O. Hoge and Jane Marcus. New York: Scholars' Facsimiles, 1978.
"Not a New 'Sensation.'" *All the Year Round* (25 July 1863): 517–20.

"Not Proven." *Saturday Review* (11 July 1857): 32–34.
"Novel-Reading." *Saturday Review* (16 Feb. 1867): 196–97.
"Novel-Reading as a Vice." *Saturday Review* (9 Oct. 1875): 452–53.
"Novels, Past and Present." *Saturday Review* (14 April 1866): 438–39.
An Old Law Reporter. Letter. *Times* [London] (12 Dec. 1887): 9.
[Oliphant, Mrs.] "Novels." *Blackwood's Edinburgh Magazine* 102 (September 1867): 257–80.
[———.] "Sensation Novels." *Blackwood's Edinburgh Magazine* 91 (May 1862): 564–84.
"Our Female Sensation Novelists." *Christian Remembrancer* 46 (1863): 209–36.
"Our Novels: The Sensational School." *Temple Bar* 29 (July 1870): 410–24.
Paget, Francis. *Lucretia; or The Heroine of the Nineteenth-Century*. London: J. Masters, 1868.
Palgrave, F. T. "On Readers in 1760 and 1860." *Macmillan's Magazine* 1 (1860): 487–89.
"Pecksniff and Poison." Editorial. *Pall Mall Gazette* [London] (16 Dec. 1886): 1.
"The Publication of Obscene Reports." *Pall Mall Gazette* (30 May 1887): 6.
"The Purity of the Press." *Saturday Review* (26 June 1858): 656–57.
"The Question of Indecent Literature." *The Lancet* (19 Nov. 1898): 1344–45.
Reade, Charles. *Griffith Gaunt, or Jealousy*. London: Chatto, 1887.
"Realism and Decadence in French Fiction." *Quarterly Review* 171 (1890):
"Recent Novel Writing." *Macmillan's Magazine* 13 (1866): 202–9.
"Reports of Divorce Cases." *Times* [London] (3 Jan. 1887): 8.
Sala, George Augustus. "On the 'Sensational' in Literature and Art." *Belgravia* 4 (1868): 449–57.
"Sensation Novels." *Blackwood's Magazine* 91 (1862): 564–84.
"Sensation Novels." *Medical Critic and Psychological Journal* 3 (1863): 513–19.
"Sensation Novelists: Miss Braddon." *North British Review* 43 (September 1865): 92–105.
"Should Scandals in High Life Be Hushed Up?" *Pall Mall Gazette* [London] (4 Feb. 1887): 1–2.
Sigma. "The 'Code of Honour'—Adultery Plus Perjury." Letter. *Pall Mall Gazette* (22 Dec. 1886): 3.
Skilton, David. Ed. *The Early and Mid-Victorian Novel*. [Reviews and Essays 1833–1888] London: Routledge, 1993.
Stack, Herbert. "Some Recent English Novels." *Fortnightly Review* 15 (June 1871): 731–46.
[Stephen, Fitzjames]. "Madame Bovary." *Saturday Review* (11 July 1857): 40–41.
[Stephen, Leslie]. "Art and Morality." *Cornhill Magazine* 32 (1875): 91–101.
Sumner, John. "Obscene Literature—Its Suppression." *Publishers Weekly* (8 July 1916): 94–97.
The Times. [London] Letters to the Editor. 1857–1914.
"The Trial of *Madame Bovary*." In *Madame Bovary* by Gustave Flaubert. Trans. Evelyn Gendel. New York: Signet, 1964. 325–403.
Trollope, Anthony. *He Knew He Was Right*. 1869. London: Penguin, 1983.
———. "Novel Reading." *Nineteenth Century* (1879): 24–43.

———. *The Small House at Allington*. 1864. London: Penguin, 1995.
"Uncle Silas." *Saturday Review* (4 Feb. 1865): 145–46.
"The Uses of Fiction." *Saturday Review* (15 Sept. 1866): 323–24.
Warlow, W. H. Letter. *Times* [London] (20 May 1913): 6.
Wolff, Robert Lee. "Devoted Disciple: The Letters of Mary Elizabeth Braddon to Sir Edward Bulwer-Lytton, 1862–1873." *Harvard Library Bulletin* 22 (1974): 5–35, 129–61.
Wood, Mrs. Henry. *East Lynne*. Ed. Sally Mitchell. New Brunswick, N.J.: Rutgers University Press, 1984.
"The Working of the New Divorce Bill." *English Woman's Journal* 1 (1858): 339–41.
Wright, Thomas. "Concerning the Unknown Public." *Nineteenth Century* 13 (February 1883): 279–98.
The Yelverton Marriage Case, Thelwall v. Yelverton, Comprising an Authentic and Unabridged Account of the Most Extraordinary Trial of Modern Times, With Its Revelations, Incidents and Details Specially Reported. London: Vickers, [1861].

Secondary Sources

Acland, Alice. *Caroline Norton*. London: Constable, 1948.
Adams, James T. "Discrepancies in the Time-Scheme of *The Good Soldier*." *English Literature in Transition* 34.2 (1991): 153–64.
Altick, Richard. *The English Common Reader: A Social History of the Mass Reading Public, 1800–1900*. Chicago: University of Chicago Press, 1957.
Anderson, Charles R. *Person, Place, and Thing in Henry James's Novels*. Durham, N.C.: Duke University Press, 1977.
Armstrong, Judith. *The Novel of Adultery*. London: Macmillan, 1976.
Armstrong, Nancy. *Desire and Domestic Fiction: A History of the Novel*. New York: Oxford University Press, 1987.
Armstrong, Paul B. *The Challenge of Bewilderment: Understanding and Representation in James, Conrad, and Ford*. Ithaca: Cornell University Press, 1987.
Auchard, John. *Silence in Henry James: The Heritage of Symbolism and Decadence*. University Park: Pennsylvania State University Press, 1986.
Auerbach, Nina. *Woman and the Demon: The Life of a Victorian Myth*. Cambridge: Harvard University Press, 1982.
Barickman, Richard, Susan MacDonald, and Myra Stark. *Corrupt Relations: Dickens, Thackeray, Trollope, Collins and the Victorian Sexual System*. New York: Columbia University Press, 1982.
Barthes, Roland. *The Pleasure of the Text*. Trans. Richard Miller. Evanston, Ill.: Northwestern University Press, 1957.
Basch, Françoise. *Relative Creatures: Victorian Women in Society and the Novel*. New York: Schocken, 1974.
Beisel, Nicola. "Constructing a Shifting Moral Boundary: Literature and Obscenity in Nineteenth-Century America." In *Cultivating Boundaries: Symbolic Boundaries and the Making of Inequality*. Ed. Michele Lamont and Marcel Fournier. Chicago: University of Chicago Press, 1992. 104–28.

———. "Morals Versus Art: Censorship, the Politics of Interpretation, and the Victorian Nude." *American Sociological Review* 58 (1993): 145–62.
Beizer, Janet. *Ventriloquized Bodies: Narratives of Hysteria in Nineteenth-Century France*. Ithaca: Cornell University Press, 1994.
Bell, Ian, ed. *Henry James: Fiction as History*. Totowa, N.J.: Barnes and Noble, 1984.
Bender, John. *Imagining the Penitentiary: Fiction and the Architecture of Mind in Eighteenth-Century England*. Chicago: University of Chicago Press, 1987.
Bersani, Leo. *A Future for Astyanax: Character and Desire in Literature*. Boston: Little, Brown 1969; 1976.
———. "The Subject of Power." *Diacritics* 73 (1977): 2–21.
Blake, Andrew. *Reading Victorian Fiction: The Cultural Context and the Ideological Content of the Nineteenth-Century Novel*. London: Macmillan, 1989.
Bolton, Richard, ed. *Culture Wars: Documents from the Recent Controversies in the Arts*. New York: New Press, 1992.
Boone, Joseph A. *Tradition-Counter-Tradition: Love and the Form of Fiction*. Chicago: University of Chicago Press, 1987.
Booth, Michael R. *English Melodrama*. London: Jenkins, 1965.
Booth, Wayne C. *Rhetoric of Fiction*. Chicago: University of Chicago Press, 1961.
Bourdieu, Pierre. *Distinction: A Social Critique of the Judgement of Taste*. Trans. Richard Nice. Cambridge: Harvard University Press, 1984.
———. "The Force of Law: Toward a Sociology of the Juridical Field." Trans. Richard Terdiman. *Hastings Law Journal* 38 (1987): 805–53.
———. *In Other Words: Essays Towards a Reflexive Sociology*. Trans. Matthew Adamson. Stanford: Stanford University Press, 1990.
———. *Language and Symbolic Power*. Trans. Gino Raymond and Matthew Adamson. Cambridge: Harvard University Press, 1991.
Boyle, Thomas. *Black Swine in the Sewers of Hampstead: Beneath the Surface of Victorian Sensationalism*. New York: Viking, 1989.
Bradbury, Nicola. *Henry James: The Later Novels*. Oxford: Oxford University Press, 1979.
Bragdon, Claude. *Henry James: The Critical Heritage*. Ed. Roger Gard. New York: Routledge, 1968.
Brantlinger, Patrick. "What Is 'Sensational' About the 'Sensation Novel'?" *Nineteenth-Century Fiction* 37 (1982): 1–28.
Brooks, Peter. *Body Work: Objects of Desire in Modern Narrative*. Cambridge: Harvard University Press, 1993.
———. *The Melodramatic Imagination: Balzac, Henry James, Melodrama, and the Mode of Excess*. New Haven: Yale University Press, 1976.
———. *Reading for the Plot: Design and Intention in Narrative*. New York: Knopf, 1984.
Brown, Lucy. *Victorian News and Newspapers*. Oxford: Clarendon, 1985.
Burger, Peter. *The Decline of Modernism*. Trans. Nicholas Walker. University Park: Pennsylvania State University Press, 1992.
———. *Theory of the Avant-Garde*. Trans. Michael Shaw. Minneapolis: University of Minnesota Press, 1984.

Burgin, Victor, James Donald, and Cora Kaplan, eds. *Formations of Fantasy.* New York: Methuen, 1986.
Butler, Judith. *Bodies That Matter: On the Discursive Limits of "Sex."* New York: Routledge, 1993.
———. "The Force of Fantasy: Feminism, Mapplethorpe, and Discursive Excess." *differences: A Journal of Feminist Cultural Studies* 2, no. 2 (1990): 105–25.
———. *Gender Trouble: Feminism and the Subversion of Identity.* New York: Routledge, 1990.
Chartier, Roger. *The Cultural Origins of the French Revolution.* Trans. Lydia G. Cochrane. Durham, N.C.: Duke University Press, 1991.
Chatman, Seymour. *The Later Style of Henry James.* London: Oxford University Press, 1972.
Cheng, Vincent. "The Spirit of *The Good Soldier* and *The Spirit of the People.*" *English Literature in Transition* 32.3 (1989): 303–16.
Cockshut, A. O. J. *Man and Woman: A Study of Love and the Novel, 1740–1940.* New York: Oxford University Press, 1987.
Cohen, William A. *Sex Scandal: The Private Parts of Victorian Fiction.* Durham: Duke University Press, 1996.
Crary, Jonathan and Sanford Kwinter, eds. *Incorporations.* New York: Zone, 1992.
Cruse, Amy. *The Victorians and Their Books.* London: George Allen, 1935.
Cvetkovich, Ann. *Mixed Feelings: Feminism, Mass Culture, and Victorian Sensationalism.* New Brunswick, N.J.: Rutgers University Press, 1992.
Davis, Lennard. *Factual Fictions: The Origins of the English Novel.* New York: Columbia University Press, 1983.
Davis, Sara. "Feminist Sources in *The Bostonians.*" *American Literature* 50 (1979): 570–87.
Dean, Carolyn. "Pornography, Literature, and the Redemption of Virility in France, 1880–1930." *differences: A Journal of Feminist Cultural Studies* 5, no. 2 (1993): 62–91.
Donoghue, Denis. "Listening to the Saddest Story." *Sewanee Review* 88 (1980): 557–71.
Douglas, Mary. *Purity and Danger: An Analysis of the Concepts of Pollution and Taboo.* London: Routledge, 1978.
Dreiser, Theodore. "The Saddest Story." In *Critical Essays on Ford Madox Ford.* Ed. Richard A. Cassell. Boston: Hall, 1987. 41–43.
Eagleton, Terry. *The Ideology of the Aesthetic.* Oxford: Blackwell, 1990.
Edel, Leon. *Henry James, 1843–1870: The Untried Years.* New York: Lippincott, 1953.
———. *Henry James: The Conquest of London: 1870–1881.* New York: Avon, 1962.
———. *Henry James: The Middle Years: 1882–1895.* New York: Avon, 1962.
———. *Henry James: The Treacherous Years: 1895–1901.* New York: Avon, 1969.
———. *Henry James: The Master: 1901–1916.* New York: Avon, 1972.
Edelstein, T. J. "Augustus Egg's Triptych: A Narrative of Victorian Adultery." *Burlington Magazine* 125 (1983): 202–10.
Fahnestock, Jeanne. "Bigamy: The Rise and Fall of a Convention." *Nineteenth-Century Fiction* 36 (1981): 47–71.

Flint, Kate. *The Woman Reader, 1836–1914*. Oxford: Oxford University Press, 1993.
Foucault, Michel. *Discipline and Punish: The Birth of the Prison*. Trans. Alan Sheridan. New York: Vintage, 1979.
——. "The Discourse on Language." *The Archaeology of Knowledge and the Discourse on Language*. Trans. A. M. Sheridan Smith. New York: Harper, 1976.
——. *History of Sexuality, Volume 1: An Introduction*. Trans. Robert Hurley. New York: Random, 1980.
——. *Power/Knowledge: Selected Interviews and Other Writings, 1972–1977*. Ed. Colin Gordon. Trans. Colin Gordon, Leo Marshall, John Mepham, and Kate Soper. New York: Pantheon, 1980.
Forster, E. M. *Aspects of the Novel*. 1927. New York: Harcourt, 1954.
Freud, Sigmund. "The Antithetical Sense of Primal Words." Vol. 4 of *Collected Papers*. Trans. and ed. James Strachey. London: Hogarth, 1950
——. *Dora: An Analysis of a Case of Hysteria*. Ed. Philip Rieff. New York: Collier, 1963.
——. *The Interpretation of Dreams*. Trans. James Strachey. New York: Avon, 1965.
——. "Totem and Taboo." In *The Origins of Religion*. Trans. and ed. James Strachey. London: Penguin, 1985. 43–224.
Gallagher, Catherine. *The Industrial Reformation of English Fiction: Social Discourse and Narrative Form, 1832–1867*. Chicago: University of Chicago Press, 1985.
Gargano, James, ed. *Critical Essays on Henry James: The Late Novels*. Boston: G. K. Hall, 1987.
Gay, Peter. *Education of the Senses*. Vol. 1 of *The Bourgeois Experience: Victoria to Freud*. 2 vols. New York: Oxford University Press, 1984.
——. *The Tender Passion*. Vol. 2 of *The Bourgeois Experience: Victoria to Freud*. 2 vols. New York: Oxford University Press, 1986.
Giddens, Anthony. *Modernity and Self-Identity: Self and Society in the Late Modern Age*. Stanford: Stanford University Press, 1991.
Gilbert, Sandra M., and Susan Gubar. *The Madwoman in the Attic: The Woman Writer and the Nineteenth-Century Literary Imagination*. New Haven: Yale University Press, 1979.
Gledhill, Christine. "The Melodramatic Field: An Investigation." In *Home Is Where the Hearth Is*. Ed. Christine Gledhill. London: British Film Institute, 1987. 5–42.
Goode, John. "The Art of Fiction: Walter Besant and Henry James. In *Tradition and Tolerance in Nineteenth-Century Fiction: Critical Essays on Some English and American Novels*. Eds. David Howard, John Lucas, and John Goode. London: Routledge, 1966. 243–81.
Green, Robert. *Ford Madox Ford: Prose and Politics*. Cambridge: Cambridge University Press, 1981.
Greenblatt, Stephen. "Culture." In *Critical Terms for Literary Study*. Chicago: University of Chicago Press, 1990. 225–31.
Griest, Guinevere L. *Mudie's Circulating Library and the Victorian Novel*. Bloomington: Indiana University Press, 1970.
Hadley, Elaine. *Melodramatic Tactics: Theatricalized Dissent in the English Marketplace, 1800–1885*. Stanford: Stanford University Press, 1995.

Hall, David D. *Cultures of Print: Essays in the History of the Book*. Amherst: University of Massachusetts Press, 1996.
Hartman, Mary S. *Victorian Murderesses: A True History of Thirteen Respectable French and English Women Accused of Unspeakable Crimes*. New York: Schocken, 1977.
Hays, Michael, and Anastasia Nikolopoulou. *Melodrama: The Cultural Emergence of a Genre*. New York: St. Martin's Press, 1996.
Helsinger, Elizabeth K., Robin Lauterbach Sheets, and William Veeder. *The Woman Question: Society and Literature in Britain and America, 1837–1883*. Vol. 3: *Literary Issues*. New York: Garland, 1983.
Herr, Cheryl. *Joyce's Anatomy of Culture*. Chicago: University of Chicago Press, 1986.
Hertz, Neil. "Dora's Secret, Freud's Techniques." In *Dora's Case: Freud-Hysteria-Feminism*. Ed. Charles Bernheimer and Claire Kahane. New York: Columbia University Press, 1985. 221–42.
Heywood, Christopher. "Flaubert, Miss Braddon, and George Moore." *Comparative Literature* 12, no. 2 (1960): 151–58.
———. "A Source for *Middlemarch*: Miss Braddon's *The Doctor's Wife* and *Madame Bovary*." *Revue de Littérature Comparée* 44 (1970): 184–94.
Hiley, Nicholas. "'Can't You Find Me Something Nasty': Circulating Libraries and Literary Censorship in Britain from the 1890s to the 1910s." In *Censorship and the Control of Print in England and France, 1600–1910*. Eds. Robin Myers and Michael Harris. Winchester: St. Paul's, 1992. 123–47.
Hoffman, Charles. *Ford Madox Ford*. Boston: Twayne, 1990.
Holland, Laurence. *The Expense of Vision*. Baltimore: Johns Hopkins University Press, 1982.
Hood, Richard A. "'Constant Reduction': Modernism and the Narrative Structure of *The Good Soldier*." *Journal of Modern Literature* 14.4 (1988): 445–64.
Horstman, Allen. *Victorian Divorce*. London: Croom Helm, 1985.
Hughes, Winifred. *The Maniac in the Cellar: Sensation Novels of the 1860s*. Princeton: Princeton University Press, 1980.
Humphreys, Anne. "Coming Apart: The British Newspaper Press and the Divorce Court." In *Defining Centres: Nineteenth-Century Media and the Construction of Identities*. Eds. Laurel Brake, William Bell, and David Finkelstein. London: Macmillan, 1999.
Hunter, Ian, David Saunders, and Dugald Williamson. *On Pornography*. London: Macmillan, 1992.
Hunter, J. Paul. *Before Novels: The Cultural Contexts of Eighteenth Century English Fiction*. New York: Norton, 1990.
Hynes, Samuel. *The Edwardian Turn of Mind*. Princeton: Princeton University Press, 1968.
———. "The Epistemology of *The Good Soldier*." In *Critical Essays on Ford Madox Ford*. Ed. Richard A. Cassell. Boston: Hall, 1987. 49–55.
Jacobs, Carol. "The (too) Good Soldier: 'A Real Story'." *Glyph* 3 (1978): 32–51.
Jacobus, Mary. *Reading Woman: Essays in Feminist Criticism*. New York: Columbia University Press, 1986.
Jameson, Fredric. *The Political Unconscious: Narrative as a Socially Symbolic Act*. Ithaca: Cornell University Press, 1981.

Jenkins, Roy. *Victorian Scandal: A Biography of the Right Honorable Sir Charles Dilke*. New York: Chilmark, 1965.
Jolly, Roslyn. *Henry James: History, Narrative, Fiction*. Oxford: Clarendon, 1993.
Kaplan, E. Ann. *Motherhood and Representation: The Mother in Popular Culture and Melodrama*. London: Routledge, 1992.
Keating, Peter. *The Haunted Study: A Social History of the English Novel, 1875–1914*. London: Secker, 1989.
Kendrick Walter. *The Secret Museum: Pornography in Modern Culture*. New York: Viking, 1987.
Kermode, Frank. *The Sense of an Ending*. New York: Oxford University Press, 1967.
Kierkegaard, Soren. *The Concept of Dread*. Trans. Walter Lowrie. Princeton: Princeton University Press, 1957.
Kristeva, Julia. *Revolution in Poetic Language*. Trans. Margaret Waller. New York: Columbia University Press, 1984.
LaCapra, Dominick. *"Madame Bovary" on Trial*. Ithaca: Cornell University Press, 1982.
Lanser, Susan Snaider. *The Narrative Act: Point of View in Prose Fiction*. Princeton: Princeton University Press, 1981.
Levine, George. "Introduction: Reclaiming the Aesthetic." *Aesthetics and Ideology*. Ed. George Levine. New Brunswick, N.J.: Rutgers University Press, 1994. 1–30.
Levine, Michael. *Writing Through Repression: Literature, Censorship, Psychoanalysis*. Baltimore: Johns Hopkins University Press, 1994.
Litvak, Joseph. *Caught in the Act: Theatricality in the Nineteenth-Century English Novel*. Berkeley: University of California Press, 1992.
Loesberg, Jonathan. "The Ideology of Narrative Form in Sensation Fiction." *Representations* 13 (1986): 115–38.
MacKinnon, Catharine A. *Only Words*. Cambridge: Harvard University Press, 1993.
MacShane, Frank, ed. *Ford Madox Ford: The Critical Heritage*. London: Routledge, 1972.
Maison, Margaret M. "Adulteresses in Agony." *The Listener* (19 Jan. 1961): 133–34.
Manchester, Colin. "Lord Campbell's Act: England's First Obscenity Statute." *Journal of Legal History* 9, no. 2 (1988): 223–41.
Marcus, Steven. "Freud and Dora: Story, History, Case History." In *Dora's Case: Freud-Hysteria-Feminism*. Ed. Charles Bernheimer and Claire Kahane. New York: Columbia University Press, 1985. 56–91.
——. *The Other Victorians: A Study of Sexuality and Pornography in Mid-Nineteenth-Century England*. New York: Basic, 1966.
Margolis, Anne. *Henry James and the Problem of Audience: An International Act*. Ann Arbor, Mich.: UMI, 1985.
Marsh, Joss. *Word Crimes: Blasphemy, Culture, and Literature in Nineteenth-Century England*. Chicago: University of Chicago Press, 1998.
Matlock, Jann. *Scenes of Seduction: Prostitution, Hysteria, and Reading Difference in Nineteenth-Century France*. New York: Columbia University Press, 1994.
May, Brian. "Ford Madox Ford and the Politics of Impressionism." *Essays in Literature* 21.1 (1994): 82–96.

McCarthy, Patrick A. "In Search of Lost Time: Chronology and Narration in *The Good Soldier*." *English Literature in Transition* 40.2 (1997): 133–49.
McKeon, Michael. *The Origins of the English Novel, 1600–1740*. Baltimore: Johns Hopkins University Press, 1987.
Merkel, Jayne. "Art on Trial." *Art in America* (December 1990): 41–50.
Miller, D. A. *Narrative and Its Discontents*. Princeton: Princeton University Press, 1981.
———. *The Novel and the Police*. Berkeley: University of California Press, 1988.
Miller, J. Hillis. "The Problematic of Ending in Narrative." *Nineteenth-Century Fiction* 33 (1978): 3–7.
Mitchell, Sally. *The Fallen Angel: Chastity, Class, and Women's Reading, 1835–1880*. Bowling Green, Ohio: Bowling Green University Popular Press, 1981.
Mizener, Arthur. *The Saddest Story: A Biography of Ford Madox Ford*. New York: World, 1971.
Moi, Toril. "Representation and Patriarchy: Sexuality and Epistemology in Freud's Dora." In *Dora's Case: Freud-Hysteria-Feminism*. Ed. Charles Bernheimer and Claire Kahane. New York: Columbia University Press, 1985. 181–99.
Moon, Heath. "James's 'A London Life' and the Colin Campbell Divorce Scandal." *American Literary Realism* 13, no. 2 (1980): 246–58.
Moore, Gene. "The Tory in a Time of Change: Social Aspects of Ford Madox Ford's *Paradise's End*." *Twentieth-Century Literature* 8 (1982): 49–68.
Moretti, Franco. *Signs Taken For Wonders: Essays in the Sociology of Literary Forms*. London: Verso, 1988.
———. *The Way of the World: The* Bildungsroman *in European Culture*. London: Verso, 1987.
Moser, Thomas. *The Life in the Fiction of Ford Madox Ford*. Princeton: Princeton University Press, 1980.
Nead, Lynda. *Myths of Sexuality: Representations of Women in Victorian Britain*. London: Blackwell, 1988.
Ohmann, Carol. *Ford Madox Ford: From Apprentice to Craftsman*. Middletown, Conn.: Wesleyan University Press, 1964.
Ortega y Gasset, Jose. *The Dehumanization of Art and Other Essays on Art, Culture, and Literature*. Princeton: Princeton University Press, 1968.
Pacey, Desmond. "Flaubert and His Victorian Critics. *University of Toronto Quarterly* 16 (Oct. 1946): 74–84.
Patterson, Annabel. *Censorship and Interpretation: The Conditions of Writing and Reading in Early Modern England*. Madison: University of Wisconsin Press, 1984.
Pearsall, Roland. *The Worm in the Bud: The World of Victorian Sexuality*. Toronto: Macmillan, 1969.
Petrey, Sandy. *Realism and Revolution: Balzac, Stendal, Zola and the Performances of History*. Ithaca: Cornell University Press, 1988.
Poole, Roger. "The Real Plot Line of Ford Madox Ford's *The Good Soldier*: An Essay in Applied Deconstruction." *Textual Practice* 4.3 (1990): 390–427.
Poovey, Mary. *Uneven Developments: The Ideological Work in Gender in Mid-Victorian England*. Chicago: University of Chicago Press, 1988.

Porter, Carolyn. "History and Literature 'After the New Historicism.'" *New Literary History* (1990): 253–72.

———. *Seeing and Being: The Plight of the Participant Observer in Emerson, James, Adams, and Faulkner.* Middletown, Conn.: Wesleyan University Press, 1981.

Prendergast, Christopher. *The Order of Mimesis: Balzac, Stendhal, Nerval, Flaubert.* Cambridge: Cambridge University Press, 1986.

Radway, Janice A. *Reading the Romance: Women, Patriarchy, and Popular Literature.* Chapel Hill: University of North Carolina Press, 1984.

Rajchman, John. "Foucault's Art of Seeing." *October* 44 (1988): 89–117.

Randall, Richard S. *Freedom and Taboo: Pornography and the Politics of a Self Divided.* Berkeley: University of California Press, 1989.

Rivkin, Julie. *False Positions: The Representational Logics of Henry James's Fiction.* Stanford: Stanford University Press, 1996.

Roberts, M. J. D. "Morals, Art, and the Law: The Passing of the Obscene Publications Act, 1857." *Victorian Studies* 28 (1985): 609–29.

Rycroft, Charles. "The Analysis of a Detective Story." *Imagination and Reality: Psycho-Analytical Essays, 1951–1961.* London: Hogarth, 1968.

Said, Edward. *Culture and Imperialism.* New York: Knopf, 1993.

———. *The World, the Text, and the Critic.* Cambridge: Harvard University Press, 1983.

Saunders, Max. *Ford Madox Ford: A Dual Life.* Oxford: Oxford University Press, 1996.

Savage, Gail. "The Operation of the 1857 Divorce Act, 1860–1910, A Research Note." *Journal of Social History* (1988): 103–10.

Scheman, Naomi. "From Hamlet to Maggie Verver: The History and Politics of the Knowing Subject." *Poetics* 18 (1989): 449–69.

Schorer, Mark. "An Interpretation." *The Good Soldier: A Tale of Passion.* New York: Vintage, 1989. vii–xvii.

Scott, James B. "Coincidence or Irony? Ford's Use of August 4th in *The Good Soldier*." *ELN* 30.4 (1993): 53–58.

Sears, Sallie. *The Negative Imagination: Form and Perspective in the Novels of Henry James.* Ithaca: Cornell University Press, 1963.

Sedgwick, Eve Kosofsky. "Epidemics of the Will." In *Incorporations.* Ed. Jonathan Crary and Sanford Kwinter. New York: Zone, 1992. 582–595.

———. *Epistemology of the Closet.* Berkeley: University of California Press, 1990.

———. "Queer Performativity: Henry James's *The Art of the Novel*." *GLQ* 1 (1993): 1–16.

Seltzer, Mark. *Henry James and the Art of Power.* Ithaca: Cornell University Press, 1984.

Shanley, Mary. "'One Must Ride Behind': Married Women's Rights and the Divorce Act of 1857." *Victorian Studies* 25 (1982): 355–76.

Showalter, Elaine. "Family Secrets and Domestic Subversion: Rebellion in the Novels of the Eighteen-Sixties." In *The Victorian Family: Structure and Stresses.* Ed. A. Wohl. London: Croom, 1978.

———. *A Literature of Their Own: British Women Novelists from Brontë to Lessing.* Princeton: Princeton University Press, 1977.

Shuttleworth, Sally. "'Preaching to the Nerves': Psychological Disorder in Sensation Fiction." In *A Question of Identity*. Ed. Marina Benjamin. New Jersey: Rutgers University Press, 1993. 192–222.

Silverman, Kaja. *Masculinity at the Margins*. New York: Routledge, 1992.

Spanos, William V. *Martin Heidegger and the Question of Literature: Toward a Postmodern Literary Hermeneutics*. Bloomington: Indiana University Press, 1979.

Spilka, Mark. "Henry James and Walter Besant: 'The Art of Fiction' Controversy." *Novel* (1973): 101–19.

Stallybrass, Peter, and Allon White. *The Politics and Poetics of Transgression*. Ithaca: Cornell University Press, 1986.

Stang, Richard. *The Theory of the Novel in England, 1850–1870*. New York: Columbia University Press, 1966.

Stang, Sondra J., ed. *The Presence of Ford Madox Ford: A Memorial Volume of Essays, Poems, and Memoirs*. Philadelphia: University of Pennsylvania Press, 1981.

Steiner, Wendy. *The Scandal of Pleasure: Art in an Age of Fundamentalism*. Chicago: University of Chicago Press, 1995.

Stone, Lawrence. *Broken Lives: Separation and Divorce in England, 1660–1857*. Oxford: Oxford University Press, 1993.

———. *The Family, Sex, and Marriage in England, 1500–1800*. New York: Harper, 1977.

———. *Uncertain Union: Marriage in England, 1660–1753*. Oxford: Oxford University Press, 1992.

Tanner, Tony. *Adultery in the Novel: Contract and Transgression*. Baltimore: Johns Hopkins University Press, 1979.

Thomas, Keith. "The Double Standard." *Journal of the History of Ideas* 20 (1959): 195–216.

Thomas, Ronald A. *Dreams of Authority: Freud and the Fictions of the Unconscious*. Ithaca: Cornell University Press, 1990.

Thompson, E. P. *The Making of the English Working Class*. New York: Vintage, 1966.

Tillotson, Kathleen. "The Lighter Reading of the Eighteen-Sixties." Introduction to *The Woman in White* by Wilkie Collins. Boston: Houghton, 1969.

Tintner, Adeline R. *The Pop World of Henry James: From Fairy Tales to Science Fiction*. Ann Arbor, Mich.: UMI, 1989.

Torgovnick, Marianna. *Closure in the Novel*. Princeton: Princeton University Press, 1981.

———. *The Visual Arts, Pictorialism, and the Novel: James, Lawrence, and Woolf*. Princeton: Princeton University Press, 1985.

Tracy, Laura. *"Catching the Drift": Authority, Gender, and Narration*. New Brunswick, N.J.: Rutgers University Press, 1988.

Trodd, Anthea. *Domestic Crime in the Victorian Novel*. London: Macmillan, 1989.

Trudgill, Eric. *Madonnas and Magdalens: The Origins and Development of Victorian Sexual Attitudes*. New York: Holmes and Meier, 1976.

Vicinus, Martha. "'Helpless and Unfriended': Nineteenth-Century Domestic Melodrama." *New Literary History* 13 (Autumn 1981): 127–43.

Vrettos, Athena. *Somatic Fictions: Imagining Illness in Victorian Culture*. Stanford: Stanford University Press, 1995.

Wagner, Peter. "The Pornographer in the Courtroom: Trial Reports About the Cases of Sexual Crimes and Delinquencies as a Genre in Eighteenth-Century

Erotica." In *Sexuality in Eighteenth-Century Britain*. Ed. Paul-Gabriel Bouce. Manchester: Manchester University Press, 1982. 120–40.

Walkowitz, Judith. *City of Dreadful Delight: Narratives of Sexual Danger in Late-Victorian London*. Chicago: University of Chicago Press, 1992.

——. "The Politics of Prostitution." *Women: Sex and Sexuality*. Ed. Catharine R. Stimpson and Ethel Spector Person. Chicago: University of Chicago Press, 1980. 145–57.

Watt, Ian. *The Rise of the Novel: Studies in Defoe, Richardson, and Fielding*. Berkeley: University of California Press, 1964.

Weinstein, Arnold. "The Fiction of Relationship." *Novel: A Forum on Fiction* 15.1 (1981): 5–22.

Williams, Linda. *Hard Core: Power, Pleasure, and the "Frenzy of the Visible."* Berkeley: University of California Press, 1989.

Williams, Raymond. *Culture and Society, 1790–1950*. Middlesex: Penguin, 1982.

——. *The Long Revolution*. New York: Columbia University Press, 1961.

Wilson, R. B. J. *Henry James's The Ultimate Narrative: "The Golden Bowl."* London: University of Queensland Press, 1981.

Wolff, Robert Lee. *Sensational Victorian: The Life and Fiction of Mary Elizabeth Braddon*. New York: Garland, 1979.

Wright, Walter. "Maggie Verver: Neither Saint nor Witch." *Nineteenth Century Fiction* 12 (1957): 59–71.

Yeazell, Ruth Bernard. *Language and Knowledge in the Late Novels of Henry James*. Chicago: University of Chicago Press, 1976.

Acknowledgments

It is a pleasure to be able to thank those people who contributed to the development of this book. Several friends and colleagues offered insightful and much appreciated readings of the manuscript or discussions of issues related to the project at crucial stages. I am deeply grateful to Maggie Berg, Frances Berkman, Michael Bristol, Peter Brooks, Tony Cascardi, Daniel Cottom, Casey Finch, Jill Frank, Peter Halewood, David Hensley, Mette Hjort, Ehud Isacoff, Dominick LaCapra, Stephen Leckie, George Levine, Paisley Livingston, Sarah Luria, Seth Moglen, Franny Nudelman, and Gary Wihl. I am especially indebted to Alison MacKeen, whose fierce intelligence always leaves me in awe and whose friendship I value immensely.

I was lucky enough to have two dedicated and incredibly industrious research assistants, Nevena Nikolova and Stella Kostova. Nevena's work in tracking down slippery sources, attending to lots of boring details, and bringing to this project a lively intelligence and a wonderful competence were much appreciated. Stella's contribution to bibliographic citations was indispensable.

My colleagues at Carleton University have provided me with an excellent environment in which to work, and think, and talk. Brenda Carr has been a colleague extraordinaire and if we talk a lot, this talking makes the working, thinking, and teaching that much more enjoyable. Larry MacDonald, Robert Lovejoy, and Barbara Gabriel also deserve a special thank-you. And thanks to Joy Dufour, Lori Dearman, and Ruth Hill-Lapensee. Carleton University has been liberal in its financial support, for which I am grateful. In addition, this project was generously funded by the Social Sciences and Humanities Research Council of Canada.

Jerome Singerman, Ellen Fiskett, Noreen O'Connor, and Gail Kienitz at the University of Pennsylvania Press have made the process of turning an unwieldy manuscript into a book remarkably streamlined and painless. Their smart suggestions and scrupulous editing have been very much appreciated.

More personally, I want to thank my parents, Robin and Rosemary Leckie, and my siblings for tolerating my books and papers on every family vacation and for their consistent support in the face of that infamous question: are you finished yet? My mother's creativity and intelligence have always been a source of inspiration. She also indulged my early fiction addiction and to her I owe a passion for reading that motivates the writing of this book. My father's unwavering confidence, sharp questions, and funny book-title suggestions were all deeply appreciated. A big thank-you, also, to Steve, Ted (and his long-distance hotline), and Annie Leckie. Ruth Westheimer, Miriam Westheimer, and Joel Einleger supported me in more ways than they probably know, and to them, and to a place — Oscawana — I will always be grateful.

It is impossible adequately to thank the person without whom this book would never have been completed. From biking in Europe to swimming at Oscawana, Joel Westheimer has listened to me talk about censorship, adultery, and readers with amazing patience, perceptiveness, and good humor. At once my most exacting and my most enthusiastic critic, he is the reader I vividly imagine when I write. My best thanks to Joel for giving me such remarkable support and for making life such a pleasure in the process.

And finally I want to thank the little miracle, Michal, whose wonderful smiles make every day amazing.

Index

Page numbers in *italics* refer to illustrations.

Acland, Alice, 266n3
Addiction metaphors: in criticism of sensation novel, 115; in divorce court journalism, 94; in *The Doctor's Wife*, 147; in *Madame Bovary* trial, 24; rhetoric of, 116–119, 144, 149. *See also* Drug metaphors; Fiction addictions
Adulteresses, 59; in novel's development, 262n6; omission in English novel, 244; point of view in French novel, 34–35; reader and, 150
"Adulteresses in Agony" (Maison), 266n2
Adultery: censorship and (*see* Censorship); as domestic detective story, 14, 89, 130–134, 171, 172–174, 182, 186–190, 230–232; in English literary tradition, 1–2, 25–26; English representations of, 20, 34, 92, 110–111, 141–142, 164, 165, 244–245, 252 (*see also* Betrayed party); epistemology of, 14, 35, 59–60, 166, 218–229; French Reign of Terror and, 191; graphic renditions of, *69, 70,* 73–76, *74–76,* 218–220, 221–228, 267n13; history of, 3; identity and, 217; as knowledge, 60, 130–134, 157, 166, 170, 172–174, 176–177, 228, 242; legitimation of, 110–111, 141–142; men's role in causation of, 263–264n15; proof of, 89, 133, 175–176; in public sphere, 9, 15, 18–19, 64–65 (*see also* Publicity, associated with adultery); punishment of, 185–186, 233–234, 271–272n14; reading synonymous with, 75, 95, 142; religious symbolism in, 74, 214–215; sensation novel and (*see* Sensation novel); as transgression and taboo, 2, 4–6, 33, 57–58. *See also* Divorce court; Divorce court journalism; French novel; Knowledge; Sensation novel

Adultery in the Novel (Tanner), 1, 262n6
Aesthetics and Ideology (Levine), 11–12
Aesthetic values: James on, 160, 162, 166–167; versus moral values, 22–23, 24, 26–27, 30, 259n5; nationality and, 21, 160, 163–164; versus realism, 14, 22
All the Year Round, 118
Altick, Richard, 16, 20
The Ambassadors (James), 184, 221, 223–225
"Angel in the house," 28, 60, 77, 268n16
"An Animated Conversation" (James), 164
Anteros (Lawrence), 33
Aristotle, 194–195
Armstrong, Judith, 19
Armstrong, Nancy, 248–249
Arnold, Matthew, 6–7, 10, 11, 14, 98
Arsenic, 51–52, 261n21. *See also* Poison metaphors
Art, versus obscenity, 24, 40–42, 44–45
The Art of Fiction (Besant), 7
"The Art of Fiction" (James), 160–162, 169, 227
"The Aspern Papers" (James), 185
Atherton, Gertrude, 197
Auerbach, Nina, 73
Aurora Floyd (Braddon), 140
Austin, Alfred, 28, 109, 118
"The Author of Beltraffio" (James), 169
The Awkward Age (James), 170, 199, 269n6

"Bad" books, 40–41, 46. *See also* Pornography
Balzac, Honoré de, 210
Barthes, Roland, 113
Basch, Françoise, 64
Basil (Collins), 188, 267n14
Bayley, J., 100–101
Beecher, Henry Ward, 184–185, 263n13
Beecher-Tilton divorce case, 184–185, 263n13
Beisel, Nicola, 29

Beizer, Jane, 24
Bender, John, 106
Bennett, Arnold, 62, 89–90, 108
Bersani, Leo, 182
Besant, Walter, 7, 161, 162
Betrayed party: in English representations of adultery, 34, 35, 60, 63, 74–75, 108–109, 158, 166, 171, 186–189, 218–220, 221, 269n7; narrative and, 9; testimony in divorce court journalism, 106, 108–109, 127
Blushing, as barometer of acceptable versus unacceptable subject matter, 27, 28, 95, 269n5
Body: cravings metaphors and, 119, 144; desire and, 115–116; impact of reading on conception of, 17, 23–24, 28; invisibility of, 163; reading and disciplined, 188; visibility of, 114, 144–145, 201
Boone, Joseph A., 108, 194, 265–266n28, 270n10
Booth, Wayne, 107
Bourdieu, Pierre: on attention to form, 205; on "categories of perception," 4–5, 23; on points of resistance, 14; on taboo and transgression, 2
Bourgeoisie, marriage and, 13–14
Braddon, Mary Elizabeth, 8–9, 257n1; compared with James, 154–155; critics on, 114, 120; works of: *Aurora Floyd,* 140; *Lady Audley's Secret,* 140, 145, 153; *The Lady's Mile,* 153. See also *The Doctor's Wife;* Sensation novel
Brooke, Stopford, 199
Brooks, Peter: on adultery and the listener, 242; on erotics of reading, 113; Freudian criticism of, 257n4; on melodrama, 126, 127, 156; on modernism, 105
Brougham, Lord, 40, 41
Brown, Ford Madox, 220
Buchanan, Robert, 120, 260n13
Burger, Peter, 10
Burgin, Victor, 12, 13
Butler, Josephine, 110
Butler, Judith, 37, 257n6

A Call (Ford), 9; critics on, 270n2; plot of, 208–210; scandal in, 230. See also Ford, Ford Madox
Campbell, Lord, 36, 39–40, 41–43
Campbell v. Campbell and Others, 67, 79; influence on James, 185; James on, 88; press coverage of, 83, 85–89, *86–88,* 90–91; publicity and, 263n9, 265n25
"A Case of Identity" (Doyle), 68, 71
"Categories of perception," 4–5, 23, 199, 203, 243, 245
Censorship, 8; adultery and, 17–18; circulating libraries and, 162, 258n1, 260n12; critical neglect of English novel and, 11; definition of, 20, 155; divorce court journalism and, 102, 127; effect on nationality, 21, 160, 163–164; female readers role in debates on, 94–95, 121–122, 149, 249–250; Ford and, 271n11; Foucault on, 5, 19; implicit print, 28; influence on narrative development, 14; James on, 155, 157, 158–162, 168–169, 179–180, 183–184, 197, 201; juridical costs of, 101; law versus vulnerable reader and, 94–95, 149; legal definition of, 7; melodrama and, 126–127, 156; nationality, art and effect of, 21, 160, 163–164; Oliphant on, 28, 259n7; press on, 28, 254n24; pressure on novelists, 30, 158–159; productive function of, 6, 159; as regulation, 39; representations in *The Doctor's Wife,* 146; of sex, 3–4, 161–162. See also "The Art of Fiction" (James); Divorce court journalism; Madeleine Smith murder trial; Robinson adultery case
Century Magazine, 228
Chartier, Roger, 118–119
Chedzoy, Alan, 266n3
Cheng, Vincent, 230
Children, sexuality of, 67, 262n5
Christian Remembrancer, 118
Circulating libraries, 162, 258n1, 260n12
Classics, regulation of, 43
Closure, absence of, 107–108, 192, 194, 195, 237–238
Cockburn, Lord, 45, 46–47, 48
Colby, F. M., 197–198
Colet, Louise, 21
Collinge, Florence, 206–207
Collins, Wilkie, 166; on body awareness, 23–24; divorce court journalism influence on, 104; female reader and, 260n10; as transitional modernist, 257n1; works of: *Basil,* 188, 267n14; *Legacy of Cain,* 16–18, 23–24, 48–49; "The Unknown Public," 27; *The Woman in White,* 119, 145, 153, 268n20

Condom metaphor, 21
The Confessional Unmasked (Scott), 44, 47, 48
Conrad, Joseph, 104, 206, 236
Contagious Diseases Act (1864), 263n12
Craik, Dinah Mulock, 267n15
Cravings, language of, 116–119, 144. *See also* Addiction metaphors
Crawford v. *Crawford and Dilke,* 67, 79; influence on James, 81, 185; influence on novelists, 264n16,17; press coverage of, 80–83, *81, 82, 84*
Criminals, as characters, 106
Culture, definitions of, 6–7, 9
Culture and Anarchy (Arnold), 6, 10, 14
Culture and Imperialism (Said), 12, 259n8

Daily Telegraph, 89, 98
Dallas, E. S., 115, 265n27
Daudet, Alphonse, 160
Davis, Lennard, 265n26
Davis, Sara, 184, 263n13
Default reader. *See* Female readers
Defoe, Daniel, 58
Democracy and Liberty (Lecky), 97–98
Democracy of print: literature versus obscenity and, 43; opponents of, 94–95; press on, 57
Derrida, Jacques, 257n4
Dickens, Charles, 27, 104, 168
Dilke, Charles, 80–83, *84*
Dilke divorce case. *See Crawford* v. *Crawford and Dilke*
Dirt, metaphors for, 40, 93
"The Discourse on Language" (Foucault), 38
Disease metaphors: in divorce court journalism, 93; in *The Doctor's Wife,* 147, 150–151; in *Madame Bovary,* 24, 150–151; in Obscene Publications Act debates, 45–46
Divorce, 33–34; Beecher-Tilton case, 184–185, 263n13; Crawford case coverage, 80–83, *81, 82, 84;* description of, 263n8; Ford and, 206; men's role in causation of, 72; procedure for, 79–80; reform laws of, 63–64, 67–68, 206, 262n4; as topic for novels, 103; tracts on, 71–73; in United States, 263n13; Yelverton trial, 65–66, 262–263n7
"Divorce a Vinculo; or, The Terrors of Sir Cresswell Cresswell," 76–78

Divorce court: common features of cases in, 90–91; examples of cases in, 206–208; in France, 263n11; jokes about, 265n25; juries in, 91–92; justice in, 100; perjury in, 89–90; petitions against, 97; public interest and, 99–100, 263nn8, 9, 10; public opinion on, 265n23; role of publicity in, 96, 101, 185, 263n9, 265n25, 271–272n14; surveillance and suspicion in, 91; wife's defense in, 83; witnesses in, 90–91; women's attendance at, 264–265n22. *See also specific cases*
Divorce court journalism: absence of closure in, 107–108; betrayed party testimony in, 106, 108–109, 127; causality and, 106; censorship and, 102, 127; content of, 92, 93, 206; critics on, 203; female readers and, 94–95, 202–203; form of, 92, 104–105; in France, 263n11; French novel versus, 93, 103; illustrations of, *69, 70;* influence on Ford, 104, 203, 204, 205–206, 230, 253; influence on James, 88, 157–158, 175–176, 181, 183–185, 192–194, 196, 252–253, 266n29; influence on Norton, 124–125; influence on Collins, 104; legitimation of adultery in, 110–111; medical discourse in, 93, 94, 249; melodrama relationship to, 127–128; metaphor usage in, 93, 94; modernist novel and, 92, 104–110, 196, 252; multiple points of view and, 107; narrative in, 110, 237; novel form and influence of, 92, 104–110, 196, 252; opponents of, 93–98; pornography versus, 59; as portrait of Victorian era, 66–67, 78–79; proscandal argument for, 101; publications of, 68; readers of, 83, 85; resemblance to medical case studies, 249; similarities to novel of adultery, 63; social space results of, 102–103, 107; supporters of, 98–101; unreliable narration and, 106–107; writing style in, 66. *See also* Press
The Divorce Court Reporter, 68
Divorce courts: press on. *See* Divorce court journalism
The Doctor's Wife (Braddon), 8–9, 120, 139–151; censorship representations in, 146; critics on, 140–141, 143–146, 149; deletions in reprints, 146, 268n18; fiction addictions in, 148–149; French novel influences on, 114; metaphors in, 147, 150–151; plot of, 142–143; portrait of

The Doctor's Wife (Braddon) (*cont.*)
female reader in, 142, 147–148, 150; on reading, 142, 147–148; relationship to *Madame Bovary,* 140, 260n11; representation of adultery in, 141–142; sensation novel theme of, 140, 149–150. *See also* Braddon, Mary Elizabeth

Domestic surveillance. *See* Surveillance: domestic

Donald, James, 12, 13

Donoghue, Denis, 270n1

Dora case history (Freud), 246–250, 253–255

Double standard, 63–64, 130, 263n12, 269n10

Douglas, Mary, 6, 40, 46, 220–221

Doyle, Arthur Conan, 68, 71, 78, 104

Dread versus fear, James on, 195–196

Dreiser, Theodore, 236

Drug metaphors: in criticism of sensation novel, 115; in divorce court journalism, 93; in *The Golden Bowl,* 180–181; in sensation novel, 146. *See also* Addiction metaphors

Dumas, Alexandre (fils), 42, 228, 260n17

East Lynne (Wood), 268n17

Edel, Leon, 178–179, 184, 269n9

Edelstein, T. J., 73, 75

Egg, Augustus, 73–76, 218–220, 221, 267n13

Eliot, George, 104, 115

Ellis, Havelock, 260n19

English Laws (Norton), 125

Epistemology: adultery as question of, 14, 35, 59–60, 166, 218–229; *Lost and Saved* and, 139

Essay in Criticism (Arnold), 98

Fantasy, 14, 37

Female authors, James on, 168

Female readers: as betrayed party (*see* Betrayed party: in English representations of adultery); characteristics of, 168–169; classics and, 45; Collins and, 260n10; critics on, 260n16; as default readers, 29; definition of obscenity and, 47–48; divorce court journalism debates and, 94–95, 202–203; *The Doctor's Wife* and, 142, 147–148, 150; versus educated readers, 23, 36, 199–200; education of, 258–259n3; fiction addictions and, 115 (*see also* Fiction addictions); *The Golden Bowl* and, 156, 157, 158–159; James on, 156, 157, 158–159, 164–165, 167, 168–169, 198; *Lost and Saved* and, 136–137; as new reading public, 27; press on, 27 (*see also* Press); reading practices of, 17–18, 249–250; Robinson case and, 58; role in censorship debates, 94, 121–122, 149, 249–250; Stephen on, 31; Trollope on, 151–152. *See also* Censorship, female readers' role in debates on; Fiction addictions; Sensation novel

Fenn, Henry, 264–265n22

Fiction addictions, 8, 112, 114–122; cravings rhetoric and, 116–119; in *The Doctor's Wife,* 148–149; female readers and, 115; French novel influences on, 116, 117

Fielding, Henry, 58

Flaubert, Gustave, 21, 36, 260nn10, 11. *See also Madame Bovary*

Flint, Kate, 27–28

Ford, Ford Madox, 9, 257n1; aesthetics of suppression of, 229–230; censorship and, 271n11; critics on, 204, 219, 270nn1, 2; debt to Victorian tradition, 243; on detective story, 271n12; divorce court journalism influence on, 104, 203, 204, 205–206, 230, 253; on French novel, 210, 271n6; narrative techniques of, 92, 212, 215–216, 221, 222–223, 235; *Parade's End,* 272n16; personal life of, 206; readership of, 205; subject versus technique in works of, 204–205; on *The Turn of the Screw,* 271n13; writing style of, 205. *See also A Call* (Ford); *The Good Soldier* (Ford)

Formations of Fantasy (Burgin et al.), 12

Forster, E. M., 106

Fort comme la mort (Maupassant), 210

Foucault, Michel: on authorship, 250–251; on censorship, 5, 19; on sexuality, 2–4, 14, 67–68; on Victorian period sexual discourse, 67; works of: "The Discourse on Language," 38; *The History of Sexuality,* 3, 257n7

Freedom of speech, law and, 98, 161

French novel. *See also* Sensation novel: adulteress point of view in, 34–35; Campbell on, 42–43; content of, 26, 104; critics on, 25–26; versus divorce court journalism, 93, 103; Ford on, 210, 271n6; influence on *The Doctor's Wife,* 114; influence on fiction addictions, 116, 117; influence on Ford, 210, 271n6; James on, 32–33, 191, 269n6, 270n12; *Madame Bovary* trial as representative of, 20–24; as models for English novels, 245; synonymous with novels of adultery, 35, 264n21

Freud, Sigmund: "'Civilized' Sexual Morality," 101; Dora case history of, 246–250, 253–255; Foucault criticism of repressive hypothesis of, 3; influence on Brooks, 257n4; Lacan and Derrida on, 257n4; on taboo and transgression, 2, 5

"Future of the Novel" (James), 159, 166–169

Garbage (dirt) metaphors, in divorce court journalism, 93

Gay, Peter, 96

Gender, melodrama and, 126. *See also* Female readers

Giddens, Anthony, 107

"The Given Case" (James), 184

Gladstone, William Ewart, 261–262n3

The Golden Bowl (James), 9, 138, 221. *See also* James, Henry; absence of closure in, 192, 194; betrayed party perspective in, 158; censorship and, 179–180; critics on, 156, 183–184, 187, 194, 196, 197–198, 200; divorce court journalism influence on, 157–158, 175–176, 181, 184–185, 192; dread versus fear in, 195–196; drug metaphors in, 180–181; female readers and, 156, 157, 158–159; form of, 192; Foucaldian readings of, 182–183, 197; graphic "framing" technique in, 226–228, 229; James's notes on, 165–166; narrative in, 192–193; plot of, 170–171; point of view in, 182; punishment of adultery in, 185–186; structure of, 193–194

Goncourt, Edmond de, 160

Goode, John, 269n3

The Good Soldier (Ford), 9, 92, 267n13. *See also* Ford, Ford Madox; adultery as theme in, 211, 216–217; Brand case, 240–242; censorship and, 271n11; closure in, 237–238; critics on, 235; domestic surveillance in, 230–232, 235; form in, 221, 235–236; Kilsyte case, 239–240; narrative in, 212, 215–216, 221, 222–223, 235; point of view in, 213; protest in, 214–215; punishment of adultery in, 233–234; reader's response to, 242; religious elements in, 214–215; repetitive techniques in, 237; seduction as theme in, 210–211, 213

Gosse, Edmund, 266n29

Greenblatt, Stephen, 6

Greg, W. R., 120; on English representation of adultery, 20; on sensation novel, 122, 266–267n5; on subject matter of French novel, 26; use of cravings language by, 116, 117

Hadley, Elaine, 123–124

Hall, David, 177

"Happy endings," 108

Hardy, Thomas, 104, 257n1

Harker, Harold Edward, 207

Harrison, Frederic, 259n6

Hartman, Mary, 52

Hartright, Walter, 153

Hawthorne, Nathaniel, 215–216

Heidegger, Martin, 195

He Knew He Was Right (Trollope), 91

Herr, Cheryl, 6

Hertz, Neil, 249

Hicklin standard, 36–39, 45–48

History of England (Macaulay), 251

The History of Sexuality (Foucault), 3, 257n7

Hoffman, Charles, 270n1

Holywell Street, 40, 43, 44, 59, 265n24

Honor, women and, 262–263n7

Howells, William Dean, 64, 103, 116, 269n4

Hunt, Violet, 206, 270n3

Hunter, Ian, 8, 37, 38–39, 257n5

Hunter, J. Paul, 265n26

Hynes, Samuel, 212, 229, 232

Hysteria: Crawford case and, 83; link to public sphere sexuality, 73; reading and, 24; Robinson case and, 56. *See also* Freud, Sigmund

Identity, 217, 257n6

Illustrated London News, 135

Illustrated Police News, 80, 85, 95

"Immoral Books," 119–120

Indecent Advertisements Act (1889), 7, 258n1

Infant's Custody Act (1839), 263n12

Infidelity, female: in *The Ambassadors*, 224; in *Crawford* v. *Crawford and Dilke*, 80–83; in "Divorce a Vinculo; or, The Terrors of Sir Cresswell Cresswell," 76–78; in "Old

Infidelity, female (*cont.*)
Bachelor" story, 71–73; in *Past and Present* painting, 73–76, 74–76. See also *Madame Bovary*
Insanity, in Robinson case, 56
"In the Cage" (James), 170

Jacobs, Carol, 235
James, Henry, 7, 9, 257n1, 258n10; on aesthetic values, 160, 162, 166–167; betrayed party perspective in works of, 158, 269n7; on *Campbell*, 88; on censorship, 155, 157, 158–162, 168–169, 179–180, 183–184, 197, 201; compared with Norton and Braddon, 154–155; on *Crawford*, 81, 185; critics on, 162, 199–200, 268–269n1 (see also *The Golden Bowl* (James): critics on); debt to *Lost and Saved*, 138; divorce court journalism influence on, 88, 157–158, 175–176, 181, 183–185, 192–194, 196, 252–253, 266n29; on dread versus fear, 195–196; on Dumas, 42, 228; on female authors, 168; on female readers, 156, 157, 158–159, 164–165, 167, 168–169, 198; on French naturalists, 160; on French novel, 32–33, 191, 269n6, 270n12; graphic "framing" technique of, 221–228, 229; on "happy ending" and closure, 108; readership of, 165, 167, 197, 198–200; on representation of adultery, 164; on Robert Louis Stevenson, 185; works of (see also *The Golden Bowl* (James)); *The Ambassadors*, 184, 221, 223–225; "An Animated Conversation," 164; "The Art of Fiction," 160–162, 169, 227; "The Aspern Papers," 185; "The Author of Beltraffio," 169; *The Awkward Age*, 170, 199, 269n6; "Future of the Novel," 159, 166–169; "The Given Case," 184; "In the Cage," 170; "A London Life," 169–170, 185; "Mora Montravers," 184; *Notebooks*, 165, 185, 192; *Portrait of a Lady*, 222; "The Real Thing," 184; *The Reverberator*, 185; *The Sacred Fount*, 199; *Turn of the Screw*, 107, 271n13; *What Maisie Knew*, 170, 197, 199, 270n12; *The Wings of the Dove*, 170, 199–200, 221, 225–226; on Zola, 164–165
Jameson, Fredric, 107
Jenkins, Roy, 263n14, 264n16
Jeune, Francis, 154, 200–201
Jolly, Roslyn, 179, 268–269n1, 269n3

Josey (Malot), 264n17
Juries, 53, 91–92

Kaplan, Cora, 12, 13
Kardon, Janet, 204–205
Keating, Peter, 11, 20
Kierkegaard, Søren A., 195–196
Knowledge: domestic, adultery as, 60, 130–134, 157, 166, 170, 172–174, 176–177, 228, 242; the novel and, 166, 178–179; reading and women's, 137, 153, 175. See also Surveillance
Kristeva, Julia, 244

Lacan, Jacques, 257n4
Lady Audley's Secret (Braddon), 140, 145, 153
The Lady of the Camellias (Dumas), 42
The Lady's Mile (Braddon), 153
The Lancet, 260n19
Lane, Dr., 55
L'Angelier, Emile, 50, 53
Lanser, Susan, 182
Law: canon to secular change in, 257n2; divorce, 63–64, 67–68, 206, 262n4; double standard and, 130, 263n12, 269n10; entanglement in Victorian adultery, 78, 233–234; fantasy and, 37; freedom of speech and, 98, 161; importance of audience in maintenance of, 99; melodrama and, 126; publicity and, 186; quest for truth and the, 182; relationship between fantasy and, 37; versus vulnerable reader and censorship, 94–95, 149. See also Divorce court; *Lost and Saved* (Norton); Matrimonial Causes Act (1857)
Lawrence, George Alfred, 33
Law Times, 42
Lecky, W. E. H., 97–98
Legacy of Cain (Collins), 16–18, 23–24, 48–49
"Letter to the Queen" (Norton), 130
Levine, George, 11–12, 258n13
Liberalism, literature and, 12–13, 37, 257n8
A Life for a Life (Craik), 267–268n15
Litvak, Joseph, 269n8
Lloyd's newspaper, 98, 264n18
London *Evening News*, 64, 85, 99, 100, 105, 263n10
"A London Life" (James), 169–170, 185
London *Times*, 40, 58, 64, 97, 100, 138, 265n23

Lost and Saved (Norton), 8, 122–139; autobiographical aspects of, 123–124; critics on, 114, 135–136, 138–139; critique of medical establishment in, 134–135, 138; divorce court journalism influence on, 124–125; epistemology and, 139; female readers and, 136–137; James's debt to, 138; melodrama in, 124, 125–126, 128–129; political purpose of, 123, 137–138; as protest novel, 125, 126, 135–137; reprint of, 266n3; second volume of, 129–130; sensation novel and, 139. *See also* Norton, Caroline

Lucretia; or The Heroine of the Nineteenth Century (Paget), 112–113, 152

Lyndhurst, Lord, 40–41, 43–44, 264n19

Macaulay, Thomas, 251
MacCarthy, Justin, 162; on *The Doctor's Wife,* 140–141; on *Lost and Saved* as protest novel, 125, 126, 135–136; on *Lost and Saved* association with sensation novel, 139; on stereotype of English women, 163
MacKinnon, Catharine, 37–38, 260n15
Madame Bovary (Flaubert), 112; adulteress point of view in, 34–35; Eleanor Marx's response to, 32; English response to, 30–33, 260n11; James's response to, 32; metaphors in, 23, 24, 150–151; omniscient narrative in, 109; Stephen's review of, 30–32, 260n11; trial of, 18, 20–24. *See also The Doctor's Wife* (Braddon)
Madeleine Smith murder trial, 18, 49–55, 261n20
Maiden Tribute case, 262n5
Maison, Margaret, 266n2
Male readers, 37–38
Malot, Hector, 264n17
Manchester Guardian, 52
Mansel, Henry, 117, 118, 119, 266n5
Mapplethorpe, Robert, 204–205
Marcus, Steven, 247, 248
Margolis, Anne, 165, 166, 268–269n1
Marriage: bourgeois ideology and, 13–14; as English versus French adultery, 26
Marsh, Joss, 258n1
Martindale, Elsie, 206
Marx, Eleanor, 32
Mass democracy: role of literature in, 11–13; role of print in, 20. *See also* Democracy of print

Massillon, Jean-Baptiste, 22
Matrimonial Causes Act (1857), 1; canon to secular law change in, 257n2; influence on obscene publications, 261n2; influence on representation of adultery, 18, 62; law courts and, 67; sexual double standard and, 263n12; visibility of adultery and, 68, 109
Matthews, Mr., 264n21
Maupassant, Guy de, 210, 242
McClellan, Mary Marcy, 185
McKeon, Michael, 265n26
Medical Critic, 116
Medical discourse: criticism of, 134–135, 138; in divorce court journalism, 93, 249; sensation novel and, 267n6; sexuality and, 247, 268n20. *See also* Addiction metaphors; Dora case history (Freud); Drug metaphors
Melodrama: censorship and, 126–127, 156; critics on, 126, 127, 156; definition of, 126; divorce court journalism relationship to, 127–128; as fiction technique, 124, 125–126; gender and, 126; in Norton's work, 124, 125–126, 128–129; plots of, 128–129
Metaphors. *See* Disease metaphors; Drug metaphors; Fiction addictions; Poison metaphors
Middlemarch (Eliot), 268n20
Mill, John Stuart, 12, 257n8
Miller, D. A., 13, 91, 105, 232
Minnoch, William, 51, 53
Modernist novel: divorce court journalism impact on, 92, 104–110, 196, 252; *Dora* compared to, 248–249; literature development and, 10, 252–253; narrative innovations associated with (*see* Narratives: innovations associated with modernist novel); Ortega y Gasset on, 198–199; transitional, 257n1
Moon, Heath, 85
Moore, George, 103, 104, 162–163
"Mora Montravers" (James), 184
Mordaunt v. *Mordaunt,* 263nn8, 14
Moretti, Franco, 1, 13, 14
Murray, Gilbert, 96
My Secret Life, 66, 67

Narratives: betrayed party and (*see* Betrayed party); in divorce court journalism, 110, 237; in Dora case history, 247; innova-

Narratives (*cont.*)
  tions associated with modernist novel, 9–10, 14, 106–109, 192–193, 236, 239, 243, 265–266n28; limited third person, 236; omniscient, 109; of sleeping versus waking body, 245; unreliable, 106–107. *See also The Golden Bowl* (James): narrative in; *The Good Soldier* (Ford): narrative in; Point of view
The Nation, 185, 263n13
Nationality, art and effect of censorship on, 21, 160, 163–164
National Social Purity Crusade, 270–271n5
National Vigilance Association, 93–94, 99
"A New Censorship of Literature" (Moore), 162–163
New York Times, 262n5
Norton, Caroline, 8, 154, 268n17; on "angels in the house," 268n16; biographies of, 266n3, 267n12; compared with James, 154–155; critics on, 114, 135–136, 138–139; divorce court journalism influence on, 124–125; melodrama usage of, 124, 125–126, 128–129; political agenda in works of, 123–124; sensation novel and, 139, 267n9; works of: *English Laws,* 125; "Letter to the Queen" (Norton), 130. *See also Lost and Saved* (Norton)
Norton, Charles, 123
Notebooks (James), 165, 185, 192
Novel, the: absence of closure in, 107–108, 192, 194, 195, 237–238; of adultery, 7–8, 35, 63, 264n21 (*see also* French novel; Sensation novel); audiences for, 166–167, 197; causality and, 106; development strategies of, 14; divorce and adultery as topics for, 103; freedom of, 167–168; ideal role of, 146–147; influence of divorce court journalism on form of, 92, 104–110, 196, 252; James on censorship and, 155, 157, 158–162, 168–169, 179–180, 183–184, 197, 201; knowledge and, 166, 178–179; as medium of social issues communication, 125; multiple points of view and, 107; nationality associations of, 21, 160, 163–164; reasons for hostility toward, 181; role in new public sphere, 21; serial novel form, 105, 265n27; as social practice, 29; traditional, 106, 251; unreliable narration and, 106–107. *See also* Modernist novel; Sensation novel

Obscene Publications Act (1857), 7, 18, 48; amendments to, 36; content of debates on, 36–44, 258n1; metaphors in debates on, 36, 45–46; opponents of, 40–41; privacy and, 264n19; trials involving, 44–45
Obscenity: versus art, 24, 40–42, 44–45; context of, 46; definition of, 40–41, 46–47; literature versus democracy of print and, 43. *See also* Aesthetic values: versus moral values
Observer, 85
Observer, in novels, 222. *See also* Surveillance: domestic
"Old Bachelor," 71–73
Oliphant, Margaret: on censorship, 28, 259n7; on *The Doctor's Wife,* 141, 149; on French versus English novel, 25–26, 117; on sensation novel, 115, 118, 120; on *The Woman in White,* 119
Omniscient narrative, in *Madame Bovary,* 109
On Pornography, 41
Ortega y Gasset, José, 198–199
Our Mutual Friend (Dickens), 27, 145

Pacey, Desmond, 260n11
Paget, Francis: *Lucretia; or The Heroine of the Nineteenth Century,* 112–113, 152; on novels, 8, 10, 11; on sensation novel and society, 11, 26, 120, 122, 152–153
Pall Mall Gazette, 64; on coverage of *Campbell* case, 83, 85; on divorce court, 66; letters to, 89; Maiden Tribute case and, 262n5; opinion pieces in, 100, 162–163; on readers and divorce court reporting, 99
Palmerston, Viscount, 63
Parade's End (Ford), 272n16
Parnell divorce trial, 184
Past and Present (painting) (Egg), 73–76, 74–76, 218–220, 221, 267n13
Paternalism, readers and, 38–39
Patmore, Coventry, 28
Patterson, Annabel, 215
Penny dreadfuls, 14, 264n21
Phillips v. *Phillips,* 236–237
Pinard, Ernest, 21, 22–23, 31, 32, 112
Plot: of *A Call,* 208–210; definition of, 106; of *The Doctor's Wife,* 142–143; of *The Golden Bowl,* 170–171; of melodrama, 128–129
Poetry, versus obscenity, 41

Point of view: of adulteress in French novel, 34–35; in *The Golden Bowl*, 182; in *The Good Soldier*, 213; ideological consequences of, 187; in *Madame Bovary*, 34–35, 109; multiple, 107. *See also* Betrayed party; Narratives

Poison metaphors: in criticism of sensation novel, 120–121; in debates on light literature, 58–59; in divorce court journalism, 93; in *Legacy of Cain*, 17; in *Madame Bovary* trial, 23, 24; in obscene publications debates, 36. *See also* Madeleine Smith murder trial

Politics, versus literature, 11–13

Poovey, Mary, 92, 123–124, 125, 266n3

Pornography: current debate on, 37–38, 204–205, 257n5, 260nn15, 18, 19; versus divorce court and light literature, 59; versus literature, 39; *On Pornography*, 41; vulnerable public and, 8. *See also* Obscene Publications Act (1857); Obscenity

Portrait of a Lady (James), 222

Press: on censorship, 28, 265n24; coverage of *Campbell v. Campbell and Others*, 83, 85–89, 86–88, 90–91; coverage of *Crawford v. Crawford and Dilke*, 80–83, 81, 82, 84; divorce courts and critiques of, 66, 98–99. *See also names of individual newspapers and journals*

Privacy, 40; in novels, 105; Obscene Publications Act and, 264n19; as personal right, 68; violations of, 83, 89, 95–96, 185. *See also* Publicity, associated with adultery

Prohibition versus proliferation, 7, 8, 36–37

Prostitutes, 28, 263n12

Publicity, associated with adultery, 96, 101, 185, 186, 234, 263n9, 265n25, 271–272n14. *See also* Public sphere

Public sphere, 9, 15, 18–19, 21, 64–65, 73. *See also* Publicity, associated with adultery

Pump Court, 98, 99

Reading: associated with adultery, 75, 95, 142; associated with youth and class, 29–30; censorship and impact of, 8; definition of new public for, 27, 200; disciplined body and, 188; *The Doctor's Wife* on, 142, 147–148; erotics of, 113, 150; hysteria and, 24; impact of on conception of body, 17, 23–24, 28; knowledge and, 137, 153, 175 (*see also* Knowledge); paternalism and, 38–39; politics of, 163–164, 259n8; regulation of women and, 120–121, 152, 259n3; revolution linked with, 30, 161, 191; social threats posed by, 21–23, 30; somatic effects of, 122, 242–243. *See also* Female readers; Fiction addictions

Realism, versus aesthetic value, 14, 22

"The Real Thing" (James), 184

Regina v. *Hicklin*, 7, 36–39, 45–48, 258n1

Religious symbolism, in representations of adultery, 74, 214–215

Repression, 2, 39, 159

The Reverberator (James), 185

Revolution, link with reading, 30, 161, 191

Revolution in Poetic Language (Kristeva), 244

The Rhetoric of Fiction (Booth), 107

Roberts, M. J. D., 38, 44

Robinson v. *Robinson* adultery case, 55–58

Rodker, John, 271n6

"Une Ruse" (Maupassant), 242

R v. *Curll*, 37

The Sacred Fount (James), 199

Said, Edward, 10, 12, 259n8

"Sarrasine" (Balzac), 210

Saturday Review, 72; on censorship, 265n24; criticism of novel reading by, 120–121; on democracy of print, 57; on divorce court journalism, 94; on female readers, 27; on Madeleine Smith murder case, 54; on Matrimonial Causes Act, 261n2; on obscene literature, 44; on Robinson adultery case, 56; on sensation versus French novel, 141; on women and adultery cases, 59

Saunders, David, 8, 37, 38–39, 257n5

Saunders, Max, 219, 229, 270n1

Scandal, 13, 98, 101–102, 109–110, 184

The Scarlet Letter (Hawthorne), 215–216, 268n20

Schorer, Mark, 235

Scott, Henry, 44, 47, 48

Scott, Walter, 168

Sedgwick, Eve, 121

Seltzer, Mark, 105, 183, 186–187

Senard, Marie-Antoine-Jules, 21, 22, 32

Sensation novel, 266n2; addictive reading and, 113; audiences for, 119, 121; critics on, 113–114, 115, 118–119, 120–121, 266–267n5; *Dora* case history compared to, 248–249; literature development and, 14; medical discourse and, 267n6; meta-

Sensation novel (*cont.*)
  phors in, 115, 120–121, 146; Norton and, 139, 267n9; Paget on, 11, 26, 120, 122, 152–153; representations of adultery in, 113–114; sexuality in, 151. *See also The Doctor's Wife* (Braddon)
Serial novel form, 105, 265n27
Sexual Inversion (Ellis), 260n19
Sexuality: censorship and, 3–4, 161–162; Foucault on, 2–4, 14, 67–68; hysteria link to public sphere, 73; medical frame of reference and, 247, 268n20 (*see also* Dora case history (Freud)); repression and, 2–3; in sensation novel, 151. *See also* Divorce court journalism; Freud, Sigmund
Shurbutt, S. Bailey, 266n3
Shuttleworth, Sally, 267n6
Smith, S., 93–94, 264nn20, 21
Sontag, Susan, 113
Spanos, William, 195
Spectator, 25, 27
Sporting Times, 265n25
Stack, J. Herbert, 33–34, 165
Stallybrass, Peter, 1
Stang, Richard, 11, 259n7
Stephen, Fitzjames, 20, 25, 30–32, 58, 162
Stephen, Leslie, 121
Stevenson, Robert Louis, 162, 185
"The Subject of Power" (Bersani), 182
Sumner, John, 45
Sunday Echo, 72
Surveillance: as domestic detective story: in divorce court trials, 91; divorce law and, 67–68; domestic, 73, 182, 186–190, 230–232, 235. *See also* Adultery

Taboo, adultery as, 2, 5–6, 33
Tanner, Tony, 1, 110, 201, 262n6
Temple Bar, 145
The Tenant of Wildfell Hall (Brontë), 188, 267n14
La Terre (Zola), 258n1, 260n14
The Theory of the Novel in England (Stang), 11
Thomas, Keith, 261n3
Thompson, E. P., 9
Tilton, Elizabeth, 185, 263n13
Tilton, Theodore, 184
Tintner, Adeline, 184, 269n9
Torgovnick, Marianna, 194, 222

Tracy, Laura, 216, 235
Tragedy, 194–195
Transgression, 2, 4–6, 33, 57–58
La Traviata (opera), 260n17
Trollope, Anthony, 91, 151–152
Trudgill, Eric, 265n24
Turner, Victor, 77
Turn of the Screw (James), 107, 271n13

United States, divorce in, 263n13
"The Unknown Public" (Collins), 27

"The Vice of Reading" (Austin), 118
Victoria, Queen of England, 66, 93, 94, 103
Victorian era: divorce court journalism as portrait of, 66–67, 78–79; Ford debt to, 243; law entanglement with adultery in, 78, 233–234
Viewpoint. *See* Point of view
Vizetelly and Company, 260n14
Vizetelly trial (1888), 258n1
Vulnerable reader, category of. *See* Female readers

Watt, Ian, 106
Weinstein, Arnold, 271n7
What Maisie Knew (James), 170, 197, 199, 270n12
White, Allon, 1
Whom God Hath Joined (Bennett), 89–90, 108
Wilde, Oscar, 266n29
Williams, Linda, 260n18
Williams, Raymond, 9
Williamson, Dugald, 8, 37, 38–39, 257n5
The Wings of the Dove (James), 170, 199–200, 221, 225–226
The Woman in White (Collins), 119, 145, 153, 268n20
Woman reader. *See* Female readers
The Woman Reader (Flint), 27–28
Wood, Mrs. Henry, 268n17
Word Crimes: Blasphemy, Culture, and Literature in Nineteenth-Century England (Marsh), 258n1
Wright, Thomas, 27, 166

Yelverton divorce trial, 65–66, 262–263n7

Zola, Emile, 160, 258n1